우루과이라운드

서비스 분야 양허 협상 3

우루과이라운드

서비스 분야 양허 협상 3

한국학술정보

| 머리말

우루과이라운드는 국제적 교역 질서를 수립하려는 다각적 무역 교섭으로서, 각국의 보호무역 추세를 보다 완화하고 다자무역체제를 강화하기 위해 출범되었다. 1986년 9월 개시가 선언되었으며, 15개 분야의 교섭을 1990년 말까지 진행하기로 했다. 그러나 각 분야의 중간 교섭이 이루어진 1989년 이후에도 농산물, 지적소유권, 서비스무역, 섬유, 긴급수입제한 등 많은 분야에서 대립하며 1992년이 돼서야 타결에 이를 수 있었다. 한국은 특히 농산물 분야에서 기존 수입 제한 품목 대부분을 개방해야 했기에 큰 경쟁력 하락을 겪었고, 관세와 기술 장벽 완화, 보조금 및 수입 규제 정책의 변화로 제조업 수출입에도 많은 변화가 있었다.

본 총서는 우루과이라운드 협상이 막바지에 다다랐던 1991~1992년 사이 외교부에서 작성한 관련 자료를 담고 있다. 관련 협상의 치열했던 후반기 동향과 관계부처회의, 무역협상위원회 회의, 실무대책회의, 규범 및 제도, 투자회의, 특히나 가장 많은 논란이 있었던 농산물과 서비스 분야 협상 등의 자료를 포함해 총 28권으로 구성되었다. 전체 분량은 약 1만 3천여 쪽에 이른다.

2024년 3월

한국학술정보(주)

| 일러두기

· 본 총서에 실린 자료는 2022년 4월과 2023년 4월에 각각 공개한 외교문서 4,827권, 76만여 쪽 가운데 일부를 발췌한 것이다.

· 각 권의 제목과 순서는 공개된 원본을 최대한 반영하였으나, 주제에 따라 일부는 적절히 변경하였다.

· 원본 자료는 A4 판형에 맞게 축소하거나 원본 비율을 유지한 채 A4 페이지 안에 삽입하였다. 또한 현재 시점에선 공개되지 않아 '공란'이란 표기만 있는 페이지 역시 그대로 실었다.

· 외교부가 공개한 문서 각 권의 첫 페이지에는 '정리 보존 문서 목록'이란 이름으로 기록물 종류, 일자, 명칭, 간단한 내용 등의 정보가 수록되어 있으며, 이를 기준으로 0001번부터 번호가 매겨져 있다. 이는 삭제하지 않고 총서에 그대로 수록하였다.

· 보고서 내용에 관한 더 자세한 정보가 필요하다면, 외교부가 온라인상에 제공하는 『대한민국 외교사료요약집』 1991년과 1992년 자료를 참조할 수 있다.

| 차례

정 리 보 존 문 서 목 록					
기록물종류	일반공문서철	등록번호	2020030072	등록일자	2020-03-10
분류번호	764.51	국가코드		보존기간	영구
명 칭	UR(우루과이라운드) / 서비스 분야 양허협상, 1992. 전6권				
생 산 과	통상기구과	생산년도	1992~1992	담당그룹	
권 차 명	V.5 11-12월				
내용목차					

0001

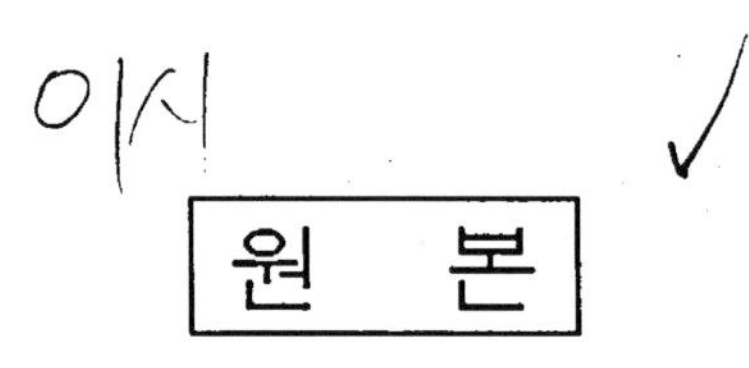

관리 번호	92-785

원 본

외 무 부

종 별 :

번 호 : JAW-5837 일 시 : 92 1102 1821

수 신 : 장관(통기)

발 신 : 주 일 대사(일경)

제 목 : 대일 시청각분야 MFN 일탈

대: WJA-4570

연: JAW-5758

1. 주재국 외무성측은 '엔도' 국제경제(UR 등) 담당대사가 11.4.(수) 오후 당관 이재춘 공사를 외무성으로 초치, 표제관련 일측 입장을 설명 예정이라고 알려온 바, 당관은 동일 이 공사의 부재(지방 출장)로 일측의 요청에 따라 이준일 참사관이 동 대사를 면담할 예정임

2. 상기 관련 지시사항 있을시 회시바람. 끝

(대사 오재희-국장)

예고: 92.12.31. 까지

통상국 아주국

PAGE 1 92.11.02 20:44

* 원본수령부서 승인없이 복사 금지 외신 2과 통제관 CH

0002

관리번호	92-795

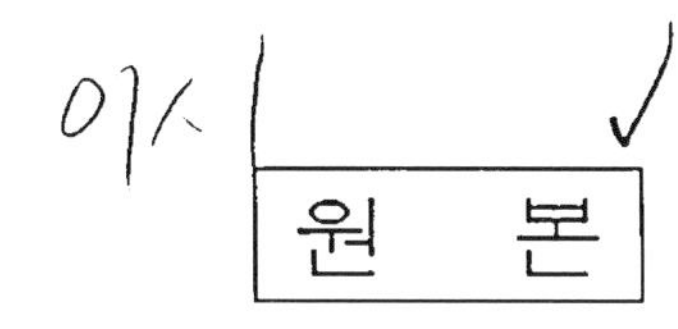

외 무 부

종 별 : 지 급

번 호 : JAW-5888 일 시 : 92 1104 2147

수 신 : 장관(통기 아일 사본:주제네바 대사--본부중계필)

발 신 : 주 일대사(일경)

제 목 : 대일시청각분야 MFN 일탈

대 : WJA-4570

연 : JAW-5667, 5837

1. 연호, 금 11.4(수) 오후 주재국 외무성 "엔도" 국제경제 담당대사는 당관 이준일 참사관을 외무성으로 초치, 대호 아측 제안에 대한 일측 입장을 아래와 같이 설명함. (당관 황순택 서기관, 쯔루오까 일측 협상대표 배석)

가. 한. 일간의 시청각분야 문제는 매우 민감한 문제로서, 잘못 처리하게 되면 양호한 양국 관계에 해를 끼칠 우려가 있으며, 현재 UR 내에서 원만한 양국간 여타 분야 협상 진행에도 악영향을 미칠 수 있다고 생각됨.

나. 일측으로서는 한국의 시청각분야 대일 MFN 일탈 등록 조치를 방치할 수 없는 입장이므로, 이의 등록 철회 요구는 당연한 조치로 생각되는 바, 만일 한국이 이를 추진하려 한다면 일본은 기타 서비스 협상 참가국에 대하여 개별 접촉을 하여야 하는 등 문제가 확대될 가능성이 있음.

다. 이러한 문제의 확산을 미연에 방지하는 것이 양국 외무 당국의 책임이라고 생각되는 바, 일측의 10.23(금) 제안 (구두멧세지 및 NON-PAPER 형식 문서 교환) 을 한국측이 수용하는 방향으로 재검토하여 주기 바람.

라. 일측의 제안은 양국이 공히 수용할 수 있다고 보며 현실적 관점에서 해결 가능한 최선의 제안으로 생각되는 바, 한국도 일본과 같은 타협 자세로 대응해 주기를 기대하며, 조속한 시일내 한국측 입장을 듣고자 함.

2. 상기 일측입장 설명에 대해, 이 참사관은 일측제안 내용만으로는 부적절함을 설명하고 우리측 주장인 토의록 (RECORD OF DISCU- SSIONS) 작성에 대한 일측 검토 결과를 재차 문의한 바, 이에 대해 동대사는 아래와 같이 부연 설명함.

가. 일측은 가능한한 동건을 양국간에 합리적이며 원만하게 처리하는 것이 바람직

통상국	장관	차관	2차보	아주국	분석관	청와대	안기부	중계

PAGE 1 92.11.04 22:53

* 원본수령부서 승인없이 복사 금지 외신 2과 통제관 CM

0003

하다고 생각, 연호 제의대로 일부는 구두로 상호 이해하고, 중요 부분에 대해서는 한.일 양국간만에 NON-PAPER 로 상호 확인코자 하였던 것임.

나. 한국측의 토의록은 형식이나 내용면에 있어 법적인 의미를 갖는 문서로서, 동 문제가 ESCALATE 될 경우 일본 국회에서도 문제가 될 소지가 있어 경우에 따라서는 양국 우호관계에 손상을 끼칠 수 있다고 봄.

다. 또한, 모든 내용을 토의록으로 처리하면, 일측으로서도 일측 견해를 전부 기록하지 않을 수 없으며, 법률적인 의미에서 국제 약속의 성격을 띄게되면 일측도 양보할 수 없는 부분도 있어 결국 문서내용 작성이 어렵게 됨. 양국간의 교섭이 이렇게 ESCALATE 된다면, 당초 의도인 양국간 만의 합리적이며 원만한 해결 모색이 어렵다고 판단, 기존 일측제의를 반복 하는 것임.

3. 또한, "쯔루오까" 일측 협상대표는 동건 처리에 있어 아래 사항을 한국측이 이해해 줄 것을 요망함.

가. 동 시청각분야 협상경위를 볼때, 일측은 91.10. 동건관련 최초협의시 한국측에 공식 요구의 입장으로부터 점차 약화된 경위가 있으며, 만일 동건이 일측 제안대로 해결될 경우 앞으로 더이상의 요구가 없어질 것임, 즉 동 문제는 UR 과 관계없는 기존의 양국간의 문제로 처리되는 결과가 될것임.

나. UR 내 서비스교섭 측면에서도 지금까지 양국간 많은 성과가 있었으며, 이러한 양국간의 분위기에 동건이 장애가 되지 않도록 가능한 조속한 시일내 동건을 타결하고, 기타 문제에 대해 상호 협력해 나가길 희망함.

4. 한편, 쯔루오까 일측 협상대표는 11.5(목) 서울개최 한. 일 다자경제. 통상 협의의 일측대표로 참석, 동건 협의를 계속코자 한다함을 참고바람. 끝.

(대사 오재희 - 국장)

예고 : 92.12.31. 까지

o 기획원 실무 검토의견대로 일측이 제시한 대안을 중심으로 동건을 조속 종결하는 것이 바람직.

o 일측의 ROD 안을 기초로 양측이 수락할 만한 문안을 도출해 내는 것이 가장 바람직하나, 일측 문안의 3항 및 4항은 아측이 그대로 수용하기 어려우므로 일측이 문안의 수정을 적극 반대하는 경우에는 대안으로 일측의 수석대표서한 제안을 검토함.

o 수석대표서한의 문안은 일측으로 하여금 제안토록 하되, 합의 형태에 있어서 아측이 양보하는 만큼 아측이 수락가능한 내용으로 작성되어야 할 것임을 일측에 전달. 끝.

※ 외무부 실무검토의견 없음

0005

경 제 기 획 원

우 427-760 / 경기도 과천시 중앙동1 정부제2청사 / 전화 503-9149 / 전송 503-9141

문서번호 통조삼 10502-132
시행일자 1992. 11. 3
(경유)
수신 수신처참조
참조 통상기구과장

선결			지시		
접수	일자 시간	92 . 11 . 4	결재·공람		
	번호	38586			
처리과					
담당자		이 시 경			

제목 UR/서비스 양자협상결과 및 검토과제 통보

1. 통조삼 10502-125('92.10.9) 관련입니다.

2. 당원 제2협력관을 수석대표로 하여 경제기획원, 재무부, 체신부, KIEP자문관 및 현지대표부 관계관으로 구성된 정부대표단은 '92.10.13~10.16기간중 스위스 제네바에서 미, EC, 일본, 캐나다, 호주, 뉴질랜드, 중국, 스웨덴, 핀랜드등 9개국과 제5차 UR/서비스 국별자유화 약속에 관한 양허협상을 가진 바 있습니다.

3. 이번 협상과정에서 각국은 MFN일탈문제, 인력이동범위 확대문제, 외국인 토지취득문제등의 공통분야외에 우리의 금융자유화 계획 추가양허, 기본통신분야의 다자간 협상 추진문제등을 주요한 의제로 제기하였는 바, 이에 대응하여 우리측 대표단은 10.7 개최된 UR대책 서비스 실무소위원회 회의결과에 의거 대처하는 한편 각국의 요구사항 및 동향파악에 주력한 바 있습니다.

4. 다음번의 양허협상일정은 아직 확정되어 있지 않으나 정부로서는 전체 UR협상이 급속히 진전될 경우에 대비하여 협상준비에 만전을 기해야 할 것입니다.

0006

우 427-760 / 경기도 과천시 중앙동1 정부제2청사 / 전화 503-9149 / 전송 503-9141

5. 따라서 그동안 양허협상과정에서 제기된 주요한 쟁점에 대한 정부입장을 명확히 하고 최종양허표를 작성하는 작업을 진행시키고자 합니다. 이에 금번 협상 회의록 및 주요검토과제를 별첨과 같이 송부하니 이를 참고하여 귀부(처, 청) 소관 사항에 대한 검토의견을 11.13(금)까지 당원으로 송부하여 주기 바라며 아울러 각국에 대한 추가요구사항(request)이 있으면 함께 통보하여 주시기 바랍니다.

첨부 : UR/서비스 제5차 양자협상회의록, UR/서비스협상 분야별 검토과제 1부.

경 제 기 획 원 장

대외경제조정실장 전결

수신처 : 외무부장관, 내무부장관, 재무부장관, 법무부장관, 교육부장관, 문화부장관, 농림수산부장관, 상공부장관, 보건사회부장관, 건설부장관, 교통부장관, 노동부장관, 동력자원부장관, 체신부장관, 과학기술처장관, 환경처장관, 공보처장관, 해운항만청장, 한국개발연구원장, 대외경제정책연구원장,

0007

UR/서비스協商 分野別 檢討課題

檢 討 課 題	要求國家	所管部處
1. 共通適用事項 (1) 外國人投資 - 外國人投資持分 制限이 없어지면 당연히 自由化業種으로 되어 申告制對象이 되는지 여부 ○ 制限業種에서 自由化業種으로 변경되는 경우 포함 ○ 특히 94, 96年부터 一般建設 및 專門建設業의 100% 外國人投資許容時 동 업종이 自由化業種이 되어 申告對象이 되는지 여부	日本	財務部, 建設部, 遞信部
○ VAN서비스에 대해 外國人 投資持分 制限이 없어지면 당연히 申告對象 自由化業種으로 되는지 여부 · 美側은 한·미간 MOU에 '94.1부터 自由化業種으로 변경되는 것으로 記載되어 있다고 주장	美國	
(2) 外國人 土地取得 - 外國人 土地取得에 있어서 임차권까지 상호주의를 적용하는 필요성 재검토 ○ 外國人 土地取得 許可時 상호주의에 대한 MFN逸脫 申請이 임차권까지 포함하는 것은 土地取得이 원천적으로 허용되지 않고 있는 상황에서 사실상 임차에 의한 영업행위마저도 불안정한 상태에 놓이게 하는 내용이며 그에 따라 양허의 수준이 全般的으로 크게 低下되므로 申請撤回를 요구	美國	內務部
- 개방서비스 업종에 대한 外國人 土地取得 허용 ○ 外國人 土地取得 許容 확대계획(중기계획 포함)	美國, 日本	內務部

0008

檢 討 課 題	要求國家	所管部處
- 土地와 建物의 분리소유 가능성 여부 ㅇ 土地所有가 안되므로 건물만 소유할 수는 있는지 여부	EC	內務部
(3) 人力移動		
- 日本 人力移動 讓許計劃(기송부)의 (b)범주에 대한 평가 및 우리입장 점검 ㅇ 專門職서비스中 유자격직종의 경우 人力移動 허용 ㅇ 會計 및 法律서비스에서 affiliation과의 관계	日本	勞動部, 法務部, 財務部, 海運港灣廳
- 핀랜드의 문서『勞動力市場 統合協定과 GATS의 範圍』(기송부)에 대한 검토	핀랜드	勞動部, 法務部
- 서비스 輸入國內에 상업적주재의 설립이 없는 상태에서의 專門職業人(specialty occupation professionals)의 一時的 移動을 양허할 것인가에 대한 우리입장 점검 ㅇ 美國의 讓許(案)에 대한 검토의견 및 우리가 同一要求를 받을 경우의 對應立場 마련	美國,캐나다	勞動部, 法務部, 財務部, 建設部, 保社部, 敎育部
- 계약조건부(contractual basis)입국자에 대한 인력이동 허용여부 ㅇ 例: 中國系 建設會社가 한국의 호텔과 계약해 中國庭園을 만들 경우 中國 建築士와 技術者가 일시적으로 입국해 동 업무를 수행할 수 있는지 여부	中國	勞動部

0009

檢　討　課　題	要求國家	所管部處
2. MFN逸脫		
- 對日 視聽覺서비스 MFN逸脫問題 o 캐나다와 EC의 視聽覺서비스 供給制限의 제도적 방식에 대한 檢討意見 마련 o 우리가 계속 유지코자 하는 日本 視聽覺서비스의 製作, 供給制限에 대한 명료한 기준자료 정비	日本	文化部
3. 金融分野		財務部
- 金融分野 Blueprint內容을 binding commitment로 반영해 달라는 요구에 대한 검토	美國, EC	
- 金融分野 현 offer에서 제외되어 있는 sector를 기제하고 향후 최소한 差別을 하지 않겠다는 약속을 해달라는 요구에 대한 검토 o 특히, 銀行業務에 있어서 신용카드를 포함한 送金서비스, leasing, money broking 등이 누락	美國, EC	
- 金融分野讓許를 understanding에 따라 해줄 것	EC	
- 金融ENT 基準의 명료화	EC	
- 外國換銀行의 換포지션 제한폐지	캐나다	
- 中小企業 貸出義務 폐지	〃	
- 擔保不動産의 독자처분요구	〃	
- 外國銀行의 同一人 대출한도 폐지	〃	
- 信託業務許容 제한완화	〃	
- 銀行서비스의 국경간공급 및 해외소비 허용	EC	
- 外換分野에서 9.1발표한 새 外國換管理規定에 Blueprint 1,2段階 措置內容 반영여부 확인	美國	

0010

檢　　討　　課　　題	要求國家	所管部處
4. 保險		財務部
- 新規保險商品 인가과정의 단순화	캐나다	
5. 事業서비스		
(1) 會計서비스		財務部
- 濠洲 CPA가 韓國內에 있는 濠洲會社의 支社, 子會社 등에 대해 회계서비스를 제공하는 것이 가능한지 여부	濠洲	
(2) 法務서비스中 외국법과 국제법 자문서비스 허용요구	美國, 핀랜드	法務部
(3) 컴퓨터 및 관련서비스중 CPC 845(컴퓨터를 포함한 사무기계 및 장비 수선·유지서비스)에 대한 양허요구	中國	商工部
(4) 教育서비스과 관련 事務所(representative office)의 設置가 가능한 지 여부	뉴질랜드	教育部
(5) 試險檢査서비스(CPC 8676)의 양허요구	캐나다	科學技術處, 動力資源部, 環境處
(6) 廣告서비스中 방송광고대행사가 KOBACO로부터 認可를 받고 동 공사의 放送廣告 代行規程을 준수해야 하는 이유	中國	公報處
6. 通信		遞信部
- 基本通信 多者間協商 參與要求에 대한 우리입장 검토 o 美國등은 한국의 참여가 同 協商의 成功與否에 매우 중요하기 때문에 韓國政府의 立場이 최종적인 것으로 보지 않고 계속 이 문제를 제기할 것임을 강조함.	美國, 캐나다, 스웨덴	

0011

檢 討 課 題	要求國家	所管部處
- 基本通信分野 非公式協議時(10.5~10.6) 논의된 의제에 대한 우리입장 검토		
o 협상개시시점 및 기간, 협상대상분야 및 참가범위, 협상결과의 이행등 協商推進 基本構造에 대한 검토		
o 협상기간중 MFN問題에 대한 우리입장		
· 代案1, 代案2에 대한 검토		
7. 海運		海運港灣廳
- 海運分野 非公式協議時(10.14) 논의된 사항에 대한 우리입장 점검		
o 서비스協定의 수혜자, 해운분야 보조금문제, 항구 설비에 대한 접근 및 이용등		
- 貨物留保制度 對象品目의 점진적 축소요구에 대한 대응 입장 마련		
o 철강을 對象品目에서 削除해 주도록 요구	日本	
o 對象貨物의 점진적 감축 요구	濠洲	
- 外國船社가 새로운 정기선 서비스를 개시하려고 할때 거쳐야 하는 절차(海運港灣廳의 認可與否등)	中國	
- 外國船社에 대한 內國民待遇 附與要求	中國	
- 合作海運船社(선박리스회사 포함) 設立에 따른 제한사항 완화요구	〃	
- 우리 offer에 기재되어 있지 않은 海運補助서비스에 대한 讓許要求	스웨덴	
8. 航空		交通部
- 航空 CRS MFN일탈 철회요구	EC	

0012

檢 討 課 題	要求國家	所管部處
9. 流通		商工部
(1) 小賣業		
- 流通業 ENT는 그 범위가 본래 허용되는 ENT를 벗어나고 부적절	美國	
- 流通業 ENT, 賣場面積 및 賣場數制限 철폐요구	中國	
(2) 貿易業		
- 綜合貿易商社의 업무확대(輸入業 許容)요구	日本	
10. 環境		環境處
- 環境서비스中 CPC 9403, 9404, 9405, 9406, 9409에 대한 讓許要求	핀랜드, 캐나다	
11. 建設		建設部
- 현재 시행되고 있는 建設業 認可基準	日本	
- 免許發給週期 및 都給限度制의 폐지요구	//	
o '94년이후 都給限度制를 어떻게 개선할 것인가에 대한 檢討結果를 질의		
- 都給限度制 關聯資料 요구	中國	
o 현재의 制度 및 基準, 現況등		
- 協會加入등에 있어서의 內外國人 差別有無確認	//	
12. 其他		
- 兩者間에 논의된 사항을 서신교환등의 형태로 追加約束하는 문제에 대한 검토	濠洲	經濟企劃院

0013

檢　討　課　題	要求國家	所管部處
- 서비스協定의 발효가 과거 양자간 합의사항에 영향을 미치게 되는지 여부에 대한 법률적 검토 ㅇ 韓·美間 서비스分野 市場開放에 관한 여러 합의 사항의 향후 효력문제와 관련 서비스협정이 발효될 경우 新協定이 과거협정의 效力을 대체(override) 한다는 것이 自國 法律專門家들의 견해라고 하면서 과거의 모든 韓·美間 合意事項을 준수하겠다는 내용의 별도의 ROU, MOU등이 있어야 함을 요청	美國	經濟企劃院, 法務部
13. 最終讓許表(案) 作成		
- 서비스供給形態(modes)를 구분한 最終讓許表(National Schedule) 草案作成 ㅇ UR의 早期妥結에 대비하기 위해 내부적으로 最終讓許表 草案作成이 필요 - 作成方式 i) 네가지형태의 서비스 供給形態를 명시적으로 구분, 작성 ※ 美國, EC, 日本등 주요국도 모두 서비스 供給形態를 구분한 讓許表(案)을 作成하였음을 밝힘. ii) '92.2 수정양허표제출이후 讓許協商過程을 통하여 最終讓許表에 반영하기로 하였던 追加自由化內容의 反映 iii) 修正讓許表에 기재하였던 투명성 제고목적 추가 정보 기재사항의 처리 ※ 最終讓許表에는 여하한 형태의 별도 information 도 기재하지 않도록 한다는 것이 대부분 국가의 立場	美國, 日本, EC등	全部處

0014

UR 서비스 협상관련 대일 시청각 서비스 제한

11. 6.

한·일 외무장관회담 자료

(말씀 요지)

o 그동안 UR 협상의 모든분야에서 양국은 원만한 협조관계를 유지하여 왔으며, 앞으로도 UR 협상이 타결될 때까지 이러한 협조관계가 지속되기를 희망함.

o 한국내 일본의 시청각 서비스 문제는 양국내에서의 민감성에 비추어 다자차원에서 거론되어 제3국 또는 양국 국민에 대해 양국간 충돌이 있는 것처럼 비쳐지는 것은 바람직하지 않음.

o 현재 국내 관련부처간 진지한 협의가 진행되고 있으므로 조만간 이 문제를 조용히 매듭짓고 종전과 같이 양국간 현안으로 계속 조용하고 조심스럽게 다루어 나갈 수 있게 될 것으로 생각함.

0015

(참고자료)

1. UR/서비스협상과 대일 시청각서비스 제한문제

(경　　위)

o UR관련 한.일 양자서비스협상(92.10.14-15, 제네바)에서 우리측은 시청각서비스 분야에서 일본에 대하여는 MFN원칙을 배제하는 MFN 일탈 신청서를 GATT사무국에 제출하고, 일본측에도 이를 설명
 - 동 일탈신청은 서비스 일반협정(GATS)제2조에 근거한 조치

o 일본측은 이에 반대의사와 함께 한국의 기존 차별정책에 대해 GATS 차원에서 이의를 제기하지 않겠다는 내용의 서면 보장을 해주겠다는 의사를 표명, 아측은 일단 동 일탈 신청을 보류

o 일본측은 10.23(금) 아측에 전화로 동 문안(별첨 Non-Paper)과 전달 방법을 제의

2. 일측 제의내용

o 주한 일본대사가 경제기획원장관을 면담(UR/서비스협상 대표 동석), 아래 구두메시지 및 NON-PAPER(법적 성격을 가지는 문서를 교환할 수없기 때문) 전달

(구두 메시지)

- 대일 시청각서비스 규제를 자유화하기 위한 한국의 노력필요
- 한국의 MFN 일탈을 다자협상에서 취급하는 것은 부적절
- 일본의 Non-Paper 전달이 GATS상 양국의 권리.의무에 영향을 미치지 않음.
- 동건 교섭내용을 대외적으로 공표하지 않을 것을 희망.

0016

(NON-PAPER 요지)

- 일본 정부는 한국의 대일 시청각서비스 관련문제가 정치.사회적으로 매우 민감한 문제임에 비추어 이를 다자차원에서 논의하는 것은 적절치 않다고 생각함.
- 일본은 현재 한국이 취하고있는 일본의 시청각서비스에 대한 조치에 관하여 한국이 GATS상의 MFN일탈을 하지않았다는 사실을 이용(take advantage) 할 의사가 없음.

아측 대응~~(10.16. 부내회의 및 10.27 관계부처 회의결과)~~

o 국내적 민감성에 비추어 단순한 Non-Paper 만으로는 부적절

o ~~양측 UR/서비스 협상 수석대표(아측 : 경기원 제2협력관)가 서명하는~~ 아래 요지의 Record of Discussions~~(별첨 문안)~~을 남기도록 10.29. 일측에 제시

- 본건의 한국내 민감성을 감안, 다자차원 협의는 부적절
- 일본은 한국의 UR 서비스 협상에서 MFN 일탈하지 않는다는 사실을 이용(take advantage)하지 않기로 함.

일측 반응

o 11.4. 일 외무성 국제경제담당 "엔도" 대사가 주일 참사관을 초치, 일측의 당초 제의 재검토 요망

- 일측으로서는 한국이 UR 협상차원에서 본건 MFN 일탈하는 것을 방치할 수 없음.
- 법적 성격의 문서교환은 일본 국내사정상 곤란하며, Non-Paper 전달 정도로 해결하고 나면 이 문제는 UR과는 관계없는 기존의 양국간 문제로 처리될 것임. 끝.

0017

0535U

(Draft)

With regard to the initial commitment negotiations under the draft General Agreement on Trade in Services of the Uruguay Round (GATS), I wish to inform you of the following in view of the practical solution of the issue:

1. It is the view of the Government of Japan that under the current circumstances the issue of the existing Korean measures on Japanese audio-visual services in the Republic of Korea is a sensitive socio-political issue. In light of the sensitivity of this issue, Japan considers inappropriate to address the issue further in the multilateral context.

2. In view of the above, Japan has no intention of taking advantage of the lack of derogation by the Republic of Korea from the most favoured nation treatment obligation under Article II of the GATS with respect to the existing Korean measures on Japanese audio-visual services in the Republic of Korea.

10.23자 日側 Non-Paper 안

0018

RECORD OF DISCUSSIONS

10.29자 합의 ROD 안

——, ——, 1992

1. WITH REGARD TO THE INITIAL COMMITMENT NEGOTIATIONS UNDER THE DRAFT GENERAL AGREEMENT ON TRADE IN SERVICES OF THE URUGUAY ROUND(GATS), REPRESENTATIVES OF THE GOVERNMENTS OF THE REPUBLIC OF KOREA AND OF JAPAN HELD A SERIES OF BILATERAL CONSULTATIONS.

2. AS A RESULT OF THE CONSULTATIONS, THE FOLLOWING UNDERSTANDINGS WERE REACHED ON THE ISSUE OF THE MFN DEROGATION IN THE AREA OF AUDIO-VISUAL SERVICES.

   1) THE GOVERNMENTS OF THE REPUBLIC OF KOREA AND JAPAN SHARED THE VIEW THAT UNDER THE CURRENT CIRCUMSTANCES THE ISSUE OF THE EXISTING KOREAN MEASURES ON JAPANESE AUDIO-VISUAL SERVICES IN THE REPUBLIC OF KOREA IS SENSITIVE SOCIO-POLITICALLY. IN LIGHT OF THE SENSITIVITY OF THE ISSUE, THE TWO SIDES CONSIDERED IT INAPPROPRIATE TO ADDRESS THE ISSUE FURTHER IN THE MULTILATERAL CONTEXT.

   2) IN VIEW OF THE ABOVE, THE GOVERNMENT OF JAPAN AGREED NOT TO TAKE ADVANTAGE OF THE LACK OF DEROGATION BY THE REPUBLIC OF KOREA FROM THE MFN TREATMENT OBLIGATION UNDER ARTICLE II OF THE GATS WITH RESPECT TO THE EXISTING KOREAN MEASURES ON JAPANESE AUDIO-VISUAL SERVICES IN THE REPUBLIC OF KOREA.

FOR THE GOVERNMENT OF THE REPUBLIC OF KOREA	FOR THE GOVERNMENT OF JAPAN
/S/	/S/
HEAD OF KOREAN DELEGATION TO THE INITIAL COMMITMENT NEGOTIATIONS UNDER THE GATS	HEAD OF JAPANESE DELEGATION TO THE INITIAL COMMITMENT NEGOTIATIONS UNDER THE GATS

0019

to. 외무부 통상기구과 이시형 서기관
FAX 725-1737

Draft

November , 1992

Dear Mr. Lee,

On behalf of the Japanese delegation to the initial commitment negotiations under the draft General Agreement on Trade in Services of the Uruguay Round (GATS), I wish to inform you of the following in view of the practical solution of the issue, on the basis of the understanding shared by the Japanese and Korean sides in the course of their consultations:

1. It is the view of the Japanese side that under the current circumstances the issue of the existing Korean measures on Japanese audio-visual services in the Republic of Korea is a sensitive socio-political issue. In light of the sensitivity of this issue, the Japanese side considers it inappropriate to address the issue further in the multilateral context of the Uruguay Round.

2. In view of the above, the Japanese side has no intention of taking advantage of the lack of derogation by the Republic of Korea from the most favoured nation treatment obligation under Article II of the GATS with respect to the existing Korean measures on Japanese audio-visual services in the Republic of Korea.

3. It is confirmed that this letter does not affect the legal rights and obligations of the Japanese side under the GATS.

Sincerely yours,

Koji Tsuruoka
Head of Japanese delegation
to the initial commitment
negotiations under the GATS

0020

RECEIVED FROM 5039141 1992.11.12 16:51 P. 1

외무부 통상기구과 이시형 [illegible]

(본 검토내용은 실무적인 선에서 검토한 것이며, 업무에 참고하시기 바랍니다)

1. 經過

- 10.23 日本側은 駐韓日本大使가 구두멧시지와 함께 non-paper 를 傳達하는 方案을 제안

- 10.29 우리측은 상기 non-paper 내용의 일부표현만 수정하여 보다 公式化된 討議錄(兩國 首席代表가 署名)으로 하자고 修正 提案

- 11.4 日本側은 討議錄은 形式, 內容面에서 법적인 의미의 문서여서 의회에서 문제될 소지가 있으며 서로 양보할 수 없는 부분을 포함시키고자 할 것이므로 文書作成도 현실적으로 매우 어려울 것이라는 點등 문제를 제기하고 既存 提議를 반복

- 11.6 日本側은 11.4일의 의견을 반복하면서 日本側 首席代表가 우리 수석대표에게 書翰을 보내는 方案(내용은 non-paper내용에 일부내용추가, 상호의견 조정작성)이 하나의 代案이 될 수도 있다는 의견을 피력(exchange of letter는 아님)

2. 檢討意見

- 同件과 관련한 兩國間의 그동안의 協議過程에서 일단 일본이 우리가 MFN逸脫登錄을 하지 못하게 한 후 이를 악용하여 GATT 次元에서 同件 MFN 違背問題를 제기코자 하는 의도는 없다는 점은 확인할 수 있었다고 봄.

  ㅇ 日本과 韓國이 여사한 형태의 兩者間 合意를 하더라도 그것이 日本의 GATT 提訴權限을 제한한다는 내용을 포함하고 있지 않는 한 日本은 법률적으로는 항상 제소가능한 것임. 그러므로 日本의 多者的 問題提起與否는 일본이 어떠한 형태로든 한국과 약속한 사항을 위반하는 外交的, 政治的 負擔을 감수하고도 문제제기를 할 것인가에 달려 있는 것이지 문서의 형식에 따라 日本에게 法的拘束力을 부과하게 되는 것은 아니라고 봄.

0021

- 이러한 日本側의 立場에 따라 우리가 현존 對日 視聽覺措置를 당분간 유지하더라도 日本이 多者次元에서 문제제기를 하지 않도록 하려는 목적은 어떤 형식으로든 日本의 書面保障이 있는 한 達成되는 것으로 보아야 할 것임.

  ○ 물론 이것은 영구적인 약속이 될 수도 없으며 또 雙務的인 次元에서의 문제제기를 배제하는 것이 아님. MFN逸脫 申請時의 시한도 UR協定發效後 再協商期間(5年)까지이며 일본측도 non-paper로서 이 기간동안에 多者次元의 문제 제기가 없을 것이라는 點을 확인해 주려는 의도임을 분명히 함.

  ○ 오히려 MFN逸脫을 우리가 고집하고 日本側이 11.4 암시한 대로 제3국을 동원하여 MFN逸脫認定을 막으려고 할 경우에는 오히려 多者體制에서 우리의 조치가 불가능함을 확인하게 되는 결과가 될 수 있음(이 문제는 MFN逸脫申請決定時에도 우려사항으로 고려하였던 점이나 日本側의 이번 암시에 따라 보다 可能性이 높아질 수 있다고 보임)

- 한편 현 시점에서 MFN逸脫申請을 다시 추진할 경우에 야기될 수 있는 兩國間 關係에 있어서의 파장에 대한 충분한 고려가 있어야 할 것임.

  ○ 일단, 그동안의 노력으로 同件에 대한 兩國의 立場에 대한 이해가 근접해 있는 상황에서 同 問題가 공개적인 양국간의 쟁점으로 등장할 경우 兩國關係의 特性上 그 해결이 매우 어렵고 상호 도움이 되지 않는 방향으로 발전할 可能性이 농후함.

  ○ 이경우 全般的인 兩國의 協力關係에도 영향이 파급될 것임.

- 따라서 日本側이 제시한 대안중 가장 실효성이 높다고 판단되는 代案을 중심으로 同件을 조속히 종결하는 것이 바람직 하다고 봄.

0022

0546U a

Record of Discussions

. . 1992

1. The delegations of Japan and the Republic of Korea have held a series of bilateral negotiations as a part of initial commitment negotiations under the draft General Agreement on Trade in Services of the Uruguay Round (GATS), in which the Japanese side requested the removal of the existing Korean measures restricting Japanese audio-visual services in the Republic of Korea. The Korean side responded negatively to the Japanese request. The Japanese side expressed its strong view that further efforts on the part of the Korean side aimed at the removal of the said measures are necessary in order to avoid raising unnecessary conflict between the two countries.

2. With regard to the notification made by the Korean side in the above negotiations that exemption from most favoured nation treatment obligation under Article II of the GATS would be sought on the measures, Japanese side stated that, in light of the socio-political background of the measures, it was inappropriate to address the issue further in the multilateral context. With a view to achieving a practical solution of the issue, the Japanese side informed the Korean side of the following Japanese position:

0023

92-11- 7 :10:16AM :

0546U a

1) It is the view of the Government of Japan that under the current circumstances the issue of the existing Korean measures on Japanese audio-visual services in the Republic of Korea is a sensitive socio-political issue. In light of the sensitivity of this issue, Japan considers inappropriate to address the issue further in the multilateral context.

2) In view of the above, Japan has no intention of taking advantage of the lack of derogation by the Republic of Korea from the most favoured nation treatment obligation under Article II of the GATS with respect to the existing Korean measures on Japanese audio-visual services in the Republic of Korea.

3. The Japanese side and the Korean side confirmed that the above Japanese position would not affect the rights and obligations of Japan and the Republic of Korea under the GATS.

4. The Japanese side and the Korean side shared the view that further consultation on this issue within the framework of the bilateral relations should proceed with the aim of achieving a rational solution of the issue within a reasonable period of time.

/S/

Head of Japanese delegation to the initial commitment negotiations under the GATS

/S/

Head of Korean delegation to the initial commitment negotiations under the GATS

0024

일측 서한 문안에 대한 의견

92.11.16.
외 무 부

o 합의를 위해서는 세부문안에 대해 구체적 검토가 더 필요하나, 전체적으로 3항을 제외하고는 수락 가능할 것으로 봄. 3항에 대하여는 ① 삭제하거나 ② 구두로 전달토록 하던지 ③ 최소한 '양측'의 GATS상 권리의무를 유보 한다는 내용으로 수정해야 할 것임.

o 그 이유로서

- 여사한 권리의무 유보가 종래 GATT 차원에서는 공식적인 합의나 결정시에 상용되어 왔던 형태이나, 금번 일측이 제시한 서한의 성격으로 보아 공식적 형태의 유보조항 삽입은 필요없음.

- 또한 1.2항의 약속이 공식적이거나 법적 구속력이 있는 약속이 아니므로 공식적 성격의 3항을 삽입하는 것은 서한 전체 내용면에서도 균형이 맞지 않음.

- 본건이 일본 국내적으로 민감한 만큼 한국으로서도 민감한 것임.

o 관계부처간 회의를 통해 아측 입장을 수립하기 전에 일측 의사를 타진해 보기 위해 금일중 주일 대사관을 통해 '3항삭제' 의견을 제시해 보는 것이 좋을 것으로 사료됨. 끝.

0025

일측 서한 문안에 대한 의견

92.11.16.
외 무 부

o 합의를 위해서는 세부문안에 대해 구체적 검토가 더 필요하나, 전체적으로 3항을 제외하고는 수락 가능할 것으로 봄. 3항에 대하여는 ① 삭제하거나 ② 구두로 전달토록 하던지 ③ 최소한 '양측'의 GATS상 권리의무를 유보 한다는 내용으로 수정해야 할 것임.

o 그 이유로서

- 여사한 권리의무 유보가 종래 GATT 차원에서는 공식적인 합의나 결정시에 상용되어 왔던 형태이나, 금번 일측이 제시한 서한의 성격으로 보아 공식적 형태의 유보조항 삽입은 필요없음.

- 또한 1.2항의 약속이 공식적이거나 법적 구속력이 있는 약속이 아니므로 공식적 성격의 3항을 삽입하는 것은 서한 전체 내용면에서도 균형이 맞지 않음.

- 본건이 일본 국내적으로 민감한 만큼 한국으로서도 민감한 것임.

o 관계부처간 회의를 통해 아측 입장을 수립하기 전에 일측 의사를 타진해 보기 위해 금일중 주일 대사관을 통해 '3항삭제' 의견을 제시해 보는 것이 좋을 것으로 사료됨. 끝.

0026

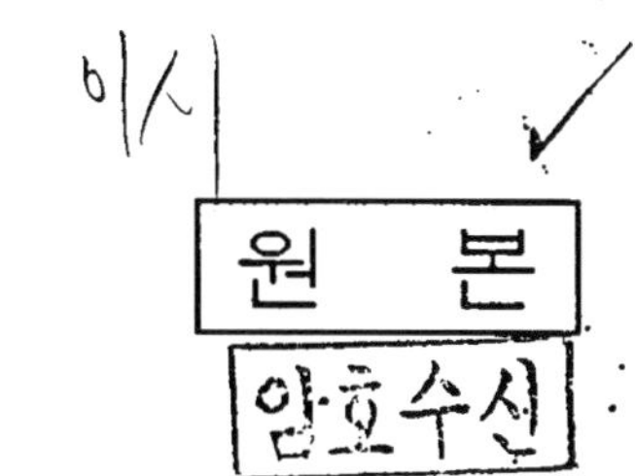

외 무 부

종 별 :

번 호 : ECW-1446　　　　일 시 : 92 1116 1800

수 신 : 장관(통기,통삼,경기원,재무부,상공부,기정동문)

발 신 : 주 EC 대사 사본: 주 제네바-필, 주미대사-중계필

제 목 : UR 협상(서비스분야)

연: ECW-1445

1. EC 집행위는 UR 서비스분야 협상관련, 아래부문에 걸쳐 MFN 원칙적용의 예외를 주장하고 있는것으로 알려짐

가. 시청각분야

0 EC 회원국의 방송시간중 적정부분을 유럽프로그램에 배정하여 이를 유럽내 EC 비회원국에도 확대

0 특정 언어프로그램에 대한 최소한 방영보장

0 EC 의 MEDIA, EURIMAGES 프로그램을 특정 EC 비회원국에 대해 공여하도록허용

0 EC 와의 문화협력 관계를 갖고 있는 나라에대해 양자협정을 통해 프로그램 배분및 기금접근면 내국민 대우부여

0 EC 는 이들 분야가 EC 의 이익보다는 제 3 국에대해 공여되는 것임을 강조하고 있음

나. 해운

0 유엔 해운협정(UN LINER CODE) 에 기초하여, 아프리카제국의 국적선에 대한 EC 의 특혜부여를 인정

다. 육상운송

0 EC 비회원국 업자가 회원국으로부터 제 3 국으로 재화를 운송하는 문제와관련, EC 는 EC 와 양자협정을 맺은 국가에 등록된 차량에 대해서만 운송권 부여를 희망 (주로 동구권제국 대상)

라. 내수로 운송

0 라인강과 마인-다뉴브강 운송권을 특정 사업자에게만 제한 희망

2. EC 집행위는 상기내용을 포함하여, 현재 이미 GATT 에 제출한 서비스분야 양허

통상국	장관	차관	1차보	통상국	분석관	청와대	안기부	경기원
재무부	상공부	중계						

PAGE 1　　　　92.11.17 04:48

외신 2과 통제관 FK

0027

OFFER 를 수정하는 문제를 검토중이며, 곧 113 조 위원회의 검토를 거쳐, 재네바로 보낼 예정인 것으로 알려짐

3. UR 서비스 분야 양허협상 관련, EC 는 최근에 싱가폴을 포함, 동남아제국에 금융서비스 관련 OFFER 의 개선을 요구하는 서한을 보낸바 있으며, 미국에 대해서도 해운 써비스분야 OFFER 를 개선할 것을 요구하고 있음. 한편 써비스분야에서 EC 가 제시한 OFFER 에 대한 반응으로서는 여러 개도국들이 노동인력의 EC 권 입국거부에 대한 시정을 요구하고 있으며, 미국은 EC 의 시청각분야의 예외주장에 대한 반대및 통신분야, 그중 특히 부가가치 전산망및 데이터통신 (DATATRANSMISSION) 등 OFFER 에대해 불만을 표시하고 있다함. 끝

(대사 권동만-국장)

0028

관리 번호	92 - 832

분류번호	보존기간

발 신 전 보

번 호 : WJA-4867 921117 1120 WH 종별 : 지급

수 신 : 주 일 대사. 총영사

발 신 : 장 관 (통 기)

제 목 : 대일 시청각 서비스 MFN 일탈

연 : WJA-4570

대 : JAW-5888

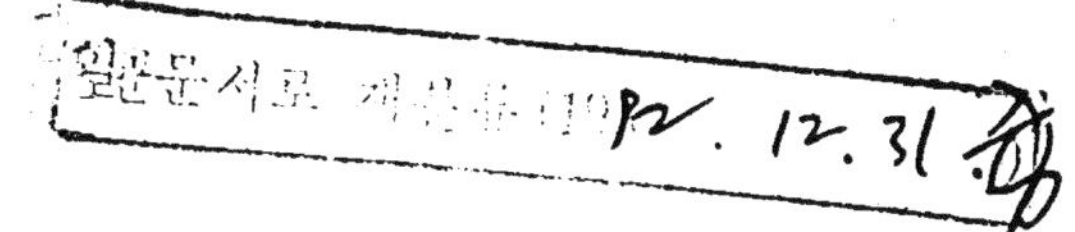

1. UR 서비스 양자협상 일측 수석대표인 쯔루오까는 11.6. 아측 수석대표를 면담, 일측의 ROD 문안을 제시하고 협의하였으나 합의하지 못하였음.

2. 일측은 11.11(수) 주한대사관을 통해 일측 수석대표 명의의 서한을 일방적으로 아측에 전달하는 방식을 제의하면서 그 문안을 별첨과 같이 제시하여 왔으며, 이에 대해 아측은 추후 검토결과를 알려 주기로 ~~하였음~~ 한 바 있음.

3. 일측 대표 서한 문안에 대한 검토결과를 아래 통보하니 이를 외무성 관계관에게 전달 바람.

가. 아측은 본건이 일본에게 국내적으로 민감한 사안임을 고려하여 기본적으로 본건의 조용한 해결을 희망하며 가급적 일측이 제시한 서한 문안을 기초로 하여 타결하기를 희망함.

나. 일측 문안은 대체로 수락가능하나, 3항은 다음과 같은 이유를 감안하여 삭제하는 것이 좋겠음. / 계속...

하거나 서한전달시에 아측이 구두로 전달

보안 통제	

앙고재	92년 11월 16일	통상기구과	기안자 성명		과 장	심의관	국 장	제2차관보	차 관	장 관
									전결	

외신과통제

아주국장 :

0029

1) 여사한 권리의무의 유보표현은 GATT 차원의 공식적 합의나 결정시에 사용되는 것으로서, 금번 일측이 제시한 서한의 성격에 비추어 이러한 공식적인 형태의 유보조항을 삽입하는 것은 서한의 형식면에서 격에 맞지 않음.

2) 또한 1항 및 2항의 약속이 공식적이거나 법적 구속력이 강한 약속이 아니므로 공식적 결정이나 합의문에 사용되는 3항과 같은 유보조항을 삽입하는 것은 서한 전체의 내용면에서도 균형이 맞지 않음.

3) 본건이 일본 국내적으로 민감한 것과 마찬가지로 한국으로서도 민감한 것이므로 3항과 같은 유보조항이 포함되어서는 곤란함.

다. 아측은 11.20(금) 관계부처 회의를 통해 대일 시청각 서비스 MFN 일탈신청 문제에 대한 최종입장을 결정할 예정이므로 가급적 그 이전에 아측 제안에 대한 일측 의견을 듣기를 희망함.

첨부 : 일측 서한 문안. 끝.

(차 관 노 창 희)

0030

(첨부)

November, 1992

Dear Mr. Lee,

On behalf of the Japanese delegation to the initial commitment negotiations under the draft General Agreement on Trade in Services of the Uruguay Round (GATS), I wish to inform you of the following in view of the practical solution of the issue, on the basis of the understanding shared by the Japanese and Korean sides in the course of their consultations :

1. It is the view of the Japanese side that under the current circumstances the issue of the existing Korean measures on Japanese audio-visual services in the Republic of Korea is a sensitive socio-political issue. In light of the sensitivity of this issue, the Japanese side considers it inappropriate to address the issue further in the multilateral context of the Uruguay Round.

2. In view of the above, the Japanese side has no intention of taking advantage of the lack of derogation by the Republic of Korea from the most favoured nation treatment obligation under Article II of the GATS with respect to the existing Korean measures on Japanese audio-visual services in the Republic of Korea.

3. It is confirmed that this letter does not affect the legal rights and obligations of the Japanese side under the GATS.

Sincerely yours,

Koji Tsuruoka
Head of Japanese delegation
of the initial commitment
negotiations under the GATS

0031

관리 번호	92-836

원 본

외 무 부

종 별 : 지 급

번 호 : JAW-6144 일 시 : 92 1117 1820

수 신 : 장관(통기)

발 신 : 주 일 대사(일경)

제 목 : 대일 시청각 MFN 일탈

대 : WJA - 4867

연 : JAW - 5888

1. 대호, 당관 황순택서기관은 금 11.17(화) UR 서비스 양자협상 일측 수석대표 쯔루오까를 접촉, 대호 일측 서한문안에 대한 우리측 검토의견을 전달 하고, 일측 의견을 늦어도 11.19(목)까지 회답해 줄 것을 요청함.

2. 상기 우리측 입장 전달에 대해, 쯔루오까 대표는 우리측 검토 의견중 (대호 3 항 (나)의 (2)) "법적 구속력이 강한 약속이 아니므로" 라고 하는 표현에 대해 일단 아래와 같이 자신의 견해를 제시하고, 우리측 협상대표와 직접 전화 통화하여 이에대한 우리측 인식을 분명히 확인 한후 일측 검토 의견을 제시하겠다고 언급하였음.

가. 기본적으로 동 문제 처리에 있어 양측이 공통된 이해와 인식에 입각, 서한 문안 작성 등을 해야 한다고 생각함.

나. 일측은 대호 서한을 법적 구속력이 강하거나 또는 약한 약속이라고 하는 차원에서 생각하지 않고, 법적 구속력이 없는 정치적.도의적 성격의 서한으로이해하고 작성한 것임.

다. 한국측이 동 서한을 법적 구속력이 없는 약속으로 이해하고 있다면, 일단 개인적 으로는 금번 한국측 검토 의견대로 제 3 항을 삭제 또는 구두전달이 가능하다고 생각하나, 그렇지 않을 경우는 다른 문제가 될 것임.

라. 일측이 대호 3 항을 서한에 삽입시키게 된것도 동 서한이 법적 구속력을 갖고있지 않기 때문인바, 만일 한국측이 동 서한을 강하던, 약하던 간에 법적 구속력이 있는 서한으로 이해하고 있다면 대호 3 항의 삭제는 오히려 동 서한이 법적 구속력이 있다고 하는 한국측의 인식을 강하게 하는 결과가 될 것으로 우려됨.

통상국	장관	차관	2차보	아주국	분석관	청와대	안기부

경기92

PAGE 1 92.11.17 18:55

* 원본수령부서 승인없이 복사 금지 외신 2과 통제관 CM

0032

마. 따라서, 한국측이 대호 서한 1 항 및 2 항의 약속을 정치적 또는 도의적 약속으로 이해하고 있는가 아닌가 하는 여부가 한국측 제안에 대한 일측 검토에 있어 대단히 중요한 점임을 강조함. 끝.

(대사 오재희 - 국장)

예고 : 92. 12. 31. 까지

이시 V

관리번호	92-846

원 본

외 무 부

종 별 :

번 호 : JAW-6177 일 시 : 92 1119 1645

수 신 : 장관(통기, 아일)

발 신 : 주 일 대사(일경)

제 목 : 대일 시청각 MFN 일탈

대:WJA-4867

연:JAW-6144

대호 주재국 UR 서비스 양자협상 일측 수석대표 쯔루오까는 금 11.19. 당관황순택 서기관에게 대호 일측 서한관련 우리측 제안에 대해 아래와 같이 일측입장을 회답하여옴.

1. 한국측이 UR 시청각 분야 대일 MFN 일탈 문제를 대호 일측 서한을 기초로해결코자 희망하고 있는 점을 고려, 일측은 다음과 같은 방향으로 본건의 최종타결을 기대함.

가. 한국측 희망대로 대호 일측서한 제 3 항을 삭제함.

나. 동 3 항 내용은 서한 전달시 구두로 전달함

2. 또한 일측은 상기 일측 입장에 대한 한국측 입장을 가급적 조속 알려주기를 희망함

3. 일측 서한 전달 시기등 세부 사항은 한국측 입장을 들은후 최종적으로 협의코자 함

(대사 오재희-국장)

예고:92.12.31. 까지

일반문서로 재분류(1992.12.31)

통상국	장관	차관	2차보	아주국	분석관	청와대	안기부	경기원

PAGE 1 92.11.19 17:29

외신 2과 통제관 FW

0034

외 무 부

종 별 :

번 호 : GVW-2177 일 시 : 92 1120 1700

수 신 : 장관(통기, 경기원, 해운항만청)

발 신 : 주 제네바대사

제 목 : UR/서비스(해운)

UR/서비스 해운분야 복수국간 협의와 관련하여 EC측에서 그간의 비공식협의 사항을정리한자료를 당관에 보내왔는바, 이를 별첨 송부하니, 검토후 의견회신 바람.

첨부 : 1. EC측 서신 및 토의문서 각 1부.

2. 동 문서의 ANNEX 3,4,5 각 1부.

3. 동 문서의 ANNEX 1(91. 12.25 카알라일 사무차장작성 문서) 및 ANNEX 2(EC 제안 MODELSCHEDULE)는 기 송부.(GVW(F)-0698). 끝.

(대사 박수길 - 국장

통상국 경기원 해항청

PAGE 1

92.11.21 07:49 CJ

외신 1과 통제관

0035

주 제 네 바 대 표 부

번 호 : GVW(F) - 0698 년월일 : 21120 시간 : 1700

수 신 : 장 관 (통기, 경기원, 해운항만청)

발 신 : 주 제네바대사

제 목 : UR/서비스(해운) GVW-2177 첨부

보 안	
통 제	

총 7 매(표지포함)

외신국	
통 제	

698-7-1

0036

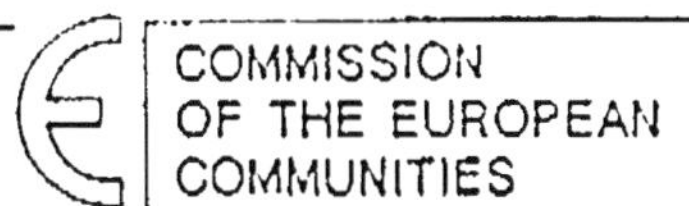
COMMISSION
OF THE EUROPEAN
COMMUNITIES

Brussels, 16 November 1992

DIRECTORATE-GENERAL
EXTERNAL RELATIONS
I.D.3 (Services)

Dear Colleague,

The attached paper has been prepared following a series of informal consultations in June and October 1992 regarding the treatment of the maritime transport sector in the GATS. It follows the circulation of some informal suggestions from the Secretariat setting out a possible "common approach" for commitments in this sector by a number of participants. In consultations on these ideas, there was a generally perceived need, before any participant could commit itself to the approach, to achieve a higher degree of technical clarity as to its content. We have thus focused on the scope rather than the level of possible commitments.

I have chaired the informal consultations in my personal capacity. The paper thus represents my own personal assessment of the state of our discussions and sets out my understanding of the degree of consensus which has been reached on the various technical issues which we have addressed. Although there are still some outstanding issues, I believe we are now approaching the point where, having made a good deal of progress on the technical parameters of the exercise, each participant will have to make the political decision as to how far it can accept the scale of commitment envisaged. Before seeking such a decision, I would be grateful for confirmation from participants in the discussions that this note is in fact a correct presentation of the situation.

There will also be a need to expand the circle of those involved in the discussions to seek a similar level of commitment from certain other participants in the Round. Before doing so, I understand that participants in the informal discussions would like to reflect both on the substance and the form of such a broader involvement of others.

Finally, reactions from any participant, to the extent possible in writing, would be very helpful for future progress.

Yours sincerely,

Jonathan SCHEELE

To participants in Informal Consultations
on Maritime Transport

/u/js/TRANS/marlett

6P8-7-2

Rue de la Loi 200 – B-1049 Brussels – Belgium

0037

Brussels, 16 November 1992
JS/js

GATS - MARITIME TRANSPORT

Discussion Paper

Elements of a Common Approach on Maritime Transport

Discussion in informal consultations has been based principally on the informal text prepared by the Secretariat in December 1991, supplemented by a non-paper circulated on 17 June 1992 at the first session of these informal consultations. Both are attached in Annexes 1 and 2. Discussion was also helped by the tabling, by Japan, of a statistical paper and, by Norway, of a draft schedule for this sector. The following text addresses the different elements of that approach :

A. International Maritime Transport

Scope : There is agreement that this does not cover cabotage, nor operation of vessels which do not have a transportation purpose (e.g. towing assistance services). The latter are seen as auxiliary services and are addressed under that heading.

Level of commitment : In accordance with the Secretariat informal paper, there seems to be a widening consensus that some transitional restrictions, to be phased out over a specified time period, should be possible for participants making commitments for the provision of cross-border services, which would normally be unlimited. Consumption abroad would also be unlimited. There is also increasing agreement that, for commercial presence and movement of persons, the commitment could be limited to the shore-based presence necessary for commercial activities or managing the operation of vessels. Keeping in mind the difficulties involved in drawing clear lines in the multimodal chain, a first attempt to list the type of operation involved in this respect is set out in Annex 3. No commitment would be implied regarding registration of vessels under the flag of the Member concerned.

MFN Exemptions : In line with the generally accepted interpretation of the GATS, MFN exemptions cannot reduce the effect of the scheduled commitments regarding market access/national treatment . To the extent that any Member sought an exemption to give preferential treatment better than its GATS commitment, others Members would need to evaluate the impact of such an exemption (depending on its scope) on the overall balance of commitments under the GATS.

Beneficiaries : A first discussion of this very complex issue suggests the provisional conclusion that the basic criterion, established in Article XXXIV of the GATS, of the country of origin of the service supplier, or operator, should apply equally to this sector. In most

0038

6P8-7-3 ./.

instances this would cover the concerns of participants to limit the benefits of the GATS to service suppliers of other Members, the flag of registration of the vessel being irrelevant; at the same time, this would not require a Member to give identical treatment to all vessels, irrespective of their flag, when such differences are justified by objective requirements such as safety. There are however instances where vessels may be owned by nationals of a Member and carry the flag of that Member, but are controlled through a company established in a non-Member; in other cases, a vessel may be owned and flagged in a Member, but chartered to an operator, i.e. a service supplier, of a non-Member. Given the interests of participants in these more complex cases, the applicability of the GATS to them needs further reflection, particularly in the light of the conditions specified in Article XXXIV. To the extent that the basic GATS origin criterion does not address them, there will be a need to determine whether any specific additional provisions are necessary.

Access to and Use of Port Facilities : There was consensus that, as a general rule, a commitment to allow market access in international maritime transport would, under Articles VIII and XXXIV(c) of the GATS, also give the right of access on a non-discriminatory basis to port facilities. At the same time there was a tendency to seek to clarify this right by establishing a list of services which were considered as covered by such a right. A revised draft of such a list is attached as **Annex 4**.

Subsidies : The applicability of the national treatment obligation with regard to subsidies in this sector was discussed. It was recognised that clarification is still required on the implications of national treatment in the cross-border mode, which is particularly relevant in the maritime transport sector. Further discussion on this in relation to the sector should however await more general clarification in the technical discussions on scheduling.

B. Auxiliary Services

Classification/Scope : There is a clear feeling that the CPC classification in this sector is in some instances inadequate and should, where appropriate, be adapted in country schedules. There is also recognition of the difficulty of extending the scope of liberalisation to cover the actual provision of labour itself (i.e. dockers' monopolies). A possible approach to classification in schedules is set out in **Annex 5** for consideration by participants.

Infrastructure Limitations : All participants recognised that the concept of total liberalisation of certain auxiliary services would in fact be untenable given the existence of physical limitations on the infrastructure of ports. In these circumstances, it was suggested that the objective of liberalisation be addressed in terms of permitting competition between a limited number of suppliers, who might also have specific obligations regarding service to users. In any case, the requirements regarding access to and use of port facilities on a non-discriminatory basis still apply (see A. above). If this approach is followed it may be necessary to determine the categories of service which are in fact affected by infrastructure limitations. A possible approach to this issue is also set out in **Annex 5**.

/u/js/TRANS/chairmar

6P8-7-4

0039

ANNEX 3

Operations involved in commercial presence for the purposes of provision of international maritime transport services

Ability for the maritime transport service supplier to undertake locally all activities which are necessary for the supply to their customers of a partially or fully integrated transport service, within which maritime transport constitutes a substantial element.

These activities include, but are not limited to:

(a) marketing and sales of maritime transport and related services through direct contact with customers, from quotation to invoicing, whether these services are operated or offered by the service supplier itself or by service suppliers with which the service seller has established standing business arrangements;

(b) acquisition, on their own account or on behalf of their customers (and the resale to their customers) of any transport and related services, including inward transport services by any mode, particularly inland waterways, road and rail, necessary for the supply of the integrated service;

(c) preparation of documentation concerning transport documents, customs documents, or other documents related to the origin and character of the goods transported;

(d) provision of business information by any means, including computerised information systems and electronic data interchange (subject to the provisions of the Annex on Telecommunications);

(e) establishment of any business arrangement, including participation in the company's stock and the appointment of personnel recruited locally (or, in the case of foreign personnel, subject to the horizontal commitment on movement of personnel), with any locally established shipping agency;

(f) management of vessels operated for the supply of the above services.

0040

6P8-7-5

ANNEX 4

Draft illustrative list of port facilities which should be made available to shipping service suppliers on reasonable and non-discriminatory terms:

- Pilotage;
- Towing and tug assistance;
- Anchorage, berths and berthing services;
- Lightering and water taxi services;
- Provisioning, fuelling and watering;
- Garbage collection and ballast waste disposal;
- Stevedoring and terminal services, including storage and warehousing;
- Port captains' services;
- Navigation aids;
- Shore based operational services essential to ship operations including communications, water and electrical supplies;
- Emergency repair facilities;
- Documentation and certification services for cargoes and vessels;
- Customs and other essential public services;
- Shipping agency services.

688-7-6

0041

ANNEX 5

Draft classification of auxiliary services which should be subject to liberalisation commitments under Articles XVI and XVII, in the context of "Attachment A" to the Carlisle Paper.

(1) Maritime cargo handling services (ad hoc definition to be elaborated);

[N.B. this encompasses "loading and unloading", "cargo handling within the port (but not inland) terminal confines", "stevedoring" in the Carlisle Paper; the definition should clarify this scope, while at the same time carving out the issue of the direct dockers' workforce]

(2) Storage and Warehousing services (CPC 742 seems adequate);

(3) Customs clearance services (ad hoc definition to be elaborated)

[N.B. this should cover "clearing cargo with customs, including making cargo available for inspection when required" in the Carlisle Paper; the substance of this activity lies within a normally accredited profession; the definition should clarify these elements]

(4) Container station services (ad hoc definition to be elaborated)

[N.B. this should cover "handling within inland terminal confines", including crating and decrating of containers, together with storage and repair of containers, whether or not in the confines of the port]

(5) Maritime agency services (ad hoc definition to be provided)

[N.B. this should cover the same type of activities as those described in Annex 3 above under Commercial Presence of shipping companies, when the service provider does not establish such a direct commercial presence. Given the description of the activities under Annex 3, the three last indents in Attachment A to the Carlisle Paper are covered; the definition should however clarify these points.]

Additional note: Services under points (1), (2) and (4) above may imply the occupation of public domain and/or land occupation capacity constraints; such constraints are not contrary to commitments which would be undertaken, provided the procedures for allocation of available surfaces are fair and transparent. [This issue may need to be further adressed.]

6P8-7-7

0042

수신: 외무부 통상3과 이윤영 사무관 (FAX: 725-1353)
발신: 재무부 국제금융과 김ㅇㅇ

주한 영국대사 서한 답신

- 서한 요지

* 주한 영국대사 D.J.Wright가 EC집행위 금융담당 부위원장인 sir Leon Brittan과 EC 재무장관 협의회의장인 영국 N.Lamont 재무장관의 다음과 같은 공동명의 서신을 재무장관에게 전달

o UR협상의 성공적 타결을 위해서는 현재 각국이 제출한 금융분야의 offer개선을 통한 추가적인 금융자유화 약속이 필요하므로

o 협상 참가국들이 금융분야 offer 개선 가능성 여부를 검토해 주기를 희망

- 답신 요지

o 우리나라는 UR협상 타결을 위하여 적극적으로 협상에 참여하고 있으며 UR 협상 타결을 위해서는 협상 참가국간의 이익이 균형되어야 함.

o offer 개선과 관련하여 일부 국가의 경우 offer를 개선할 필요가 있다는 것에 동의하고 있으며, 우리나라의 경우는 현재 Geneva에서 진행되고 있는 양자협상 결과를 반영하여 추후 합의될 협상 일정에 따라서 National Schedule을 제출할 계획임.

o UR 협상의 성공적 타결을 위한 귀하의 노력에 경의를 표함.

0043

0011 P02 NOV 24 '92 17:48

British Embassy
Seoul

HE Mr Rhee Yong-man
Minister
Ministry of Finance

22 October 1992

Your Excellency,

I have been asked to convey to you the text of a joint letter from the British Chancellor of the Exchequer, the Rt Hon Norman Lamont MP who is President of the European Community Finance Minister and Sir Leon Brittan of the European Commission.

Text Begins:

Uruguay Round and Financial Services

We are writing to you jointly, on behalf of the European Community and the Member States, to invite you to address a remaining problem in the crucial matter of the negotiations on financial services in the Uruguay Round. We believe it is axiomatic that a satisfactory outcome to the already protracted Uruguay Round negotiations is a very important ingredient in ensuring global prosperity and renewed non-inflationary growth.

As you know, the financial services offers of some of the major parties to the round are conditional upon acceptable offers being tabled by other parties to the round. Some progress was made in the recent bilateral discussions in Geneva, but there is still some way to go if we are to achieve widespread liberalisation on an MFN basis. There continues to be a serious risk that if the overall level of offers is not improved, the more generous ones may be withdrawn, which could effectively remove financial services from the round as a whole. The financial services agreement is one aspect where Finance Ministers can have direct influence on the stance Governments take, given our responsibility for the important sectors and markets concerned.

We would therefore invite you personally to examine the content of your offer and to consider how best it may be improved.

SIGNED
NORMAN LAMONT
SIR LEON BRITTAN

0044

I should like to take this opportunity to convey to Your Excellency the assurances of my highest consideration.

Yours sincerely

David Wright

D J Wright
HM Ambassador

0045

Ministry of Finance

KWACHON, KOREA

OFFICE OF THE MINISTER

November 20, 1992

Rt. Hon. Norman Lamont MP,
Chancellor of the Exchequer

Your Excellency :

Thank you very much for your letter of Oct. 22 relayed through the Ambassador of United Kingdom in Korea, and I would like to take this opportunity to first acknowledge my wholehearted support in your continuing efforts to successfully conclude the Uruguay Round.

In this regard, I fully agree with your belief that a satisfactory outcome to the already protracted Uruguay Round negotiations is a very important ingredient in ensuring global prosperity and renewed non–inflationary growth.

As you know, Korea is one of the active participants in the on–going Uruguay Round negotiations. Thus we believe it is essential to agree on a balance of benefits among the participants.

With regard to the improvement of the offer list, I also agree that the overall level of offers needs to be improved in some aspects. However, Korea will submit a national schedule which will reflect the outcome of the bilateral meetings in Geneva at the future agreed time.

0046

Finally, let me again pay my respects to your negotiation efforts, hoping for a very positive and fruitful coutcome.

Sincerely,

Yong-Man Rhee
Minister of Finance

0047

Ministry of Finance

KWACHON, KOREA

OFFICE OF THE MINISTER

November 20, 1992

Sir Leon Brittan,
Vice President of the European Commission

Your Excellency :

Thank you very much for your letter of Oct. 22 relayed through the Ambassador of United Kingdom in Korea, and I would like to take this opportunity to first acknowledge my wholehearted support in your continuing efforts to successfully conclude the Uruguay Round.

In this regard, I fully agree with your belief that a satisfactory outcome to the already protracted Uruguay Round negotiations is a very important ingredient in ensuring global prosperity and renewed non–inflationary growth.

As you know, Korea is one of the active participants in the on–going Uruguay Round negotiations. Thus we believe it is essential to agree on a balance of benefits among the participants.

With regard to the improvement of the offer list, I also agree that the overall level of offers needs to be improved in some aspects. However, Korea will submit a national schedule which will reflect the outcome of the bilateral meetings in Geneva at the future agreed time.

0048

Finally, let me again pay my respects to your negotiation efforts, hoping for a very positive and fruitful coutcome.

Sincerely,

Yong-Man Rhee
Minister of Finance

0049

관리번호	92 - 878

분류번호	보존기간

발 신 전 보

WGV-1810 921125 1124 WG

번 호 : 종별 :

수 신 : 주 제네바 대사. 총영사

발 신 : 장 관 (통 기)

제 목 : 대일 시청각 서비스 MFN 일탈 문제

연 : (1) WGV-1655, (2) JAW-5888

대 : GVW-2034

검 토 필 (1992.12.31.)

표제건 관련, 그간의 일측과 협의 경과를 아래 알리니 참고바람.

1. 연호(1) 아측의 토의록(ROD) 제안에 대하여, 일측(엔도 UR 담당대사)은 연호(2)와 같이 국내 정치적 어려움을 강하게 표시하고 일측의 당초 제안인 non-paper 로서 타결할 것을 희망한 바 있음. (11.5 한.일 외무부 다자경제 협의에 참석한 일 외무성 오구라 경제국장도 필요한 경우 일측이 이문제를 11.8 양국 외무장관 회담에서 제기할 수도 있다는 점을 표명한 바 있음)

2. 이에 대해 아측은 non-paper는 수락하기 어려우므로 양측이 다른 방법을 모색할 것을 요청하고 협의한 결과, 연호 non-paper 내용을 일측 수석대표가 아측 수석대표앞 서한으로 전달하는 방안에 대해 원칙적으로 합의한 바 있음.

검 토 필 (1993.6.30.)

3. 그러나, 최근 국내 대책협의 과정에서 문화부가 입장을 후퇴시켜 구속력 있는 법적보장 확보 또는 MFN 일탈신청 강행을 주장함에 따라, 관계부처간 협의가 계속되고 있음. 끝.

(통상국장 홍 정 표)

보안통제	

앙고재	92년 11월 25일	통상기구과	기안자 성명		과 장	심의관	국 장		차 관	장 관
							전결			

외신과통제

0050

관리 번호	92 - 865

	분류번호	보존기간

발 신 전 보

번 호 : WJA-4970 921124 1453 WG 종별 :

수 신 : 주 일 대사. 총영사

발 신 : 장 관 (통 기)

제 목 : 한.일 시청각 서비스 MFN 일탈문제

대 : JAW-6177

연 : WJA-4867

연호, 표제건에 대한 아측의 최종입장 마련을 위한 관계부처 회의가 11.20(금) 개최되었으나, 부처간 의견 조정에 다소 시간이 필요할 것으로 보이는 바, 일측의 문의가 있는 경우 관계부처간 의견 조정중임을 우선 설명바람. 끝.

(통상국장 홍 정 표)

보 안 통 제	(서명)

앙 고 재	92년 11월 24일	통상기구과	기안자 성 명		과 장	심의관	국 장		차 관	장 관
			이시형		(서명)	(서명)	전결			(서명)

외신과통제

0051

원 본

외 무 부

종 별 :

번 호 : FRW-2439 일 시 : 92 1127 1730

수 신 : 장 관 (통기,경일,사본:재무부,상공부)

발 신 : 주 불 대사

제 목 : OCED/서비스 교역 분야 합동회의

1. OECD 무역위 및 재무위는 UR 에서서비스교역에 관한 일반 협정(GATS:GENERALAGREEMENT ON TRADE IN SERVICES)이 타결되기 전에 동협정 초안상 최혜국 대우와 내국민대우 원칙을 조세에 적용하는 문제(협정 2, 11, 14, 22, 23조)에대해 OECD 내에서 검토키로 결정하고, 오는 12.7 양위원회간 합동위를 개최키로 함.

2. OECD 사무국은 상기 회의에 아국이 옵서버자격으로 참석하여 줄것을 희망하면서,동 회의의특성을 고려 가급적 조세 및 서비스 분야전문가의(각분야 1명씩) 참석을 요청하여왔는바, 동 회의의 중요성을 감안 가급적 본부대표를 파견하여 주시고, OECD 사무국이 제안한 문제점과 협정초안 수정안에 대한 아국 입장을알려주시기 바람.

3. 상기 회의 의제 및 회의자료는 FAX(FRW(F)-0045)편 송부함.끝.

(대사 노영찬-국장)

통상국 경제국 재무부 상공부

PAGE 1 92.11.28 05:32 DX

외신 1과 통제관

0052

주 불 대 사 관

FRW(F) : 046 (92. 1127 1800)

수 신 : 장 관 (통기)

발 신 : 주불대사

제 목 : OECD/서비스 교역 분야 회의 (출처 :)

보안 통제

배부처	장관실	차관실	一차보	二차보	외정실	분석관	아주국	미주국	구주국	중아국	국기국	경제국	통상국	문협국	외연원	청와대	안기부	공보처	경기원	상공부	재무부	농수부	동자부	환경처	과기처		
													O														

(046-10-1)

0053

ORGANISATION FOR ECONOMIC CO-OPERATION AND DEVELOPMENT

DIRECTORATE FOR FINANCIAL, FISCAL AND ENTERPRISE AFFAIRS

COMMITTEE ON FISCAL AFFAIRS

RESTRICTED

Paris, drafted: 26-NOV-1992

English text only

DRAFT AGENDA

AD HOC INFORMAL MEETING BETWEEN TRADE IN SERVICES AND TAX EXPERTS ON THE TREATMENT OF TAXES IN THE GENERAL AGREEMENT ON TRADE IN SERVICES (GATS)

to be held at the Château de la Muette on
Monday 7 December 1992 beginning at 10:00 a.m.
and continuing until 18:00

I. ADOPTION OF THE AGENDA

II. CURRENT STATE OF PLAY ON GATS

-- Statements by Delegates

III. THE TREATMENT OF TAXES IN GATS

-- Discussion of main problems DAFFE/CFA/WP1/WD(92)4/5/13*

1. General Principles on the treatment of taxes

-- Presentation by the OECD Secretariat

2. Difficulties with the present text and alternative solutions:

-- Art. XIV	(Chapeau)	-- Introductory remarks by Canada
-- Art. XIV d)		-- Introductory remarks by the United Kingdom and the United States
-- Art. XIV e)		-- Introductory remarks by the United Kingdom
-- Art. XXII		-- Introductory remarks by Canada
-- Art. XI		-- Introductory remarks by United States

3. Suggested Drafting Amendments to the present discussion

-- Discussion of proposed draft amendments

IV. OTHER BUSINESS

---

* This document has already been distributed to Working Party No. 1 Delegates of the Committee on Fiscal Affairs.

045-10-2

0054

ORGANISATION FOR ECONOMIC CO-OPERATION AND DEVELOPMENT

DIRECTORATE FOR FINANCIAL, FISCAL AND ENTERPRISE AFFAIRS

COMMITTEE ON FISCAL AFFAIRS

RESTRICTED

Paris, drafted: 9 September 1992
OLIS: >
disc.: >

Scale I

DAFFE/CFA/WP1/WD(92)4
(3rd Revision)

English Text Only

WORKING PARTY No. 1 ON DOUBLE TAXATION OF THE COMMITTEE ON FISCAL AFFAIRS

THE TREATMENT OF TAXES IN THE GENERAL AGREEMENT ON TRADE IN SERVICES

(Note by the Secretariat)

The attached information note, which has been prepared by the Secretariat, summarises the Working Party's discussion on this issue.

046-10-3

0055

+33 1 47538838 1992-11-27 18:01 G3-96 S #9

OCDE

ORGANISATION DE COOPÉRATION ET DE DÉVELOPPEMENT ÉCONOMIQUES

OECD

ORGANISATION FOR ECONOMIC CO-OPERATION AND DEVELOPMENT

DIRECTION DES AFFAIRES FINANCIÈRES, FISCALES ET DES ENTREPRISES
DIRECTORATE FOR FINANCIAL, FISCAL AND ENTERPRISE AFFAIRS

CFA(92)860
JO/fk

Paris, 26 November 1992

TO THE MAIN DELEGATES OF THE COMMITTEE ON FISCAL AFFAIRS AND THE TRADE COMMITTEE

THE TREATMENT OF TAXES IN GATS

Dear Colleague,

An examination of the present text of the GATS suggests that there are a number of serious difficulties that arise in the treatment of taxes. The Secretariat, in cooperation with Working Party No. 1 on double Taxation of the Committee on Fiscal Affairs, has prepared a note outlining these problems and alternative solutions.

Consultations with a number of trade and tax experts suggests that a joint meeting between tax experts and the trade negotiators at the GATS would help resolve these problems. Consequently, the Secretariats of the Committee on Fiscal Affairs and the Trade Committee, in consultation with the respective Chairmen, propose to arrange a special one day meeting here in Paris on the 7th December. An agenda for the meeting, as well as a discussion document is attached.

We apologise for the very short notice in organisising this meeting but, as you will appreciate it is now urgent to agree upon the treatment of taxes since the text of GATS is likely to be finalised quickly.

Given the importance of this issue we hope that you would be able to send two senior representatives (one from tax and one from trade in services) to this meeting who are familiar with the issues. It would be helpful if the representative for the trade side was your trade in services negotiator in Geneva.

Although, the meeting is limited to OECD countries, Mexico and Korea will be invited as observers (both countries already have observer status in the Trade Committee). It is proposed that the Secretariat chair this informal ad hoc meeting.

The names of your representatives should be communicated to Miss Karat Francine (Fax (33-1) 45 24 78 52) before the 2nd December 1992.

Sincerely yours,

Jeffey Owens
Head of Fiscal Affairs Division

Gerhard Abel
Head of Trade Directorate

cc.: M. Vinde, M. Cornell, M. Llewellyn,
M. Burgeat, M. de Miramon Fitz-James
M. Witherell, M. Geiger

0056

2, rue André Pascal 75775 PARIS CEDEX 16 Tél. : 45 24 82 00
TÉLÉGRAMMES DÉVELOPÉCONOMIE / TÉLEX 640048 / TÉLÉFAX (33-1) 45 24 78 52

045-10-4

E APPELE: +33 1 47538838 1992-11-26 15:01 G3-96 S BIEN RECU #2

DAFFE/CFA/WP1/WD(92)2
(3rd Revision)

A. INTRODUCTION

1. This note has been prepared by the Secretariat of the Committee on Fiscal Affairs on the basis of the discussions at the meeting of the Working Party No. 1 on Double Taxation held on 8th-10th September 1992.

2. The note is intended to provide a contribution to the current discussions underway in Member countries and other international fora on the treatment of taxes in the General Agreement on Trade in Services (GATS). The note is written from the perspective of tax experts and does not address the wider trade issues that are raised in the GATS. The first section sets out some of the technical problems that arise with the present GATS text in the tax area, after first noting some of the broad principles which should determine the treatment of taxes in international agreements which are not primarily focusing on tax issues. The next section of the note puts forward suggested technical drafting amendments to the relevant Articles of the GATS. These amendments are intended to clarify the treatment of taxes in the GATS.

3. When proposing amendments the Group has tried to follow as closely as possible the present wording of the GATS and has only addressed problems which are of concern to a number of countries, it being understood that country specific problems will be raised bilaterally and may be dealt with by "scheduling" (1). The proposed amendments, all of which are of a technical nature, have drawn upon well-defined taxation principles that have been established by the UN and by the OECD and which are followed by most developed and developing countries.

4. Whilst the note sets out the opinions of the tax experts represented in Working Party No. 1 of the Committee on Fiscal Affairs, the main tax policy body of the OECD - it cannot necessarily be taken as representing the views of the Member governments of the OECD since tax considerations are only one of many issues that need to be examined in reviewing these proposals. Tax Experts would be pleased to discuss further the proposals set out in this note with trade experts and with the GATT Secretariat.

B. THE MAIN ISSUES

General principles

5. A general conclusion which can be drawn from the discussions of the Working Party is that there are fundamental and well known difficulties in applying the principles of most-favoured nation treatment or national treatment to tax measures and that the provisions of bilateral tax conventions with respect to taxes on income and on capital provide a much more appropriate way to deal with these measures.

---

1. Scheduling, however, would not be appropriate for tax measures which are of a permanent and essential feature of tax systems and which affect a number of countries.

0057

045-10-5

6. Whilst bilateral conventions are patterned on generally recognised principles, they differ from each other in many respects. These differences result from a process of negotiations through which the various aspects of the bilateral relationship between two countries are taken into account in order to arrive, sometimes with great difficulty, at an agreement that strikes a delicate balance between the demands of each Contracting State. By its very nature, the most-favoured-nation principle, if it were applied without restrictions, would extend to all States the concessions granted to one particular State in the context of these bilateral negotiations. In effect, this would be equivalent to replacing each of the provisions of the bilateral conventions concluded by one State by the corresponding provision which, in all the conventions concluded by that State, proves to be the most favourable for the other Contracting State. This would run counter to the methods of bilateral tax conventions which provide individual solutions tailored to the particular needs of the treaty partners.

7. Most-favoured-nation clauses also present difficulties with respect to certain provisions found in domestic tax legislation. One example is that of "Sub-part F" type legislation intended to prevent abusive schemes involving the use of tax havens. In many cases, such legislation can be said to differentiate between countries insofar as it results in different treatment of income from investments in countries that are considered as tax havens. Given the purpose of this type of anti-avoidance legislation, it would be clearly inappropriate to apply the most-favoured-nation principle to it.

8. National treatment clauses can be even more problematic than most-favoured-nation clauses where they purport to ensure similar treatment of residents and non-residents. The distinction between residents and non-residents is a fundamental aspect of the application of both domestic laws and tax conventions of all countries. Thus there are important differences between the tax obligations of residents and those of non-residents. While the non-discrimination provisions of tax conventions recognise these differences, national treatment clauses ignore the significance of tax measures that necessarily differentiate between residents and non-residents. Thus, in the case of tax measures, the application of the non-discrimination provisions found in double taxation conventions should be preferred to that of the principles of the most-favoured-nation and national treatment clauses.

9. It follows from these principles that disagreements with respect to the interpretation or application of the non-discrimination provisions of double taxation conventions should be dealt with through the mechanism provided by these conventions, namely the mutual agreement procedure, rather than through the general dispute settlement mechanisms found in more general agreements. Apart from the fact that this avoids a duplication of the procedure for the settlement of disputes dealing with tax measures, it ensures a consistent application of the provisions of domestic tax legislation and double taxation conventions. It is also important to note that whilst taxpayers can directly claim the benefits of the provisions of double taxation conventions this does not appear to be the case with respect to many of the provisions of these more general agreements (such as trade agreements). Therefore, if dispute settlements mechanisms found in the latter agreements were to apply to cases

0058

045-10-6

involving the application of the non-discrimination provisions of double taxation conventions, there would a potential for conflicts between judicial decisions and solutions arrived at through these dispute settlement mechanisms.

10. Therefore, where provisions relating to non-discrimination exist, any dispute dealing with the application of these provisions should be dealt with through the mechanisms provided for by the convention rather than by the dispute settlement mechanisms of more general agreements. There thus appear to be good reasons to exclude as far as possible tax measures from the scope of general provisions dealing with most-favoured-nation treatment, national treatment or dispute settlement.

11. It is, however, recognised that there is a need to reconcile tax policy objectives with the objectives pursued during the negotiations of bilateral or multilateral trade agreements. For that reason, it may not always be possible to provide that tax measures will generally be excluded from the application of these provisions. Nevertheless, it remains essential that potential conflicts between tax measures and agreements, on the one hand, and trade agreements, on the other, should be minimised.

(ii) Difficulties that arise with the present text of the GATS

12. The difficulties encountered with the draft GATS relate to Article II (the most-favoured-nation clause), Article XI (relating to restrictions on transfers), Article XVII (the national treatment clause) and Articles XXII and XXIII (relating to the settlement of disputes).

13. When these provisions are read in relation with the general exceptions provided for under sub-paragraphs (d) and (e) of Article XIV, it is clear that an attempt has been made to follow some of the principles discussed above. However, the proposed wording of Articles XIV, XXII and XXIII still present a number of technical difficulties, most important of which are:

- Article XIV (d) is confined to tax measures relating to service suppliers and would, as presently drafted, not cover measures affecting the consumers of services. Thus, for example, tax measures which enable participants in approved (usually resident) pension funds to deduct their contributions to such funds but which deny such deductions for contributions to unapproved (usually non-resident) funds would not be carved out even though the purpose of such measures is to ensure an equitable and efficient taxation. Consequently, most tax experts would prefer to cover these measures in the scope of the carve-out. It is recognised that trade negotiators may have concerns about some specific tax provisions that apply to consumers of services;

- the most-favoured nation clause in Article II should not be applicable in respect of tax measures found in domestic tax legislation which counteracts tax evasion and avoidance. Such anti-avoidance legislation includes, amongst other things, sub-part F type legislation (see para. 7 above),

0059

MS-10-7

- Article XIV(d) and (e) as presently drafted would not apply to taxes on capital gains or capital taxes such as net wealth and inheritance taxes. Since these taxes are used by many countries and are usually covered by tax agreements it would be appropriate to bring them into the scope of Article XIV (d) and (e);

- the text of Article XIV(e) limits its application to international agreements relating to the avoidance of double taxation. There are, however, international agreements, other than double taxation agreements, which contain provisions relating to double taxation (e.g. shipping agreements, road transportation agreements) which should be included in the scope of the Article;

- whilst Article XIV(e) provides a general exclusion for the most favoured nation clause in respect of differences resulting from double taxation conventions, there is no such exclusion for the national treatment clause since the exclusion in XIV(d) applies to a "Party's relevant tax measures." Thus, for example, this exception would not cover the case of a country refusing to extend treaty benefits to residents of a non-treaty country;

- the dispute settlement mechanism provided for in Articles XXII and XXIII should not apply where a tax agreement containing provisions relating to non-discrimination is applicable. In these circumstances any disputes should be resolved under the procedures provided for in the tax agreement (see paragraph 9 above for a further discussion of this point);

- the preamble to Article XIV provides a general limitation on the measures which can be treated as general exceptions by specifying that they would only qualify insofar as they are not applied in a manner which would constitute a means of arbitrary or unjustifiable discrimination. Whilst tax experts can accept this general limitation, most believe that in Article XIV(d) it is not necessary to subject tax measures to the additional test of being aimed at ensuring an equitable or effective imposition or collection of taxes. It is an accepted principle of domestic and international taxation arrangements that they should be equitable or effective and, if these conditions are not met, then a measure would generaly be considered to be arbitrary or unjustified. Consequently, most tax experts would prefer to delete these conditions altogether (this explains the brackets around these words in the proposed revised text);

There were a number of other problems raised in the discussions, but since these concerned only a limited number of countries, they will be raised bilaterally.

5

0060

046-10-8

14. Problems may also arise with Article XI which deals with restrictions to transfers and payments. The Group's view is that this Article should not apply to tax measures. No modifications to the text are suggested at this stage since it is understood that the IMF has been asked to confirm that under its principles, withholding taxes would not be considered as restriction on transfers or payments.

C. SUGGESTED AMENDMENTS

15. The discussions of the present text of GATS showed that there is a need for a different approach to the treatment of taxes in the GATS. It is recognised, however, that at this stage in the negotiations it is unlikely that a radically different approach would be acceptable to all Parties (2). The suggestions set out below take into account these constraints:

Modifications to Article XIV: (General Exception):

16. No changes are suggested to the preamble to Article XIV and sub-items (a) to (c). The folowing technical changes are proposed to (d) and (e):

(d) inconsistent with Article XVII, [provided that any tax measure giving rise to a difference in treatment has as its purpose the equitable or effective imposition or collection of] relating to (3) taxes on income, or on capital gains or on capital in respect of services or on service suppliers, where the service supplier is not a resident, under the Party's relevant tax measures, of the Party's territory;

---

2. For example, from a tax perspective, it would be preferable to use the following text for Article XIV(d): "inconsistent with Article XVII relating to taxes on income, or on capital gains, or on capital in respect of services or service suppliers".

3. If the bracketed text is dropped (see para. 13) then the underlined words should be inserted.

0061

045 10-9

(c) inconsistent with Article II, provided that any difference in treatment is the result of:

(i) a double taxation agreement, or provisions relating to double taxation in any other international agreement or arrangement by which the Party is bound; or

(ii) a measure which imposes a charge to tax on a person who, under the Party's relevant tax measures, is a resident of the Party's territory, and which is intended to counteract tax evasion and avoidance.

Modifications to "Article XXII (3) (Consultations)

A Party may not invoke Article XVII, either under this Article or Article XXIII (Dispute Settlement and Enforcement), with respect to a measure of another Party if there is an international agreement between the Parties concerned relating to the avoidance of double taxation that contains a provision relating to non-discrimination or equivalent provisions which apply to the measure concerned."

17. It should also be noted that it would help to resolve some of the problems referred to above if the negotiating history could have an acceptable degree of force and where appropriate be incorporated into the agreement. In particular, this may help clarify that the agreement would not apply to taxes on service suppliers other than in their capacity as service suppliers.

18. Tax experts would be pleased to discuss these suggestions with trade experts and they would also be prepared to assist in drafting any negotiating notes which would clarify some of the issues addressed above.

7

0062

045-10-10

NOMBRE P.10

	분류번호	보존기간

발 신 전 보

번 호 : WFR-2419 921201 1439 WG 종별 :

수 신 : 주 불 대사. 총영사

발 신 : 장 관 (통 기)

제 목 : OECD/서비스 교역분야 합동회의

대 : FRW-2439

대호 12.7. 개최되는 서비스 교역에 관한 표제회의와 관련 동기간중 제네바에서 개최될 예정인 UR/서비스 양자협상에 본부대표 참석으로 인해 본부대표의 표제회의 파견이 어려우니, 현지에서 참석하기 바라며 동회의 의제에 대한 아국입장을 조속 송부 예정임. 끝.

(통상국장 홍 정 표)

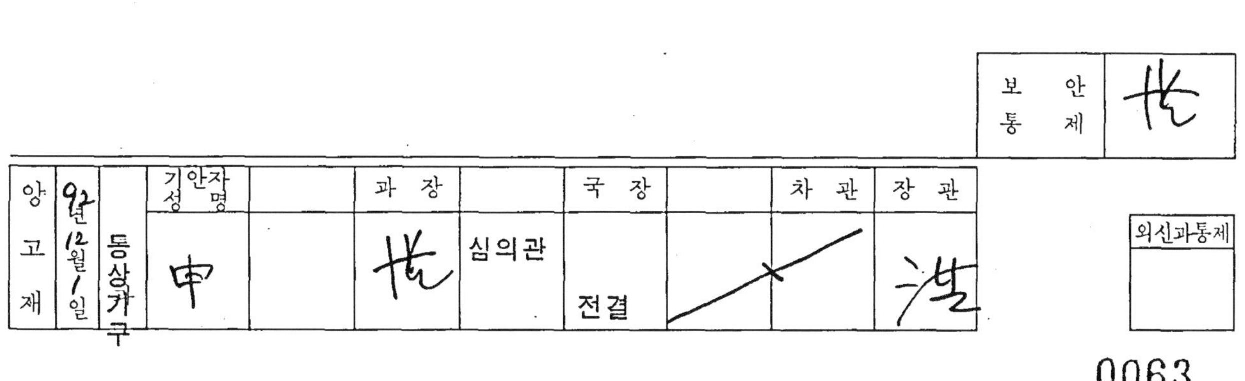

보안 통제	

앙 고 재	92년 12월 1일	통상기구	기안자 성명		과장	심의관	국장	차관	장관
							전결		

외신과통제

0063

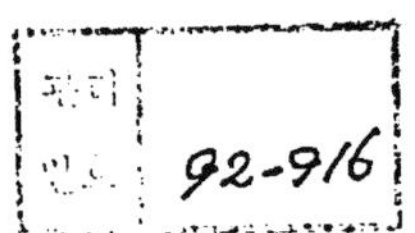

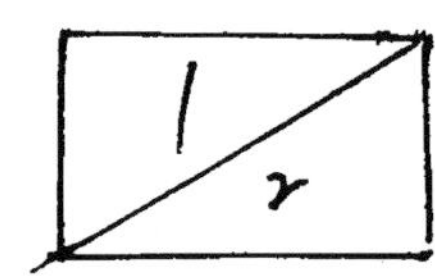

문 화 부

우110-703 서울 종로구 세종로 82-1 / 전화 720 - 3821 / 전송 736-8513

문서번호 영진 35175-83

시행일자 1992. 12. 1.

(경유)

수신 외무부장관

참조 통상국장

선결			지시	
접수	일자 시간	1992.12.2.		
	번호	48090	결재·공람	
처리과				
담당자		이시형		

제목 **대일 시청각서비스 MFN일탈 관련 회신**

1. UR/서비스협상의 대일 시청각서비스 문제는 지금까지 견지되어온 정부의 일본영화, 가요 등 대중문화의 국내수입 불허 시책과 직결되는 중대한 사안으로, 그 동안 최혜국대우(MFN)일탈 문제를 두고 한.일간에 추진되어온 교섭경과와 국내외의 종합적인 상황을 검토하고 다음과 같이 우리부의 입장을 통보하오니 협조하여 주시기 바랍니다.

가. 그동안 일본측이 제안해온 방식은 일본 자국내의 정치, 사회적인 민감성을 반영하긴 하였으나 구체적인 보장이 없는 내용으로 사료되어 수용하기 어려움.

나. 일본 대중문화의 국내수입 문제는 현재 국내여론이 압도적으로 반대하고 있는 관계로, 우리정부의 문화시책에 의하여 단계적으로 해결되지 못하고 대일협상의 불리한 결과로 불가피하게 수용하게 될 경우 국민감정의 악화와 정부 신뢰의 실추가 예상됨.

다. 따라서 UR/서비스협상의 전반적 추세와 한.일간의 현안문제를 종합적으로 고려하여 다음과 같이 제안함.

- o 제안사항 : MFN일탈 신청안의 내용 수정
- o 수정내용
  - 대 상 : 일본영화(비디오 포함) 및 일본대중가요에 국한
  - 기 한 : 향후 10년간.

2. 위 내용은 영진 35175-91 ('92.11.24)로 경제기획원에 회신하였음을 알려드립니다. 끝.

문 화 부 장 관

0064

경 제 기 획 원

우 427-760 / 경기도 과천시 중앙동1 정부제2청사 / 전화 503-9149 / 전송 503-9141

문서번호 통조삼 10502-137

시행일자 1992. 12. 1

(경유)

수신 수신처 참조

참조 통상기구과장

선결			지시	
접수	일자 시간	92.12.2	결재	
	번호	41581	·	
처리과			공람	
담당자		이시		

제목 UR/서비스협상 참고자료 송부

1. 최근의 UR협상 진전동향에 대응하여 정부는 서비스분야의 최종양허표 초안을 작성중에 있습니다.

2. 동 양허표는 UR협상결과가 발효될 경우 "서비스교역에 관한 일반협정(General Agreement on Trade in Services)"의 일부가 되어 우리정부가 이에 따른 국제적인 의무를 부담하게 되므로 동 양허표상의 내용을 정확하게 작성하는 일이 무엇보다도 중요하다고 하겠습니다.

3. 이와같은 관점에서 당원에서는 "서비스교역에 관한 일반협정의 해설자료"와 "최종양허표 초안작성시 주요점검사항"등을 작성하였는 바, 동 자료들을 별첨 송부하오니 각 부,처,청에서는 이를 숙지하시어 소관분야의 양허표 초안작성에 차질이 없도록 만전을 기하여 주시기 바랍니다.

첨부 : 1. 서비스교역에 관한 일반협정 요약해설 2부.
2. 서비스교역의 정의 및 범위(서비스협정 제1조에 대한 해설) 2부.
3. 최종양허표 초안작성관련 주요점검사항 2부.
4. 서비스교역에 관한 일반협정안(국·영문 대역) 2부. 끝

경 제 기 획 원 장

제2협력관 전결

수신처 : 외무부장관, 내무부장관, 재무부장관, 법무부장관, 교육부장관, 문화부장관, 농림수산부장관, 상공부장관, 보건사회부장관, 건설부장관, 교통부장관, 노동부장관, 동력자원부장관, 체신부장관, 과학기술처장관, 환경처장관, 공보처장관, 공업진흥청장, 특허청장, 해운항만청장

0065

신 구이시

원 본

외 무 부

종 별 :

번 호 : GVW-2254 일 시 : 92 1202 1800

수 신 : 장 관(통기,경기원)

발 신 : 주 제네바 대사

제 목 : UR/서비스 협상 비공식 협의

1. 12.2(수) 10:00 홍콩 대표부 주관으로 일부 국가간에 내주 이후 서비스 분야협상 관련 비공식 협의가 있었는바, 주요 논의 내용 아래와 같음.

(아국, 호주, 알젠틴, 브라질, 싱가폴, 스웨덴, 뉴질랜드, 스위스, 멕시코 10개국)

가. 12.4(금) 15:00 향후 서비스 협상 작업 계획 토의를 위한 비공식 협의가 있을 것이며 서비스 양자 협상은 12.7-18 까지 진행 예정인바 GNS 의장은 호주 호스 (HAWS) 대사가 대행할것임.

나. 동 협의시는 현재의 서비스 협상 진행 상황에 대한 종합적인 평가와 앞으로 GNS 에서 논의해야 할 과제 (OUTSTANDING ISSUES)에 대한 CHECK LIST 및 제 21조, 제34조 와 SCHEDULING 관련 최근 TEXT 가 배포될것임.

다. T3 에서 배포된 서비스 협정문안 (1161) 중 T3에서 추가 논의해야 할 것으로 사무국이 지적한 사항중 일부 (5조 6항 A, 31조)는 GNS 에서 논의가 있어야 할 것으로 보며 T3 에서는 서비스 협정중 MTO 관련 사항으로 논의를 국한 하여야 할것임.

라. GNS 가 앞으로 크리스마스 이전 까지 논의 완료해야 할 주요 과제는 다음과같음. (DFA상의 ANOTATION 사항)

- TEXT : 21조 34조(1조, 31 조 포함) 및 SCHEDULING 관련 사항 (14조 TAXATION 관련 조항 포함)

- SECTOR : 통신 부속서, 항공부속서

- MFN 관련: 기본 통신, 해운

0 기본 통신에 관해서는 현재 QUAD 간에 현재의 접근 방법에 의견을 같이하고 있는 것으로 보이며 남은 문제는 MFN 관련 사항을 어떻게 처리하느냐임.

0 해운 분야는 스케쥴링 관련하여 FLAG 와 OWNER SHIP, 국제해운, 해운 보조 서비스의 정의등 많은 문제가 남아 있으나, 지난번 미. EC간에는 MFN 관련 실질

통상국 경기원

PAGE 1

92.12.03 05:29 FO

외신 1과 통제관 ✓

0066

문제에관해서는 논의가 없었던 것으로 보이며 당분간 현행대로 기술적 문제에 대한 논의의지속이 불가피할 것으로 보임.

- 기타: LLDC 의 NATIONAL SCHEDULE 제출 여부

마. 상기 사항중 상당수 국가는 시간적 제안을 고려 CHECK LIST 에 대부분의 국가가 이해를 갖는 분야에 한정해야 한다고 하고 (예: TAXATION 제외) 또한 2조의 MFN주석과 관련 수평적 협정에 관한 범위를 정할 필요가 있다고 함.

2. 던켈 총장이 11.26 TNC 회의시 제시한 년내 정치적 결정을 요하는 사항의 완결과 관련, 서비스 협상의 관점에서 볼때 이는 MFN 문제, 양허수준 및 TEXT 수정등이이에 해당하나 년내 TEXT 수정 완료만을 목표로 할수 밖에 없을 것이며 따라서 내년초의 협상일정 (양허표 및 MFN 일탈 목록의 초안 및 최종 제출시기)도 년내 고려하기 어렵다고 봄.

3. 참고로 호주는 내주 양자 협상시 수정 OFFER 및수정 MFN 리스트를 동시 제출하겠다고 하며, 멕시코는 지난번 양자 협상시 기본 통신에 대한 OFFER 를 공식 철회하 겠다고 하였다함. 끝

(대사 박수길-국장)

원 본

외 무 부

종 별 :

번 호 : GVW-2257 일 시 : 92 1202 1930

수 신 : 장 관(통기,경기원,재무부,교통부)

발 신 : 주 제네바 대사

제 목 : UR/서비스협상 자료 송부

항공 부속서 관련 뉴질랜드 제안 및 서비스 협정 14조의 조세관련 OECD PAPER 를별첨 FAX 송부 하오니 검토후 의견 조속 회신 바람.

첨부: 1. 항공 부속서 관련 뉴질랜드 제안 1부

2. 조세관련 OECD PAPER 1부.(GVW(F)-723)

(대사 박수길-국장)

통상국 교통부 경기원 재무부

PAGE 1

92.12.03 05:30 FO

외신 1과 통제관

0068

주 제 네 바 대 표 부

번 호 : GVW(F) - 723   년월일 : 92. 12. 2 시간 :

수 신 : 장 관 (통기, 경기원, 재무부, 교통부)

발 신 : 주 제네바대사

제 목 : UR/서비스협상 자료송부

보 안	
통 제	

총 10 매(표지포함)

외신과	
통 제	

배부처	장관실	차관실	一차보	二차보	외정실	분석관	아주국	미주국	구주국	중아국	국기국	경제국	통상국	문협국	외연원	청와대	안기부	공보처	경기원	상공부	재무부	농수부	동자부	환경처	과기처	교통부	
													O						/		/					/	

723-10-1

0069

NEW ZEALAND PERMANENT MISSION TO THE
OFFICE OF THE UNITED NATIONS AT GENEVA

28 A, CHEMIN DU PETIT-SACONNEX
P.O. BOX 334
1211 GENEVA 19 • TEL (022) 734 95 30 • FAX (022) 734 30 62

17 March 1992

H.E. Mr F Jaramillo
Chairman
Group of Negotiations on Services
General Agreement on Tariffs and Trade
Centre William Rappard
rue de Lausanne 154
1211 Geneva 21

Dear Ambassador Jaramillo

Following your informal consultation New Zealand has been giving some further thought to the suggested changes to the Air Transport Annex presented in the Secretariat draft of 27 February. New Zealand considers that the definition of traffic rights suggested by Sweden as an additional subparagraph 7(d) provides a valuable clarification and should be added to the Annex text.

However, having thus defined traffic rights as they appear in subparagraph 2(a) of the annex, the addition to that subparagraph of the words 'however granted' we believe carries the text beyond the intent of the annex as negotiated in the draft Final Act of 20 December 1991.

New Zealand's understanding is that the excepting of measures affecting traffic rights from the Agreement relates solely to the wish to avoid the necessity, given the current international aviation regime, of parties having to individually seek MFN derogations for MFN inconsistent granting of traffic rights. This intent might be more accurately captured by the following drafting (suggested changes to the Secretariat's draft of 27 February are shown in bold typeface):

2. The Agreement shall not apply to measures affecting:

(a) traffic rights, when granted in a manner not consistent with Article II.1 of the Agreement;

(b) the supply of directly related services, when such measures would limit or affect the ability of parties to negotiate, to grant or receive traffic rights pursuant to subparagraph 2(a) above, or which would have the effect of limiting their exercise;

except as provided in paragraphs 3 and 4 of this Annex.

0070

923-10-2

2

New Zealand would be happy to discuss this matter further at your convenience.

Yours sincerely

A M Bisley
Permanent Representative

ORGANISATION FOR ECONOMIC
CO-OPERATION AND DEVELOPMENT

DIRECTORATE FOR FINANCIAL, FISCAL
AND ENTERPRISE AFFAIRS

COMMITTEE ON FISCAL AFFAIRS

RESTRICTED

Paris, drafted: 9 September 1992
OLIS: >
dist.: >

Scale I

DAFFE/CFA/WP1/WD(92)4
(3rd Revision)

English Text only

WORKING PARTY No. 1 ON DOUBLE TAXATION OF THE COMMITTEE ON FISCAL AFFAIRS

THE TREATMENT OF TAXES IN THE GENERAL AGREEMENT ON TRADE IN SERVICES

(Note by the Secretariat)

The attached information note, which has been prepared by the Secretariat, summarises the Working Party's discussion on this issue.

923-10-4

0072

(3rd Revision)

A. INTRODUCTION

1. This note has been prepared by the Secretariat of the Committee on Fiscal Affairs on the basis of the discussions at the meeting of the Working Party No. 1 on Double Taxation held on 8th-10th September 1992.

2. The note is intended to provide a contribution to the current discussions underway in Member countries and other international fora on the treatment of taxes in the General Agreement on Trade in Services (GATS). The note is written from the perspective of tax experts and does not address the wider trade issues that are raised in the GATS. The first section sets out some of the technical problems that arise with the present GATS text in the tax area, after first noting some of the broad principles which should determine the treatment of taxes in international agreements which are not primarily focusing on tax issues. The next section of the note puts forward suggested technical drafting amendments to the relevant Articles of the GATS. These amendments are intended to clarify the treatment of taxes in the GATS.

3. When proposing amendments the Group has tried to follow as closely as possible the present wording of the GATS and has only addressed problems which are of concern to a number of countries, it being understood that country specific problems will be raised bilaterally and may be dealt with by "scheduling" (1). The proposed amendments, all of which are of a technical nature, have drawn upon well-defined taxation principles that have been established by the UN and by the OECD and which are followed by most developed and developing countries.

4. Whilst the note sets out the opinions of the tax experts represented in Working Party No. 1 of the Committee on Fiscal Affairs, the main tax policy body of the OECD - it cannot necessarily be taken as representing the views of the Member governments of the OECD since tax considerations are only one of many issues that need to be examined in reviewing these proposals. Tax Experts would be pleased to discuss further the proposals set out in this note with trade experts and with the GATT Secretariat.

B. THE MAIN ISSUES

General principles

5. A general conclusion which can be drawn from the discussions of the Working Party is that there are fundamental and well known difficulties in applying the principles of most-favoured nation treatment or national treatment to tax measures and that the provisions of bilateral tax conventions with respect to taxes on income and on capital provide a much more appropriate way to deal with these measures.

---

1. Scheduling, however, would not be appropriate for tax measures which are of a permanent and essential feature of tax systems and which affect a number of countries.

0073

121-10-5

6. Whilst bilateral conventions are patterned on generally recognised principles, they differ from each other in many respects. These differences result from a process of negotiations through which the various aspects of the bilateral relationship between two countries are taken into account in order to arrive, sometimes with great difficulty, at an agreement that strikes a delicate balance between the demands of each Contracting State. By its very nature, the most-favoured-nation principle, if it were applied without restrictions, would extend to all States the concessions granted to one particular State in the context of these bilateral negotiations. In effect, this would be equivalent to replacing each of the provisions of the bilateral conventions concluded by one State by the corresponding provision which, in all the conventions concluded by that State, proves to be the most favourable for the other Contracting State. This would run counter to the methods of bilateral tax conventions which provide individual solutions tailored to the particular needs of the treaty partners.

7. Most-favoured-nation clauses also present difficulties with respect to certain provisions found in domestic tax legislation. One example is that of "Sub-part F" type legislation intended to prevent abusive schemes involving the use of tax havens. In many cases, such legislation can be said to differentiate between countries insofar as it results in different treatment of income from investments in countries that are considered as tax havens. Given the purpose of this type of anti-avoidance legislation, it would be clearly inappropriate to apply the most-favoured-nation principle to it.

8. National treatment clauses can be even more problematic than most-favoured-nation clauses where they purport to ensure similar treatment of residents and non-residents. The distinction between residents and non-residents is a fundamental aspect of the application of both domestic laws and tax conventions of all countries. Thus there are important differences between the tax obligations of residents and those of non-residents. While the non-discrimination provisions of tax conventions recognise these differences, national treatment clauses ignore the significance of tax measures that necessarily differentiate between residents and non-residents. Thus, in the case of tax measures, the application of the non-discrimination provisions found in double taxation conventions should be preferred to that of the principles of the most-favoured-nation and national treatment clauses.

9. It follows from these principles that disagreements with respect to the interpretation or application of the non-discrimination provisions of double taxation conventions should be dealt with through the mechanism provided by these conventions, namely the mutual agreement procedure, rather than through the general dispute settlement mechanisms found in more general agreements. Apart from the fact that this avoids a duplication of the procedure for the settlement of disputes dealing with tax measures, it ensures a consistent application of the provisions of domestic tax legislation and double taxation conventions. It is also important to note that whilst taxpayers can directly claim the benefits of the provisions of double taxation conventions this does not appear to be the case with respect to many of the provisions of these more general agreements (such as trade agreements). Therefore, if dispute settlements mechanisms found in the latter agreements were to apply to cases

. . .

Revision)

involving the application of the non-discrimination provisions of double taxation conventions, there would a potential for conflicts between judicial decisions and solutions arrived at through these dispute settlement mechanisms.

10. Therefore, where provisions relating to non-discrimination exist, any dispute dealing with the application of these provisions should be dealt with through the mechanisms provided for by the convention rather than by the dispute settlement mechanisms of more general agreements. There thus appear to be good reasons to exclude as far as possible tax measures from the scope of general provisions dealing with most-favoured-nation treatment, national treatment or dispute settlement.

11. It is, however, recognised that there is a need to reconcile tax policy objectives with the objectives pursued during the negotiations of bilateral or multilateral trade agreements. For that reason, it may not always be possible to provide that tax measures will generally be excluded from the application of these provisions. Nevertheless, it remains essential that potential conflicts between tax measures and agreements, on the one hand, and trade agreements, on the other, should be minimised.

(ii) Difficulties that arise with the present text of the GATS

12. The difficulties encountered with the draft GATS relate to Article II (the most-favoured-nation clause), Article XI (relating to restrictions on transfers), Article XVII (the national treatment clause) and Articles XXII and XXIII (relating to the settlement of disputes).

13. When these provisions are read in relation with the general exceptions provided for under sub-paragraphs (d) and (e) of Article XIV, it is clear that an attempt has been made to follow some of the principles discussed above. However, the proposed wording of Articles XIV, XXII and XXIII still present a number of technical difficulties, most important of which are:

- Article XIV (d) is confined to tax measures relating to service suppliers and would, as presently drafted, not cover measures affecting the consumers of services. Thus, for example, tax measures which enable participants in approved (usually resident) pension funds to deduct their contributions to such funds but which deny such deductions for contributions to unapproved (usually non-resident) funds would not be carved out even though the purpose of such measures is to ensure an equitable and efficient taxation. Consequently, most tax experts would prefer to cover these measures in the scope of the carve-out. It is recognised that trade negotiators may have concerns about some specific tax provisions that apply to consumers of services;

- the most-favoured nation clause in Article II should not be applicable in respect of tax measures found in domestic tax legislation which counteracts tax evasion and avoidance. Such anti-avoidance legislation includes, amongst other things, sub-part F type legislation (see para. 7 above).

0075

123-10-7

DAFFE/CFA/WP1/WD(92)4
(3rd Revision)

- Article XIV(d) and (e) as presently drafted would not apply to taxes on capital gains or capital taxes such as net wealth and inheritance taxes. Since these taxes are used by many countries and are usually covered by tax agreements it would be appropriate to bring then into the scope of Article XIV (d) and (e);

- the text of Article XIV(e) limits its application to international agreements relating to the avoidance of double taxation. There are, however, international agreements, other than double taxation agreements, which contain provisions relating to double taxation (e.g. shipping agreements, road transportation agreements) which should be included in the scope of the Article;

- whilst Article XIV(e) provides a general exclusion for the most favoured nation clause in respect of differences resulting from double taxation conventions, there is no such exclusion for the national treatment clause since the exclusion in XIV(d) applies to a "Party's relevant tax measures." Thus, for example, this exception would not cover the case of a country refusing to extend treaty benefits to residents of a non-treaty country;

- the dispute settlement mechanism provided for in Articles XXII and XXIII should not apply where a tax agreement contains provisions relating to non-discrimination is applicable. In these circumstances any disputes should be resolved under the procedures provided for in the tax agreement (see paragraph 9 above for a further discussion of this point);

- the preamble to Article XIV provides a general limitation on the measures which can be treated as general exceptions by specifying that they would only qualify insofar as they are not applied in a manner which would constitute a means of arbitrary or unjustifiable discrimination. Whilst tax experts can accept this general limitation, most believe that in Article XIV(d) it is not necessary to subject tax measures to the additional test of being aimed at ensuring an equitable or effective imposition or collection of taxes. It is an accepted principle of domestic and international taxation arrangements that they should be equitable or effective and, if these conditions are not met, then a measure would generaly be considered to be arbitrary or unjustified. Consequently, most tax experts would prefer to delete these conditions altogether (this explains the brackets around these words in the proposed revised text);

There were a number of other problems raised in the discussions, but since these concerned only a limited number of countries, they will be raised bilaterally.

5

0076

123-10-8

14. Problems may also arise with Article XI which deals with restrictions to transfers and payments. The Group's view is that this Article should not apply to tax measures. No modifications to the text are suggested at this stage since it is understood that the IMF has been asked to confirm that under its principles, withholding taxes would not be considered as restriction on transfers or payments.

C. SUGGESTED AMENDMENTS

15. The discussions of the present text of GATS showed that there is a need for a different approach to the treatment of taxes in the GATS. It is recognised, however, that at this stage in the negotiations it is unlikely that a radically different approach would be acceptable to all Parties (2). The suggestions set out below take into account those constraints:

Modifications to Article XIV: (General Exception):

16. No changes are suggested to the preamble to Article XIV and sub-items (a) to (c). The folowing technical changes are proposed to (d) and (e):

(d) inconsistent with Article XVII, [provided that any tax measure giving rise to a difference in treatment has as its purpose the equitable or effective imposition or collection of] relating to (3) taxes on income, or on capital gains or on capital in respect of services or on service suppliers, where the service supplier is not a resident, under the Party's relevant tax measures, of the Party's territory;

---

2. For example, from a tax perspective, it would be preferable to use the following text for Article XIV(d): "inconsistent with Article XVII relating to taxes on income, or on capital gains, or on capital in respect of services or service suppliers".

3. If the bracketed text is dropped (see para. 13) then the underlined words should be inserted.

92-10-P

(3rd Revision)

(e) inconsistent with Article II, provided that any difference in treatment is the result of:

(i) a double taxation agreement, or provisions relating to double taxation in any other international agreement or arrangement by which the Party is bound; or

(ii) a measure which imposes a charge to tax on a person who, under the Party's relevant tax measures, is a resident of the Party's territory, and which is intended to counteract tax evasion and avoidance.

Modifications to "Article XXII (3) (Consultations)

A Party may not invoke Article XVII, either under this Article or Article XXIII (Dispute Settlement and Enforcement), with respect to a measure of another Party if there is an international agreement between the Parties concerned relating to the avoidance of double taxation that contains a provision relating to non-discrimination or equivalent provisions which apply to the measure concerned."

17. It should also be noted that it would help to resolve some of the problems referred to above if the negotiating history could have an acceptable degree of force and where appropriate be incorporated into the agreement. In particular, this may help clarify that the agreement would not apply to taxes on service suppliers other than in their capacity as service suppliers.

18. Tax experts would be pleased to discuss these suggestions with trade experts and they would also be prepared to assist in drafting any negotiating notes which would clarify some of the issues addressed above.

0078

123-10-10

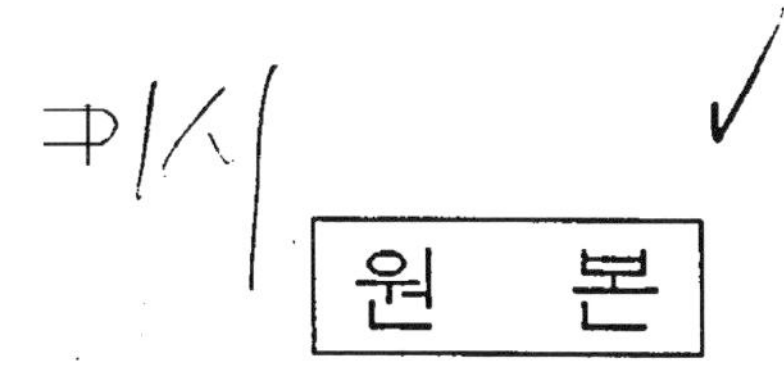

외 무 부

종 별 :

번 호 : GVW-2275 일 시 : 92 1204 1950

수 신 : 장 관 (수신처 참조)

발 신 : 주 제네바 대사

제 목 : UR/GNS 비공식협의

표제회의가 12월 4일(금) 15:00 호주대사 주재하에 향후 서비스 협상작업 계획 관련 비공식 협의가있었는바, 그요지 아래와 같음.

1. 의장은 11월 26일 TNC 결과에 따라 INITIALCOMMITMENT 에 관한 협상을 가급적연내에 종결하고, 서비스 협정문안에 대한 기술적 작업도빠른 시일안에 완결해야 할것이라고 언급하고,향후 협상 일정 및 작업 과제를 다음과 같이제시함.

- INITIAL COMMITMENT 에 관한 양자협상: 12월7일(월) 부터 2주간
- 기술적 과제에 관한 협의 : 12월 8일(화) 부터개시
- 추가작업이 필요한 기술적 과제.

0 DFA 상의 주석에 적시된 4개 사항(항공 및통신부속서, 34조, 21조)0 스케쥴링관련 사항0 분쟁해결

0 서비스 협정 밖의 조치(예: SOCIAL SECURITY,노동력이동 협정등)

0 조세문제

2. 상기 의장이 제시한 작업 과제에 대해 인도,알젠틴등 일부 개도국은 이들중에는 기술적사항외에 정치적 결정을 요하는 문제(예:통신부속서, 항공부속서의 적용범위 및 동 부속서4항등)도 있으므로 별도 논의가 필요함을지적하였으며,또한 협상 조기종결을 위해 MFN문제(기본통신, 해운등)도 조속히 처리되어야할것이며, 스케쥴링관련 보조금에 대한 논의필요성도 제기함. 한편 탄자니아는 최빈개도국을대표하여 이들 국가에 대한 NATIONAL SCHEDULE 제출면제 문제도 토의되어야 할것이라고 한바, 의장은 동 문제는 상당한 정치적 결정을 요하는사항이라고 지적함.

첨부: 사무국 배포자료(FAX 송부)

1. 스케쥴링 EXPLANATORY NOTE2. 34조 TEXT

3. 21PA TEXT 각 1부

통상국	법무부	보사부	문화부	교통부	체신부	경기원	재무부	농수부
상공부	건설부	노동부	과기처	해항청	환경처	공보처		

PAGE 1 92.12.05 06:47 DX

외신 1과 통제관

0079

(GVW(F)-0729).끝

수신처:통기,경기원,재무부,법무부,농림수산부,상공부,건설부,보건사회부,노동부,교통부,체신부,문화부,과학기술처,공보처,환경처,해운항만청)

(대사 박수길-국장)

첨부물 필요시 원본부서에 요청 바람

주 제 네 바 대 표 부

번호 : GVW(F) - 72P 년월일 : 21204 시간 : 1P00

수신 : 장 관(통기, 경기원, 재무부, 법무부, 농림수산부, 상공부, 문화부, 보사부, 건설부, 교통부, 체신부, 과기처, 공보처, 항만청, 환경처)

발신 : 주제네바대사

제목 : UR/서비스협상 비공식 협의

보 안 통 제	

총 32 매(표지포함)

외신관 통 제	

첨부물 분리시 인간부서에 요청 바람

부처	장관실	차관실	一차보	二차보	외정실	분석관	아주국	미주국	구주국	중아국	국기국	경제국	통상국	문협국	외연원	청와대	안기부	공보처	경기원	상공부	재무부	농수부	동자부	환경처	과기처	법무부	문화부	보사부	건설부	교통부	체신부	과기처	해항청
													O					/	/	/	/	/				/	/	/	/	/	/	/	/

0081

72P-32-1

DRAFT
4.12.92

Group of Negotiations on Services

In the light of informal consultaions, the text of Article XXI (as contained in MTN.TNC/W/FA) has been revised by the Secretariat. The attached document contains the revision of Article XXI along with Draft Procedures for the Implementation of Article XXI. The document should be considered as a draft which is distributed as a basis for discussion.

0082
19-ART2

72P-32-2

DRAFT
4.12.92

Group of Negotiations on Services

ARTICLE XXI: MODIFICATION OF SCHEDULES

1. (a) A Member (hereafter in this Article referred to as the "modifying Member") may modify or withdraw any commitment in its Schedule, at any time after three years have elapsed from the date on which that commitment entered into force, if the modifying Member has complied with the provisions of this Article.

(b) A modifying Member shall notify its intent to modify or withdraw a commitment pursuant to this Article to the Council on Trade in Services no later than three months before the intended date of implementation of the modification or withdrawal.

2. (a) At the request of any Member whose interests under this Agreement may be affected (hereafter "an affected Member") by a proposed modification or withdrawal notified under paragraph 1(b), the modifying Member shall enter into negotiations with a view to reaching agreement on any necessary compensatory adjustment. In such negotiations and agreement, the Members concerned shall endeavour to maintain a general level of mutually advantageous commitments not less favourable to trade than that provided for in schedules of specific commitments prior to such negotiations.

(b) Compensatory adjustments shall be made on a most-favoured-nation basis.

3. (a) If agreement is not reached between the modifying Member and all affected Members before the end of the period provided for negotiations, any affected Member may refer the matter to arbitration. Any affected Member that wishes to enforce a right

0083
19-ART2

72P-32-3

that it may have to compensation must participate in the arbitration.

(b) If no affected Member has requested arbitration, the modifying Member shall be free to implement the proposed modification or withdrawal.

4. (a) The modifying Member may not modify or withdraw its commitment until it has made compensatory adjustments in conformity with the findings of the arbitration.

(b) If the modifying Member implements its proposed modification or withdrawal and does not comply with the findings of the arbitration, any affected Member that participated in the arbitration may modify or withdraw substantially equivalent benefits in conformity with those findings. Notwithstanding Article II, such a modification or withdrawal may be implemented solely with respect to the modifying party.

5. The Council on Trade in Services shall provide procedures for rectification or modification of schedules of commitments. Any Member which has modified or withdrawn scheduled commitments under this Article shall modify its schedule accordingly under such procedures.

72P-32-4

0084

19-ART2

DRAFT PROCEDURES FOR THE IMPLEMENTATION OF ARTICLE XXI

Modification of Schedules
to the General Agreement on Trade in Services

Notification of Modification or Withdrawal

1. A Member intending to modify or withdraw a scheduled commitment in accordance with Article XXI (the "modifying Member") shall transmit a notification to that effect, no later than three months before the intended date of implementation of such modification or withdrawal, to the Secretariat which will distribute the notification to all other Members in a secret document.

2. The notification shall include a list of the commitments which it is intended to modify or withdraw. For each such commitment the notification shall indicate whether the intention is to modify or to withdraw it, in whole or in part; the proposed date for implementing such modification or withdrawal; and the exact nature of any proposed modification.

3. Any Member intending to invoke the provisions of Article XXI under Article X:2 of the Agreement shall transmit a request for authorization to modify or withdraw commitments to the MTO Secretariat to be circulated to all other Members in a secret document and included in the agenda of the next meeting of the Council for Trade in Services. Such a request shall indicate the matters provided for in paragraph 2 above and shall also include the cause for invoking Article X:2.

Negotiations on Compensation

4. Any Member which considers that its interests under the Agreement may be affected by the proposed modification or withdrawal ("affected Member") shall communicate its claim in writing to the modifying Member and at the

72P-32-5

19-ART2

same time inform the MTO Secretariat. Such claims of interest must be made no later than one month after the date of circulation by the MTO Secretariat of the notification referred to in paragraph 1 above. If by that date no Member has submitted a claim that it is an affected Party, the modifying Member shall be free to implement the proposed modification or withdrawal, and shall submit a notification of the date of such implementation to the MTO Secretariat, for circulation to the Members of the MTO.

5. The modifying Member and any affected Member which has identified itself under paragraph 4 above shall negotiate with a view to reaching agreement within three months following the last date on which such a claim of interest may be made. This period of negotiation may be extended by mutual agreement.

6. Upon completion of each negotiation conducted under paragraph 2(a) of Article XXI, the modifying Member shall send to the MTO Secretariat a joint letter signed by both parties, together with a report concerning the results of the negotiations which shall be initialled by both parties. The MTO Secretariat will distribute the letter and the report to all Members in a secret document.

7. A modifying Member which has reached agreement with all Members that had identified themselves under paragraph 4 above shall send to the MTO Secretariat, for distribution in a secret document, a final report on negotiations under Article XXI. Such a modifying Party will be free to implement the changes agreed upon in the negotiations as from the date of this report or any later date agreed upon in those negotiations, and it shall notify the date of implementation to the Secretariat, for circulation to the Members of the MTO.

Arbitration

8. If the modifying Member and a Member that had identified itself under paragraph 4 above do not reach agreement before the end of the period of negotiations referred to in paragraph 5, such an affected Member may request arbitration. Such a request shall be made in writing to the modifying Member and the Secretariat no later than [one month] after the end of that period.

9. If no Member that had identified itself under paragraph 4 above submits a timely arbitration request under paragraph 8, the modifying Member shall be free to implement [the changes agreed upon in negotiations] [the proposed modification or withdrawal], and it shall notify the date of implementation to the Secretariat, for circulation to the Members of the MTO.

10. If an affected Member submits a timely arbitration request under paragraph 8, the modifying Member must suspend the implementation of its proposed modification or withdrawal until it has received the arbitrator's findings and has implemented compensatory adjustments in accordance with those findings.

11. If the parties to the arbitration cannot agree on an arbitrator within ten days from the date of the request for arbitration, the arbitrator shall be appointed by the Director-General of the MTO, after consulting both parties, within ten days thereafter.

12. Any affected Party that wishes to enforce a right that it may have to compensation must participate in the arbitration. [If a modifying Party has reached agreement with an affected Party under paragraph 5 above, that affected Party shall be deemed to have participated in any arbitration with respect to the modification or withdrawal in question.]

13. The arbitrator shall have the following terms of reference unless the parties to the arbitration agree otherwise within ten days from the request for arbitration:

72P-12-7

"To examine the compensatory adjustments offered by (name of modifying Member) or requested by (affected Member requesting the arbitration), together with any compensatory adjustment proposed by (affected Member requesting the arbitration), and to find whether the resulting balance of rights and obligations maintains a general level of mutually advantageous commitments not less favourable to trade than that provided for in Schedules of specific commitments prior to the negotiations".

14. The arbitrator's findings and recommendations shall be communicated to the parties to the arbitration within three months of the appointment of the arbitrator.

15. When an arbitration has been conducted in accordance with paragraphs 8 through 14 above, the modifying Member shall be free to implement a modification or withdrawal which is in conformity with the findings of the arbitrator. Any affected Member shall then be free, no later than three months after such action is taken, to modify or withdraw benefits in conformity with those findings.

16. When an arbitration has been conducted in accordance with paragraphs 8 through 14 above, and the modifying Member implements a modification or withdrawal and does not comply with the findings of the arbitrator, an affected Member that participated in the arbitration may, within [one month] from the date of such implementation, request the arbitrator to further find the appropriate level of retaliatory modification or withdrawal of commitments by that affected Member. The arbitrator may recommend that such a retaliatory modification or withdrawal be implemented solely with respect to services or service suppliers of the modifying Member.

17. The arbitrator's further findings and recommendations shall be communicated to the parties to the arbitration within one month of the request for such findings and recommendations. The affected Member that requested such findings or recommendations will then be free to modify or

7니-32-8

19-ART2

withdraw commitments in conformity with those findings or recommendations, within [three months] thereafter.

18. Retaliatory modifications or withdrawals implemented in accordance with paragraph 16 shall be terminated if the modifying Member complies with the findings and recommendations of the arbitrator under paragraph 14.

19. The modifying Member may withdraw at any time its notification under Article XXI:1 of the Agreement and paragraph 1 above, by notice to the MTO Secretariat. Upon receipt of such a withdrawal, Article XXI and these procedures shall cease to apply and the modifying Member shall be obligated to maintain the commitment in question in conformity with its Schedule and Part III of the Agreement.

Formal aspects of the procedures for modification or rectification of schedules of commitments

20. These procedures are also valid for invocation of Article XXI pursuant to Article V, paragraph 5; Article VIII, paragraph 4; Article X, paragraph 2; and Article XXIII, paragraph 4.

21. Changes in the authentic texts of Schedules annexed to the General Agreement which reflect modifications resulting from such invocation shall be certified by means of Certifications. A draft of such changes shall be communicated to the Secretariat within three months after the changes have been implemented.

22. Changes in the authentic texts of Schedules shall be made when amendments or rearrangements which do not alter the scope of a commitment are introduced in measures of a Members in respect of bound items. Such changes and other rectifications of a purely formal character shall be made by means of Certifications. A draft of such changes shall be communicated to the Director-General where possible within three months but not later than six months after the amendment or rearrangement has been introduced in

72P-32-P

19-ART2 0089

measures of a Members or in the case of other rectifications, as soon as circumstances permit.

23. The draft containing the changes described in paragraphs 21 and 22 shall be communicated by the MTO Secretariat to all Members and shall become a Certification provided that no objection has been raised by a Member within three months on the ground that, in the case of changes described in paragraph 21, the draft does not correctly reflect the modifications or, in the case of changes described in paragraph 22, the proposed rectification is not within the terms of that paragraph.

24. Certifications shall record the date of entry into force of each modification and the effective date of each rectification.

Review

25. These procedures shall be reviewed and shall be adapted in the light of experience as the Council for Trade in Services deems appropriate.

72P-32-10

DRAFT
3.12.92

Group of Negotiations on Services

INFORMAL NOTE BY THE SECRETARIAT

Definitions: Article XXXIV

The annotations to the Draft Final Act provide that, in addition to the legal clarification to be undertaken with respect to the Agreement as a whole, participants will examine technical matters with respect to Article XXXIV (Definitions).

A revised version of Article XXXIV (Definitions) was prepared by the Secretariat, 14 May 1992. In the light of comments received by the Secretariat from delegations, this text has been further revised and is attached.

The present draft is being made available for further consultations and comments from delegations.

72P-32-11

18-ART2

DRAFT
3.12.92

TECHNICAL REVISION TO ARTICLE XXXIV: DEFINITIONS

FINAL ACT	14 MAY TEXT	PROPOSED REVISED TEXT
Article XXXIV Definitions	Article XXXIV Definitions	Article XXXIV Definitions
For the purpose of this Agreement: (a) "measure" means any measure by a Party, whether in the form of a law, regulation, rule, procedure, decision, administrative action, or any other form;	For the purpose of this Agreement: (a) "measure" means any measure by a Member, whether in the form of a law, regulation, rule, procedure, decision, administrative action, or any other form;	For the purposes of this Agreement: (a) "measure" means any measure by a Member, whether in the form of a law, regulation, rule, procedure, decision, administrative action, or any other form;
(b) "supply of a service" includes the production, distribution, marketing, sale and delivery of a service;	(b) "supply of a service" includes the production, distribution, marketing, sale and delivery of a service;	(b) "supply of a service" includes the production, distribution, marketing, sale and delivery of a service;
(c) "measures by Parties affecting trade in services" include measures in respect of	(c) "measures by Members affecting trade in services" include measures in respect of	(c) "measures by Members affecting trade in services" include measures in respect of
i) the purchase, payment or use of a service,	i) the purchase, payment or use of a service,	i) the purchase, payment or use of a service,
ii) the access to and use of, in connection with the supply of a service,	ii) the access to and use of, in connection with the supply of a service,	ii) the access to and use of, in connection with the supply of a service, services which are required by those Members to be offered to the public generally;
1. distribution and transportation systems, and	1. distribution and transportation systems, and	

0092

92P-12-12

- 2 -

FINAL ACT	14 MAY TEXT	PROPOSED REVISED TEXT
2. public telecommunications transport networks and services, and	2. public telecommunications transport networks and services, and	
iii) the presence, including commercial presence, of persons of a Party for the supply of a service in the territory of another Party.	iii) the presence, including commercial presence, of persons of a Member for the supply of a service in the territory of another Member;	iii) the presence, including commercial presence, of persons of a Member for the supply of a service in the territory of another Member;
(d) "commercial presence" means any type of business or professional establishment, including through	(d) "commercial presence" means any type of business or professional establishment, including through	(d) "commercial presence" means any type of business or professional establishment, including through
i) the constitution, acquisition or maintenance of a juridical person, or	i) the constitution, acquisition or maintenance of a juridical person, or	i) the constitution, acquisition or maintenance of a juridical person, or
ii) the creation or maintenance of a branch or a representative office,	ii) the creation or maintenance of a branch or a representative office,	ii) the creation or maintenance of a branch or a representative office,
within the territory of a Party for the purpose of supplying a service.	within the territory of a Member for the purpose of supplying a service.	within the territory of a Member for the purpose of supplying a service;
	(..) "sector" of a service means one or more, or all, sub-sectors of that service, as specified in a Member's schedule	(e) "sector" of a service means, i) with reference to a specific commitment, one or more, or all, sub-sectors of that service, as specified in a Member's schedule ii) otherwise, the whole of that service sector, including all of its sub-sectors.

0093

72P-32-13

- 3 -

FINAL ACT		14 MAY TEXT		PROPOSED REVISED TEXT	
		(..)	"service of a Member" means a service which originates in the territory of the Member	(f)	"service of another Member" means a service which is either i) supplied from or in the territory of that other Member or, ii) in the case of the supply of a service through commercial presence or through the presence of natural persons, supplied by a service supplier of that other Member;
(e)	"service supplier" of another Party means any person of that Party that supplies a service;	(e)	"service supplier" means any person that supplies a service;	(g)	"service supplier" means any person that supplies a service;
		(..)	"monopoly supplier of a service" means any person, public or private, which in the relevant market of the territory of a Member is authorized or established formally or in effect by that Member as the sole supplier of that service.	(h)	"monopoly supplier of a service" means any person, public or private, which in the relevant market of the territory of a Member is authorized or established formally or in effect by that Member as the sole supplier of that service;
(f)	"service consumer" of a Party means any person of that Party that receives or uses a service;	(f)	"service consumer" means any person that receives or uses a service;	(i)	"service consumer" means any person that receives or uses a service;
(g)	"person" of a Party is either a natural or a juridical person of that Party	(g)	"person" means either a natural person or a juridical person	(j)	"person" means either a natural person or a juridical person;
(h)	"natural person" of a Party means	(h)	"natural person of a Member" means a natural person who	(k)	"natural person of another Member" means a natural person who

0094

72P-32-1X

FINAL ACT	14 MAY TEXT	PROPOSED REVISED TEXT
i) a natural person who is a national of the Party under the law of that Party, or	i) is a national of the Member or,	i) is a national of that other Member or,
ii) in the case of a Party which does not have nationals, a natural person who has the right of permanent residence under the law of that Party,	ii) in the case of a Member which does not have nationals, or a Member which makes a special declaration to the Council on Trade in Services, has the right of permanent residence in the Member	ii) in the case of a Member which 1. does not have nationals, or 2. has given written notification to the Council on Trade in Services that, for the purpose of this Agreement, it treats its permanent residents as its nationals, has the right of permanent residence
and who resides in the territory of that Party or any other Party.	under the law of that Member, and who resides in the territory of that Member or any other Member;	under the law of that other Member, and who resides in the territory of that Member or any other Member;
(i) "juridical person" of another Party means any corporation, partnership, joint venture, sole proprietorship or association, whether constituted for profit or otherwise, and whether privately-owned or governmentally-owned, which is	(..) "juridical person" means any legal entity duly constituted or otherwise organized under applicable law, whether for profit or otherwise, and whether privately-owned or governmentally-owned, including any corporation, trust, partnership, joint venture, sole proprietorship or association.	(1) "juridical person" means any legal entity duly constituted or otherwise organized under applicable law, whether for profit or otherwise, and whether privately-owned or governmentally-owned, including any corporation, trust, partnership, joint venture, sole proprietorship or association;

0095

72-32-15

- 5 -

FINAL ACT	14 MAY TEXT	PROPOSED REVISED TEXT
	(i) "juridical person of another Member" means a juridical person which is	(m) "juridical person of another Member" means a juridical person which is either
i) constituted under the law of that Party and is engaged in substantive business operations in the territory of that Party or any other Party, or	i) constituted or otherwise organized under the law of that other Member, and is engaged in substantive business operations in the territory of that Member or any other Member; or	i) constituted or otherwise organized under the law of that other Member, and is engaged in substantive business operations in the territory of that Member or any other Member; or
ii) owned or controlled by	ii) in the case of the supply of a service through commercial presence, owned or controlled by	ii) in the case of the supply of a service through commercial presence, owned or controlled by
1. natural persons of that Party, or	1. natural persons of that Party, or	1. natural persons of that Member, or
2. juridical persons of that Party as defined under paragraph (i);	2. juridical persons of that other Member identified under subparagraph (i).	2. juridical persons of that other Member identified under subparagraph (i);
(j) A juridical person is	(j) A juridical person is	(n) A juridical person is
i) "owned" by persons of a Party if more than 50 per cent of the equity interest in it is beneficially owned by persons of that Party;	i) "owned" by persons of a Member if more than 50 per cent of the equity interest in it is beneficially owned by persons of that Member;	i) "owned" by persons of a Member if more than 50 per cent of the equity interest in it is beneficially owned by persons of that Member;
ii) "controlled" by persons of a Party if such persons have the power to name a majority of its directors or to otherwise legally direct its actions;	ii) "controlled" by persons of a Member if such persons have the power to name a majority of its directors or to otherwise legally direct its actions;	ii) "controlled" by persons of a Member if such persons have the power to name a majority of its directors or otherwise to legally direct its actions;

0096

92P-32-16

FINAL ACT	14 MAY TEXT	PROPOSED REVISED TEXT
iii) "affiliated" with another person when it controls, or is controlled by, that other person; or when it and the other person are both controlled by the same person.	iii) "affiliated" with another person when it controls, or is controlled by, that other person; or when it and the other person are both controlled by the same person.	iii) "affiliated" with another person when it controls, or is controlled by, that other person; or when it and the other person are both controlled by the same person;

<u>Article I</u> <u>Scope and Definition</u>	<u>Article I</u> <u>Scope and Definition</u>	<u>Article I</u> <u>Scope and Definition</u>
1. This Agreement applies to measures by Parties affecting trade in services.	1. This Agreement applies to measures by Members affecting trade in services.	1. This Agreement applies to measures by Members affecting trade in services.
2. For the purposes of this Agreement, trade in services is defined as the supply of a service:	2. For the purposes of this Agreement, trade in services is defined as the supply of a service:	2. For the purposes of this Agreement, trade in services is defined as the supply of a service:
(a) from the territory of one Party into the territory of any other Party;	(a) from the territory of one Member into the territory of any other Member;	(a) from the territory of one Member into the territory of any other Member;
(b) in the territory of one Party to the service consumer of any other Party;	(b) in the territory of one Member to the service consumer of any other Member;	(b) in the territory of one Member to the service consumer of any other Member;
(c) through the presence of service providing entities of one Party in the territory of any other Party;	(c) by a service supplier of one Member, through commercial presence in the territory of any other Member;	(c) by a service supplier of one Member, through commercial presence in the territory of any other Member;
(d) by natural persons of one Party in the territory of any other Party.	(d) by a service supplier of one Member, through presence of natural persons of a Member in the territory of any other Member.	(d) by a service supplier of one Member, through presence of natural persons of a Member in the territory of any other Member.

0097

724-32-17

FINAL ACT	14 MAY TEXT	PROPOSED REVISED TEXT
3. For the purposes of this Agreement:	3. For the purposes of this Agreement:	3. For the purposes of this Agreement:
"measures by Parties" means measures taken by:	(a) "measures by Members" means measures taken by:	(a) "measures by Members" means measures taken by:
(i) central, regional or local governments and authorities; and	(i) central, regional or local governments and authorities; and	i) central, regional or local governments and authorities; and
(ii) non-governmental bodies in the exercise of powers delegated by central, regional or local governments or authorities;	(ii) non-governmental bodies in the exercise of powers delegated by central, regional or local governments or authorities;	(ii) non-governmental bodies in the exercise of powers delegated by central, regional or local governments or authorities;
In fulfilling its obligations and commitments under the Agreement, each Party shall take such reasonable measures as may be available to it to ensure their observance by regional and local governments and authorities and non-governmental bodies within its territory.	In fulfilling its obligations and commitments under the Agreement, each Member shall take such reasonable measures as may be available to it to ensure their observance by regional and local governments and authorities and non-governmental bodies within its territory.	In fulfilling its obligations and commitments under the Agreement, each Member shall take such reasonable measures as may be available to it to ensure their observance by regional and local governments and authorities and non-governmental bodies within its territory.
3. (...) (b) "services" includes any service in any sector except services supplied in the exercise of governmental functions.* *The terms of the exclusion of services supplied in the exercise of governmental functions will be reviewed in the context of the work on Article XXXIV.	3. (...) (b) "services" includes any service in any sector, except a service supplied in the exercise of governmental authority. A service supplied in the exercise of governmental authority shall not be understood to include a service supplied on a commercial basis, or in competition with one or more service suppliers.	3. (...) (b) "services" includes any service in any sector, except a service supplied in the exercise of governmental authority.

0098

724-32-18

FINAL ACT	14 MAY TEXT	PROPOSED REVISED TEXT
		(c) A service supplied in the exercise of governmental authority means any service which is supplied neither on a commercial basis, nor in competition with one or more service suppliers.

FINAL ACT	14 MAY TEXT	PROPOSED REVISED TEXT
<u>Article XXXI</u> <u>Denial of Benefits</u>	<u>Article XXXI</u> <u>Denial of Benefits</u>	<u>Article XXXI</u> <u>Denial of Benefits</u>
1. A Party may deny the benefits of this Agreement: (a) to the supply of a service, if it establishes that the service originates in the territory of a country that is not a Party to this Agreement, or in the territory of a Party to which the denying Party does not apply this Agreement; and	1. A Member may deny the benefits of this Agreement: (a) to the supply of a service, if it establishes that the service originates in the territory of a country that is not a Member to this Agreement, or in the territory of a Member to which the denying Member does not apply this Agreement; and	1. A Member may deny the benefits of this Agreement: (a) to the supply of a service, if it establishes that the service is supplied from the territory of a country that is not a Member to this Agreement, or in the territory of a Member to which the denying Member does not apply this Agreement; and
(b) to a service supplier that is a juridical person, if it establishes that ultimate ownership or control of such person is held by persons of a country that is not a Party to this Agreement, or of a Party to which the denying Party does not apply this Agreement.	(b) to a service supplier that is a juridical person, if it establishes that ultimate ownership or control of such person is held by persons of a country that is not a Member to this Agreement, or of a Member to which the denying Member does not apply this Agreement.	(b) to a service supplier that is a juridical person, if it establishes that ultimate ownership or control of such person is held by persons of a country that is not a Member to this Agreement, or of a Member to which the denying Member does not apply this Agreement.

FINAL ACT	14 MAY TEXT	PROPOSED REVISED TEXT
<u>ANNEX ON FINANCIAL SERVICES</u> 1. <u>Scope and Definition</u>	<u>ANNEX ON FINANCIAL SERVICES</u> 1. <u>Scope and Definition</u>	<u>ANNEX ON FINANCIAL SERVICES</u> 1. <u>Scope and Definition</u>

0099

72P-32-1P

- 9 -

FINAL ACT	14 MAY TEXT	PROPOSED REVISED TEXT
1.2 For the purposes of Article I:3(b) of the Agreement, "services supplied in the exercise of governmental functions" means the following:	1.2 For the purposes of Article I:3(b) of the Agreement, "services supplied in the exercise of governmental authority" means the following:	1.2 For the purposes of Article I:3(b) of the Agreement, "services supplied in the exercise of governmental authority" means the following:
1.2.1 activities conducted by a central bank or monetary authority or by any other public entity in pursuit of monetary or exchange rate policies;	1.2.1 activities conducted by a central bank or monetary authority or by any other public entity in pursuit of monetary or exchange rate policies;	1.2.1 activities conducted by a central bank or monetary authority or by any other public entity in pursuit of monetary or exchange rate policies;
1.2.2 activities forming part of a statutory system of social security or public retirement plans; and	1.2.2 activities forming part of a statutory system of social security or public retirement plans; and	1.2.2 activities forming part of a statutory system of social security or public retirement plans; and
1.2.3 other activities conducted by a public entity for the account or with the guarantee or using the financial resources of the Government.	1.2.3 other activities conducted by a public entity for the account or with the guarantee or using the financial resources of the Government.	1.2.3 other activities conducted by a public entity for the account or with the guarantee or using the financial resources of the Government.
1.3 For the purposes of Article I:3(b) of the Agreement, if a Party allows any of the activities referred to in paragraph 1.2.2 or 1.2.3 to be conducted by its financial service providers in competition with a public entity or a financial service provider, "services" shall include such activities.	1.3 For the purposes of Article I:3(b) of the Agreement, if a Member allows any of the activities referred to in paragraph 1.2.2 or 1.2.3 to be conducted by its financial service providers in competition with a public entity or a financial service provider, "services" shall include such activities.	1.3 For the purposes of Article I:3(b) of the Agreement, if a Member allows any of the activities referred to in paragraph 1.2.2 or 1.2.3 to be conducted by its financial service providers in competition with a public entity or a financial service provider, "services" shall include such activities.
		1.4 Article I:3(c) of the Agreement shall not apply to services covered by this Annex.

0100

DRAFT
4.12.92

SCHEDULING OF INITIAL COMMITMENTS IN TRADE IN SERVICES:

EXPLANATORY NOTE[1]

Introduction

1. This informal note is intended to assist in the preparation of offers, requests and national schedules of initial commitments. Its objective is to explain, in a concise manner, how commitments should be set out in schedules in order to achieve precision and clarity. It is based on the view that some standardization of format is necessary to ensure comparable and unambiguous commitments. The note cannot answer every question that might occur to persons responsible for scheduling commitments; it does attempt to answer those questions which are most likely to arise. The answers should not be considered as an authoritative legal interpretation of the GATS.

2. The GATS contains two sorts of provisions: general obligations which apply uniformly; and specific commitments, which are negotiated sectoral undertakings particular to each GATS signatory. Specific commitments, upon the conclusion of negotiations, are to be recorded in national schedules which will be attached to, and form an integral part of, the GATS. By virtue of Article XXVIII:1, every signatory must attach to the GATS its national schedule.

---

[1]This note is circulated by the Secretariat in response to requests by participants. It is a revised version of a draft entitled Scheduling of Commitments in Trade in Services: Explanatory Note 11 February 1992. It is subject to further revision as thought necessary by participants. References to the General Agreement on Trade in Services (GATS) are based on the text contained in MTN.TNC/W/FA of 20 December 1991, as adjusted by the Legal Drafting Group and distributed as an Informal Note by the Secretariat (Review of Individual Texts in the Draft Final Act, No. 1161, 25 June 1992.

0101

72P-32-21

F-INIT2

This note addresses two main questions: what items should be entered on a schedule, and how should they be entered.

PART I

WHAT ITEMS SHOULD BE SCHEDULED?

3. A schedule contains three main types of information: limitations[2] to market access, limitations to national treatment, and additional commitments other than market access and national treatment. If a Member undertakes a commitment in a sector then it must indicate, for each mode of supply in that sector:

- what limitations, if any, it maintains on market access;
- what limitations, if any, it maintains on national treatment; and
- what further commitments, other than market access and national treatment, it may decide to undertake.

A. Limitations on Market Access (Article XVI)

4. A Member grants full market access in a given sector and mode of supply when it does not maintain in that sector or mode any of the types of measures listed in Article XVI. The measures listed comprise four types of quantitative restrictions (subparagraphs a-d), as well as limitations on forms of legal entity (subparagraph e) and on foreign equity participation

---

[2] The term "limitations" will be used throughout this note to refer to the "terms", "conditions", "limitations", and "qualifications" used in the GATS, in particular in Articles XVI and XVII.

0102

72P-32-22 F-INIT2

(subparagraph f). The list is exhaustive and includes measures which may also be discriminatory according to the national treatment standard (Article XVII). The quantitative restrictions can be expressed numerically, or through any other criteria that do not relate to the quality of the service supplied, or to the ability of the supplier to supply the service (i.e. technical standards or qualification of the supplier).

> <u>Example</u>: A law specifies that a restaurant will be granted a license to operate only if the applicant demonstrates that market conditions justify an additional restaurant. This is a measure contrary to paragraph 2(a) of Article XVI.

A Member which maintains a measure listed in Article XVI in a sector and mode of supply in which it is making a commitment has a choice: in the light of the results of negotiations it may either remove the measure, or it may record the measure on its schedule as a limitation to market access.

B. Limitations on National Treatment (Article XVII)

5. A Member grants full national treatment in a given sector and mode of supply when it accords in that sector and mode conditions of competition no less favourable to services or service suppliers of other Members than those accorded to its own like services and service suppliers. This requirement may result from treatment which is either formally identical or formally different; the standard thus covers both <u>de jure</u> and <u>de facto</u> discrimination. Unlike Article XVI, the national treatment commitment is not defined through an exhaustive listing of the types of measure which would constitute limitations.

> <u>Example</u>: A law requires that all accountants practising in a country be its nationals. Such a measure discriminates explicitly on the basis of the origin of the service

0103

F-INIT2

supplier and thus constitutes formal, or de jure, denial of national treatment.

Example: A law requires that all accountants be graduates of local universities. Although the measure does not formally distinguish service suppliers on the basis of national origin, it de facto offers less favourable treatment to foreign service suppliers by modifying in an unfavourable way the conditions of competition in relation to the like service supplier of national origin.

6. Article XVII applies to subsidy-type measures in the same way that it applies to all other measures. Article XV (Subsidies) merely obliges Members to "enter into negotiations with a view to developing the necessary multilateral disciplines" to counter the distortive effects caused by subsidies. Therefore, any subsidy which is a discriminatory measure within the meaning of Article XVII would have to be either scheduled as a limitation on national treatment or brought into conformity with that Article. Subsidy-type measures are also not excluded from the scope of Article II (M.f.n.). An exclusion of such measures would require a legal definition of subsidies which is currently not provided for under the GATS.

7. Measures may exist which are inconsistent with both Articles XVI and XVII. Article XX:2 stipulates that such measures shall be inscribed in the column relating to Article XVI on market access. Thus, while there may be no limitation entered in the national treatment column, there may exist a discriminatory measure inconsistent with national treatment inscribed in the market access column. However, in accordance with the footnote to Article XVI:2, any discriminatory measure can be challenged as a violation of Article XVII.

C. Additional Commitments (Article XVIII)

92-32-24

0104

F-INIT2

8. A Member may, in a given sector, make commitments other than market access and national treatment. Such commitments can include, but are not limited to, undertakings with respect to professional qualifications, technical standards, licensing procedures, and other domestic regulations referred to in Article VI, even though these measures may be consistent with full market access (Article XVI) and national treatment (Article XVII). Unlike market access and national treatment, additional commitments are expressed in the form of undertakings, not limitations.

D. Exceptions

9. All measures falling under Article XIV (General Exceptions) are excepted from all obligations and commitments under the Agreement, and therefore need not be scheduled. Clearly, such exceptions cannot be negotiated under Part III of the Agreement. Likewise, any prudential measure justifiable under paragraph 2:1 of the Annex on Financial services constitutes an exception to the Agreement and should not be scheduled. Measures falling under Article XII are also exceptions and should not be scheduled. Article XII provides for separate disciplines for such measures, including notification and consultation.

E. Specific Commitments and MFN Exemptions

10. A Member taking a national treatment or a market access commitment in a sector must accord the stated minimum standard of treatment specified in its schedule to all other Members. The m.f.n. obligation requires that the most favourable treatment actually accorded must also be accorded to all other Members. Where an m.f.n. exemption has been granted in a sector, a Member is free to deviate from its Article II obligations, but not from its Article XVI and XVII commitments. Therefore, in such cases, a Member may accord treatment in that sector more favourable than the minimum standard to some Members, as long as all other Members receive at least that minimum standard of Article XVI or XVII appearing in its schedule.

72P-32-25

0105
F-INIT2

PART II

HOW SHOULD ITEMS BE SCHEDULED?

11. Schedules record, for each sector, the legally enforceable commitments of each Member. It is therefore vital that schedules be clear, precise and based on a common approach and terminology. This section describes how commitments should be entered in schedules.

The main elements are:

A. horizontal measures;
B. sector-specific measures;
C. sectoral classification;
D. modes of supply; and
E. use of common terms.

A. Scheduling of horizontal measures

12. A horizontal measure is a measure which affects trade in services in a number of service sectors. In order to avoid repetition, it is practicable to enter these measures in a separate section at the beginning of the schedule. The entry should describe the measure concisely, indicating the elements which make it inconsistent with Articles XVI or XVII. Some horizontal measures may be specific to only one mode of supply:

Example: Legislation may refer to foreign investment, formation of corporate structures or land acquisition regulations. Such measures affect above all commercial presence.

Example: Legislation may stipulate requirements regarding entry, temporary stay and work as well as define the scope of personnel movement covered by a particular offer. Such measures affect above all the presence of natural persons.

0106
F-INIT2

72P-32-26

Other horizontal measures may affect more than one mode of supply:

Example: Legislation may provide for tax measures which are contrary to national treatment. Such measures would normally affect the supply of services in several modes.

B. Scheduling of sector-specific measures

13. A sector-specific measure is a measure which affects trade in services in only one sector. Such a measure, if maintained and contrary to Articles XVI or XVII, must be entered as a limitation in the appropriate column (either market access or national treatment) for the relevant sector. The entry should describe the measure concisely, indicating the elements which make it inconsistent with Articles XVI or XVII.

14. Given the legal nature of a schedule, it should contain only descriptions of bound measures. Any additional information for clarification purposes should not be entered in the schedule. A reference to the legal basis of a scheduled measure (i.e. the relevant law or regulation) may be entered if thought necessary. In any event, such information will be subject to the obligations of Article III.

C. Sectoral Classification

15. The classification of sectors and sub-sectors should be based on the secretariat's revised Services Sectoral Classification List.[3] Each sector contained in the secretariat list is identified by the corresponding Central Product Classification (CPC) number. Where it is necessary to refine further a sectoral classification, this should be done on the basis

---

[3]Document MTN.GNS/W/120, dated 10 July 1991.

of the CPC. The most recent breakdown of the CPC, including explanatory notes for each sub-sector, is contained in the UN Provisional Central Product Classification.[4]

Example: A Member wishes to indicate an offer or commitment in the sub-sector of map-making services. In the secretariat list, this service would fall under the general heading "Other Business Services" under "Related scientific and technical consulting services" (see item 1.F.m). By consulting the CPC, map-making can be found under the corresponding CPC classification number 86754. In its offer/schedule, the Member would then enter the sub-sector under the "Other Business Services" section of its schedule as follows:

Map-making services (86754)

If a Member wishes to use its own sub-sectoral classification or definitions it should, for the purpose of ensuring legal certainty, provide concordance with the CPC in the manner indicated in the above example.

D. Modes of supply

16. The four modes of supply listed in the schedules correspond to the scope of the GATS as set out in Article I:2. The modes are essentially defined on the basis of the origin of the service supplier and consumer, and the degree and type of territorial presence which they have at the moment the service is delivered. This classification is intended to

---

[4] Statistical Papers Series M no. 77, Provisional Central Product Classification, Department of International Economic and Social Affairs, Statistical Office of the United Nations, New York, 1991.

0108

72P-32-28 F-INIT2

correspond to the categories of regulatory measures which commonly affect trade in services. The modes of supply may be illustrated as follows:

MODES OF SUPPLY

Supplier Presence	Other Criteria	Mode
Service supplier not present within the territory of the Member	Service delivered within the territory of the Member, from the territory of another Member	CROSS-BORDER SUPPLY
	Service delivered outside the territory of the Member, in the territory of another Member, to a service consumer of the Member	CONSUMPTION ABROAD
Service supplier present within the territory of the Member	Service delivered within the territory of the Member, through the commercial presence of the supplier	COMMERCIAL PRESENCE
	Service delivered within the territory of the Member, with supplier present as a natural person	PRESENCE OF NATURAL PERSON

17. It is important to have a common interpretation of what each mode covers along the lines of what is suggested above. Further examples and explanations are given below.

(a) Cross-border supply

18. The supply of a service through telecommunications, mail, and services embodied in goods (e.g. a computer diskette, or drawings) are all examples of cross-border supply, since the service supplier is not present within the territory of the Member where the service is delivered.

0109

72P-32-2P

F-INIT2

(b) Consumption abroad

19. This mode of supply is often referred to as "movement of the consumer". The essential feature of this mode is that the service is delivered outside the jurisdiction of the Member taking the measure. Often the actual movement of the consumer is necessary as in tourism services. However, activities such as ship repair abroad, where only the property of the consumer "moves", or is situated abroad, are also covered.

20. Whatever the mode of supply, obligations and commitments under the Agreement relate directly to the treatment of services and service suppliers. They only relate to service consumers insofar as services or service suppliers of other Members are affected.

21. The "service consumer of any other Member" mentioned in Article I:2(b) may be from any Member. In practice however, a Member may only be able effectively to impose restrictive measures affecting its own consumers, not those of other Members, on activities taking place outside its jurisdiction.

(c) Commercial Presence

22. This mode covers not only the presence of juridical persons in the strict legal sense, such as corporations, but also other legal entities such as partnerships, joint ventures, representative offices, and branches, which share some of the same characteristics (see Definitions: Article XXXIV).

(d) Presence of natural persons

23. This mode covers natural persons who are themselves service suppliers, as well as natural persons who are employees of service suppliers.

(e) Relationship between modes of supply

0110

92P-32-30

F-INIT2

24. Where a service transaction requires in practical terms the use of more than one mode of supply, coverage of the transaction is only ensured when there are commitments in each relevant mode of supply.

<u>Example</u>: A Member has made a commitment in the cross-border supply of architectural services (e.g. by telecommunications or by mail). This commitment alone does <u>not</u> extend to the presence of natural persons (e.g. visits by architects). A separate commitment would have to be taken under "Presence of natural persons" to cover this case.

E. How should commitments be recorded?

25. Since the terms used in a Member's schedule create legally binding commitments, it is important that those expressing presence or absence of limitations to market access and national treatment be uniform and precise. Depending on the extent to which a Member has limited market access and national treatment, for each commitment four cases can be foreseen:

(a) Full commitment

26. In this case the Member does not seek in any way to limit market access or national treatment in a given sector and mode of supply through measures inconsistent with Article XVI and XVII. The Member in this situation should mark in the appropriate column: <u>NONE</u>. However, any relevant horizontal limitations will still apply.

(b) Commitment with limitations

27. Two main possibilities can be envisaged in this case. The first is the binding of an existing regulatory situation ("standstill"). The second is the binding of a more liberal situation where some, but not all, of the measures inconsistent with Articles XVI or XVII will be removed ("rollback"). Here, the Member must describe in the appropriate column the

72P-32-31

0111
F-INIT2

measures maintained which are inconsistent with Articles XVI or XVII. The entry should describe each measure concisely, indicating the elements which make it inconsistent with Articles XVI or XVII. It would not be sufficient to merely enter in a column words such as "bound", "freeze" or "standstill".

(c) No commitment

28. In this case, the Member remains free in a given sector and mode of supply to introduce or maintain measures inconsistent with market access or national treatment. In this situation, the Member must record in the appropriate column the word: UNBOUND. This case is only relevant where a commitment has been made in a sector with respect to at least one mode of supply. Where all modes of supply are "unbound", and no additional commitments have been undertaken in the sector, the sector should not appear on the schedule.

(e) No commitment technically feasible

29. In some situations, a particular mode of supply may not be technically feasible. An example might be the cross-border supply of hair-dressing services. In these cases the term UNBOUND* should be used. The asterisk should refer to a footnote which states "Unbound due to lack of technical feasibility". Where the mode of supply thought to be inapplicable is in fact applicable, or becomes so in the future, the entry should be understood to mean "unbound".

0112
F-INIT2

92-12-32

관리 번호	92 - 928

	분류번호	보존기간

발 신 전 보

번 호 : WJA-5156 921205 1510 FY 종별 :

WGV -1912

수 신 : 주 일 대사. 총영사 (사본 : 주 제네바 대사)

발 신 : 장 관 (통 기)

제 목 : 대일 시청각 MFN 일탈 문제

대 : JAW-6177

연 : WJA-4970

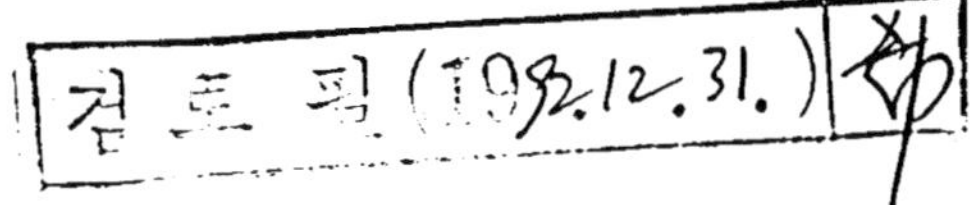

1. 표제관련 관계부처 협의결과, 그간 한.일간에 최종 절충한 방식대로 우리측이 UR/서비스협상 일측 대표의 서한을 접수하고 현재 GATT 사무국에 보류되어 있는 동건 관련 MFN 일탈신청을 철회키로 하였으니 이를 주재국 외무성에 통보바람.

2. 상기와 관련, 세부사항에 대한 아측 의견을 아래와 같이 일측에 통보바람.

가. 서한 내용

- 대호 1항(11.19자 일측 입장)대로 함. (당초 일측 서한의 제3항 삭제)
- 아측 수석대표의 full title(Yoon Jae LEE, Head of Korean delegation to the initial commitment negotiations under the GATS)을 서한의 왼쪽 아래에 표기

나. 서한 전달방식

일반문서로 재분류(1993 . 6 . 30)

- 가급적 조속히 주한 일본 대사관을 통해 아측 수석대표에 전달. 끝.

(통상국장 홍 정 표)

보 안 통 제	

아주국장: 제2차관보:

앙 고 재	92 년 12 월 5 일	통상기구과	기안자 성 명		과 장	심의관	국 장		차 관	장 관
							전결			

외신과통제

0113

	분류번호	보존기간

발 신 전 보

번 호 : WFR-2458 921205 1556 FY 종별 :

수 신 : 주 불 대사. 총영사 WGV -1914 (사본 : 주 제네바대사)

발 신 : 장 관 (통 기)

제 목 : OECD/서비스 교역분야 합동위원회

대 : FRW-2439, GVW-2257

연 : WFR-2419

1. 표제회의 의제에 대한 검토의견을 별첨 송부함.

2. 연호 통보한 바와 같이 본부대표단 파견이 어려우니 귀관에서 동 회의에 참가하고, 회의결과 본부 보고시에는 주 제네바 대표부로도 사본 송부바람.

첨 부(FAX) : 의제 검토의견. 끝.

(통상국장 홍 정 표)

보안통제	

앙고재	92년 12월 5일	통상기구과	기안자 성명		과 장	심의관	국 장		차 관	장 관
							전결			

외신과통제

0114

외 무 부

번 호: WFRF-0067 921205 1557 FY 년월일: 시간: WGVF-0521

수 신: 주 불, 제네바 대사(총영사)

발 신: 외무부장관(통 기)

제 목: OECD/ 서비스 교역분야 합동위원회

총 5 매 (표지포함)

보 안 통 제	
외신과 통 제	

0115

OECD貿易委 및 財務委 合同會議 關聯

1. 會議槪要

- 會議日時 및 場所 : 12.7(月), 파리

  議題 : UR/서비스 일반협정문중 租稅關聯條項에 대한 논의
  (協定文 제2, 11, 14, 22, 23조)

- OECD事務局은 상기 회의에 아국이 옵서버 資格으로 참석해 줄 것을 희망

  ○ 租稅 및 서비스分野 專門家 각1명

2. OECD事務局 提案內容에 대한 檢討

가. 14條(d)項 관련

① 서비스협정문 내용

- 다른 회원국의 서비스 공급자들의 所得(income)에 대한 조세의 공정하거나 효과적인 부과 혹은 징수를 위한 것일 경우 內國民待遇 예외인정

② OECD事務局 修正案

- 所得(income), 資本所得(capital gains), 서비스관련 資本[1] (Capital in respect of services), 당해 회원국 영토내의 거주자가 아닌 서비스 공급자등에 대한 조세의 공정하거나 효과적인 賦課 혹은 徵收를 위한 것일 경우 내국민대우 예외인정

1. 例 : 資産稅와 相續稅(net wealth or inheritance taxes)

0116

② 檢討意見

- 租稅問題와 관련 미국, 캐나다등은 지난 10.8 GNS 非公式 協議에서 14조(d)항의 예외허용요건인 equitable or effective test의 삭제 또는 조세정책상의 조치로의 대체를 要求한 바 있음. 그 논리로서

  i) 동 기준이 매우 주관적이기 때문에 紛爭이 제기되었을 경우 패널이 판단하기 어렵고

  ii) 14조 서두의 요건(자의적이거나 정당화될 수 없는 차별이 아닐 것)과 함께 이중 test의 결과가 되며

  iii) test대상이 조세정책이 아니라 租稅措置의 영향을 검토하는 것이기 때문에 고도로 복잡한 조세체계의 성격상 많은 문제가 야기될 수 있음을 든 바 있음.

- 금번 OECD事務局에서 제시한 14조(d)항의 수정안 내용을 보면 지난번 會議에서 equitable or effective test의 삭제문제에 대해 우리나라를 비롯 日本, 濠洲, 브라질 등이 反對意見을 피력한 바 이에 대한 대안으로서 마련된 것으로 판단됨.

  o OECD事務局은 상기 문구를 삭제하는 것이 바람직(preferable)하나 현재 시점에서 協定文의 급격한 변경 (radically different approach)은 다른 회원국의 지지를 받기 어려운 점을 감안 위와 같은 내용의 修正案을 제시한 것이라고 밝힘.

- 이번 수정안에서 사무국측은 美國, 캐나다등의 의견을 받아 所得뿐만 아니라 資本所得, 資本 및 서비스供給者에 대한 조세조치로 그 범위를 넓혀 內國民待遇 例外許容範圍의 擴大를 모색하려는 것으로 볼 수 있음.

  o 이는 고도로 발달된 복잡한 조세체계를 가진 美國, EC, 캐나다와 기타국가의 조세제도와의 차이에서 문제가 비롯된 것임.

0117

- 동 문제는 결국 조세체계가 복잡한 美, 캐나다등이 현재 시행하고 있는 內國民待遇 例外的인 課稅措置에 대해 MFN일괄신청을 하기보다 서비스 협정문상의 권리로서 당연히 인정을 받기위해 所得외에 資本所得, 資本自體, 서비스 供給者등에 대해 例外認定範圍를 擴大하려는 것으로 보임.

- 따라서 우리는 동 문제가 서비스協定文 改正을 필요로 하므로 Track 4(Fine Tuning)에서 다루어져야 할 사항임을 강조하되, 우리측의 의견을 開陳할 필요가 있다면 반대입장 표명

나. 14條 (e)項 關聯

① 서비스協定文 內容

- 현재의 서비스協定文에는 서로 다른 대우가 당해 회원국이 서명국인 이중과세방지와 관련한 國際協定의 結果일 경우에만 예외를 인정하도록 한정하고 있음(協定文 제14조 e항)

② 事務局 提案內容

- OECD事務局이 제안한 내용은 이중과세 방지협정 뿐만 아니라 당해 회원국이 체결한 다른 國際協定이나 協約에 二重課稅 防止條項이 들어있는 경우 그 조항도 포함시키는 것으로 되어 있음(事務局文書 14조 e항(i))

- 또한 당해 회원국의 조세조치하에서 居住者로 분류되는 자에 대해 조세회피를 방지할 목적으로 과세하도록 책임을 부과하는 措置까지 포함(事務局文書 14조 e항(ii))

③ 檢討意見

- 二重課稅 防止協定이외에 기타 국가간 협정상의 이중과세 방지조항에 따른 조치도 MFN 例外範圍에 해당한다는 것은 지난 6월의 조세관련 GNS 非公式協議에서 합의된 바 있으므로 (i)項은 문제없는 것으로 판단됨.

- (ii)項은 결국 국가간 협정에 의하지 않고 例外範圍가 한 나라의 일방적 조치에 의하여 결정되는 결과가 되므로 受容할 수 없음.

0118

다. 22條 (3)項

① 서비스協定文 內容

- 無差別原則 條項을 포함하고 있는 이중과세 방지관련 국제 협정의 당사국인 회원국간에는 同 協定의 適用對象인 타 회원국의 조치에 대하여 한 회원국은 동 협상의 분쟁해결 조항을 원용하고 또한 합리적인 기간내에 동 분쟁에 대한 만족스러운 타결이 이루어지지 않지 않는 한 본조 또는 제23조에 의거하여 제17조(內國民待遇 條項)을 원용할 수 없다고 규정

② 事務局 提案內容

- 提案內容은 관련당사국간 무차별원칙 관련조항 또는 관련 조치에 적용할 수 있는 유사한 조항이 포함된 二重課稅 防止協定이 당사국간에 체결되어 있을 경우에는 17조를 원용할 수 없다고 규정

③ 檢討意見

- 事務局 提案內容은 MTO의 통합분쟁해결 절차의 정신에 어긋나는 것으로 보인다는 點을 지적하고

- 지난 6월 EC가 租稅問題關聯 GNS 非公式協議에서 제안한 대로 동 문제를 제14조(예외)에 반영하여 二重課稅 防止 協定에 해당하는 어떤 조치가 14조 서두의 자의적이거나 정당화될 수 없는 차별이 아닌 경우에 한하여 同 協商의 紛爭解決에 맡기는 방안은 검토할 수 있다는 정도로 대응

0119

관리 번호	92-931

원 본

외 무 부

종 별 :

번 호 : JAW-6448 일 시 : 92 1207 1900

수 신 : 장 관 (통기, 주제네바 대사 - 중계필)

발 신 : 주 일 대사(일경)

제 목 : 대일시청각 MFN 일탈

대 : WJA-5156

연 : JAW-6177

1. 표제관련, 당관 황서기관은 주재국 외무성 국제기관 1 과 사사끼 담당관에게 대호 우리측 의견을 전한 바, 동인은 이를 주제네바 일본대표부를 통해 제네바 출장중인 쯔루오까 일측 협상 수석대표에게 전달하겠다고 함.

2. 한편, 동인은 대호 서한의 전달방식과 관련, 쯔루오까 협상대표가 당분간 계속 제네바에 체류하면서 협상 추진 예정임을 감안, 현지에서 접촉 예정인 우리측 협상 대표에 직접 또는 주제네바 아국대표부를 통해 전달하는 방식이 좋겠다고 언급하였는 바, 이에대한 본부방침 회시바람. 끝.

(대사 오재희 - 국장)

예고 : 1993.6.30. 까지

검 토 필(1992. 12. 31.)

일반문서로 재분류(1993. 1. 30)

통상국 중계

PAGE 1

92.12.07 19:22

외신 2과 통제관 DI

0120

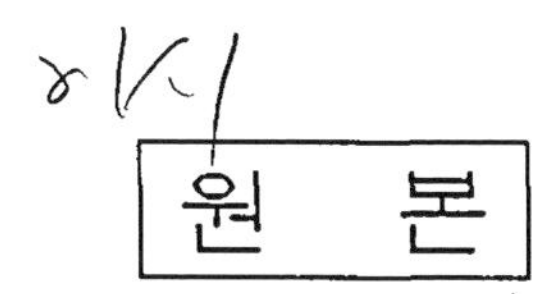

외 무 부

종 별 :

번 호 : GVW-2285 일 시 : 92 1207 1850

수 신 : 장관(통기,경기원,재무부,과학기술처,환경처)

발 신 : 주제네바대사

제 목 : UR 서비스 협상관련 카나다측 서한

카나다 서비스 수석대표인 P.D.LEE 가 아측 수석대표앞으로 UR 서비스 양허 협상관련 카나다측 요구사항을 담은 서한을 보내온바, 별첨 FAX 송부하니 카나다측과의 12월양자협상대비에 참고 바람.

첨부: 카나다측 서한 1부

(GVW(F)-0731).끝

(대사 박수길-국장)

통상국 경기원 재무부 과기처 환경처

PAGE 1 92.12.08 07:00 CJ

외신 1과 통제관

0121

7/12/92 19:20 KOREA MISSION GENEVA → 736 7790 NO.598 P01

주 제 네 바 대 표 부

번 호 : GVW(F) - 0732　　년월일 : 21207　　시간 : 1820

수 신 : 장　　관 (통기, 경기원, 재무부, 과학기술처, 환경처)

발 신 : 주 제네바대사

제 목 : UR 서비스 협상 관련 카나다측 서한

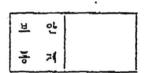

총 3 매(표지포함)

보 안	
통 제	

외신국	
통 제	

배부처	장관실	차관실	一차보	二차보	외정실	분석관	아주국	미주국	구주국	중아국	국기국	경제국	통상국	문협국	외연원	청와대	안기부	공보처	경기원	상공부	재무부	농수부	동자부	환경처	과기처		
				/	/								0						/		/			/	/		

0122

732-3-1

ernal Affairs and International Trade Canada Affaires extérieures et Commerce extérieur Canada

Canada

OTTAWA, ONTARIO
K1A OG2

December 1, 1992

Chief Services Negotiator
for Korea
Permanent Mission of Korea
Geneva

My dear Colleague:

This is further to the bilateral exchanges which have taken place between Canada and Korea concerning the market access requests and offers in the services negotiations in the Uruguay Round.

In addition to the offer of 19 February 1992 and improvements which Korea has indicated that it would make to this offer, Canada has requested that Korea schedule the full range of environmental services (CPC 9401- 9409), as well as technical testing and analysis services (CPC 8676).

With respect to financial services, Canada has outlined in previous discussions the problems of Canadian banks in Korea including restricted access to local currency funding, credit allocation requirements in favour of the small business sector, and lack of transparency in regulations governing banking and insurance operations. Our concerns were reflected in a letter of 10 November from the Canadian Minister of Finance to Minister Rhee and specific requests were reiterated during a visit to Seoul earlier this month by representatives of the Canadian Department of Finance. Here I wish to emphasize once again that it is essential that Korea improve its offer on banking and insurance if we are to achieve our objective of a major result for services in the Uruguay Round.

...\2

732-3-2

- 2 -

For its part, Canada will enscribe our revised offer of February 14,1992 in a draft schedule which will also reflect to the extent possible Korea's requests. Moreover, we are exploring the scope to extend temporary access for certain foreign professional services suppliers. I also confirm that Canada is prepared to remove certain financial services sector limitations, as requested by Korea, subject to a substantial over-all package in that sector.

Yours sincerely,

P.D. Lee
Chief Services Negotiator
for Canada

732-3-3

0124

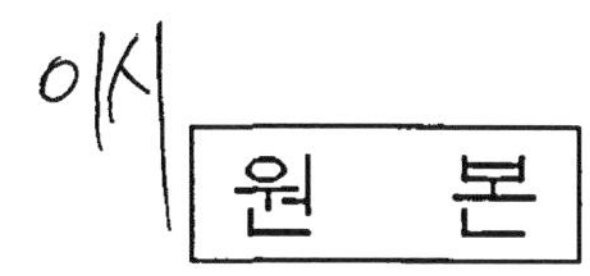

외 무 부

종 별 :

번 호 : FRW-2531 일 시 : 92 1208 1930

수 신 : 장관(통기,경일,재무부),사본:주제네바대사-직송필

발 신 : 주 불대사

제 목 : OECD/서비스 교역분야 합동위 참가 보고

대:WFR-2458

1. 표제회의는 12.7 재무국 RAINER GEIGER 부국장주재로 개최된 바,회의결과 아래 보고함.(당관최혁공사,조서기관 참석)

가. GATS 협정안 제14조 D 항

1) EQUITABLE OR EFFECTIVE 삭제 문제

- 칸다,미국이 14조 서두의 요건(자의적 이거나 정당화될수 없는 차별이 아닌것)에 비추어 중복되는 테스트 결과가 되며 테스트 대상이 조세정책 자체가 아니라 조세조치가 무역에 미치는 영향을 검토하는 것이기 때문에 복잡한 조세체계의 성격상 문제가 야기될수 있고 분쟁발생시 PANEL 판단이 어렵다는 점등을 들어삭제를 주장

- 이에대해,여타국들은 삭제 제의 배경을 이해하면서도 14조 서두는 기본 방향을규정한 것에 불과함으로 PROPORTIONALITY 원칙에 따라 무역에 미치는 효과를 검토하도 록 해야하므로 D 항에 별도요건을 두어야한다는 점(EC) 및 NAFTA협정에도 동일 여건 이 규정되어 있는점(일본)등을 들어 삭제에 유보적 입장을 견지

2) 내국민 대우 인정 범위

- 카나다,미국,멕시코등은 서비스 공급자에 부과하는 조세가 자본소득,서비스관련 자등에 대한 조세로 세분되어 있음을 들어 내국민 대우 예외 인정범위를 확대하자는 사무국안을 지지(EC 도 이에부분적 동조)

- 그러나,호주,일본은 서비스 공급자의 소득에 대한조세범위에 일반적으로 자본소득이 포함되며 예외범위를 너무 확대하는것은 바람직하지않다는 점등을 들어 유보입장을 표명

- 사무국은 본건이 국별로 상이한 조세체계에 기인함을 지적하였으며 THIN CAPITALIZATION관행에 대한 대응,전문서비스 제공에 따른 조세문제등 현실적이며

통상국 경제국 재무부

PAGE 1

92.12.11 16:15 FY

외신 1과 통제관

0125

기술적 문제에 대한해결방안은 계속 검토가 필요하다는 견해 표명나. 동 14조 E 항

1) 2중과세방지 협정외의 여타 협정 및 협약에대한 MFN 예외 인정 문제:

- 2중과세방지 협정이외의 여타 국제 협정상의 2중과세방지 조항에 따른 조치도 MFN예외범위에 해당한다는 원칙에는 이의가없었으나,카나다가 국제관행을 국내법으로규정하는 경우에는 해당국내의 규정도 예외범위에 포함할 것을 제의

2) 조세회비에 대한 대응목적에 과징금부과조치에 대한 예외 적용 문제:

- 멕시코가 '회원국의 조세조치하에서 거주자로 분류되는 자' 의 요건을 삭제할것을 제의한외에 대체로 사무국안에 문제를 제기치않았으나,아국 및 일본이 UR 협상이 최종단계에 있으며 동 문제가 실질 권리의무관계를 규정한 것이므로 조세 회피를 방지하는 목적의모든 조세 추가 부과 조치를 예외로 인정하는데 문제가 있음을 지적

-조세회피에 대한 대응문제가 14조 C 항의예외조항 (기만,사기관행 방지조치) 으로 처리될수있는지에 대한 의문이 제기되었으나 부정적해석이 유력하였음.

다.동 22조3항 (협의조항)

-관련당사국간 문제된 조치에 적용할수 있는 무차별원칙 또는 이와 유사한 조항이 포함된 2중과세 방지 협정이 체결 되어 있을 경우, GATS의 분쟁해결 절차에 의거 17조를 원용할수없도록 하는 문제는 1) 해당조치가 어느 범주에속하는지에 대한 판정문제 2) 판정주체를 제소국또는 PANEL 로 할 것인지의 판단주체 문제로 귀착된다는데 대체로 의견이 모아짐. 다만 일본은 해당조치를 보다 한정적으로 규정할 것을 제의

2.관찰 및 건의

가.금번회의 결론 도출보다도 문제점을 제기하여 해결방안을 검토하는데 의의가있었음(사무국이쟁점별 토의 요록을 준비하되, 결론이나 방향은 제시치 않기로 함)

나.회의 전체 분위기로 보아 일본, 아국, 호주등 일부국을 제외하고는 대체로 사무국 수정안에 동조적 입장을 표명한 바, 미.카나다 등이 UR관련회의에서 동 문제를적 극 제기할 것에대비, 사무국안에 대한 아측입장과 대응논리를보다 면밀히 검토하여 대응토록 할 것을 건의함.끝

(대사 노영찬-국장)

관리 번호	92 - 941

	분류번호	보존기간

발 신 전 보

WJA-5189 921209 1125 WG

번 호 : 종별 :

수 신 : 주 일 대사. 총영사

발 신 : 장 관 (통 기)

제 목 : 대일 시청각 MFN 일탈

대 : JAW-6448

대호 서한전달 관련, 우리측 서비스 협상 대표단이 12.12(토) 제네바 도착 예정이므로 제네바에서 일측 서비스협상 수석대표가 아측 서비스협상 수석대표에게 전달하는 방식이 좋을 것으로 보이니 이를 일측에 통보바람. 끝.

(통상국장 대리 오 행 겸)

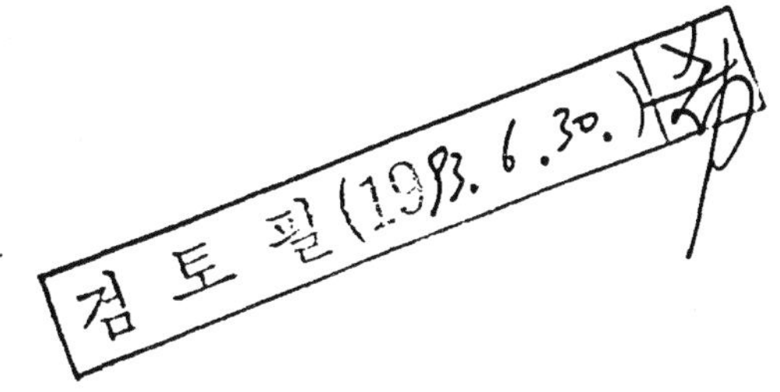

보 안 통 제	

앙 고 재	92 년 12 월 9 일	통상기구과	기안자 성명		과 장	심의관	국 장		차 관	장 관
							전결			

외신과통제

0127

원 본

외 무 부

종 별 :

번 호 : GVW-2307 일 시 : 92 1209 1100

수 신 : 장관(수신처참조)

발 신 : 주 제네바 대사

제 목 : UR/서비스 양자 협상 일정

수신처:(통기,경기원,재무부,법무부,농림수산부,상공부,문화부,건설부,교통부,체신부,보사부,과기처,공보처,환경처,항만청)

1. 12.12 주간 개최예정인 표제 협상 관련 12.8현재 확정된 아국의 양자 협상일정을 하기 보고함.

- 12.14(월) 11:00 스웨덴

11:00 EC (금융분야)

- 12.15(화) 10:00 일본

15:00 인도네시아(잠정)

18:00 호주(금융분야)

- 12.16(수) 09:00-12:00 미국(금융포함)

15:00 호주(금융이외)

- 12.17(목) 10:00 EC (금융 이외)

14:30 캐나다

- 12.18(금) 09:00 태국

- 상기 이외 뉴질랜드는 아국에 양자 협상을 요청중이나 미정(월요일 오후)이며중국은 본부대표단 파견 여부 자체의 미정으로 일정 미확정

2. 금번 양자 협상 관련 파악된 각국의 대표단 규모는 아래와 같음.

- 미국: 13명(명단 별첨)

- 호주: 본부 5명(금융전문가 1명 포함)

- 일본: 본부대표 15명

- 카나다: 6-7 명(금융, 통신, 인력이동 전문가 각1인 포함)

- EC, 스웨덴, 뉴질랜드 : 92.10월 협상시 수준

통상국 법무부 보사부 문화부 교통부 체신부 경기원 농수부 상공부
건설부 과기처 해항청 환경처 공보처 재무부

PAGE 1

92.12.09 22:27 EI

외신 1과 통제관

0128

- 인도네시아, 태국: 미정

3. 상기 각국대표단 수준을 감안, 아국 대표단규모는 10여명선(금융 3인 포함)으로 구성함이 적절한 것으로 사료됨.

(첨부:GVW(F)-739)

(대사 박수길-국장)

주 제 네 바 대 표 부

번 호 : GVW(F) - 739　　　　년월일 : 2120ｐ　　　　시간 : 1800

수 신 : 장 관 (통기, 경기원, 재무부, 법무부, 농림수산부, 상공부, 문화부, 건설부 교통부, 체신부, 보사부, 과기처, 공보처, 환경처, 항만청)

발 신 : 주 제네바대사

제 목 : UR/서비스 양자협상 일정

보 안	
통 제	

총 3 매(표지포함)

외신국	
통 제	

배부처	장관실	차관실	一차보	二차보	외정실	분석관	아주국	미주국	구주국	중아국	국기국	경제국	통상국	문협국	외연원	청와대	안기부	공보처	경기원	상공부	재무부	농수부	동자부	환경처	과기처		

739-3-1

0130

List of U.S. Services Delegates Attending Bilateral with Korea

Bonnie Richardson
Director of Multilateral Services Negotiations
Office of Services, Investment, and Science & Technology

Christina Lund
Attache (USTR/Geneva)

Fred Elliott
International Trade Specialists
Office of Services
US Department of Commerce

Todd Kushner
International Economist
Developed Country Trade Office
U.S. State Department

Ron Dobson
International Economist
Office of International Economic Affairs
U.S. Department of Labor

Laura Sallstrom
Deputy Director of Multilateral Services Negotiations
Office of Services, Investment, and Science & Technology
USTR

Larry MacDonald
International Economist Treasury 6명.
Office of Financial Services Negotiations
Treasury

Ida May Mantel
Deputy Director of Financial Services Negotiations
Office of Financial Services Negotiations
Treasury

Art MacMahon
International Economist
Office of Financial Services Negotiations
Treasury

Jerry Newman
Director of Office of Financial Services Negotiations
Office of Financial Services Negotiations
Treasury

1/2

73P-3-2

0131

Keith Palzer
Attorney/Advisor
General Council
Treasury

Deborah Katz
Legal Advisor
Office of Comptroller of the Currency
OCC

James Fall
Deputy Assistant Secretary for Developing Nations
U.S. Treasury

73P-3-3

2/2

0132

외 무 부

110-760 서울 종로구 세종로 77번지 / (02)720-2188 / (02)720-2686 (FAX)

문서번호 통기 20644-

시행일자 1992.12. 9.( )

수신 내부결재

참조

취급		차 관	장 관
보존		전결	
국 장	출장		
심의관		제2차관보	
과 장			
기안	이 시 형		협조

제목 UR/서비스 협상 정부대표 임명

92.12.14-18간 제네바에서 개최되는 UR/서비스 양자협상에 참가할 정부대표를 "정부대표 및 특별사절의 임명과 권한에 관한 법률"에 의거, 아래와 같이 임명하고자 건의하오니 재가하여 주시기 바랍니다.

- 아 래 -

1. 정부대표

수석대표 :	경제기획원	제2협력관	이윤재
대 표 : (11명)	경제기획원	통상조정3과장	장항석
		통상조정3과 사무관	이성한
		통상조정3과 사무관	한철수
		통상조정1과 사무관	주형환
	재 무 부	국제금융과 사무관	최희남
		은행과 사무관	윤용로
		보험정책과 사무관	변상구
	법 무 부	국제법무심의관실 검찰관	김영철
	체 신 부	통신협력단 과장	김재섭

/ 계속...

0133

자　　문 : 대외경제연구원 연구위원　　　　　성극제
　　　　　통신개발연구원 연구위원　　　　　최병일

2. 출장기간 및 장소 : 92.12.12-19, 제네바
(경기원 이윤재 협력관, 이성한 사무관 및 재무부 소속대표는 12.12-12.20간)

3. 경　　비 : 소관부처(기관) 부담

4. 훈　　령 : 별첨. 끝.

0134

(첨부)

훈 령(안)

1. 기본훈령

o 그동안의 협상결과를 토대로 다음과 같은 방향으로 대응

가. 한국정부는 그동안 협상의 성공적 타결을 위해 노력해온 바와 같이 협상의 완결시까지 최선의 협조와 노력을 계속해 나갈 것임을 강조

나. 양허범위는 수정양허표 제출이후 추가자유화가 이루어졌거나 향후의 자유화계획이 마련된 분야를 대상으로 그동안의 양허협상을 통해 추가양허가 가능한 부분을 밝힌 상태이므로 이번 협상에서는 이러한 기본입장을 견지하되 지난번 양허협상이후 추가로 검토된 통신, 환경등 분야에서는 동 검토내용을 표명

다. 아울러 우리의 최종양허표 초안을 다음 양허협상시 제시하겠다는 의사를 밝히고 금융, 기본통신, 해운, MFN 일탈 문제등 주요쟁점에 대한 각국의 입장과 최종양허표 제출 동향등을 파악

2. 분야별 세부훈령

가. 인력이동부문

o 인력이동부문 양허계획에 서비스 세일즈인력, 상업적주재의 설치를 위한 대표인력을 포함시킨다는 방침을 협상대상국에 통보

o 미국, 일본등이 요구한 전문직업인의 일시적 이동과 중국의 계약 조건부(contractual basis) 입국자에 대한 인력이동 요구에 대해서는 국내노동시장 수급여건상 추가양허가 어렵다는 입장을 표명(미국, 일본, 중국)

0135

나. 외국인 투자기업의 토지취득

o 자유화된 서비스 업종에 대한 외국인 투자기업의 토지취득 허용 요구에 대해서는 현시점에서 추가 양허하기는 어려우나 외국인 투자기업의 토지취득을 확대 허용하기 위한 제도개선 계획이 있음을 표명(미국, 일본)

- 아울러 12.1부터 시행된 보험업 및 첨단서비스 업종에 대한 외국인 토지취득 내용을 설명

o 외국인이 토지와 별개로 건물만 취득 가능한지 여부에 대해서는 제도적으로는 건물취득이 가능함을 표명(EC)

다. 외국인투자

o 외국인 투자지분 제한이 없어지면 신고대상 자유화업종으로 되는지 여부에 대해서는 신고만으로 사업영위가 가능하나 개별법상의 등록요건, 면허요건은 충족해야 함을 설명(미국, 일본)

라. 금융분야

o Blueprint등 금융개방계획의 offer 반영요구에 대해서는 blueprint 내용과 보험시장개방계획중 최종양허표 제출 시점까지의 자유화 내용을 양허표에 반영할 용의가 있음을 표명

o Standstill 요구에 대해서는 우리 양허표가 사실상 standstill을 전제로 하고 있음을 설명하고 최종양허표에 우리의 standstill 의도를 보다 명맥하게 표현할 용의가 있음을 표명

마. 사업서비스

o 법무서비스는 양허가 곤란하다는 기존입장 견지(미국, 핀랜드)

0136

o 회계서비스와 관련 외국 C.P.A가 한국내에 있는 자국회사의 지사, 자회사등에 대해 회계서비스를 제공하는 것이 가능한지 여부에 대해서는 단독으로 회계서비스를 제공하는 것은 불가하다는 입장을 표명(호주)

- 다만, 외국회계법인과 국내회계법인과의 업무제휴를 통해 외국 회계법인 소속 C.P.A가 국내회계법인에 일정계약기간동안 근무 하면서 자국회사의 지사, 자회사등에 대해 회계제도에 관한 자문, 회계감사자문, 감사기술을 전수하는 것 등은 가능

o 교육서비스와 관련 사무소(representative office)의 설치가 가능한 지 여부에 대해서는 국내사무소 설치가 가능하나 국내에서의 활동은 홍보 활동, 자료모집등에 제한됨을 설명(뉴질랜드)

o 컴퓨터 관련서비스중 CPC 845(사무기기 및 장비 수선유지) 양허요구에 대해서는 최종양허표에 추가로 등재할 계획임을 표명(중국)

o 시험조사서비스(CPC 8676)의 양허요구에 대해서는 CPC 86761중 측정 대행업(대기, 수질, 소음, 진동)과 검사대행업(대기, 소음, 진동) 및 CPC 86764(기술검사 서비스)를 추가로 양허할 계획임을 표명(캐나다)

바. 통 신

o 기본통신 다자간협상 참여요구에 대해서는 다음과 같은 전제하에 협상에 참여할 의사가 있다는 우리측 기본입장을 표명(미국, 캐나다, 스웨덴)

- 다자간협상이 진행되는 동안 쌍무협상을 요구하지 않을 것
- 다자간협상이 반드시 참여국의 기본통신 시장개방을 의미해서는 안되며 시장개방의 정도는 각국의 통신산업 발전정도를 고려해야 함.
- MFN 원칙은 협상기간중 그리고 협상이 끝난 후에도 적용될 것

0137

사. 해 운

o 화물유보제도 대상품목의 축소요구에 대해서는 향후 점진적으로 대상품목을 축소해 나갈 방침이나 구체적 내용을 양허표에 반영할 단계는 아님을 설명(일본, 호주)

o 합작해운선사 설립에 대한 제한사항 완화요구 및 해운보조 서비스 추가양허요구에 대해서는 추가양허가 곤란함을 설명(중국, 스웨덴)

아. 항 공

o 항공 CRS MFN 일탈 철회요구에 대해서는 철회곤란 입장 견지(EC)

자. 유 통

o 유통업 ENT, 매장면적 및 매장수 제한 철폐요구에 대해서는 기존 입장 고수(미국, 중국)

o 종합무역상사의 수입업 허용요구에 대해서는 곤란함을 표명(일본)

차. 환경관련 서비스

o 환경서비스중 CPC 9403, 9404, 9405, 9406, 9409에 대한 양허요구에 대해서는

- CPC 9406중 환경영향평가대행업 및 CPC 9409중 환경영향평가 대행업을 추가로 양허할 계획임을 표명(캐나다, 핀랜드)
- CPC 9404중 대기오염 방지시설업 및 CPC 9405중 소음진동 방지 시설업은 건설 및 엔지니어링분야에 기반영되어 있음을 설명

0138

카. MFN 일탈문제

o 이번 양허협상기간중 항공 CRS, 한.일 항로, 외국인 토지취득 및 리스관련 상호주의등 세분야에 대한 MFN 일탈 신청서를 GATT에 공식제출('92.3.12. 제출하였던 일탈신청서를 대체)

- 대일 시청각 서비스분야는 제외

o 단, 외국인 토지취득 및 리스관련 상호주의에 대한 MFN 일탈 신청은 ① 현재까지 한번도 적용된 사례가 없었고 ② 사실상 대부분의 나라가 양허표에서 토지취득.리스와 관련하여 아무런 제한사항을 기재하지 않고 있는 상황에서 경제적 실익이 크지 않고 ③ 동종의 MFN 일탈신청을 했던 일본이 이를 철회하기로 했고 ④ 토지취득 허용도 되지 않는 상황에서 리스의 경우까지 제한가능성을 유지 하는데 따라 우리 양허의 전반적인 질이 저하된다는 미국등의 강력한 불만표명이 있는 등 문제가 있으므로 이번 양허협상의 결과를 본 후 그 유지여부를 다시 검토

타. 기 타

o 한.미 양자간에 논의된 사항을 서신교환등의 형태로 추가 약속하는 문제에 대해서는 기존 한.미간 합의가 UR 협정에 의해 무효화되지 않는다는 것이 우리 법률전문가들의 견해이며 우리정부는 기존의 한.미간 합의를 충실히 이행할 의지가 확고하나 새로운 문서화는 곤란함을 표명(미국). 끝.

0139

경 제 기 획 원

우 427-760 / 경기도 과천시 중앙동1 정부제2청사 / 전화 503-9149 / 전송 503-9141

문서번호 통조삼 10502-141

시행일자 1992. 12. 7

수신 외무부장관

참조 통상국장

선결			지시	
접수	일자 시간	92.12.8	결재·공람	
	번호	42098		
처리과				
담당자		이시형		

제목 : UR/서비스 양허협상 참석

1. 스위스 제네바에서 개최되는 UR/서비스 양허협상에 다음과 같이 참석코자 하니 협조하여 주기 바랍니다.

- 다 음 -

가. 출장자

- 수석대표 :	경제기획원	제2협력관	이윤재
- 대 표 :	경제기획원	통상조정3과장	장항석
		통상조정3과 사무관	이성한
		〃 〃	한철수
		통상조정1과 사무관	주형환
- 자 문 관 :	KIEP	연구위원	성극제

나. 출장기간 : '92. 12.12~12.19(제2협력관은 12.12~12.20)

다. 출 장 지 : 스위스 제네바

라. 경비부담 : 경제기획원, KIEP

첨부 : 출장일정 1부.

경 제 기 획 원 장

0140

出張日程(暫定)

'92. 12.12(土)	12:55	서울 발 (KE 905)
	18:05	프랑크푸르트 착
	21:05	〃 발 (SR 545)
	22:15	제네바 착
12.14(月) ~ 12.18(金)		UR/서비스 讓許協商

< 제2협력관 >

'92. 12.19(토)	16:45	제네바 발(BA 729)
	17:15	런던 착
	19:30	〃 발(KE 908)
12.20(日)	17:35	서울 착

< 기타 >

'92. 12.18(金)	16:15	제네바 발(SR 726)
	17:20	파리 착
	20:30	파리 발(KE 902)
12.19(土)	17:35	서울 착

0141

법 무 부

우 : 427-760 경기 과천시 중앙동 1 / 전화 : (02)503-9505 / 전송 : (02)504-1378

문서번호 국심 23016-91
시행일자 1992.12. 9.
(경 유)
수 신 외무부장관
참 조

선결			지시		
접수	일자 시간	92.12.9 :	결재·공람		
	번호	42284			
처리과					
담당자					

제 목 UR/서비스협상 당부대표 추천

'92.12.14.부터 12.19.까지 스위스 제네바에서 개최되는 UR/서비스 협상의 우리나라 대표단 구성과 관련하여 당부대표로 아래와 같은 사람을 추천합니다.

- ㅇ 소 속 : 국제법무심의관실
- ㅇ 직위(직급) : 검사(검찰관)
- ㅇ 성 명 : 김 영철
- ㅇ 생년월일 : 1959. 2. 27.

첨 부 국·영문 이력서 각 1부. 끝.

법 무 부 장관

0142

재 무 부

우 427-760 경기도 과천시 중앙동 1 / 전화 503-9266 / 전송 503-9324

문서번호 국금 22251- 377
시행일자 '92. 12. ( )

선결			지시		
접수	일자 시간	92.12.11	결재·공람		
	번호	42484			
처리과					
담당자		1481			

수신 외무부장관
참조

제목 UR 금융협상 참석

UR금융서비스 협상과 관련 스위스 제네바에서 '92.12.14~18간 개최 예정된 양자협상에 참석할 당부대표를 다음과 같이 파견코자 하오니 결재하여 주시기 바랍니다.

다 음

성 명	소 속	기 간
최 희 남	국제금융과 사무관	'92.12.12~20
윤 용 로	은행과 사무관	"
변 상 구	보험정책과 사무관	"

재 무 부 장 관

0143

관리 번호	92-957

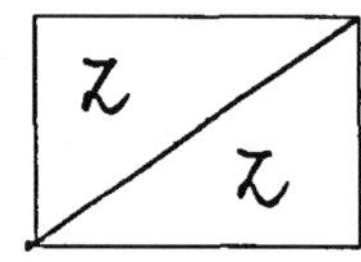

체 신 부

우110-777 서울 종로구 세종로 100번지 /전화(02)750-2360 /전송 (02)750-2915

문서번호 통협 34475-146	선결		지시	
시행일자 1992. 12. 11 ( )	접수	일자 시간 1992.12.11 :	결재·공람	
(경유)		번호 4643		
수 신 수신처참조	처리과			
참 조	담당자	이시형		

검 토 필(1992.12.31.)

제 목 UR/서비스 양허협상 참가

1. UR협상의 급진전에 따른 통신서비스분야 협상에 효율적으로 대처하기 위하여 우리부에서는 아래와 같이 UR/서비스 양허협상에 참가하고자 하오니 필요한 조치를 취하여 주시기 바랍니다.

가. 출장기간 : '92.12.12(土)~'92.12.19(土), 8일간

나. 출 장 지 : 스위스 제네바

다. 출 장 자

소 속	직 급	성 명
체신부 통신협력단	서 기 관	김 재 섭
통신개발연구원	연 구 위 원	최 병 일

라. 출장목적 : UR/GNS 양허협상 참가

마. 출장일정 : 붙임

바. 대응입장 : 붙임

검 토 필(1993.6.30.)

붙임 1. 출장일정 1부

2. 대응입장 1부. 끝.

첨부문에 (분리되면 일반문서)

체 신 부 장 관

수신처 : 경제기획원장관(대외경제조정실장), 외무부장관(통상국장).

0144

2/2

출 장 일 정

일 시		편 명	일 정
12.12(토)	12:55 18:05 21:05 22:15	KE905 SR545	서울출발 프랑크푸르트 도착 프랑크푸르트 출발 제네바 도착
12.13(일)			대표단 대책회의
12.14(월)			UR/GNS 양허협상 참가
12.15(화)			"
12.16(수)			"
12.17(목)			"
12.18(금)	16:15 17:20 20:30	SR 726 KE 902	제네바 출발 파리 도착 파리 출발
12.19(토)	17:35		서울 도착

0145

3-1

제6차 UR/서비스 양허협상 대응입장

1. 최근 협상동향

o 서비스일반협정 제정작업은 최종협정 문안에 대해 기술적 사항을 중심으로 논의가 진행되고 있으며, 현재 협정문안에 대한 큰 수정없이 마무리될 전망

o 서비스 양허협상은 '93.2월말까지 2~3차례 마무리협상이 있을 것으로 예상되며, 미.EC가 금융, 통신, 해운등 주요사항에 대하여 공동대응할 것으로 전망됨.

o 기본통신분야 개방을 위한 협상은 UR종료후에도 계속될 것임

- EC의 시장개방협상 참여동의, 미국의 MFN일탈 철회로 타결될 가능성

2. 제6차 양허협상 개요

o 11.26의 무역협상위원회 합의에 따라 12.7일부터 2주간 개최

o 우리나라는 12.4부터 1주간 참여

- 미, 일, EC, 캐나다, 호주등과 협상예정

0146

3-2

3. 대응입장

o 기본방향

- 금번 양허협상시 UR협상 전체의 마무리를 위하여 주요쟁점의 타결노력이 본격화될 것으로 예상되므로

- 주요쟁점에 대한 각국 입장과 최종양허표 제출동향 등 전반적 동향을 파악하고

- 기본통신협상 협의시 아래와 같이 우리의 입장을 제시

o 기본통신협상관련

- 협상과정에는 계속적으로 참여하되 협상초기에는 적극적인 입장표명을 유보하고

- 각국의 협상동향 및 관련정보입수에 주력

- 협상참여조건

. GATS체제내 다자간협상방식 : 양자간 협상 또는 제한된 국가간 협상반대
. 국가별 통신발전수준에 따른 개방범위의 차등인정
. 개방된 서비스에 관하여는 MFN원칙 적용

- 협상관련 기본구조

. 협상개시시점 : UR종료후 협상시작
. 참 가 범 위 : UR/GNS협상 참가국 모두에 기회개방
. 협상결과이행 : 양허계획에 수정사항으로 기록, GATS 규정에 따라 협상결과 적용
. MFN적용 : 협상기간중 MFN원칙의 적용

0147

3-3

외 무 부

110-760 서울 종로구 세종로 77번지 / (02)720-2188 / (02)720-2686 (FAX)

문서번호 통기 20644-423
시행일자 1992.12.10.( )

취급		장 관
보존		
국 장	전 결	
심의관		
과 장		
기안	이 시 형	협조

수신 수신처참조
참조

제목 UR/서비스협상 정부대표 임명 통보

UR/서비스 협상에 참가할 정부대표를 "정부대표 및 특별사절의 임명과 권한에 관한 법률"에 의거, 아래와 같이 임명하였음을 알려드립니다.

- 아 래 -

1. 정부대표

수석대표	:	경제기획원	제2협력관	이윤재
대 표 (11명)	:	경제기획원	통상조정3과장	장항석
			통상조정3과 사무관	이성한
			통상조정3과 사무관	한철수
			통상조정1과 사무관	주형환
		재 무 부	국제금융과 사무관	최희남
			은행과 사무관	윤용로
			보험정책과 사무관	변상구
		법 무 부	국제법무심의관실 검찰관	김영철
		체 신 부	통신협력단 과장	김재섭

/ 계속...

0148

자　　문 : 대외경제연구원 연구위원　　　　성극제
　　　　　통신개발연구원 연구위원　　　　최병일

2. 출장기간 및 장소 : 92.12.12-19, 제네바
(경기원 이윤재 협력관, 이성한 사무관 및 재무부 소속대표는 12.12-12.20간)

3. 경　　비 : 소관부처(기관) 부담

4. 훈　　령 : ~~별첨~~ 12.8. 대책회의 자료중 Ⅱ, Ⅲ항 내용.

~~첨부 : 훈령.~~ 끝.

외 무 부 장 관

수신처 : 경제기획원, 재무부, 법무부, 체신부장관, 대외경제연구원장, 통신개발연구원장.

0149

외 무 부

110-760 서울 종로구 세종로 77번지 / (02)720-2188 / (02)720-2686 (FAX)

문서번호 통기 20644-

시행일자 1992.12. 9.( )

수신 내부결재

참조

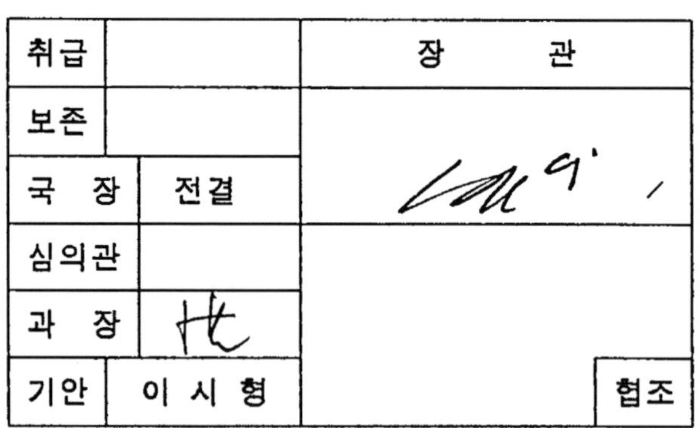

취급		장 관
보존		
국 장	전결	
심의관		
과 장		
기안	이 시 형	협조

제목 UR/서비스 협상 정부대표 추가 임명

92.12.9자 임명된 UR/서비스 협상 정부대표에 아래와 같이 1인을 추가하고자 건의하오니 재가하여 주시기 바랍니다.

\- 아 래 -

1. 인적사항
   - ㅇ 성 명 : 김 창 록
   - ㅇ 소속.직위 : 재무부 국제금융과 과장
2. 출장기간 및 장소 : 92.12.12-12.20, 제네바
3. 경 비 : 재무부 부담. 끝.

0150

재 무 부

우 427-760 경기도 과천시 중앙동 1 / 전화 503-9266 / 전송 503-9324

문서번호 국금 22251- 377
시행일자 '92. 12. 10 ( )

선결			지시		
접수	일자 시간		결재·공람		
	번호				
처리과					
담당자					

수신 외무부장관
참조

제목 UR 금융협상 참석

UR금융서비스 협상과 관련 스위스 제네바에서 '92.12.14~18간 개최 예정된 양자협상에 참석할 당부대표를 다음과 같이 파견코자 하오니 결재하여 주시기 바랍니다.

다 음

성 명	소 속	기 간
김 창 록	국제금융과장	'92.12.12~17
최 희 남	국제금융과 사무관	'92.12.12~20
윤 용 로	은행과 사무관	"
변 상 구	보험정책과 사무관	"

재 무 부 장 관

0151

외 무 부

110-760 서울 종로구 세종로 77번지 / (02)720-2188 / (02)720-2686 (FAX)

문서번호 통기 20644-426

시행일자 1992.12.11.( )

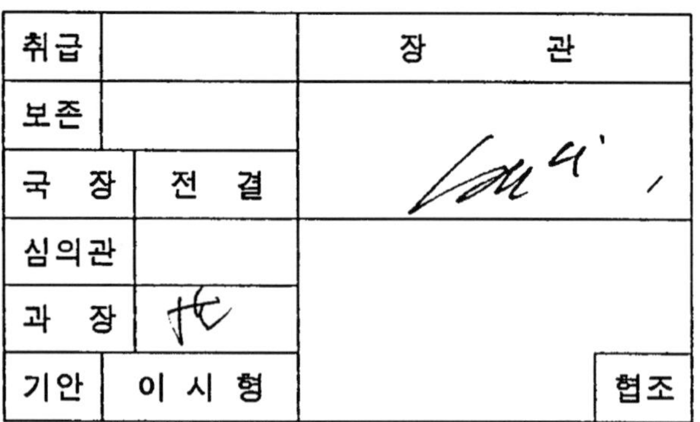

취급		장 관
보존		
국 장	전 결	
심의관		
과 장		
기안	이 시 형	협조

수신 경제기획원장관, 재무부장관

참조

제목 정부대표 임명(추가) 통보

연 : 통기20644-423

연호 UR/서비스 협상 정부대표단에 재무부 국제금융과 김창록 과장이 추가 임명되었음을 통보합니다. 끝.

외 무 부 장 관

0152

관리번호	92 - 964

	분류번호	보존기간

발 신 전 보

번 호 : WGV-1959 921211 1843 EI 종별 :

수 신 : 주 제네바 대사. 총영사

발 신 : 장 관 (통 기)

제 목 : UR/서비스 양자협상 대표단 임명 통보

대 : GVW-2307

검토필 (1992. 12. 31.)

1. 대호 92.12.14-18간 귀지 개최 예정인 표제 협상에 참가할 정부대표단이 아래와 같이 임명되어 12.12(토) 귀지 도착 예정이며, 훈령은 별첨과 같음.

- 아 래 -

검토필 (1993. 6. 30.)

가. 수석대표 :	경제기획원	제2협력관	이윤재
나. 대표(10명):	경제기획원	통상조정3과장	장항석
		통상조정3과 사무관	이성한
		통상조정3과 사무관	한철수
		통상조정1과 사무관	주형환
	재 무 부	국제금융과 과 장	김창록
		국제금융과 사무관	최희남
		은행과 사무관	윤용로
		보험정책과 사무관	변상구
	법 무 부	국제법무심의관실 검찰관	김영철
	체 신 부	통신협력단 과장	김재섭

/ 계속...

보안통제	

앙고재	92년 12월 11일	통상기구과	기안자 성명		과 장	심의관	국 장		차 관	장 관
							전결			

외신과통제

0153

다. 자문(2명) : 대외경제연구원 연구위원 성극제

통신개발연구원 연구위원 최병일

2. 금융분야의 대미 양자협상에 대비, 대호 미측 대표단을 감안하여 아측 대표단을 구성하였으니 참고바람.

첨부 : 훈령. 끝.

(통상국장 대리 오 행 겸)

0154

(첨부)

훈 령

1. 기본훈령

o 그동안의 협상결과를 토대로 다음과 같은 방향으로 대응

가. 한국정부는 그동안 협상의 성공적 타결을 위해 노력해온 바와 같이 협상의 완결시까지 최선의 협조와 노력을 계속해 나갈 것임을 강조

나. 양허범위는 수정양허표 제출이후 추가자유화가 이루어졌거나 향후의 자유화계획이 마련된 분야를 대상으로 그동안의 양허협상을 통해 추가양허가 가능한 부분을 밝힌 상태이므로 이번 협상에서는 이러한 기본입장을 견지하되 지난번 양허협상이후 추가로 검토된 통신, 환경등 분야에서는 동 검토내용을 표명

다. 아울러 우리의 최종양허표 초안을 다음 양허협상시 제시하겠다는 의사를 밝히고 금융, 기본통신, 해운, MFN 일탈 문제등 주요쟁점에 대한 각국의 입장과 최종양허표 제출 동향등을 파악

2. 분야별 세부훈령

가. 인력이동부문

o 인력이동부문 양허계획에 서비스 세일즈인력, 상업적주재의 설치를 위한 대표인력을 포함시킨다는 방침을 협상대상국에 통보

o 미국, 일본등이 요구한 전문직업인의 일시적 이동과 중국의 계약조건부(contractual basis) 입국자에 대한 인력이동 요구에 대해서는 국내노동시장 수급여건상 추가양허가 어렵다는 입장을 표명(미국, 일본, 중국)

0155

나. 외국인 투자기업의 토지취득

o 자유화된 서비스 업종에 대한 외국인 투자기업의 토지취득 허용 요구에 대해서는 현시점에서 추가 양허하기는 어려우나 외국인 투자기업의 토지취득을 확대 허용하기 위한 제도개선 계획이 있음을 표명(미국, 일본)
  - 아울러 12.1부터 시행된 보험업 및 첨단서비스 업종에 대한 외국인 토지취득 내용을 설명

o 외국인이 토지와 별개로 건물만 취득 가능한지 여부에 대해서는 제도적으로는 건물취득이 가능함을 표명(EC)

다. 외국인투자

o 외국인 투자지분 제한이 없어지면 신고대상 자유화업종으로 되는지 여부에 대해서는 신고만으로 사업영위가 가능하나 개별법상의 등록요건, 면허요건은 충족해야 함을 설명(미국, 일본)

라. 금융분야

o Blueprint등 금융개방계획의 offer 반영요구에 대해서는 blueprint 내용과 보험시장개방계획중 최종양허표 제출 시점까지의 자유화 내용을 양허표에 반영할 용의가 있음을 표명

o Standstill 요구에 대해서는 우리 양허표가 사실상 standstill을 전제로 하고 있음을 설명하고 최종양허표에 우리의 standstill 의도를 보다 명맥하게 표현할 용의가 있음을 표명

마. 사업서비스

o 법무서비스는 양허가 곤란하다는 기존입장 견지(미국, 핀랜드)

0156

o 회계서비스와 관련 외국 C.P.A가 한국내에 있는 자국회사의 지사, 자회사등에 대해 회계서비스를 제공하는 것이 가능한지 여부에 대해서는 단독으로 회계서비스를 제공하는 것은 불가하다는 입장을 표명(호주)

- 다만, 외국회계법인과 국내회계법인과의 업무제휴를 통해 외국 회계법인 소속 C.P.A가 국내회계법인에 일정계약기간동안 근무 하면서 자국회사의 지사, 자회사등에 대해 회계제도에 관한 자문, 회계감사자문, 감사기술을 전수하는 것 등은 가능

o 교육서비스와 관련 사무소(representative office)의 설치가 가능한 지 여부에 대해서는 국내사무소 설치가 가능하나 국내에서의 활동은 홍보 활동, 자료모집등에 제한됨을 설명(뉴질랜드)

o 컴퓨터 관련서비스중 CPC 845(사무기기 및 장비 수선유지) 양허요구에 대해서는 최종양허표에 추가로 등재할 계획임을 표명(중국)

o 시험조사서비스(CPC 8676)의 양허요구에 대해서는 CPC 86761중 측정 대행업(대기, 수질, 소음, 진동)과 검사대행업(대기, 소음, 진동) 및 CPC 86764(기술검사 서비스)를 추가로 양허할 계획임을 표명(캐나다)

바. 통 신

o 기본통신 다자간협상 참여요구에 대해서는 다음과 같은 전제하에 협상에 참여할 의사가 있다는 우리측 기본입장을 표명(미국, 캐나다, 스웨덴)

- 다자간협상이 진행되는 동안 쌍무협상을 요구하지 않을 것
- 다자간협상이 반드시 참여국의 기본통신 시장개방을 의미해서는 안되며 시장개방의 정도는 각국의 통신산업 발전정도를 고려해야 함.
- MFN 원칙은 협상기간중 그리고 협상이 끝난 후에도 적용될 것

0157

사. 해　　운

o 화물유보제도 대상품목의 축소요구에 대해서는 향후 점진적으로 대상품목을 축소해 나갈 방침이나 구체적 내용을 양허표에 반영할 단계는 아님을 설명(일본, 호주)

o 합작해운선사 설립에 대한 제한사항 완화요구 및 해운보조 서비스 추가양허요구에 대해서는 추가양허가 곤란함을 설명(중국, 스웨덴)

아. 항　　공

o 항공 CRS MFN 일탈 철회요구에 대해서는 철회곤란 입장 견지(EC)

자. 유　　통

o 유통업 ENT, 매장면적 및 매장수 제한 철폐요구에 대해서는 기존 입장 고수(미국, 중국)

o 종합무역상사의 수입업 허용요구에 대해서는 곤란함을 표명(일본)

차. 환경관련 서비스

o 환경서비스중 CPC 9403, 9404, 9405, 9406, 9409에 대한 양허요구에 대해서는
  - CPC 9406중 환경영향평가대행업 및 CPC 9409중 환경영향평가 대행업을 추가로 양허할 계획임을 표명(캐나다, 핀랜드)
  - CPC 9404중 대기오염 방지시설업 및 CPC 9405중 소음진동 방지 시설업은 건설 및 엔지니어링분야에 기반영되어 있음을 설명

0158

카. MFN 일탈문제

o 이번 양허협상기간중 항공 CRS, 한.일 항로, 외국인 토지취득 및 리스관련 상호주의등 세분야에 대한 MFN 일탈 신청서를 GATT에 공식제출('92.3.12. 제출하였던 일탈신청서를 대체)

- 대일 시청각 서비스분야는 제외

o 단, 외국인 토지취득 및 리스관련 상호주의에 대한 MFN 일탈 신청은 ① 현재까지 한번도 적용된 사례가 없었고 ② 사실상 대부분의 나라가 양허표에서 토지취득.리스와 관련하여 아무런 제한사항을 기재하지 않고 있는 상황에서 경제적 실익이 크지 않고 ③ 동종의 MFN 일탈신청을 했던 일본이 이를 철회하기로 했고 ④ 토지취득 허용도 되지 않는 상황에서 리스의 경우까지 제한가능성을 유지하는데 따라 우리 양허의 전반적인 질이 저하된다는 미국등의 강력한 불만표명이 있는 등 문제가 있으므로 이번 양허협상의 결과를 본 후 그 유지여부를 다시 검토

타. 기 타

o 한.미 양자간에 논의된 사항을 서신교환등의 형태로 추가 약속하는 문제에 대해서는 기존 한.미간 합의가 UR 협정에 의해 무효화되지 않는다는 것이 우리 법률전문가들의 견해이며 우리정부는 기존의 한.미간 합의를 충실히 이행할 의지가 확고하나 새로운 문서화는 곤란함을 표명(미국). 끝.

0159

경 제 기 획 원

우 427-760 / 경기도 과천시 중앙동1 정부제2청사 / 전화 503-9149 / 전송 503-9141

문서번호 통조삼 10502-143
시행일자 1992. 12. 11

수신 외무부장관
참조 통상국장

선결			지시		
접수	일자 시간	92. 12. 14 :	결재·공람		
	번호	42696			
처리과					
담당자		이시형			

제목 : UR/서비스 양허협상 참석 출장기간 연장통보

1. 통조삼 10502-141('91.12.7)호의 관련입니다.

2. 당초 UR/서비스 양허협상에만 참석하려던 일정을 변경하여 18일 오후에 개최되는 TNC회의에도 참석한 후 귀국코자 하니 협조하여 주시기 바랍니다.

- 다 음 -

가. 출 장 자 : 경제기획원 통상조정3과 사무관 이성한
나. 출장기간

당 초	변 경	비 고
'92.12.12~12.19 (7박 8일)	'92.12.12~12.20 (8박 9일)	1박 1일 연장

다. 출 장 지 : 스위스 제네바
라. 경비부담 : 경제기획원

첨부 : 출장일정(변경) 1부.

경 제 기 획 원 장 관

0160

出張日程(變更)

'92. 12.12(土)	12:55	서울 발 (KE 905)
	18:05	프랑크푸르트 착
	21:05	〃 발 (SR 545)
	22:15	제네바 착
12.14(月) ~ 12.18(金)		UR/서비스 讓許協商
12.18(金)	오 후	TNC회의 참석
'92. 12.19(토)	16:45	제네바 발(BA 729)
	17:15	런던 착
	19:30	〃 발(KE 908)
12.20(日)	17:35	서울 착

0161

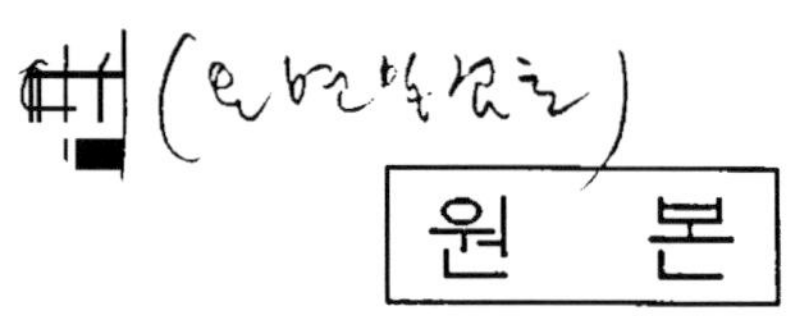

외 무 부

종 별 :

번 호 : GVW-2338　　　　일 시 : 92 1211 1130

수 신 : 장 관(수신처 참조)

발 신 : 주 제네바 대사

제 목 : UR/GNS 비공식협의(1)

연: GVW-2275

12.8(화)-12.9(수)간 개최된 스케쥴링 및 협정문제 21조 (양허표 수정)에 대한 표제협의 결과를 하기 보고함. (약 20개국 참석)

1. SCHEDULING 에 대한 토의

가. 협의개요

- 12.4 일자 사무국의 스케쥴링 EXPLANATORY NOTE 초안 (기송부)에 대한 각항별토의를 진행 하였는바, 사무국은 동 토의결과를 반영한 수정안을 제시키로 함.

나. 협의내용

1) 제 16조(시장접근 제한) 스케쥴 사항 관련 (사무국초안 제 4항)

- 아국은 제 16조 2항(A-D)이 열거적 (EXHAUSTIVE)인 수량 제한을 의미하고 있는데 반해 사무국 EXPLANATORY NOTE 4항 마지막 문장에서 양적 제한 표현 방식이 쿼타 또는 질적인 것과 관련되지 않는 'ANY OTHER CRITERIA' 라고 기술하고 있는 것은 오해의 소지가 있을 수있다고 질문한바, 사무국은 이는 쿼타외의 경제적 필요성 검토,독점등을 의미하는 것으로서 현재 협정문상 이외의 것들을 상정하는 것이 아니라고함.

0 또한 아국은 경제적 필요성 검토나 쿼타가 아닌것으로 예를 들어 건설서비스도급 한도제가 스케쥴링 대상이니 여부를 확인한바, 인도등 동 제도는 국내규제로서 PRUDENTIAL MEASURE 란 관점에서 볼수 있으므로 스케쥴 사항이 아니라고 지적 하였으며, 다른 나라도 별다른 이견을 제출하지 않았음.

- 5.29일자 스케쥴링 관련 토의 자료에 아국이 제기 하였으나 논의되지 않았던 제 16조2항(B) ((C),(D) 동일 상의) 'LIMTATIONS ON THETOTAL VALUE OF SERVICES TRANSACTIONS' 이 MAXIMUM 제한 및 MINIMUM 제한 양자를 포함 하느냐에 대해 카나다

통상국	법무부	보사부	문화부	교통부	체신부	경기원	재무부	농수부
상공부	건설부	과기처	해항정	환경처				

PAGE 1　　　　92.12.12 05:50 FO

외신 1과 통제관 0162

및 아국이 다시 이를 제기한바, 일본은 16조는 MAXIMUM 제한을 의미하여, MINIMUM 제한은제 6조 (국내규제) 사항으로 스케쥴 대상이 아니라고 하였으나 이에 대해 사무국은동 문제에 대해서는 추후 토의 자료를 작성, 추가 논의키로 함.

2) 제 17조(내국민 대우 제한) 스케쥴 사항관련 (사무국 초안 제 5-7항)

가) RESIDENCE 문제.

- 카나다가 서비스 공급자를 자국민 으로만 한정할 경우 내국민 대우 위반 뿐만아니라 경우에 따라서는 외국인이 서비스 시장 자체에 접근이 불가하다 는 점에서 영(ZERO)의 쿼타 개념으로 볼수 있으며 따라서 사실상 (DE FACTO)시장 접근에 대한 제한으로 제 16조 스케쥴 사항으로 볼수 있다는 점을 지적함

- 또한 거주 요건도 사안에 따라 그종류, 거주자격, 거주기간등이 다양한바, 내국민대우 원칙과 관련보다 자세한 검토가 필요하다는 지적에 대해 사무국은 RESIDENCE 문제도 추가 검토키로 함.

나) 차별적 보조금의 스케쥴링 여부

- 사무국 초안이 서비스에 대한 차별적 보조금도 17조 스케쥴링 사항이라고 한데대해 대부분의 나라가 사무국 초안을 원칙적으로 지지 하였으나, EC, 미국, 멕시코등이 이 문제를 제기하였음.

0 카나다는 보조금 관련 자국소재 내.외국 기업에는 차별이 없는 경우에도 자국영토 밖으로 부터의 CROSS - BORDER SUPPLIER 와 관련하여 문제가 될수 있음을 지적함.

0 EC 는 협정문 제 15조가 서비스 보조금 관련 다자간 원칙 개발을 위한 협상 및작업 계획을 규정하고 있음을 상기시키면서 보조금의 스케쥴링과 관련해서 검토해야할 문제가 많음을 지적함.

0 스웨덴은 한나라가 특징지역 기업에만 보조금을주고 있는것이 스케쥴량 대상인지 질문한바, 특징지역 에서만 보조금을 주더라도 차별적이 아니면 스케쥴 사항이 아니라고 함

0 멕시코는 협정문상 서비스 보조금에 관한 어떠한 의무 (OVLIGATION)도 아직 합의된 바 없으며, 또한 미래의 보조금은 스케쥬링 할 수 없음을 지적한바, 이에 대해 사무국은 미래에 보조금 도입시 내국민 대우 원칙하에 지급하면 문제도리 것이 없으며, 차별적인 경우에는 NATIONAL SCHEDULE 수정 문제로 될것임을 언급함.

3) 협정 문안 예외 (EXCEPTIONS)가 인정된 사항들의 스케쥴링 여부 (사무국 초안 9항)

- 사무국안에 별다른 이견이 없었으나 다만 EC가 금융분야 이외의 PRUDENTIAL MEASURE 에 상응하는 조치들의 경우 스케쥴링 예외 대상 으로 하자고 한데 대해 대부분나라 는 혼란만 가중 시키므로 14조등 으로 국한하는 것이 바람직 하다고 지적함.

4) 구체적 양허와 MFN 일탈과의 관계 (사무국초안 제 10항)

- 아국은 스케쥴링과 관련 한 나라가 특정 서비스 분야에 양허를 한 상태에서 특정 국가를 배제하는 MFN 일탈을 추구하는 경우에는 어떻게 되는지에 대해 질의한바,각국은 양허를 할경우에는 최혜국 대우에서만 일탈이 가능하고, 모든 나라에 대해 MINIMUM STANDARD 의 대우는 제공해야 한다고 함.

5) SECTROAL CLASSIFICATION (사무국 초안 제안 15항)

- 일본은 CPC CODE 의 법적 성격과 관련하여 그것이 각국 양허표를 비교하기 위해 통일적 기준으로서의 필요성과 유용성은 인정되나, REFERENCE 로 CPC CODE 를 부여하고, 구체적 SECTOR 에 대해 별도 기술을 할 경우는 그기술 내용에 대해 구속력이주어지는 것이라고한바, 대부분의 국가들이 공감을 표시함

- 사무국도 실제 기재 (ACTUAL DESCRIPTION)사항이 우선하나 다만 각국의 양허비교 를 위해 CPC CODE를 사용해야 할것임을 표명

6) 4가지 서비스 공급형태 (MODE OF SUPPLY)를 구분하여 스케쥴링하는 것에 대하여 대부분의 국가는 이견을 제시하지 않았으나 스웨덴, 카나다는 이들 MODE 간의 구분을 명확히 하기 어려운 부분이 많으며 따라서 스케쥴링 작성시 4가지 MODE 로구분하여 작성하는 것이 곤란 하다는 입장을표명함.

7) 사무국 초안이 시장접근 및 내국민 대우 제한이 없는 FULL COMMITMENT 인 경우 'NONE' 으로 표기하도록 한데 대해 인도는 오해의 소지가 있으므로 'NONE EXCEPT FOR HORIZONTAL LIMITATIONS'로 표기하는 것이 적절하다고 함.

2. 제 21조에 대한 토의

가. 12.4일자 사무국 작성 21조 수정 TEXT 를 항목별로 토의하였음.

나. 협의내용

- 21조 1항(A) 중 하단을 'IF THE MODIFYING ... OF INACCORDANCE WITH' 로 대체하고, 2항(A) 중 'WHOSEINTEREST'를 'WHOSE BENEFIT'으로

3항(A) 중 'ALL AFFECTED MEMBERS'를 'ANY AFFECTEDMEMBER'로, 동 항 ' ANY AFFECTED MEMBER'를 'SUCHAFFECTED MEMBER'로, 5항 첫째줄 'SHALL

PROVIDEPROCEDURE' 를 'SHALL ESTABLISH PROCEDURE'로 하고 동항 넷째줄 ' ACCORINGLY UNDER 를 ACCORDINGTO'로 변경함

- 미국은 양허수정 또는 철회에 대한 보상조정 (COMPENSATORY ADJUSTMENT)과 관련하여 법률적으로 서비스내에서만 가능한지 여부에 대해 문제를 제기한바, 인도, 일본등은 이는 당연히 GATS 하에서의 서비스만 대상이라고 하였으나, EC등은 당사국간 합의시 서비스이외의 보상 조치를 하는 것은 별개 문제라고 함.

- 양허수정 국가가 중재 판정에 불복할 경우에 AFFECTED MEMBER 가 보복 조치를 MFN BASIS 로 할것인지 여부에 대해 MFN BASIS 로 할지 여부는 보복조치 국가의 판단의 문제 (PLOICY QUESTION) 라고함. 다만 사무국 초안 16항 마지막 문장에서 중재판정자가 NON-MFN BASIS 로 할것을 권유할 수있다고 한데 대해서는 각국은 의문을제기함.끝

(대사 박수길-국장)

수신처:통기,경기원,재무부,법무부,농림수산부,상공부,문화부,건설부,교통부,체신부,보사부,과기처,공보처,환경처,항만청

원 본

외 무 부

종 별 :

번 호 : GVW-2350 일 시 : 92 1211 2000

수 신 : 장관(수신처참조)

발 신 : 주 제네바 대사

제 목 : UR/GNS 비공식 협의(2)

수신처:(통기,경기원,재무부,법무부,농림수산부,상공부,문화부,건설부,교통부,체신부,보사부,과기처,공보처,환경처,항만청)

연: GVW-2338

표제 협의가 12.10(목) 오전(해운) 및 오후 (34조)에개최된바, 주요 내용 아래 보고함.

1. EC 주관 해운 분야 복수국간 협의(아국 포함13개국 참석)

가. 협의 개요

- EC 측이 11.16 자로 배포한 해운 토의문서(기송부)및 금일 제시된 EC 및 일본의NON-PAPER(별첨 FAX 송부)를 중심으로 토의가 진행되었으며, 그간의 비공식 협의 결과를 12.11(금) 오후 개최 예정인 GNS 회의를 통해다자화 하기로 함.

나. 협의 내용

1) 일본은 UR 협상이 막바지 단계이므로 국제해운의 자유화를 추구하기 위해 필요한 최소한의요건(MINIMUM REQUIREMENT)를 정의하는데 협상력을 집중해야 할 것이라고 하고, 본 비공식협의 대상국에 아세안, 스위스, 중국등 주요교역 대상국들도 참여토록 해야 할 것이라고 함.

2) 국제해운의 범위(11.16 일자 EC 문서순)

- 일본이 연안 CABOTAGE 의 정의가 불분명하므로 동 정의를 'CABOTAGE WHICH IS CONSTRUED IN ACCORDANCEWITH THE ESTABLISHED INTERNATIONAL LAW '로 하자고 한데대해, 미국, EC 등은 CABOTAGE 는일반적으로는 일국내 PORT TO PORT, PORT TO POINT,POINT TO PORT 등이 대상이 되나 CABOTAGE 의일반적 정의와 관련 아직 확립된 국제법은없고, 국내법에 따라 해석이 다르므로 정의를 일률적으로 규정할수 없다고 함.

통상국	보사부	문화부	교통부	체신부	경기원	재무부	농수부	상공부
건설부	과기처	해항청	환경처	공보처				

PAGE 1

92.12.12 07:14 FY

외신 1과 통제관

0166

- 다만 CABOTAGE 가 해운 관련 본 비공식 협의문서상 논의 범위에서 배제할것이지 서비스협정상의 양허 대상에서 배제되는 것은 아니므로 각국이 이를 양허 하거나 필요시 MFN 일탈을할수는 있을 것이라는데 각국이 동의함.

3) 자유화의 수준

- EC 는 해운 업자가 상업적 주재국에서당해국의 FLAG 하에서 국제해운업을영위하려는데는 일반적으로 많은 제한이 따르나,MARITIME AGENCY 를 통해 영위하는 것은비교적자유화 될수있는 분야라고 지적함. - 캐나다는 외국 소재 해운회사가 어떤 회원국에대하여 CROSS-BORDER MODE 를 통해 해운 서비스의구매, 판촉행위등을 할수 있느냐에 대해 질의한바, EC 는 스케쥴상 그에 대한 제한사항이 없는 경우에는 가능하다고 하고, 제한을하려고 하는 경우 동 제한 사항을 스케쥴에 기재해야 한다고 한데대 해 대부분의 국가가 의견을 갑이함

- ANNEX 3(상업적 주재의 활동범위)와 관련동 부속서 E항 ESTABLISHMENT 를 SETTING UP으로 수정하고 F 항을 금일 배포 EC NON-PAPER상의 MODEL 스케쥴 4:D:F 항으로대체키로함.

4) MFN 일탈문제

- 각국이 MFN 일탈 관련 EC 문서에 별다른 이견을 제시하지 않았으나 일본은 국제해운에대한 양허를 하고 CARGO SHARING 을 MFN 일탈할 경우 양허 수준 평가가 어렵다는 점을 지적함.

5) 수혜자(BENEFICIRY)

- 수혜자와 관련 선박의 소유, FLAG 등에 불구하고 선박 운영자(SERVICE OPERATOR)가 누구냐가 판단의 기초라는 것에 별다른 이견이 없었으나,한 회원국 국민이 소유하 고 당해국 FLAG 를사용하나 (1) 비회원국내에 설립된 기업에 의해지배되고 있는경우, 또는 (2) 비회원국 OPERATOR에 의해 용선(CHARTERED)되어 있는 경우등은 추가검토 가 필요하다는 지적이 있었음.

6) 항만 시설에 대한 접근 및 이용(ANEX 4)

- ANEX 4 는 예시적인 것으로서, 항만시설 중협정문 제 1조 3(B) 형태의 서비스에 해당하는것은 이용 가능해야 한다는 지적이 있었으며,부속서 4와 부속서 5간의 관계가 명확하지 않다는각국의 지적에 대해 EC 측이 추가 검토키로 함.

0 그리고 PORT CAPTAIN'S SERVICE, STEVEDORING, DOCKER등의 개념이 보다 명확히정립되어야 한다는지적이 있었으며, 부속서 5의 MARITIME AGENCYSERVICES 와

부속서4의 SHIPPING AGENCY SERVICES 는동일한 것으로서 MARITIME AGENCY SERVICES 로통일키로 함.

7) 해운 분야에서 보조금 문제는 자세히 논의되지않았으나, 일본은 CARGO SHARING 과 관련 추가검토가 필요하다고 지적하였음.

8) EC 는 향후해운분야 협의와 관련 기술적과제와 정치적 과제가 있는바, 기술적과제에대해서는 추가 검토 필요성이 있다고 하고, 정치적과제에 대해서는 조심스럽게 양자 또는 복수간으로 논의할수 있는 방법이 있으나 복수간협의로 할 경우보다 어려 운 문제를 야기할 가능성이있다고 지적하면서, 각국은 정치적 결정이 있는경우 현행 논의되고 있는 MODEL 스케쥴에따라 해운 양허를 할수 있도록 준비해야 할것이라고지적함.

9) 끝으로 일본은 지금 논의중인 문서의 향후법적 성격과 관련, 서비스 협정문의부속서,NOTE, GUIDELINE 등 어떻게 할 것인지를 제기하고양허 GUIDELING 이 바람직하다고 언급함.

2. 협정문 34 조

가. 협의 개요

- 12.3 일자 34조 관련 사무국 비공식 문서(기송부)에대해 각항별로 논의를 하였음.

나. 협의 내용

- 사무국의 (C) II) 수정안에 대해 멕시코는 과거조문이 유통 및 운송 시스템, 공중 전기 통신망및 서비스로 한정하였던 것에 비해 너무 포괄적으로됨을 지적함.

- (F) I) 타회원국의 서비스 정의와 관련 해운,항공, 육운등과같이(회원국)-(비회원국)-(회원국)의 경로를거쳐 들어오는 서비스의 경우에 대해추가 검토키로 함.

- (K) 항의 영주권자를 시민으로 간주하는 규정과관련 일본은 별첨 문서를 통해국제법상의 국제문제등과의 상치를 들어 삭제를 주장하였는바, 캐나다, 뉴질랜드, 호주등은 자국의특수성상 동 주장을 수용할수 없다고 하였는바,추가 검토키로 함.

- 일본은 상기 별첨 자국 자료를 통해 (M) 항의타회원국의 서비스 공급자로서의법인의 정의와 관련 동항 I) 의 동 법인이 실질적 영업활동(SUBSTANTIAL BUSINESS OPERATIONS)에 종사하고있어야 한다는 요건은 (B) 항과 (G) 항에서 이미 이러한 것이전제되고 있으므로 삭제할 것을 주장하였으나, EC 는 PAPER COMPANY 등 동

PAGE 3

0168

규정삭제시많은 문제가 발생될수 있다면서 강하게반대함.

- (N) 항에서 법인이 소유되는 경우를 50 퍼센트이상이라고 한데 대해 예컨데 3개국이 각각 30퍼센트, 30 퍼센트, 30 퍼센트 씩 소유하고 있는경우 분쟁 발생시 누가AFFECTED PARTY 가 되느냐하는 문제가 제기되었으나, 법인 내부간 계약등이있을 것이므로 이는 당사국간에 해결이 가능한문제라는 것에 대체적으로 의견을 같이함.

- 일본측이 상기 자료에서 제시한 인력이동 문제는 추후 토의키로 하였음.

3. 끝으로 12.11(금) 15:00 에 해운, 기본통신,조세문제에 대한 GNS 전체회의가있을예정임.

첨부: 1. 해운 분야 EC 및 일본측 NON-PAPER

2. 34조 관련 일본측 토의 문서 각 1부.끝

(GVW(F)-745)

(대사 박수길-국장)

12/92 21:06 KORAEA MISSION GENEVA → 736 7790 NO.610 P01

주 제 네 바 대 표 부

번 호 : GVW(F) - 0745 년월일 : 21211 시간 : 2030

수 신 : 장 관 (통기, 경기원, 법무부, 재무부, 농림수산부, 상공부, 문화부, 건설부, 교통부, 체신부, 보사부, 과기처, 공보처, 환경처)

발 신 : 주 제네바대사

제 목 : UR/GNS 비공식협의 (2)

보 안	
통 제	

총 32 매(표지포함)

외신국	
통 제	

0170

545-32-1

NON PAPER

REV. 3

SCHEDULING CONSIDERATIONS FOR INTERNATIONAL SHIPPING AND AUXILIARY SERVICES

Introduction

This paper is proposing reflections in order to achieve common understandings and a scheduling methodology for the scheduling of commitments in the shipping sector, particularly in the perspective of "fleshing out" technically the substance of the Carlisle paper. It comes with an illustrative "ideal schedule" and the explanations which would need to be attached to such a schedule. It does not have the ambition of being perfect nor definitive, but may hopefully serve as a basis for further reflections and may stimulate constructive criticisms.

1. Liberalisation of International Shipping

Barriers to the activities of shipping companies can affect both operational and commercial aspects, under different modes.

a) with regard to the cross border mode of delivery :

- the commercial aspect may be essentially affected by restrictions on access to cargoes (cargo reservations and preferences) which bear on market access and/or national treatment conditions, by discriminations on access to cargoes (cargo sharing) affecting foreign service suppliers, and which violate MFN, or by a prohibition to do business on a cross-border basis (requirement of prior commercial presence). The absence of any qualifications in a schedule (a "none" entry) would imply the absence of any such services.

- the operational barriers may relate to limited or discriminatory conditions on access to and use of port facilities. This latter aspect is not directly relevant to commitments under Articles XVI and XVII, since such barriers would contradict Article XXXIV and VIII obligations when a commitment is undertaken, but raise the question whether there is a need to further interpret or clarify the provisions of Articles XXXIV and VIII. Since this question is also relevant in the context of the multimodal aspects of shipping services, it will be further discussed later in this paper.

b) With regard to the commercial presence mode of delivery, it should be acknowledged that restrictions often exist, on the operational side of shipping activities, with regard to the possibility for foreign shipping companies to operate vessels under the national flag of the country where such a commercial presence is established (restrictive flagging conditions). These restrictions do not in reality affect the possibilities for shipping companies to provide their services which, from the operational point of view, remain essentially cross-border in nature. However, restrictions on the establishment of a commercial presence of any kind (office, branch, subsidiary, ...) for the purpose of undertaking commercial activities ("doing business", "sales and marketing") or managing the operations of the vessels operated, would undermine in many instances the ability for service providers to benefit effectively from market access opportunities.

0171

1ㄷㄷ-2-2-2

Therefore, even though the purpose of liberalisation of trade in this sector may be focused on the cross-border aspect (in view of its nature) it is necessary to envisage some (limited) commitments on commercial presence which, while leaving "full fledged" establishment unbound or (at the choice of Members) qualified by any current restrictions which may apply, will ensure the effectiveness of cross-border liberalisation by allowing shipping companies to carry out their commercial business locally.

c) In this view, unlike other sectors, shipping require the clarification of the content of "doing business activities on a local basis", and also of the form under which local commercial representation can be established. This latter aspect address the issue of the status of "Shipping Agencies" : shipping companies, when they seek a local representation, do not in all instances establish a personal or direct commercial office, branch or subsidiary, but may often rely on a local agent which will undertake on their behalf their marketing and sales, often on a non exclusive basis (the shipping agency may act for many shipping companies). The agency can be a completely independent business, but may as well have such links with the shipping company (shareholding, appointment of personnel) that it can be construed as a form of commercial presence by the shipping company. Therefore, the explanations to the "ideal schedule" attempt to address these issues by defining, in an illustrative manner, "doing business" activities under commercial presence, and by dealing with the shipping agency issue both as a possible form of such a commercial presence and as a discrete maritime auxiliary service entry (see point 4(e) of the explanations to the "ideal schedule", and paragraph 3 below).

By the same token, this description of "doing business" activities starts addressing under points 4(a) and 4(b) - particularly under (b) of the explanations - the issue of "freedom to contract or sub-contract" for the provision of integrated/multimodal services, thus anticipating part of the discussion of this issue under the following paragraph.

2. Integration of Shipping Services

It is acknowledged that the evolution of technologies and the globalisation of markets has the effect of integrating transport services, particularly in the liner shipping sector. Thus, undertaking commitments for the liberalisation of international shipping services without taking account of this economic reality could in many instances severely curtail the value of commitments made. A clear understanding on the issues involved and a methodology for transcribing it in the "ideal schedule" is thus needed.

a) In practice the issue is twofold :

(i) on the one hand, shipping companies who wish to integrate their services will seek as a first step the possibility to contract freely with any local provider of any service which will be incorporated in the multimodal transport service package, in order to be able to sell the comprehensive package to their customers (including the resale or the invoicing of those sub-elements of the package they have not supplied directly

0172

themselves). Provided that there is a clear understanding that this ability is open to shipping companies which benefit from a commitment made under "International maritime transport", on the basis of the direct applicability of Articles XXXIV and VIII, and with the benefit of the further clarification of this legal implication which is proposed in the description of "doing business" activities under point (4) of the explanations to the "ideal schedule", it could be considered that this aspect of the difficulty is solved. Alternatively, the language suggested under point (5) of the explanations to the "ideal schedule" could be used to clarify the issue of the "through bill of lading".

(ii) On the other hand, shipping companies may wish to supply themselves if not all the service elements of an integrated package, at least those which may be the most crucial to the quality of the global service rendered. This will be true even if they do not provide a multimodal service, but merely a comprehensive maritime transport package. In this case they will wish to provide themselves such shipping auxiliary services as cargo handling, storage/warehousing, customs clearance services, which can be summarised as "origin related and/or destination related port and associated Services" (UNCTAD terminology).

One step further, for the provision of door-to-door services, shipping companies could wish to provide "origin related and/or destinations related inland transport services". These would in practice be limited to trucking, inland waterway barging, and access to railway services and/or infrastructures, at the most. Thus, direct commitments are less critical here provided the conclusions of point (i) above were acceptable.

b) In view of the above, it seems necessary to clarify the following scheduling issues :

(i) Firstly, how to define "origin/destination related port and associated services"? This category of activities is distinct from "doing business" activities already dealt with on the one hand, and from other port and associated services, which are not connected with the processing/forwarding of cargoes on the other. This issue will be addressed in more detail under the next paragraph (3), dealing with auxiliary services.

(ii) Secondly, how to address the issue of commitments allowing the inland transport ("onward transport on a through bill of lading")? Three possibilities can be envisaged :

- the GATS Member concerned is making effective commitments (under commercial presence) for inland transport sectors. In such a case, these general commitments could equally be used by shipping service providers;

0173

545-32-4

- the GATS Member is not in a position to make a general commitment to liberalise the supply of a given mode of transport, but could undertake to authorise shipping companies to operate such inland transport on their own behalf, while restricting the supply of these services to the "general public". In this case, ad hoc additional commitments could be made under Article XVIII, as suggested as an option in the "ideal schedule";

- the GATS Member is not ready to make either general or additional commitments, but accept the interpretations previously suggested under 4(a), (b) and/or 5 of the explanations to the "ideal schedule" (freedom to sub-contract). In this case, the possibility for the shipping company to sell door-to-door services (of which it will undertake the sea-leg) is nevertheless consolidated, this remaining the key objective suggested in the Carlisle paper.

3. Ancillary services

a) Two general observations :

- the CPC classification/descriptive notices are inadequate for certain issues : cargo handling, customs clearance, shipping agencies, at least;

- maritime ancillary services fall a priori in 3 general categories, but only the first one requires a degree of delimitation:

(i) "origin/destination - related port and associated services": those which are connected with the handling, documentation and on-carrying of the cargoes, and targeted in the Carlisle paper;

(ii) other port services which are more likely to be provided on a private, commercial basis, but which "liberalisation of supply" has no direct bearing on the liberalisation of shipping itself. Examples are lightering, provisioning, repair/maintenance ...;

(iii) other port services which are more likely to be considered as "pure" public services such as pilotage, port captain's services, navigation aid services ....

b) For the purposes of scheduling there is in fact no need to make a distinction between the second and the third category, provided that there can be a clear understanding on two points :

(i) firstly, each Member shall remain free to request and/or offer the liberalisation of these second and/or third category services, or alternatively to refuse to schedule commitments, in particular if it considers that these services are public services;

(ii) secondly, in order not to undermine the commitment made on international shipping, it must be clear that in pursuance with the provisions of the framework (Articles XXXIV and VIII) access to and use, as a consumer, of any port service shall be de facto reasonable and non-discriminatory for the shipping service suppliers who benefit of commitments under XVI and XVII. 0174

./.

c) Provided that such an understanding can be achieved and properly formalised, the only remaining issue for the implementation of the Carlisle paper in <u>this</u> area of ancillary services is the short-list and, when necessary, the description/definition of the services falling in the <u>first</u> category.

(i) So far, the following may be identified with a relative certainty :

- <u>stevedoring/terminal operator/cargo handling services</u>. There, an ad hoc definition shall be necessary to replace the inadequate CPC description and to cater for the issue of dockers monopolies;

- <u>storage and warehousing</u>;

- <u>customs clearance services</u>. Here again, an ad hoc definition is required in the absence of any clear reference in the CPC.

(ii) <u>Container station</u> (storage and repair) <u>services</u> should be an additional candidate for this category, even though it has not been explicitly identified so far. A definition would also be required;

(iii) The Carlisle paper refers to other activities in its attachment A, which are more delicate to address, since they are likely to be undertaken by different kinds of <u>entities</u>:

- <u>direct commercial representations</u> (commercial presence) of a shipping company;

- <u>shipping agencies</u> acting, as an independent business, on behalf of one or more shipping company, and

- <u>freight forwarders</u>, acting as shippers or on behalf of shippers.

All these entities will participate in the organisation and/or execution of transport operations, but with different commercial objectives and interests; they all may however:

- <u>market and sell</u> transport and/or related services;

- <u>buy</u> on their own account or on behalf of their customers, transport and related services;

- <u>operate</u> information and documentation services.

Assuming that the coverage of these activities evoked in the Carlisle paper is addressed, under the first of the three possible angles (<u>direct presence</u>, agency, freight forwarder), by commitments undertaken under "commercial presence" of shipping companies on the one hand, and assessing that the freight forwarding business is in fact not directly linked with shipping on the other, it would remain necessary to include in the short-list of "origin/destination related port and associated services" the <u>shipping agency</u> services, for which an ad hoc definition would be needed, since the CPC entry 7480 ("freight transport agency services") seems primarily to describe freight forwarding business.

0175

./.

Commitments with regard to freight forwarding should in this perspective follow the same logic as auxiliary services in the second/third category (point (b) above of the present paragraph);

d) A last point to be addressed for some of these services, when operated in the port area (cargo handling, storage/warehousing, container stations), is the issue of infrastructure limitations. Whatever the port authority is, public or private, it cannot allocate available space on an unrestricted basis. This practical restriction to market access would however not be inconsistent with the commitments undertaken, if the licensing/concession mechanism is fair and non-discriminatory. When the port authority is a private company, it is essentially an issue of private commercial negotiations, where the port authority might however have to comply with Article VIII disciplines. When the port authority is a public entity, it may, in granting concessions, intergrate a public utility criterion when processing the applications made for establishing a business. For transparency and legal security purposes, it is suggested in the draft ideal schedule to cover this eventuality by an appropriate footnote.

4. Access to and use of port infrastructures

a) Since port infrastructures can be construed to fall within either of the 3 categories of auxiliary services discussed in para. 3(a) above (examples: a crane or a warehouse, in category 1, an assistance vessel - tugboat or pilot - in category 2 or 3, a navigation aid, in category 3), a first observation would be to recall the propositions made in paragraph 3 (b) (ii) and 2 (a) (i) above, and the explanations to the "ideal schedule" under point 4(b), these being based on the interpretation of Articles XXXIV and VIII of the framework.

b) However, in view of the specificity and technicity of maritime shipping and port activities, it has been maintained by some participants that a more detailed interpretation/clarification of the relevant provisions of the framework would be necessary. Some language have been developed to this end by a group of participants in the GNS towards the end of 1991, in the context of the clarification of proposals made at the time by the Nordic countries. This language can be found in document GNS.W/135/add 2, pages 3 and 4. It is proposed to further consider this language and amend it if necessary, and, as a possible way of proceeding, a reference is made to this end in the explanations to the "ideal schedule", point 6.

5. Remaining key issues not included elsewhere

Two issues remain yet technically unclarified while important to the meaningfulness of commitments : "board to board" or "via the quay" trans-shipments (trans-shipment involving barges or other vessels being included in cabotage and thus excluded from the scope of commitment) and cargo handling activities/equipment aboard the vessel. Restrictions affecting such operations may in some instances undermine the value of commitments which could be undertaken by Members. Thus, a scheduling technique needs to be found for addressing these issues. The problem stems from the difficulty to link directly eventual restrictions to a precise heading in the schedule, except for considering such restrictions as affecting cross-border trade in international shipping.

145-32-7 0176

./.

or affecting cross-border trade in cargo handling services. Therefore, two solutions can be imagined a priori to render explicit the absence of restrictions in the "ideal schedule" : either a mention under cross-border trade in cargo handling, or an additional commitment under cross-border trade in international shipping. Tentative language is proposed to this end in the "ideal schedule" as options under both formats. A third option, possibly preferable, would be to understand that, in the absence of any restrictive qualification in the schedule, no limitations to these activities would be enforceable.

145-32-8

0177

Sector or Sub-Sector	Limitations on Market Access	Limitations on National Treatment	Additional Commitments
	DRAFT "IDEAL SCHEDULE" ON INTERNATIONAL SHIPPING		
TRANSPORT SERVICES			
MARITIME TRANSPORT SERVICES			
International Transport (freight and passengers) CPC 7211 and 7217 less cabotage transport	1) a) Liner Shipping: none	1) a) None [subsidies?]	Optional commitments, depending on scheduling option for cargo handling services, and on commitments on inland transport services (examples)
	b) Bulk, tramp, and other international shipping, including passenger transportation: none	b) None	1) No limitation on trans-shipments (board to board or via the quay).
	2) None	2) None	2) No limitation on use of on-board cargo handling equipment.
	3 a) Establishment of registered company for the purpose of operating a fleet under the national flag of the State or establishment: unbound	3) a) Unbound	3) No limitation on ownership and/or rental/lease of trucking equipment for the inland forwarding of cargoes
	b) Other forms of commercial presence: none	b) None	4) No limitation on ownership and/ or lease of barges and equipment necessary for inland forwarding of cargoes.
	4) a) Ships crews: unbound	4) a) Unbound	
	b) Shore personnel: none (subject to horizontal commitment)	b) None	5) No limitation on ownership and/ or rental/lease of railway equipment/ carriage for the inland forwarding of cargoes.

145-32-P

0178

Sector or Sub-Sector	Limitations on Market Access	Limitations on National Treatment	Additional Commitments
MARITIME AUXILIARY SERVICES			
Maritime Cargo Handling Services (as defined in ....)	1) Unbound (*) [except for - no limitation on trans-shipment (board to board or via the quay) and/or on use of on-board cargo handling equipment] 2) None 3) None (**) 4) None	1) Unbound (*) [except for no limitation on trans-shipment (board to board or via the quay) and/or on use of on-board cargo handling equipment] 2) None 3) None 4) None	
Storage and Warehousing Services CPC 742 [as amended]	1) Unbound (*) 2) None 3) None (**) 4) None	1) Unbound (*) 2) None 3) None 4) None	
Customs Clearance Services (as defined in ...)	1) Unbound (*) 2) None 3) None (**) 4) None	1) Unbound (*) 2) None 3) None 4) None	
Container Station Services (as defined in ...)	1) Unbound (*) 2) None 3) None (**) 4) None	1) Unbound (*) 2) None 3) None 4) None	

(*) A Commitment on this mode of delivery is not feasible.
(**) Public utility concession or licensing procedures may apply in case of occupation of the public domain for the conduct of these activities.

0179

145-32-10

Sector or Sub-Sector	Limitations on Market Access	Limitations on National Treatment	Additional Commitments
Maritime Agency Services (as defined in ...)	1) None 2) None 3) None 4) None	1) None 2) None 3) None 4) None	
[Subsectors which would enhance the value of commitments with regard to the multimodal dimension of shipping:			
Freight forwarding (as defined in [CPC 748] [+ 7497])			
Road Transport Services, Freight CPC 7123 (and especially 71233, containers)			
Rail Transport Services, Freight CPC 7112 (and especially 71223, containers)			
Inland Waterways Transport Services by Barges (as defined in ...)]			

0180

5KF-32-1

Explanations to the Schedule

It is understood that:

1) This schedule does not include maritime cabotage transport services, i.e. transportation of passengers or goods between a port located in ... (name of the country or, for EEC, "a Member State") and another port located in ... (name of the country or, for EEC, "the same Member State") and traffic originating and terminating in the same port located in ... (name of country, or for the EEC, "a Member State") provided that this traffic remains within ... (name of country or "this Member State") territorial waters.

2) The commitments in this schedule apply in relation to international maritime transport service suppliers of other Members, irrespective of the flag of the vessel operated for the supply of the service. International shipping services supplied by non-Members service suppliers are not covered by the commitments (However, when these services are operated with a vessel flying the flag of a Member, this vessel will normally be granted access to and use of port facilities under reasonable and non-discriminatory conditions, without prejudice to this Agreement (in particular Articles XIV, XIV bis and XXXI) nor to other existing or future international obligations suscribed by ... (name of the country or "the European Community and its Member States").

3) An international maritime transport service supplier of another Member "A" is a natural or juridical person who fulfils the conditions set forth in Article XXXIV or, if he is not established in the territory a Member, whose vessels are registered in that other Member "A" in accordance with the legislation of that other Member "A", provided that he operates his services with these vessels.

4) The commitment under commercial presence implies the ability for international maritime transport service suppliers of other Members to undertake locally all activities which are necessary for the supply to their customers of a partially or fully integrated transport service, within which the maritime transport constitutes a substantial element. (This commitment shall however not be construed as limiting in any manner the commitments undertaken under the cross border mode of delivery).

These activities include, but are not limited to:

(a) marketing and sales of maritime transport and related services through direct contact with customers, from quotation to invoicing, these services being those operated or offered by the service supplier itself or by service suppliers with which the service seller has established standing business arrangements;

(b) the acquisition, on their own account or on behalf of their customers (and the resale to their customers) of any transport and related services, including inward transport services by any mode, particularly inland waterways, road and rail, necessary for the supply of the integrated service;

(c) the preparation of documentation concerning transport documents, customs documents, or other documents related to the origin and character of the goods transported;

(d) the provision of business information by any means, including computerised information systems and electronic data interchange (subject to the provisions of the annex on telecommunications);

0181

(e) the setting up of any business arrangments, including participation in the stock of a company and the appointment of personnel recruited locally (o
the case of foreign personnel, subject to the horizontal commitment on movement of personnel) with any locally established shipping agency.

(f) acting on behalf of the companies, organising the call of the ship or taking over corgoes when required.

5) The commitments in this schedule include the possibility for the service suppliers concerned, which fufil the definition of "Multimodal Transport Operator"
forth below, to supply such multimodal services, without prejudice to the specific limitations or qualifications included in the schedule. These ser
suppliers cannot therefore supply directly or unconditionally those sub-elements of the multimodal service which are discrete transport or related services
included in the schedule, or which are subject to explicit limitations or qualifications.

Multimodal Transport Operator means the person on whose behalf the bill of lading/multimodal transport document, or any other document evidencing a contrac
multimodal carriage of goods, is issued and who is responsible for the carriage of goods pursuant to the contract of carriage.

6) Pursuant to Articles XXXIV and VIII of the Agreement, vessels operated by international maritime transport service suppliers of other Members shall be g
access to and use of all port facilities (see illustrative list) on reasonable and non-discriminatory terms and conditions. In this view, (tex
GNS.W/135/Add. 2, pages 3 and 4, with appropriate amendments?).

0182

일본측 non-paper(해운)

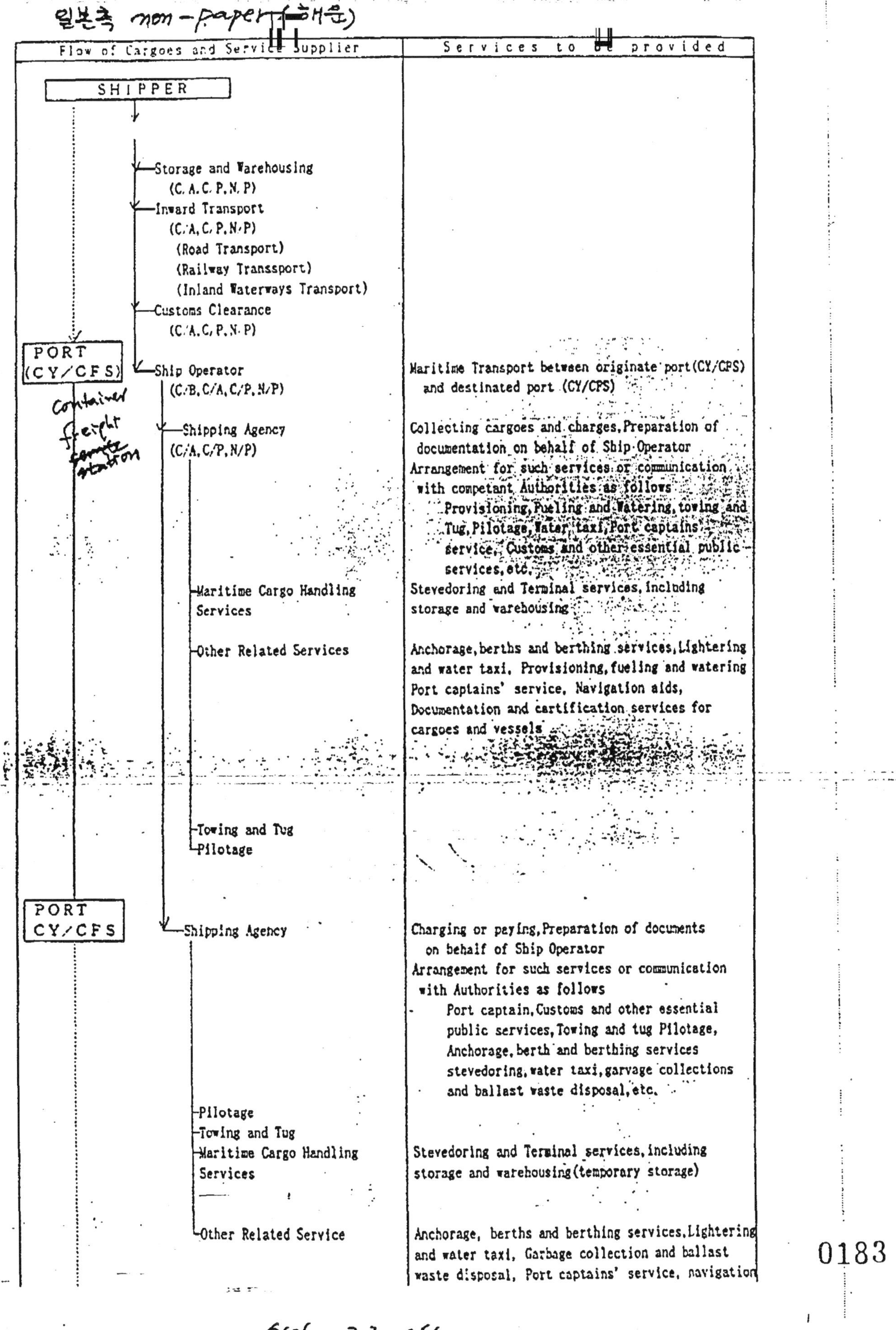

Flow of Cargoes and Service Supplier	Services to be provided
SHIPPER	
Storage and Warehousing (C.A.C.P.N.P)	
Inward Transport (C/A,C/P,N/P) (Road Transport) (Railway Transsport) (Inland Waterways Transport)	
Customs Clearance (C/A.C/P.N.P)	
PORT (CY/CFS) — Ship Operator (C/B,C/A,C/P,N/P)	Maritime Transport between originate port(CY/CPS) and destinated port (CY/CPS)
Shipping Agency (C/A,C/P,N/P)	Collecting cargoes and charges, Preparation of documentation on behalf of Ship Operator Arrangement for such services or communication with competant Authorities as follows Provisioning, Fueling and Watering, towing and Tug, Pilotage, Water taxi, Port captains' service, Customs and other essential public services, etc.
Maritime Cargo Handling Services	Stevedoring and Terminal services, including storage and warehousing
Other Related Services	Anchorage, berths and berthing services, Lightering and water taxi. Provisioning, fueling and watering Port captains' service, Navigation aids, Documentation and certification services for cargoes and vessels
Towing and Tug	-
Pilotage	-
PORT CY/CFS — Shipping Agency	Charging or paying, Preparation of documents on behalf of Ship Operator Arrangement for such services or communication with Authorities as follows Port captain, Customs and other essential public services, Towing and tug Pilotage, Anchorage, berth and berthing services stevedoring, water taxi, garvage collections and ballast waste disposal, etc.
Pilotage	
Towing and Tug	
Maritime Cargo Handling Services	Stevedoring and Terminal services, including storage and warehousing (temporary storage)
Other Related Service	Anchorage, berths and berthing services, Lightering and water taxi, Garbage collection and ballast waste disposal, Port captains' service, navigation

container freight station

0183

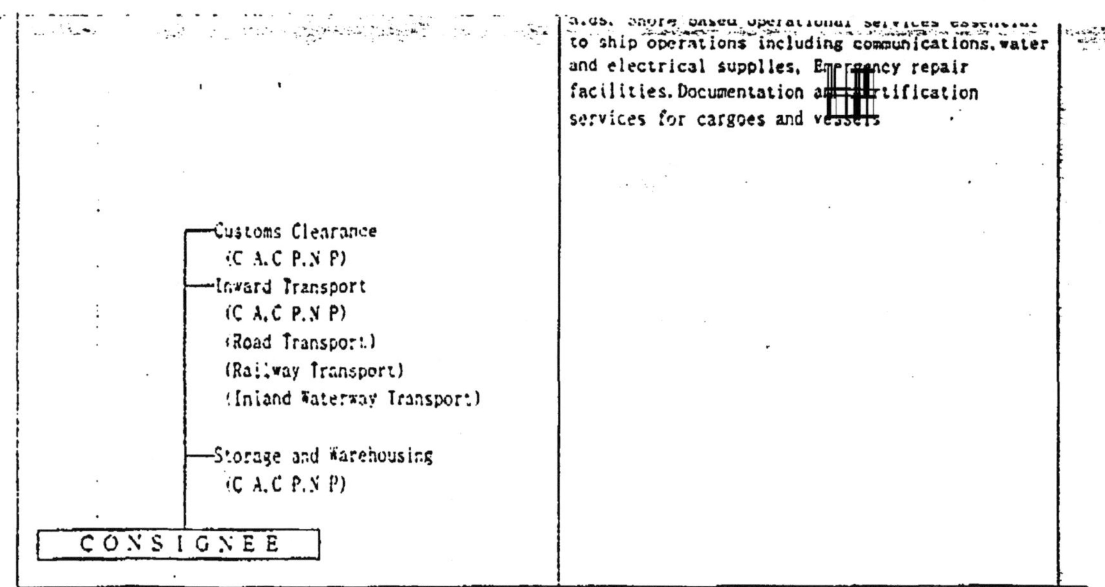

aids, shore based operational services essential to ship operations including communications, water and electrical supplies, Emergency repair facilities. Documentation and certification services for cargoes and vessels

—Customs Clearance
(C A.C P.N P)
—Inward Transport
(C A.C P.N P)
(Road Transport)
(Railway Transport)
(Inland Waterway Transport)

—Storage and Warehousing
(C A.C P.N P)

CONSIGNEE

Note:
C B Cross-border supply
C A Consumption abroad
C P Through Commercial Presence
N P Through Presence of natural persons

0184

144-32-15

11/12/92 21:12 KOREA MISSION GENEVA → 736 7790

Japan's Informal Comments on the Revised Secretariat Draft of Article XXXIV dated 3.12.92

December 9, 1992
The Japanese Delegation

945-32-16

0185

TABLE OF CONTENTS

0186

1. Definition of Nationals

A. Comments

I Questions

1. If a country wishes its permanent resident to be its citizen, then that country should give him citizenship as it sees fit. Why should the permanent resident be treated as a national only in relation to GATS?

2. Must a Member accept a unilateral notification made by another Member?

II Observations

1. If a permanent resident is a national of a Member, he would be a beneficiary of the agreement even without the notification.

2. The only category of permanent residents who would not be beneficiaries of the agreement without the notification is those permanent residents who are nationals of non-Members.

945-132-18

0187

3. Another side of this issue of notification is which Member represents the permanent resident.

(1) If there is no scheme for notification, the permanent resident's interest as a natural person will be represented by his country of nationality and not by his country of residence.

(2) If there is a scheme for notification, the permanent resident's interest as a natural person may be represented by both his country of nationality and his country of residence.

(3) In the case of a juridical person owned or controlled by the permanent resident, the juridical person's interest may be represented by:

(a) the country of his nationality when there is no notification, and

(b) the country of his nationality and the country of his residence when there is a scheme for notification.

This is so because Article 31 does allow Members to deny the benefit of the agreement to juridical persons owned or controlled by a non-Member regardless of their address of incorporation.

(4) The denial mechanism of Article 31 may not be triggered for juridical persons owned or controlled by a national of a non-Member if he is notified as being a national of a Member.

4. If the notification scheme is adopted and notification is made, Members will have to treat a permanent resident of a Member as a national of that Member as well as a national of his original nationality. Even

945-232-1 p

0188

11/12/92 21:13 KOREA MISSION GENEVA → 736 7790 NO.610

if that permanent resident has an original nationality of a non-Member or a Member to which the benefit of the agreement is denied under Article 31, Members may not deny the benefit of the agreement to him, because the notification scheme makes him a national of a Member as well.

5. If a Member takes a commitment on movement of personnel to the Members, a permanent resident notified as national of a Member will be given the same treatment accorded to the national of that Member regardless of his real nationality.

6. Nationality is the last resort to the control of foreigners in a country because, if he is to be deported, the country of his nationality has the obligation of receiving him. The nationality status of a permanent resident under the GATS does not guarantee that the country of his permanent residence will be responsible to receiving him when deported. This is just one example that makes it difficult to accept the notification scheme to be adopted.

145-32-20
3

B. Proposed Revision

- 4 -

FINAL ACT	14 MAY TEXT	PROPOSED REVISED TEXT
i) a natural person who is a national of the Party under the law of that Party, or	i) is a national of the Member or,	i) is a national of that other Member or,
ii) in the case of a Party which does not have nationals, a natural person who has the right of permanent residence under the law of that Party,	ii) in the case of a Member which does not have nationals, ~~or a Member which makes a special declaration to the Council on Trade in Services,~~ has the right of permanent residence in the Member	ii) in the case of a Member which 1. does not have nationals, or 2. has given written notification to the Council on Trade in Services that, for the purpose of this Agreement, it treats its permanent residents as its nationals, has the right of permanent residence
and who resides in the territory of that Party or any other Party.	under the law of that Member, and who resides in the territory of that Member or any other Member;	under the law of that other Member, and who resides in the territory of that Member or any other Member;
(i) "juridical person" of another Party means any corporation, partnership, joint venture, sole proprietorship or association, whether constituted for profit or otherwise, and whether privately-owned or governmentally-owned, which is	(..) "juridical person" means any legal entity duly constituted or otherwise organized under applicable law, whether for profit or otherwise, and whether privately-owned or governmentally-owned, including any corporation, trust, partnership, joint venture, sole proprietorship or association.	(1) "juridical person" means any legal entity duly constituted or otherwise organized under applicable law, whether for profit or otherwise, and whether privately-owned or governmentally-owned, including any corporation, trust, partnership, joint venture, sole proprietorship or association;

945-32-21

0190

4

11/12/92 21:14 KOREA MISSION GENEVA → 736 7790 NO.610 P21

2. Definition of a Ser[illegible]

Person

A. Comments

11/12/92 21:15 KOREA MISSION GENEVA → 736 7790 NO.610 D22

NOTE: REFERENCE GIVEN IN PARANTHESIS INDICATES THE RELEVANT PROVISIONS AS STIPULATED IN THE PROPOSED REVISED TEXT OF ARTICLE 34 OF THE SECRETARIAT DATED 3.12.92. UNDERLINE IS ADDED TO INDICATE THE ISSUE. THE DIFFERENT PATTERNS OF THE PARENTHESIS INDICATE PARTS THAT ARE INTERRELATED.

WOULD A JURIDICAL PERSON THAT HAS MET THE TESTS OF LEGAL NATURE AND THE ORIGIN AND WHO SUPPLIES A SERVICE, FOR EXAMPLE BY DELIVERING A SERVICE, NOT BE CONSIDERED AS A SERVICE SUPPLIER BECAUSE THE DELIVERY OF SERVICE IS NOT CONSIDERED TO BE A SUBSTANTIVE BUSINESS OPERATION BY A MEMBER ? THE FOLLOWING ANALYSIS ELABORATES THE CONCEPT BEHIND THIS QUESTION.

I .THE STRUCTURE OF THE REVISED VERSION

SERVICE SUPPLIER MEANS ANY PERSON THAT SUPPLIES A SERVICE(G)

SUPPLY OF A SERVICE (INCLUDES THE PRODUCTION, DISTRIBUTION, MARKETING SALE AND DELIVERY OF A SERVICE) (B)

PERSON MEANS EITHER A NATURAL PERSON OR A JURIDICAL PERSON(J)

JURIDICAL PERSON MEANS ANY LEGAL ENTITY DULY CONSTITUTED OR OTHERWISE ORGANIZED [UNDER THE APPLICABLE LAW] , WHETHER FOR PROFIT OR OTHERWISE, AND WHETHER PRIVATELY-OWNED OR GOVERNMENTALLY -OWNED, INCLUDING ANY CORPORATION, TRUST, PARTNERSHIP, JOINT-VENTURE, SOLE PROPRIETORSHIP OR ASSOCIATION(L)

JURIDICAL PERSON OF ANOTHER MEMBER MEANS A JURIDICAL PERSON WHICH IS EITHER

i) CONSTITUTED OR OTHERWISE ORGANIZED [UNDER THE

0191

LAW] OF THAT OTHER MEMBER, AND IS [ENGAGED IN SUBSTANTIVE BUSINESS OPERATIONS IN THE TERRITORY OF THAT OTHER MEMBER OR ANY OTHER MEMBER] ; OR

ii) IN THE CASE OF SUPPLY OF A SERVICE THROUGH COMMERCIAL PRESENCE, OWNED OR CONTROLLED BY

1. NATURAL PERSONS OF [THAT MEMBER]
2. JURIDICAL PERSONS OF [THAT OTHER MEMBER] IDENTIFIED UNDER SUBPARAGRAPH (i)(M)

II. THE ISSUE IS HOW A MEMBER DETERMINES WHETHER A JURIDICAL PERSON IS A SERVICE SUPPLIER THAT IS COVERED UNDER THE AGREEMENT.

THE PROVISIONS OF THE REVISED DEFINITION REQUIRE A JURIDICAL PERSON TO PASS THE FOLLOWING TESTS:

1. IT HAS TO BE A JURIDICAL PERSON IN THE SENSE OF THE AGREEMENT: RELEVANT PROVISIONS ARE (L) AND (M)
2. AFTER CLEARING THE ABOVE TEST, IT HAS TO BE A SERVICE SUPPLIER: RELEVANT PROVISIONS ARE (G) AND (B)

THE TESTS OF (L) AND (M) CONSIST OF (i) THE LEGAL NATURE, (ii) THE ORIGIN AND (iii) THE NATURE OF ITS BUSINESS ACTIVITIES.

(i) THE LEGAL NATURE REQUIREMENT IS MET BY BEING DULY CONSTITUTED UNDER THE {APPLICABLE} LAW (L) AND (M).

(ii) THE ORIGIN REQUIREMENT IS MET BY BEING CONSTITUTED IN A MEMBER (M).

(iii) THE NATURE OF ACTIVITIES TEST IS MET BY BEING ENGAGED IN SUBSTANTIVE BUSINESS OPERATIONS IN THE TERRITORY OF A MEMBER (M)

AFTER CLEARING THE ABOVE TEST, IT HAS TO BE A SERVICE SUPPLIER, WHICH IS A TEST OF THE NATURE OF ITS ACTIVITIES (G).

IN EFFECT, WHETHER IT WAS INTENDED OR NOT, A JURIDICAL PERSON WILL BE SUBJECT TO TWO DIFFERENT SETS OF TESTS CONCERNING ITS BUSINESS ACTIVITIES.

WOULD A JURIDICAL PERSON THAT HAS MET THE TESTS OF LEGAL NATURE AND THE ORIGIN AND WHO SUPPLIES A SERVICE, FOR EXAMPLE BY DELIVERING A SERVICE, NOT BE CONSIDERED AS A SERVICE SUPPLIER BECAUSE THE DELIVERY OF SERVICE IS NOT CONSIDERED TO BE A SUBSTANTIVE BUSINESS OPERATION BY A MEMBER?

6

0192

7 FF - 72 - 23

WOULD A JURIDICAL PERSON THAT MET ALL THE 3 TESTS MENTIONED ABOVE STILL NOT CONSIDERED AS A SERVICE SUPPLIER BECAUSE HE DOES NOT, FOR EXAMPLE EVEN DELIVER, A SERVICE?

DIFFICULTY ARISES FROM THE DUPLICATION OF THE ACTIVITY TEST. SINCE THE JURIDICAL PERSON HAS TO BE A SUPPLIER OF A SERVICE AS STATED IN (G), THE TEST OF SUBSTANTIVE BUSINESS ACTIVITIES IN (M) IS IN EFFECT A MERE DUPLICATION OF THE TEST, UNLESS IT IS INTENDED TO COVER JURIDICAL PERSONS WHICH ARE NOT ENGAGED IN THE SUPPLY OF SERVICE. OR, IF THE INTENTION IS TO TEST WHETHER THE JURIDICAL PERSON IS ENGAGED IN SUBSTANTIVE BUSINESS ACTIVITIES IN THE SUPPLY OF SERVICE, THE DUPLICATION OF THE TESTS BECOME OBVIOUS, AND THE REFERENCE TO SUBSTANTIVE BUSINESS ACTIVITIES BETTER BE DELETED TO AVOID UNNECESSARY CONFUSION. THIS DELETION OF COURSE DOES NOT MEAN THAT A POST BOX COMPANY WILL BE ABLE TO CLAIM THE BENEFIT OF THE AGEREEMENT, BECAUSE A JURIDICAL PERSON HAS TO BE ENGAGED IN THE SUPPLY OF SERVICE.

Ⅲ. OTHER ISSUES ARE SIMPLE WORDING CONSISTENCIES.

(L) SAYS "UNDER THE APPLICABLE LAW", WHILE i),OF (M) SAYS "UNDER THE LAW". IT WOULD BE BETTER TO SAY "APPLICABLE LAW" IN BOTH CASES.

1. ii) OF (M) STATES "NATURAL PERSONS OF THAT MEMBER". IT SHOULD SAY "NATURAL PERSONS OF THAT OTHER MEMBER".

※FOR DISCUSSIONS RELATING TO THE TEST OF SUBSTANTIVE BUSINESS ACTIVITIES WITH REGARD TO DENIAL OF BENEFITS (ARTICLE XXXI), SEE THE FOLLLOWING ANNEX.

- 745-32-28

0193

Chart on Treatment of Service

* This chart does not address financial services because the Financial Services' Annex provides a different definition for financial services.

1. Basic principle under the Agreement

Territory from which the service originates	Territory in which the service is consumed	Whether or not benefits may be denied
Member	Member	No
non-Member*	Member	Yes
Member	non-Member*	Yes

2. Principle concerning a service that involves 3 or more countries.

Territory from which the service originates	Territory through which the service passes (cf. example 1. below)	Territory in which the service is consumed	Whether or not benefits may be denied
Member	Member(s)	Member	No
Member	non-Member(s)*	Member	No
non-Member*	Member(s)	Member	Yes

e.g.1. Data processing services completed in a country which passes through telecommunications means of another country before reaching its final destination.

8

9KA - 72 - 25

0194

3. Principle concerning services to which a value is added by 2 or more countries. (cf. example 2. below)

(1) The Agreement does not address all the theoretically possible cases:(a)The one case left out is that of a service that originates in a non-Member and enters into the territory of a Member, where some value is added on it, and then is transferred from that Member's territory into another Member's territory. Whether a Member denies benefits to this service or not will be up to that Member's judgement, based on a concrete individual case. It should be noted, however, that a Member is always free to grant the benefits to any service if it wishes to do so because Article XXXI uses the word "may".

(b) Another case which will be similarly subject to a Member's judgement, based on a concrete individual case, is the case of a service which originates in a Member, enters into the territory of a non-Member where some value is added on it, and then is transferred from that non-Member's territory into another Member's territory.

(2) The difficulty of addressing the above two cases will not be resolved by changing "originates" to "supply from", because neither may be defined until more experience is gained on the basis of concrete cases. It is therefore not appropriate to pursue them further just for the sake of theoretical perfection.

---

* The term "non-Member", used above, includes a Member to which the application of the Agreement has been denied by the Member in which the service is consumed.

e.g.2. In information service, data inputs are prepared in one country, then they are transferred to another country where the data are processed by a computer, then the final processed data are transferred to the final destination.

0195

(p.2)

Chart on Treatment of Service Supplier

Owned or controlled by a person of a Member	Constituted in a Member and engaged in substantive business operations in that Member	Whether or not benefits may be denied
Yes	Yes	No
Yes	No	No
No	Yes	Yes
No	No	Yes

The Service supplier has a commercial presence as defined in Article XXXIV in a Member's territory, and the question is, whether that service supplier may be denied the benefits of the Agreement by that member.

745-32-27

0196

11

(p.1)

Which service may be denied the benefits of the Agreement?

Q.1. Does the service come from a Member's territory?

(1) Yes;

Q.2: Does it originate in that Member's territory?

(i) Yes: benefits may not be denied.

(ii) No: (a) it originates in another Member's territory and simply passes through the territory of a Member: benefits may not be denied.

(b) it originates in a Non-Member's territory and simply passes through the territory of a Member: benefits may be denied.

(2) No, it comes from the territory of a Non-Member;

Q.2: Does it originate in the territory of a Member?

(i) No: it originates in the territory of a Non-Member: benefits may be denied;

(ii) Yes: it originates in the territory of a Member and simply passes through the territory of a Non-Member: benefits may not be denied

Note: The term "Non-Member", used above, includes a Member to which the application of the Agreement has been denied by the Member in which the service is consumed.

745-32-28

0197

10

B. Proposed Revision

- 5 -

FINAL ACT	14 MAY TEXT	PROPOSED REVISED TEXT
	(l) "juridical person of another Member" means a juridical person which is	(m) "juridical person of another Member" means a juridical person which is either
i) constituted under the law of that Party and is engaged in substantive business operations in the territory of that Party or any other Party, or	i) constituted or otherwise organized under the law of that other Member, and is engaged in substantive business operations in the territory of that Member or any other Member; or	i) constituted or otherwise organized under the law of that other Member~~, and is engaged in substantive business operations in the territory of that Member or any other Member~~; or
ii) owned or controlled by	ii) in the case of the supply of a service through commercial presence, owned or controlled by	ii) in the case of the supply of a service through commercial presence, owned or controlled by
1. natural persons of that Party, or	1. natural persons of that Party, or	1. natural persons of that Member, or
2. juridical persons of that Party as defined under paragraph (i);	2. juridical persons of that other Member identified under subparagraph (i).	2. juridical persons of that other Member identified under subparagraph (i);
(j) A juridical person is	(j) A juridical person is	(n) A juridical person is
i) "owned" by persons of a Party if more than 50 per cent of the equity interest in it is beneficially owned by persons of that Party;	i) "owned" by persons of a Member if more than 50 per cent of the equity interest in it is beneficially owned by persons of that Member;	i) "owned" by persons of a Member if more than 50 per cent of the equity interest in it is beneficially owned by persons of that Member;
ii) "controlled" by persons of a Party if such persons have the power to name a majority of its directors or to otherwise legally direct its actions;	ii) "controlled" by persons of a Member if such persons have the power to name a majority of its directors or to otherwise legally direct its actions;	ii) "controlled" by persons of a Member if such persons have the power to name a majority of its directors or otherwise to legally direct its actions;

945-32-2P

0198

/3

(p.3)

Which service supplier may be denied the benefits of the Agreement?

Q.1. Where is the service supplier constituted, or otherwise organized, acquired or maintained?

(1) In a Member:

Q.2. related to Article XXXIV: Is the service supplier engaged in substantive business operations in that Member on in another Member?

(a) Yes: the service supplier is the service supplier of the Member within the meaning of Article XXXIV - Q.3. must be cleared;

(b) No: the service supplier is not the service supplier of the Member with the meaning of Article XXXIV - Q.3. asked.

Q.3. related to Article XXXI: Is the service supplier owned or controlled by a person of a Member?

(a) Yes: the service supplier is the service supplier of the Member within the meaning of Article XXXIV - no more questions asked;

(b) No: the service supplier may be denied the benefits of the Agreement.

Some questions and answers that illustrate this follow:

(a) Would a travel agent owned by a person of a Member, constituted and engaged in substantive business operations in another Member's territory, be denied the benefits of the Agreement?

No, because that travel agent meets all the conditions of Article XXXIV and XXXI;

(b) Would a travel agent owned by a person of a Non-Member, constituted and engaged in substantive business operations in another Member's territory, be denied the benefits of the Agreement?

Yes, because, although that travel agent is a service supplier of another Member under Article XXXIV, it may be denied the benefits of the Agreement under Article XXXI.

0199

5ㅆ5-32-3.

12

3. Origin Rule and Annex on Movement of Natural Persons

A. Comments

In compliance with the proposed revised text of Article 34 (k) i), and origin rule indicated therein, the provisions of the Annex on Movement of Natural Persons also should be revised accordingly as indicated in B. of the following page.

0200

745-32-14-31

B. Proposed Revision

ANNEX ON MOVEMENT OF NATURAL PERSONS

1. This Annex applies to measures affecting natural persons who are service suppliers of a Member, and natural persons of a Member who are employed by a service supplier of a Member, in respect of the supply of a service for which specific commitments relating to entry and temporary stay of such natural persons have been undertaken by another Member.

2. The Agreement shall not apply to measures affecting natural persons of a Member seeking access to the employment market of any other Member, nor shall it apply to measures regarding citizenship, residence or employment on a permanent basis.

4. The Agreement shall not prevent a Member from applying measures to regulate the entry of natural persons of any other Member into, or their temporary stay in, its territory, including those necessary to protect the integrity of, and to ensure the orderly movement of natural persons across, its borders, provided that such measures are not applied in such a manner as to nullify or impair the benefits accruing to any other Member under the terms of a specific commitment.

0201

원 본

외 무 부

종 별 :

번 호 : GVW-2359 일 시 : 92 1214 1700

수 신 : 장관(수신처참조)

발 신 : 주 제네바 대사

제 목 : UR/GNS 비공식 회의(3)

수신처:(통기,경기원,재무부,법무부,농림수산부,상공부,문화부,건설부,교통부,체신부,보사부,과기처,공보처,환경처,항만청)

연: GVW-2350

1. 협의 개요

- 12.11(금) 15:00 에 GNS 비공식 회의(약 50 개국참석)가 개최되었는바, 의장은금주 개최된 비공식 회의 결과를 참가국들에게 요약보고하였으며, 그동안 복수국간협의 형태로 진행된 해운(EC), 기본통신(스웨덴),조세문제(사무국)에 대한 보고가 있었음.

2. 협의 내용

가. 의장은 금주 논의된 협정문 관련하여 추가논의가 필요한 사항을 다음과 같이언급함.

- 스케쥴링: 16조 2항 B 에서 D 관련 MAXIMUM및 MINIMUM 제한 문제, 16조 및 17조 관련 거주요건 문제, 내국민 대우 관련 외국 소재 서비스공급자의 CROSS-BORDER SUPPLY 및 CONSUMER ABROAD통한 서비스 공급 문제

- 21조: 동조의 일부 조문의 변경이 있었고 동조관련 절차문제에 대하여는 최초서비스 이사회에서 채택할수 있도록 검토를 해두자는데 대해 대부분의 국가가 동의

- 34조: F. I(3) 해운, 항공, 철도등 운송관련 ORIGIN OF SERVICES 문제, K.I, 2(4) 영주권자의 시민으로서의 인정문제, 34 관련한 31조 문제

나. 기본통신(스웨덴 보고)

- 기본통신 분야는 일부 국가만이 OFFER 하고 일부는 MFN 일탈 신청이 되어 있는 상태에서 이를 해결키 위해 6월 및 10월에 두차례 회의를가졌음. 대부분의 국가가복

통상국	법무부	보사부	문화부	교통부	체신부	경기원	재무부	농수부
상공부	건설부	과기처	해항청	환경처	공보처			

PAGE 1 92.12.15 05:41 CJ

외신 1과 통제관

0202

잡한 국내 규제를 갖고 있고 일부는 현재 DEGULATION 을 진행중이며 또한 동 분야의 기술 발전도 급격히 변화하고 있음.

- 규제 완화는 많은 시간을 소요하므로 UR 종료후 일정기간(2년)의 협상을 통해자유화를 추구하려고 하는 것이나 아직까지 아무런 합의는 없으며, 동협상 참가에 어떤 국가를 배제하는 것은 아님.협상의 범위도 기본통신을 포함하여 모든통신분야를대상으로 하고 GATS RULE 과 MFN BASE따라 이를 추구하려는 것이나 협상기간중 MFN문제와 관련 아직 아무런 합의가 없음.

- 일본, 미국, 카나다, 호주, 멕시코 등은 동 협의의 다자화에 대해 환영을 표시하고 시간적 제약을 고려 가급적 빠른 시일내에 동 협의를 완료하고 협상이 조기 시행되기를 기대한다고 언급하였음.

- EC 는 기본 통신 협상의 명료성이 유지될 필요가 있고 그 조건이 상당히 중요하며, 협상결과가 모두에게 만족스럽게 되기를 기대한다고 함. 협상 우선 순위와 관련, FROME WORK 협상, 양허협상순이며 INITIAL COMMITMENT 와 관련해서만 MFN 문제가 제기되므로 동 기본 통신 분야협의의 우선 순위가 낮다고 하고, INITIAL COMMITMENT와MFN 모두의 문제가 해결되기전까지는 서비스협상도 종결되기는 어렵다고 함.

- 인도, 이집트등은 협상의 우선 순위와 관련 첫번째 과제는 TEXT 를 조기 종결하는 것이라고 하고 다자화에는 별다른 이의가 없으나 동협의상의 조건과 MFN 원칙이중요하다 언급함.

다. 해운(EC 보고)

- 해운분야는 사무국 작성 NON-PAPER(칼라일PAPER) 가 배포된후 6월, 10월 및 최근까지 기술적 과제에 대한 논의를 12-15 개 국가간에 협의를 해왔으나 이는 EC 의일장보다는 EC협상 대표 개인 자격으로 진행되어 온것임.

- 해운 분야는 정치적 측면과 기술적 문제 양자를 포괄하고 있고 기술적인 과제는 해운분야의 용어정의, 타분야와의 관계(항구 접근,MULTIMODEL 서비스) 등 여러문제가 있어 논의를 계속해왔으나, 아직 합의에 이른 것은 아님.정치적인 문제는 (미국의 MFN 일탈) 그간 양자협상을 통해서만이 논의가 되어 왔으나,지금은 정치적 결정이없이는 기술적 과제의협의가 시간을 허비할 뿐이라고 하고 현재논의중인 스케쥴링 관련 문서는 협정의부속서로 상정한 것은 아니라고 함.

- 일본 및 아국은 현재가 기술적인문제로 부터 정치적인 문제로 관심을 돌려야 할

것이라는 EC의 입장에 동조를 표시하였으며, 인도 및 이집트는 FORMULA 방식에 의한 자유화는 받아들일수 없다고 하였음.

라. 조세문제

- 샘슨 국장은 14조 본문 및 D 항과의 관계,동조 E 항의 이중과세 방지협정과의관계,11조 2항등 금번 6월에 논의된 조세관련문제를 설명하였으나, 각국의 발언은 없었음.

3. 12.12(토) 09:00-12:00 조세문제, 14:00-17:00 기본통신문제를 논의 예정임.

첨부: 12.1 현재 각국의 양허표 제출 현황 1부. 끝

(GVW(F)-746)

(대사 박수길-국장)

주 제 네 바 대 표 부

번 호 : GVW(F) - 0746 년월일 : 21214 시간 : 1700

수 신 : 장 관 (통기, 경기원, 재무부, 법무부, 농림수산부, 상공부, 문화부, 건설부, 교통부, 체신부, 보사부, 과기처, 공보처, 환경처, 항만청)

발 신 : 주 제네바대사

제 목 : UR/GNS 전체회의 (3)

보 안	
통 제	

총 7 매(표지포함)

외신국	
통 제	

0205

746 - 7 - 1

1.12.92

LIST OF INITIAL COMMITMENTS

1.	MTN.GNS/W/109/Rev.2	10.04.92	Comm. from Switzerland - Conditional Offer of Switzerland concerning Initial Commitments - Revision
2.	MTN.GNS/W/112/Rev.1	21.1.92	Comm. from U.S.A. - Revised Conditional Offer of the U.S.A. concerning Initial Commitments - Revision
	MTN.GNS/W/112/Rev.1/Add.1	26.3.92	Financial Services
3.	MTN.GNS/W/113/Rev.2	10.2.92	Comm. from Japan - Conditional Offer of Japan concerning Initial Commitments - Revision
	MTN.GNS/W/113/Rev.2/Corr.1*	17.2.92	Corrigendum (English only)

****

4.	MTN.TNC/W/51/Rev.1	8.11.91	Comm. from Australia - Conditional Offer of Australia concerning Initial Commitments - Revision
5.	MTN.TNC/W/53/Rev.3	1.11.91	Comm. from the EC - Preliminary Conditional Offer by the EC of Initial Commitments on Trade in Services - Revision
6.	MTN.TNC/W/54/Rev.1	2.04.92	Comm. from Hong Kong - Conditional Offer of Hong Kong concerning Initial Commitments - Revision
7.	MTN.TNC/W/55/Rev.1	14.2.92	Comm. from Canada - Conditional Offer by Canada of Specific Commitments in the UR on Trade in Services - Revision
8.	MTN.TNC/W/58/Rev.1	28.1.92	Comm. from New Zealand - Revised Conditional Offer of New Zealand concerning initial commitments on Trade in Services under the GATS - Revision
9.	MTN.TNC/W/59/Rev.1	19.2.92	Comm. from Sweden - Revised Conditional Offer by Sweden concerning Initial Commitments on Services - Revision
	MTN.TNC/W/59/Rev.1/Add.1	23.3.92	Telecommunications

스웨덴 12.11 R.) 배부함
일본 12.4 R)
EC. 12.11 R —송부

0206

ㄱ116—ㄱ-2

19-GNMIS

10.	MTN.TNC/W/61/Rev.1	19.2.92	Comm. from the Rep. of Korea - Revised Conditional Offer by the Republic of Korea concerning Initial Commitments on Trade in Services - Revision
	MTN.TNC/W/61/Rev.1/Corr.1	28.2.92	Corrigendum
11.	MTN.TNC/W/62/Rev.2	14.2.92	Comm. from Finland - Conditional Offer by Finland Concerning Initial Commitments - Revision
12.	MTN.TNC/W/63	24.1.91	Comm. from Norway - Conditional Offer by Norway concerning Initial Commitments in the Services Negotiations
	MTN.TNC/W/63/Add.1/Rev.1	21.2.92	Revision
13.	MTN.TNC/W/64	4.2.91	Comm. from Indonesia - Initial Commitments of Indonesia in the field of Services
14.	MTN.TNC/W/65/Rev.1	27.4.92	Revised Conditional Offer from Singapore - Initial Commitments - Revision
	MTN.TNC/W/65/Rev.1Corr.1	19.6.92	Comm. from Singapore - Revised Conditional Offer of the Republic of Singapore concerning Initial Commitments - Corrigendum
15.	MTN.TNC/W/66/Rev.1	27.5.92	Comm. from Austria - Conditional Offer of Austria concerning Initial Commitments in Trade in Services - Revision
16.	MTN.TNC/W/67/Rev.2	17.2.92	Comm. from Colombia - Initial Commitments - Revision
17.	MTN.TNC/W/71/Rev.2	24.2.92	Comm. from Mexico - Conditional List of Offers of Mexico - Revision
18.	MTN.TNC/W/72/Rev.1	4.3.92	Conditional Offer of the Republic of Turkey concerning Initial Commitments - Revision
19.	MTN.TNC/W/73	25.3.91	Comm. from the Czech and Slovak Federal Republic - Preliminary Conditional Offer by the Czech and Slovak Federal Republic concerning Initial Commitments to Trade in Services
	MTN.TNC/W/73/Add.1	16.12.91	Addendum

0207

20.	MTN.TNC/W/74/Rev.1	16.3.92	Comm. from Iceland - Conditional Offer by Iceland concerning Initial Commitments on Trade in Services - Revision
21.	MTN.TNC/W/78	3.5.91	Comm. from Romania - Preliminary Conditional Offer by Romania concerning Initial Commitments on Trade in Services
	MTN.TNC/W/78/Add.1/Rev.1	16.04.92	Revision

****

22.	MTN.GNS/W/115/Rev.1	17.12.91	Comm. from Chile - Offer of Chile concerning Initial Commitments on Trade in Services - Revision
23.	MTN.GNS/W/116/Rev.1	19.3.91	Comm. from Brazil - Revised Conditional Offer of Brazil concerning Initial Commitments on Trade in Services - Revision
24.	MTN.GNS/W/121	15.7.91	Comm. from Yugoslavia - Preliminary Conditional Offer of Yugoslavia concerning Initial Commitments on Trade in Services
25.	MTN.GNS/W/122/Rev.1	17.3.92	Comm. from Malaysia - Conditional Offer by Malaysia of Initial Commitments on International Trade in Services
	MTN.GNS/W/122/Rev.1/Corr.1	27.3.92	Corrigendum
26.	MTN.GNS/W/123	19.7.91	Comm. from Venezuela - Declaration by the Government of Venezuela to the Group of Negotiations on Services
	MTN.GNS/W/123/Add.1/Rev.2	9.4.92	Comm. fm Venezuela - Initial Commitment - Revision
27.	MTN.GNS/W/124	19.7.91	Comm. from China - Conditional Offer of the People's Republic of China concerning Initial Commitments
28.	MTN.GNS/W/125/Rev.2	30.3.92	Comm. from Argentina - Conditional Offer of the Rep. of Argentina concerning Initial Commitments - Revision
	MTN.GNS/W/125/Rev.2/Corr.1	25.6.92	Corrigendum

0208

19-GNMIS

29. MTN.GNS/W/126/Rev.1	30.3.92	Comm. from Poland - Revised Preliminary Conditional Offer of Poland concerning Initial Commitments - Revision
30. MTN.GNS/W/127	25.7.91	Comm. from Costa Rica - Declaration to submit offer for Initial Commitments
MTN.GNS/W/127/Add.1	27.9.91	Comm. fm Costa Rica - Condition and Provisional Offer concerning Initial Commitments on Trade in Services - Addendum
31. MTN.GNS/W/128	25.7.91	Comm. fm Uruguay - Preliminary Conditional Offer of Uruguay concerning Initial Commitments on International Trade in Services
32. MTN.GNS/W/129/Rev.1	13.4.92	Comm. fm Peru - Revised Offer of Peru concerning Commitments on Services in the Uruguay Round of Trade Negotiations - Revision
MTN.GNS/W/129/Rev.1/Corr.1	21.5.92	Corrigendum - Comm fm Peru
33. MTN.GNS/W/131/Rev.1	13.10.92	Comm. fm Philippines - Revised Conditional Offer by the Philippines on Initial Commitments to Trade in Services - Revision
MTN.GNS/W/131/Rev.1/Corr.1	16.10.92	Corrigendum
34. MTN.GNS/W/132/Rev.1	7.4.92	Comm. from Thailand - Conditional Offer by Thailand concerning Initial Commitments on Trade in Services - Revision
35. MTN.GNS/W/133/Rev.1	3.3.92	Comm. fm Hungary - Revised Conditional Offer of Hungary concerning Initial Commitments on Trade in Services - Revision
36. MTN.GNS/W/136	27.9.91	Comm. fm South Africa - Preliminary Conditional Offer of South Africa concerning Initial Commitments on Trade in Services
37. MTN.GNS/W/137	27.9.91	Comm. fm Egypt - Conditional Offer by Egypt of Initial Commitments on Trade in Services
38. MTN.GNS/W/141/Rev.1	10.04.92	Comm. fm Morocco - Revised Conditional Offer by the Kingdom of Morocco concerning Initial Commitments on Trade in Services - Revision

0209

19-GNMIS

39. MTN.GNS/W/142	25.10.91	Comm. fm El Salvador, Guatemala, Honduras and Nicaragua - Conditional and Provisional Offer concerning Initial Commitments on Trade in Services
40. MTN.GNS/W/143	1.11.91	Comm. fm Cuba - Declaration by the Government of Cuba to the GNS
MTN.GNS/W/143/Add.1	10.03.92	Comm. fm Cuba - Conditional Offer of Cuba concerning Initial Commitments on Trade in Services - Addendum
MTN.GNS/W/143/Add.1/Corr.1	17.03.92	Corrigendum
41. MTN.GNS/W/144	22.11.91	Comm. fm India - Conditional Offer by India of Initial Commitments on Trade in Services
42. MTN.GNS/W/147	26.02.92	Comm. fm Bolivia - Initial Commitments
43. MTN.GNS/W/148	03.03.92	Comm. fm Sri Lanka - Conditional Offer by Sri Lanka on Initial Commitments on Trade in Services
44. MTN.GNS/W/149	26.03.92	Comm. fm Jamaica - Conditional and Provisional Offer of Jamaica concerning Initial Commitments on Trade in Services
45. MTN.GNS/W/150	03.04.92	Comm. fm Nigeria - Conditional Offer by Nigeria of Initial Commitments in the Uruguay Round Negotiations on Trade in Services
46. MTN.GNS/W/151	06.04.92	Comm. fm Senegal - Conditional Offer of Senegal concerning Initial Commitments on Trade in Services
47. MTN.GNS/W/152/Rev.1	23.11.92	Comm. fm Paraguay - Conditional and Provisional Offer of Paraguay concerning Initial Commitments on Trade in Services
48. MTN.GNS/W/153	14.04.92	Comm. fm Côte d'Ivoire - Draft List of Initial Commitments of Côte d'Ivoire in the Negotiations on Services
49. MTN.GNS/W/154	17.06.92	Comm. fm Israel - Conditional Offer of Israel concerning Initial commitments on Trade in Services
50. MTN.GNS/W/155	30.06.92	Comm. fm Cameroon - Conditional Offer of Cameroon concerning Initial Commitments on Trade in Services

0210

19-GNMIS

51. MTN.GNS/W/156	07.08.92	Comm. fm Zimbabwe - Conditional Offer of Zimbabwe concerning Initial Commitments on Trade in Services
52. MTN.GNS/W/157	14.09.92	Comm. fm Ghana - Conditional Offer of Ghana concerning Initial Commitments on Trade in Services.
53. MTN.GNS/W/158	30.9.92	Comm. fm Tunisia - Conditional Offer by Tunisia of Initial Commitments in the UR Negotiations on Trade in Services - Revision
MTN.GNS/W/158/Rev.1 (English only)	6.10.92	Comm. fm Tunisia - Revision

19-GNMIS 0211

1 46-7-7

원 본

외 무 부

종 별 :

번 호 : GVW-2360 일 시 : 92 1214 1800

수 신 : 장관(통기,경기원,재무부,체신부)

발 신 : 주제네바대사

제 목 : UR/GNS 비공식 협의(4)

연: GVW-2350

표제회의가 12.12(토) 오전(조세문제) 및 오후(기본통신)에 개최된바, 주요 내용 하기 보고함.

1. 조세문제

가. 협의개요

- 조세문제관련 협정문제 14조(D), (E)항에 대한 토의가 별첨 EC 및 미국측 수정제안을 중심으로 T4의 구체적 내용을 논의하였으나 기존의 쟁점들에 대한 합의를 도출 하지 못하고 추가 검토키로 함.

나. 협의내용

1) 내국민 대우에 대한 예외의 범위(14조 D 항)

- 예외 인정조세의 범위

0 미국 수정안은 직접세(DIRECT TAXES) 전체, EC수정안은 서비스 또는 서비스 공급자 관련 소득,자본이득 및 자본에 대한 과세로 14조(D)항관련 내국민대우 예외인정 조세범위를 넓힌데 대해 인도,호주,일본등은 LOOHOLE 이 될수 있으므로 예외범위를확대하는 것에 유보적 입장을 표명

- EQUITABLE OR EFFECTIVE 기준의 존치 여부

0 미국.카나다는 이중 TEST 라는 종래의 입장을 되풀이하면서 14조 D 의 예외 허용 요건인 EQUITABLE AND EFFECTIVE TEST 를 삭제하자는데 대해 브라질, 인도등은 14조 서두는 14조 전체에 대한 기본원칙이므로 D 의 요건을 현행대로 존치할것을 주장하였으며 EC도 동 요건을 존치하는 수정안을 제시함.

- 법률국은 조세의 내국민 대우 관련 문제는 기본적으로 국별로 조세 체계상의 차이에 기인하고 있으므로 내국민 대우 예외인정의 범위, THINCAPITALIZATION,

통상국 체신부 경기원 재무부

PAGE 1 92.12.15 05:31 CJ

외신 1과 통제관

0212

거주자간 차별문제등은 결국 17조의CONDITIONS OF COMPETITION 에 영향을 주느냐 여부로판달할 문제라고 지적함

2) MFN 에 대한 예외허용 범위(14조 E 항)

- EC 수정 제안은 14조 E항 수정이 없는데 비해 미국은 수정제안을 통해 MFN 에대한 예외범위를 종래의 2중과세 방지 관련 국제협정이외에 2중과세 방지관련 국내조치, 조세 탈루 및 회피에 대한 조치를 포함하여 확대할것을 주장하였으나, 일본, 인도등은 이를 반대하였으며, EC도 추가 검토가 필요하다고 언급

- 조제 회피와 관련 조세천국(TAX HEAVEN)문제가 해결되어야 한다는 EC 주장에 대하여 MFN 예외로 명시되지 않더라도 14조 서두 및 C항(기만, 사기관행 방지조치)으로 대응 가능한지 않느냐 해석이 있었으나, 명확한 결론을 내리지는 못함.

- 한편 미국측 수정제안은 11조(지급 및 이전)조항의 예외로 원천징수(WITHHOLDING TAX)등 세원에 대한 조세부과를 협정 적용 예외대상으로 하고 있는데 대해 사무국측이 IMF 의 설명에 의거, 송금여부에 관계없이 비거주자의 국내외 지급 또는 이전에 대해 부과되는 진정한 소득세는 외환규제가 아닌바, 그경우와 해외로의 지급 또는이전에만 부과되는 외환규제인송금에 대한 조세(REMITTANCE TAXES)와는 구별되어야한다고 지적함.

2. 기본통신

가. 협의개요

- 12.11(금) GNS 회의에서의 기본통신 복수국간 협의의 다자화에 따라 기존의 협의 참여국외에 인도, 알젠틴,말레이지아등 기본통신에 관심있는 국가들이 참석하였으며, 협상기간,협상범위, 협상기간 동안의 MFN 문제가 주로 논의되었음.

나. 협의내용

1) 협상대상 범위

- 모든 기본통신 분야를 협상대상으로 해야 한다는데는 각국의 이견이 없었으나,카나다,홍콩,일본,인도등 다수국들이 각국의 기본통신 포괄범위가 다른만큼 기본통신 에 대한 정의가 필요하다는 지적을 하였음.

2) 협상 개시 싯점 및 기간- 스웨덴은 그간 다수국간에 협상을 UR 종료이전에 가능한한 빨리 시작하자는 것이 대체적인 의견이었다고 하면서 협상기간은 2년이 제시되었으나 결론을 내린것은 아니었다고 설명한데 대해 , 가능한한 빨리 시작하되 95년초 2-3월까지 종결(2년) 하자는 안(카나다), 내년1월에 시작하여 UR

발효전(94년)에종결 하자는안(미국,일본), 가능한 한 빨리 시작하되 사안의 성격상 시한을 너무 촉박하게 잡는 것은 곤란하므로 협상기간을 한정하지는 말자는 주장(EC, 스위스)등이제시되 어 결론을 내리지못함.

3) 협상결과의 이행문제

- 협상결과는 협상 비참가자에게도 MFN 원칙에따라 적용될 것임에도 각국이 의견을 같이하였음.

- 다만, 협상결과의 스케쥴 수정과 관련 21조에따라 각국 NATIONAL 스케쥴의 수정사항으로 기록되어야 한다고 하는 의견이 제시되었으나,인도는 24조(공동행위)에 의거 체약국단결정으로 채택가능하다는 의견을 제시한바,각국이 관심을 표명함.

4) 협상기간중 MFN 문제

- 협상 종결을 위해 MFN 일탈 문제 해결이 관건이라는데 각국이 인식을 같이하였는바, 특히EC는 협상에서 LEVEL OF PALYING FIELD 가 중요하다고 하고 협상중의 MFN일탈은 협상진행의 심각한 장애가 될것이며 특정국이 MFN 일탈을 협상력 제고 수단으로 사용할 경우다른 나라들도 대응수단을 강구할 것이므로 협상은 해결곤란한 복잡한 상황(JUNGLE SITUATION)으로 될것임을 강하게 주장함.

- 미국은 MFN 일탈과 관련하여 타국이 제기하고있는 문제는 1) MFN 일탈의 진정한 의도 2)협상기간중의 처리문제라고 하고, 미국은 EC가 지적한 협상제고 수단으로 MFN 일탈을 악용할의도는 전혀 없으며, 협상기간중에도 현존 법규에따라 개방수준은 계속 유지될 것임을 설명

0 의장은 미국의 이러한 입장을 문서화하여 제출할것을 요청한바, 미국이 이를 수용함.

- 이에 대해 카나다는 MFN 문제해결이 협상개시의 관건이라고 하고 일부 국가의 MFN일탈이 문제를 어렵게 하고 있으나 특정국 MFN일탈 철회에도 정치적 제약요인 있는 만큼 적극적 해결책 모색이 필요하다고 지적하였음.

- 일본, 인도는 MFN 일탈은 유지되나 하나 동문제를 협상종료시(THE END OF NEGOTIATIONS)에 결정하는 경우, 이는 여러가지 문제를 야기하 것이라고함.

3. GNS 비공식 협의 일정

- 의장은 협상 조기 종결을 위해 우선 TEXT관련 사항부터 마무리 지을 필요가 있다고 하고,12.14 주간에 이를 집중적으로 검토할 것임을 언급하고, 잠정적으로 하기 일정을 발표함.

- 12.14(월) 오후: 21조, 항공부속서, 통신부속서
- 12.15(화) 오후 : TAXATION
- 12.16(수) 오후 :34 조
- 12.17(목) 오후: 기본통신, 협정문 밖의 조치

첨부: 조세문제 관련 미국 및 EC측 협정문 수정제안 각 1부.끝

(GVW(F)-0747).끝

(대사 박수길-국장)

주 제 네 바 대 표 부

번 호 : GVW(F) - 0747 년월일 : 2/2/14 시간 : 1800

수 신 : 장 관 (통기, 경기원, 재무부)

발 신 : 주 제네바대사

제 목 : UR/GNS 비공식회의 (4)

보 안	
통 제	

총 4 매(표지포함)

외신과	
통 제	

배부처	장관실	차관실	一차보	二차보	외정실	분석관	아주국	미주국	구주국	중아국	국기국	경제국	통상국	문협국	외연원	청와대	안기부	공보처	경기원	상공부	재무부	농수부	동자부	환경처	과기처		
													0						/		/						

147-4-1

0216

DRAFT

12.12.92

EC DRAFTING SUGGESTIONS

Article XIV(d)

1. delete "inconsistent with Article XVII".

2. "...taxes on income, capital gains or capital, in respect of service suppliers or their services, when under the Member's relevant tax measures, the service supplier is not deemed to reside..."

0217

147-4-2

M-TX

12.12.92

Text by U.S.

GENERAL AGREEMENT ON TRADE IN SERVICES

Article XIV
General Exceptions

Subject to the requirement that such measures are not applied in a manner which would constitute a means of arbitrary or unjustifiable discrimination between countries where like conditions prevail, or a disguised restriction on international trade in services, nothing in this Agreement shall be construed to prevent the adoption or enforcement by any Party of measures:

(a) ...

(b) ...

(c) ...

(d) inconsistent with Article XVII, relating to direct taxes in respect of service suppliers or services;

(e) inconsistent with Article II, provided that the difference in treatment is the result of a tax measure relating to:

(i) the avoidance of double taxation; or

(ii) tax evasion or avoidance;

(f) notwithstanding Article XI, imposing a tax at source by withholding or other means.

Article XXII
Consultations

...

3. A Member may not invoke Article II or Article XVII, either under this Article or Article XXIII (Dispute Settlement and Enforcement), with respect to a taxation measure of another Member if there is an international agreement between the Members concerned relating to the avoidance of double taxation that contains a provision relating to non-discrimination or equivalent provision which, as determined under such agreement, applies to the measure concerned.

0218

747-4-3

Article XXXIV
<u>Definition</u>

For the purpose of this Agreement:

(xxx) "Direct taxes" include all taxes on total income, on total capital or on elements of income or of capital, including taxes on gains from the alienation of property, taxes on estates, inheritances and gifts or substantially similar taxes, taxes on the total amounts of wages or salaries paid by enterprises, as well as taxes on capital appreciation.

141-4-4

0219

교　통　부

우100-162 서울 중구 봉래동2가 122 / 전화 (02) 392-4817 / 전송(02)392-9809

문서번호 국항 10502- 1519
시행일자 1992. 12. 15. ( )
(경 유)
수 신 외무부장관
참 조

선결			지시	
접수	일자 시간	1992.12.16 :	결재·공람		
	번호	42979			
처리과					
담당자		이미경			

제 목 UR 서비스협상 관련 뉴질랜드 제안에 대한 검토의견

UR 서비스협상 항공부속서 관련 뉴질랜드 제안에 대한 검토의견을 첨부와 같이 송부합니다.

첨 부 항공부속서 관련 뉴질랜드 제안에 대한 의견 1부. 끝.

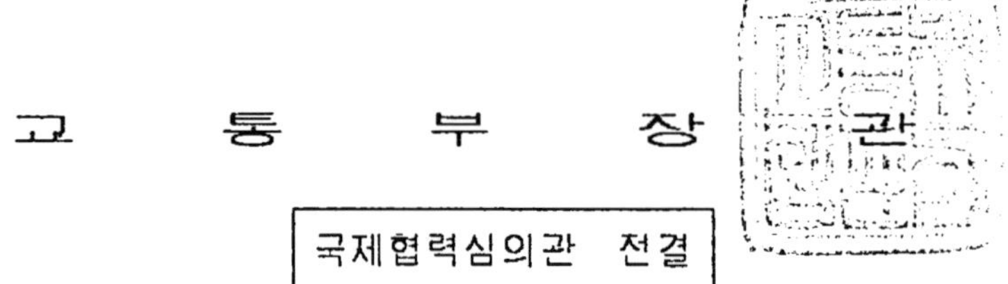

교 통 부 장 관

국제협력심의관 전결

0220

○ 항공부속서 제2항 관련 뉴질랜드 제안 검토

현 행 협 정 문(안)	뉴 질 랜 드 제 안	검 토 의 견
2. Except as set out in paragraph 3, no provision of the Agreement shall apply to measures affecting: (a) traffic rights covered by the Chicago Convention, including the five freedoms of the air, and by bilateral air services agreements; (b) directly related activities which would limit or affect the ability of parties to negotiate, to grant or to receive traffic rights, or which would have the effect of limiting their exercise. 2. 3항에 규정된 것을 제외하고 서비스협정의 어느 규정도 다음의 사항에는 적용하지 않음 (a) 시카고 협약 및 쌍무간 항공협정이 적용되는 1-5의 항공자유를 포함하는 운수권 (b) 운수권을 협상, 승인, 부여하는 체약국의 능력을 제한하거나 영향을 주는, 또는 운수권행사를 제한하는 효과를 가져오는데 직접적으로 관련된 활동	2. The Agreement shall not apply to measures affecting: (a) Traffic rights, when granted in a manner not consistent with Article II.1 of the Agreement; (b) the supply of directly related services, when such measures would limit or affect the ability traffic rights pursuant to subparagraph 2(a) above, or which would have the effect to limiting their exercise; except as provided in paragraphs 3 and 4 of this Annex. 2. 서비스협정은 본 부석서의 3.4항에 규정된 것을 제외하고 다음의 사항에는 적용하지 않음 (a) 협정문 2항1 (최혜국 대우원칙)과 부합되지 않는 않는 운수권 (b) 운수권을 교환하기 위하여, 협상하는 체약국의 능력을 제한하거나 영향을 주는, 또는 운수권의 사용을 제한하는 효과를 주는 사항과 직접적으로 관련된 서비스의 공급 ;	○ 뉴질랜드의 제안 : 협정의 배제대상을 제3.4항을 제외한 "운수권 및 운수권과 직접적으로 관련된 서비스의 공급"으로 정의하므로 제4항(공공으로 가용하는 서비스에의 접근 또는 사용)의 모든 서비스가 협정의 적용대상이 됨 ○ 기존 우리나라 입장은 "공공으로 가용한 서비스"는 그 성격에 따라 나라별로 차등적용할 수 있는 서비스드 있으므로 제4항은 제외시키는 것이 타당 ○ 따라서 뉴질랜드의 제안에 반대함

0221

관리번호	92-982

원 본

외 무 부

0151

종 별 :

번 호 : GVW-2385 일 시 : 92 1216 1720

수 신 : 장관(통기,아일,경기원,문화부) 사본:주일대사(본부중계필)

발 신 : 주 제네바 대사

제 목 : 대일 시청각 서비스 관련 일본측 서한 접수

대: WGV-1920(JAW-6448)

12.15(화) UR/ 서비스 한일간 양허 협상 시작시 일본측 서비스 양허 협상 수석대표인 KOJI TSURUOKA 는 양국간 협의를 통하여 한국의 대일 시청각 서비스 MFN 일탈 문제가 상호 만족스럽게 처리된 것을 환영하고 그간 협의 결과 합의된 문안대로 동인 명의의 서한을 아국 서비스 양허 협상 수석대표 이윤재 경기원 제 2 협력관에게 전달하였는바, 동 서한 별첨 송부함.

첨부: 대일 시청각 서비스 관련 일본측 서한 1 부. 끝

(GVW(F)-757)

(대사 박수길-국장)

예고 97.12.31. 까지

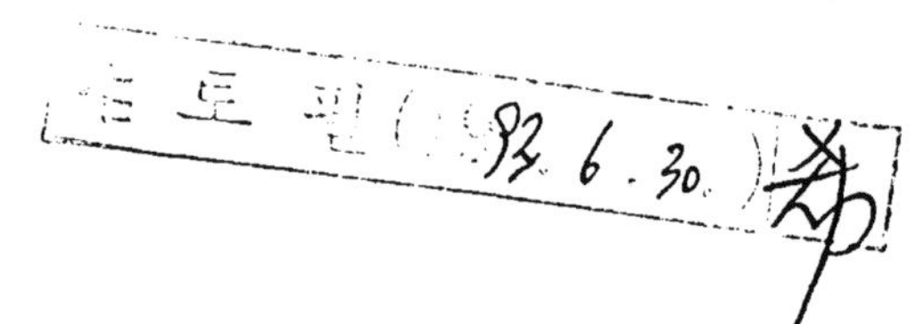

통상국 아주국 문화부 경기원 중계

PAGE 1 92.12.17 05:04

* 원본수령부서 승인없이 복사 금지 외신 2과 통제관 FR

0222

제 네 바 대 표 부

✓

번 호 : GVW(F) - 0757 년월일 : 21216 시간 : 1800

수 신 : 장 관 (통기, 아일, 경기원, 문화부) 사본: 주일대사

발 신 : 주 제네바대사

제 목 : 첨부

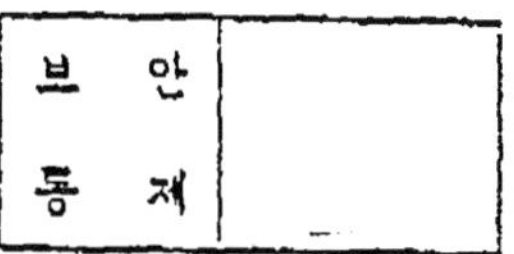

보 안	
통 제	

총 2 매(표지포함)

외신과	
통 제	

757-2-1

16/12/92 20:12 KOREA MISSION GENEVA → 736 7792 NO.640 D01

0223

MISSION PERMANENTE DU JAPON
AUPRÈS DES ORGANISATIONS INTERNATIONALES
GENÈVE - SUISSE

Geneva, 15 December, 1992

Dear Mr Lee,

On behalf of the Japanese delegation to the initial commitment negotiations under the draft General Agreement on Trade in Services of the Uruguay Round (GATS), I wish to inform you of the following in view of the practical solution of the issue, on the basis of the understanding shared by the Japanese and Korean sides in the course of their consultations:

1. It is the view of the Japanese side that under the current circumstances the issue of the existing Korean measures on Japanese audio-visual services in the Republic of Korea is a sensitive socio-political issue. In light of the sensitivity of this issue, the Japanese side considers it inappropriate to address the issue further in the multilateral context of the Uruguay Round.

2. In view of the above, the Japanese side has no intention of taking advantage of the lack of derogation by the Republic of Korea from the most favoured nation treatment obligation under Article II of the GATS with respect to the existing Korean measures on Japanese audio-visual services in the Republic of Korea.

Sincerely yours,

Koji Tsuruoka
Head of the Japanese delegation
to the initial commitment
negotiations under the GATS

Mr Yoon Jae LEE
Head of the Korean delegation
to the initial commitment
negotiations on the GATS
c/o Permanent Mission of the
Republic of Korea
20 route de Pré-Bois
Case Postale 566
1215 GENEVA 15

157-2-2

0224

16/12/92 20:13 KOREA MISSION GENEVA → 735 7792

원 본

외 무 부

0151

종 별 :

번 호 : GVW-2384 일 시 : 92 1216 1720

수 신 : 장 관(수신처 참조)

발 신 : 주제네바대사

제 목 : UR/서비스 양자협상(1)

12.14(월)-12.15(화) 까지 개최된 EC(금융),스웨덴, 뉴질랜드, 일본,인니와의 표제협상관련 주요내용 하기 보고함.

~~1. EC(금융), 스웨덴,뉴질랜드,일본,인니와의표제협상 관련 주요 내용 하기 보고함.~~

1. EC(금융)와의 양자협상(12월 14일 오전)

- EC측은 EC가 관심을 갖고 있는주요국가(한국, ASEAN, 브라질등 남미제국 및인디아등)의 양허 수준제고를 위해 최종협상결과(서비스 분야 전체 및 특정부분 모두포함)의평가시점까지 회원국내의 상호주의 규정의 존치가불가피 하다고 주장하면서 동 상호주의 조치를 12.10제출된 EC측 수정 OFFER 에 예시적으로 제시

0 양허 평가 기준으로 금융부문 전체에 대한STANDSTILL, 상기 주요 국가의 경우 ECO 및효과적인 시장접근 개념에 입각한 금융시장의실제 개방 정도 및 ROLLBACK 여부를 판단기준으로제시

- 구체적으로 EC측은 우리를 상기 주요국가중여타국가와 동일시 하지는 않으나 우리측의 수정양허표를 보지 않은 상태에서 최종적인 평가는곤란하다는 입장을 제시하면서 상기 기준에 비추어우리의 경우

I) ECONOMIC NADES TEST(ENT) 기준의 명료화

II) 업종의 확대(금융리스,크레디카드, 단자,보험대리점등)

III) STANDSTILL 약속

IV) 그리고 회원국 설득을 위해 BLUE PRINT 의양허가 필요함을 주장

0 다만 BP 양허내용(특히 미래시행 예정 조치)의기술상, 법적성격상의 어려운 점을 인정하면서,양허 방법으로 기자유화 조치는 양허하고 기발표미시행자유화조치의경우에는 예를 들어 금융분야COVER NOTE 등에 한국이 자유화

경기원 법무부 보사부 문화부 교통부 체신부 재무부 농수부 상공부
건설부 과기처 해항청 환경처 공보처

PAGE 1 92.12.17 06:34 DX

외신 1과 통제관

0225

조치를 추진중이있다는의향표시(STATEMENT OF INTENT)등을 해주는방안을 제시

- 이에 대해 우리측은 ENT 관련 표현완화,금융리스 및 단자의 경우 업체난립 및금융산업개편 가능성등을 들어 양허가 곤란함을 설명하고BP 상의 미래조치에 대해서는 기 자유화 조치를제외한 여타 미래자유화 조치의 경우 양허 의사가없다는 입장 제시

0 내년초 수정 OFFER 제출시 추후 다시 논의키로 함.

2. 스웨덴과의 양자협상(12월 14일 오후)

- 스웨덴은 지난 협의에 이어 아국 수정 OFFER 가포괄범위나 기술적 측면에서 잘만들어진 것이나인수합병금지, 합작투자요건, ENT등이 아국OFFER 의 질을 저하시키고 있다고 지적한바,아국은 인수 합병문제와 관련 주식시장 개방이직접투자 개방보다는 늦을수 밖에 없기 때문에불가피한 조치이며, 향후 주식시장 개방 진전에 따라완화될수있을 것이라고 하고,합작투자 및ENT등도 일부분야에 한정된 것임을 설명함.

- 금융분야에 있어서 스웨덴은 금융리스, MONKEYBROKING, 송금, 지불 및 정산 서비스등을포괄범위에 추가해 줄것을 요청하였으며 BLUEPRINT 상의 개방계획을 OFFER에 반영해줄것과 ECONOMIC NEDDS TEST 의 기준을 구체적으로밝혀줄 것을 요청함.

- 기본통신 분야 시장접근 협상과 관련 아국은동 협상의 준거기준과 방식등을 논의하는토의에는 계속 참여하겠으며, 동 토의 경과를감안하여 시장접근 협상에의 참여 여부를재검토하겠다고 밝힌바, 스웨덴은 긍정적진전이라고 환영함.

- 스웨덴은 자국의 2차 수정 OFFER 초안을 전달설명하였는바, 아측은 1차적 검토의견으로서 동수정 OFFER 상의 기술적 문제점을 지적함

- 한편, 아측은 MFN 의무 면제와 관련 외국인토지 취득허가시 상호주의가 추가되었으며 해운분야MFN 의무 면제 신청 내용에 일부 변경이있음을 설명함.

3. 뉴질랜드와의 양자협상(12월 14일)- 뉴질랜드는 자국 양허표를 수정하고 있는바,이것이 DRAFT NATIONAL 스케쥴이 될 가능성이높다고 하고 동 스케쥴은 내년 1월중 배포가가능할것이며, 양허표는 가능한한 스케쥴링GUIDANCE 를 준수할 것임을 설명하였음. 그리고CPC CODE 가 포함될것이며 COMPUTER 관련서비스, 광고서비스, 건축설계서비스등이 업종이포함될 것도 아울러 아측에 설명하였음.

- 아측은 뉴측의 요구사항중 교육서비스 관련대표사무소의 설치에 대해 설치는 가능하나학생모집등은 할수 없고, 자료수집,홍보활동등만 가능함을

설명하였으며, 항공서비스중 항공기 유지.수선서비스에 격납고서비스(HANGER 서비스)가 포함되는지 여부에 대한뉴측질의에 대해 우리측은 동 서비스는 포함되지않는다고 답변하였음.

4. 일본(12월 15일 오전)

- 일측 제시 수정 OFFER 에 대해 아측은 추후검토후 아측 의견을 제시하겠다고 하고, 우리는그간의 양자협상 결과 및 스케쥴링 방법상의진전을 반영하여 내년 1월에낼 예정이나, 그구체적 시기는 향후 UR 협상 진전상황을 보고결정할 것임을 표명

0 이에 대해 일측은 한국의 양허수준 평가를위해서는 DRAFT NATIONAL 스케쥴이 빨리제출되어야 할것임을 지적하였음.

- 일측은 아측 MFN 일탈사항중 한.일 항로에대하여 동 일탈 철회를 요구한바, 아측은동제한은 95년 1월부터 폐지될 것이므로 UR타결후 발효싯점을 감안할때 일본해운업체의 영업에 실질적 영향은 없을것임을 전제하고, 동 일탈은 일본을 대상으로한것이 아니라 국내 영세업체 보호를 위한 것으로역사적인 이유로 하여 미국외의 모든나라, 심지어국내업체도 기준에 합치않는 경우 불허하고있다면서 일탈 철회가 불가함을 설명하였음.

- 외국인 토지 취득 MFN 일탈과 관련 일측은자국도 당초 MFN 일탈을 신청했으나외국서비스공급자의 상업적 주재 양허를 실질화하기 위해서자국내부 조정과정이 쉽지 않았음에도 이를철회하였다고 하면서 한국의 외국인 토지 제도의개선을 희망하였음.

0 이에 대해 아측은 아국의 높은 토지가격, 투기등의경험에 비추어 어려움이 많으나 점진적으로제도개선을 하고 있으며, MFN 일탈과관련해서는 이는 현존 우리 법규를 반영한 것이나아국기업에 대해 토지취득을 불허하는 나라에대해서만 상호주의가 적용되는 것이므로 외국에큰 영향을 주는 것은 아니라고 설명하는 한편, 현재 외국인 토지취득 허용업종은 10월 협상시설며한 대로라고 하였음.

- 아측은 일본의 유통관련 개정 제도와 관련추가적으로 매장면적 500 M2 제한 완화와협의절차 단축을요구하면서 실제 유통업인가에소요되는 기간을 질의한바, 일측은 자국제도를설명하고, 법 시행기간이 얼마안되어 실제소요기간이 얼마인지는 알수 없다고 하였음.

- 일본은 건설업 신규면허 발급주기 및도급한도제에 대한 종래의 주장을 되풀이하면서건설 발급주기를 1년으로 단축한다는 한국측보도의 확인을 요청한바,

한국이 건설면허 관련제도를 개선 추진중인 것은 사실이나 발급주기등그 구체적 내용은 아직결정되지 않았으며, 법개정 소요시간을 고려시 개선제도는 내년하반기에나 알수 있을것임을 설명

5. 인도네시아(12월 15일 오후)

- 인니측은 자국 수정 OFFER 는 내년 1월단에4가지 MODE 형태로 CPC CODE 를 포함하여 제출할것이며, 은행, 보험등이 포함될 것임을 설명하는한편, 현재 자국 OFFER상의정책,규정,지침등에 따라 제한이 있음이라는표현을 보다 구체적 조치들로 대체하겠다고하였음.

- 아측은 컴퓨터 관련 서비스(CPC 841,842) 를OFFER 에 포함할 것을 요구한바, 인니측은본부에 이를 전달하겠다고 하였음.

- 아측의 건설 OFFER 요구 및 합작투자 지분제한폐지요구에 대해서는 건설의 경우(비공식적인답변임을 전제) CPC 514,516 상의 서비스가포함될것이며, 합작투자 지분제한은 49 퍼센트이며이를 폐지할 계획이 없음을 설명함.끝

(대사 박수길-국장)

수신처:통기,경기원,재무,법무부,농림수산부 ,상공부,문화부,건설부,교통부,체신부, 보사부,과기처,공보처,환경처,항만청

외 무 부

우 110-760 서울 종로구 세종로 77번지 / 전화(02)720-2331 / FAX(02)725-1737

문서번호 통이 20655-1507
시행일자 1992.12.17.( )

47565

수신 주카나다대사
참조

취급		장 관
보존		代
국 장	전 결	
심의관		
과 장		
기안	홍 지 인	협조

제목 재무부장관 서한 송부

Mazankowski 재무장관의 우리 재무장관앞 서한에 대한 재무부장관의 답신을 별첨 송부하니 적의 전달바랍니다.

첨 부 : 1. 재무부장관 서한 원본 및 사본 1매.
2. Mazankowski 장관 서한 사본 1매. 끝.

외 무 부 장 관

0229

카나다 재무장관 서한 답신('92.11.27)

- 카나다 재무장관 서한 요지

  o UR의 타결은 세계경제 성장에 활력소가 될 것이며, 이러한 관점에서 UR 금융협상에 임하는 각국의 Offer 내용 개선이 요구됨.

  o 카나다는 외국인의 은행 소유 및 지분취득 제한을 철폐하는 등 자유화 조치를 취해 나가고 있음.

  o 한국도 Blueprint의 기 자유화된 조치의 양허등 금융 Offer의 개선을 요망

- 답신 요지

  o 우리나라는 UR의 성공적 타결을 위해 처음부터 적극적으로 협상에 참여하고 있음.

  o 한국 정부도 원화자금 조달 확대, 지점설치 제한 철폐등 폭넓은 시장 개방 조치를 취했으며, 현재 제3단계 시장 개방계획을 작성중임.

  o 각국의 금융 Offer의 개선 필요성에 동감이며 양자 협상 결과를 반영한 National Schedule을 제출할 계획임.

0230

Ministry of Finance

KWACHON, KOREA

OFFICE OF THE MINISTER

December 10, 1992

The Honorable Don Mazankowski
The Minister of Finance of Canada

Your Excellency :

Thank you very much for your letter of November 10 relayed through the Ambassador of Canada in Korea. I would like to take this opportunity to first acknowledge my wholehearted support for your continuing efforts to successfully conclude the Uruguay Round.

I share your view that a satisfactory outcome to the already protracted Uruguay Round negotiations is a very important ingredient in ensuring global prosperity and renewed, non–inflationary growth. To this end, Korea has actively participated in the Uruguay Round negotiations since its inception.

On this occasion, I would like to explain you that the Korean government has begun to take extensive deregulation and market opening measures in the financial industry with regard to local currency funding, branching, foreign exchange, etc. since 1990. Additionally, we are now formulating a three stage blueprint for mid– to long–term financial deregulation and market opening. We believe that these measures will help to improve financial environments of foreign entrants.

0231

With regard to the improvement of offer lists in financial services, I feel that the overall level of offers among the participants needs to be improved. Korean delegation will meet with other delegates, including your country, next week in Geneva to discuss this issue. We will submit a national schedule which will reflect the outcome of the bilateral meetings in Geneva at the agreed time.

Finally, let me again express my appreciation for your efforts to help bring about a positive and fruitful outcome to the Uruguay Round negotiations.

Sincerely yours,

Yong-Man Rhee
Minister of Finance

0232

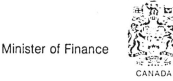

Minister of Finance 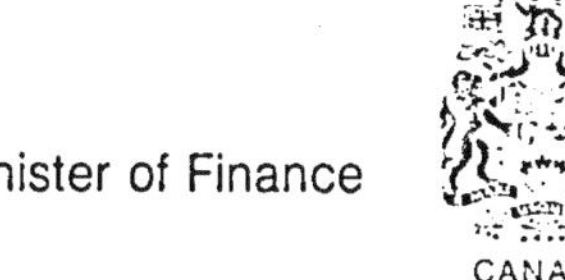 Ministre des Finances

CANADA

NOV 10 1992

Dear Minister:

I am writing to you in regard to the Uruguay Round financial services negotiations in view of our common policy responsibilities in this area. The financial services liberalization commitments undertaken by participants in the negotiations are a critical element to the success of the services negotiations and of the Round as a whole. They are important as well in strengthening support for the Round among the private sector. It is increasingly evident that a successful Uruguay Round would contribute to renewed economic growth worldwide.

With concerted effort on the part of participants in the services negotiations, we were able to develop a good draft multilateral framework of rules for trade in services. Specially adapted rules for financial services were included in recognition of the importance of the sector and the need to maintain the ability to take measures for prudential reasons. In addition to rules, however, there is need for a meaningful package of financial services liberalization commitments on the part of all participants. My colleague, the Honourable Michael Wilson, Minister for International Trade, wrote to Trade Ministers last May, stressing the importance of ensuring that key service sectors, including financial, are adequately covered by liberalization commitments.

.../2

His Excellency Mr. Rhee Yong Man
Minister of Finance
171-11 Chungang Dong
Kwachon
Kyonggi'do
427-760
Republic of Korea

0233

Ottawa, Canada K1A 0G5

Our services negotiators have reported some progress in the recent set of bilateral discussions in Geneva. However, there remain some important obstacles to market access and national treatment in a number of markets of particular importance to us. I am concerned that insufficient commitments in this sector may compromise the full involvement of financial services in the Round. I think you would agree that it would be an unfortunate development for all concerned if this involvement were reduced or eliminated.

For our part, Canada is now indicating its readiness to contribute to the Uruguay Round outcome by making an additional commitment to remove the foreign ownership and acquisition restrictions that form part of the federal financial services legislation. (These restrictions are the 10% individual and the 25% collective limitations on the foreign ownership of Canadian-controlled federally-regulated financial institutions and the 12% asset ceiling on the size of the foreign bank sector in Canada.) We view this as a significant move which will effectively fully liberalize access to Canada's financial services market. It indicates our strong commitment to these negotiations and we hope other countries will decide to take comparable steps.

Other possible improvements in the Canadian services offer have also been mentioned in bilateral discussions, notably in respect of the temporary movement of service personnel. This would be, inter alia, of direct benefit to your services exporters.

I would therefore appreciate that you reassess your current financial services offer with a view to undertaking additional liberalization commitments, notably in regard to local currency funding and the requirement for allocating 35% of loans to small- and medium-sized companies. With respect to Korea's three-stage economic liberalization plan, an undertaking to bind in Korea's GATS schedule relevant reforms as they enter into force would be in order.

Yours sincerely,

0234

0141

관리번호	92-988

원 본

외 무 부

종 별 :

번 호 : GVW-2388 일 시 : 92 1217 1900

수 신 : 장관(통기,경기원,재무부,경제수석) 사본:주미대사(본부중계필)

발 신 : 주 제네바 대사

제 목 : UR/서비스 한.미 양자 협상(금융)

연: GVW-2384

1. 협의 개요

- 12.14(월) 부터 당지 개최중인 UR 서비스 분야 양자 협상중 12.15(화) 14:00-16:00 까지 한. 미간에 금융분야에 대한 협상이 진행되었음.

- 미측은 UR 서비스 협상이 전세계적으로 현존 규제 수준의 동결(GLOBAL STANDSTILL)뿐만 아니라 실질적으로 서비스 교역의 자유화 수준을 제고시키기 위한 것임에 비추어 우리의 금융 및 보험 양허표는 이러한 기대에 미치지 못하는등양허수준이 매우 미흡하다고 상당한 불만을 제기하면서 미국의회 및 업계를 설득할수 있도록 미측 요구사항을 반영해 줄것을 구체적 예를 들어가며 요청함.

- 이에 대해 아측은 그간 FPT, BLUE PRINT 작업 계획등을 통한 미측 요구 수용 노력을 설명하고 아국의 금융 산업 발전 단계를 감안시 급속한 자유화 추진및 미측 요구사항의 추가적 반영이 어려움을 설명하였으나 미측은 미측의 입장을 본국정부에 전달 재차 검토해 줄것을 요청함.

2. 협의 내용

- 미측은 우리 금융분야 양허 수준의 제고를 위해 구체적으로 한국이 다음 조치를 취해줄 것을 요구

1) 최소한 미 양허된 업종을 포함한 금융분야 전체에 대한 STANDSTILL 약속및 양허 업종(COVERAGE)의 확대

0 금융 리스, 단자, 결제서비스, 환, 데이타처리등 중요한 금융 활동의 양허

0 특히 아직 한국에 없는 업종이라고 하더라도 양허표상에 "새로운 업종(상품)의 영업이 가능하다고 약속 또는 신규 업종 도입시 내.외국인 제한 없음"등으로 양허가 가능함을 설명

통상국 장관 차관 2차보 미주국 분석관 청와대 안기부 경기원
재무부 중계

92.12.18 10:03

외신 2과 통제관 BX

0235

2) BLUE PRINT 상의 미래 자유화 조치(주로 3 단계 조치)에 대한 시행 및 GATS 하의 양허(BINDING) 의사 표명

0 BP 상의 미시행조치(주로 제 3 단계 미래 자유화)에 대해 시행시기 및 양허의사를 분명히 하는 것은 (1) 현재 미 의회 및 업계에 BP 상의 조치가 즉시 시행되고 또 바로 BINDING 되어야 한다는 강한 움직임. (STRONG SENTIMENT)이 있고, (2) 대한 진출 미국 금융기관의 실질적 영업활동 능력 개선과 관련된 주요 조치가 BP 3 단계 사항과 직결되어 있으며,(3) 한국측으로 부터 이들 미래 시행 예정인 주요 조치에 대한 확고한 이행 담보를 얻기 위해서도 필요하고, (4) UR 협상 자체가 기자유화 및 향후 자유화 조치에 대한 양허 약속(BINDING) 을 얻기 위한 것임을 감안시 미국내 의회 및 업계 설득을 위해서도 불가피하다고 하면서

0 동 양허 내용은 "BP 상의 미래 조치를 시행한 것이며 일단 시행될 경우 이를 BINDING (즉 동 조치보다 후퇴된 조치는 채택하지 않겠다는 약속) 할것이라는 약속(COMMITMENT)" 이라고 설명하고

0 구체적 예로 "한국은 미래의 MA/NT 관련 조치를 시행시 양허표에 이를 BINDING 할것" 이라는 등의 방법을 제시

3) 미측 기 요구사항(REQUEST LIST) 중 미수용 사항에 대해 UR 협상 기간중구체적, 실질적 자유화 조치 추진과 최종 양허표의 반영

0 BP, 1,2 단계 및 FPT 등을 통한 한국의 그간의 기자유화 조치는 대한 진출 미국 금융기관의 원화 자금 조달등 제반 현안을 근본적으로 타결시키지 못하고 있고(MARGINALLY IMPROVED), 근본적 개선 조치와 직결된 BP 3 단계가 '97 년 이후로 시행시기가 잡혀있어 한국이 BP 에 대한 양허를 하더라도 당장 시급한 현안이 해결되지는 못하는바, 금번 협상기간중 원화자금 조달 개선 요구등 미측 요구사항에 대한 구체적, 가시적 조치가 시행되고 최종 양허표에 BINDIN 바 되어야대의회, 업계에 UR 금융분야 PACKAGE 설득(SELLING) 이 가능할 것임을 주장

0 구체적인 예로 CD 발행 한도의 경우 200 % 에서 225 % 로의 인상등 PIECEMEAL 조치가 아닌 최소한 본점 자본금에 연계 또는 철폐가 구체적, 가시적 조치로 간주될 수 있을 것이라고 설명하고, 아울러 단편적 조치가 여러개 이루어 졌다고 해서 근본적 개선이 이루어지는 것은 아님을 지적함.

4) 아국 서비스 분야 OFFER 상에 PRUDENTIAL REGULATIONS 으로 기재된 사항들이 정상적인 PRUDENTIAL MEASURES 의 범위를 초과하여 과도(EXCESSIVE)하며 경제적

필요성 검토(ENT) 로 기재된 사항도 매우 주관적이라고 지나침.

0 이들이 시장접근을 제한할 가능성이 많은점을 감안하여 이들을 정상적인 PRUDENTIAL REGULATIONS 으로 한정(정상적인 PRUDENTIAL CARVE-OUT 으로 금융제도의 건전성 및 안정성과 관련된 것만 규제) 한정하고 TRANSPARENCY 목적으로 열거가 필요한 경우를 제외하고는 이를 양허표에서 삭제할 것과 ENT 기준도 명료화또는 폐지가 필요함.

5) 금융 부속서상의 UNDERSTANDING 에 따른 금융분야 양허표의 작성

0 과거 UNDERSTANDING (즉 금융부속서 선진 4 개국안) 상의 한국측이 문제삼던 내국민 대우의 ECO 개념 및 자율 규제 단체(SRO)가 삭제된 이상 우리측이 협정상의 UNDERSTANDING 에 따라 양허해야 기존 입장과 일관성이 있고 또 양허 수준의 실질적 제고에도 기여할수 있을 것이라고 함.

- 이러한 미측 요구에 대해 우리측은 그간 우리측의 FPT 등을 통한 미측 요구 수용 노력을 설명하고 금융 산업의 발전단계등을 감안 시급한 자유화는 곤란하며 BP 미래 자유화 조치의 양허도 거시경제 여건과의 연계성을 고려시 기 자유화 조치 이외에는 양허하기 어렵다는 입장을 제시하였음. 아울러 현단계에서 미측 요구사항에 대한 추가적인 구체적 조치도 취할수 없음을 지적함.

- 이에 대해 미측은 아직 협상 종료전까지는 시간이 있음을 지적하면서 상기 미측 입장을 본부에 전달, 검토해 줄것을 재차 요구하였음.

나. 보험.

- 미측은 아국의 보험분야 양허 수준 제고를 위해 다음 조치를 취해줄 것예정요구

1) 미측 요구사항인 독립 대리점등의 허용시기가 너무 늦고 BINDING 도 되어 있지 않음에 비추어 이의 조속한 허용과 함께 양허를 요구함.

2) 최근 보험사에 대한 업무용 토지 취득 허용 기준, 범위등이 매우 제한적이고 또 부자용 토지 취득을 허용않는 것은 NT 위배 사항이므로 업무용 토지 취득 허용기준 및 범위의 완화 및 부자용 토지 취득 허용을 촉구

3) 국내사 우선 추재제도 및 요율 협정 철폐등 재보험 자유화의 기간(TIME SPAN)이 장기에 걸쳐 이루어지도록 되어 있는 점에 비추어 이의 조기 자유화 및BINDING 요구

4) 신상품 인가등 상품인가 절차의 명료성 제고 및 단축등을 요구

- 상기 미측 요구사항에 대한 우리측 입장 제시는 시간 관계상 12.16(수) 09:00-12:00 한미간 금융분야 이외 양자 협의시 논의키로 함. 끝

(대사 박수길-국장)
예고 93.12.31. 까지

PAGE 4

0238

이시

원 본

외 무 부

종 별 :

번 호 : GVW-2383 일 시 : 92 1217 1030

수 신 : 장관(통기,경기원,재무부,교통부,체신부)

발 신 : 주제네바대사

제 목 : UR/GNS 비공식협의(5)

연: GVW-2360

12.14(월)-12.15(화) 간의 표제관련 21조(양허수정), 항공부속서, 통신 부속서 및 조세문제에 대한 주요 협의 내용 하기 보고함.

1. 협의개요

- 21조는 12.9 일 회의결과(GVW-2338)대로 별다른 이견없이 별첨 수정안을 배포하여 논의를 종결하고 양허수정 절차에 대해서는 추후 검토키로 하였음.

- 통신부속서에 대해서는 별다른 이견이 없었으나 인도 및 이집트는 5.2항(원가지향 가격책정)과 관련 이견을 계속 제시하였음.

- 항공부속서는 사무국 수정안(12.14일자)을 중심으로 논의를 하였으나 합의에 도달하지 못하였고 조세문제에 대해서도 결론을 내리지 못하고 추후 재론키로 하였음.

2. 협의내용

1) 항공부속서

- 미국측은 서비스 협정은 항공관련 양자 또는 다자간 협정(시카고 협약등)상의권리와 의무관계에 영향을 미치지 않는다는 것이 공통인식이라고 하면서, 사무국 수정안 2항은 이러한 인식을 반영한 것이며 따라서 운수권 및 3항의 세가지 보조서비스외의 모든 운수권 관련 보조서비스는 협정 적용 배제대상으로 확인해 둘필요가 있다고 하였음.

이에 대해 EC도 별다른 이의를 제기하지 않았음.

- 뉴질랜드는 현행 부속서 수정안 2항은 운수권 관련사항의 양허 가능성 자체를봉쇄하고 있으므로 별첨과 같이 이를 수정하거나 새로운 항을 만들어 3항 보조서비스외에도 각국이 운수권 및 관련 보조서비스(특히 지상조업) 양허를 할수 있는 가능성을 개방해 놓을 필요가 있다고 주장한바, EC 는 뉴질랜드안이 너무

통상국 교통부 체신부 경기원 재무부

PAGE 1

92.12.19 00:13 EI

외신 1과 통제관 ✓

0239

호호하고 항공권자체에 영향을 줄수 있다고 하고 2항 B 에 'EXCEPT WHERE A MEMBER HAS MADE A SPECIFIC COMMITMENT INITS SCHEDULE' 로 하자고 한바, 미국은 이에 반대의견을 표시함.

- EC 는 부속서 제 4항은 2항 논의와 연계되어 있으므로 동시 검토가 필요하다고 한바 미국은 양자협정 대상인 운수권 (HARD RIGHT)과 보조서비스 (SOFT RIGHT)의 구분에 어려운 점이 많으므로 현행 규정대로 할것을 주장함.

- 수정안 5항 전단(분쟁해결)은 2항에 'THE AGREEMENT INCLUDING ITS DISPUTE SETTLEMENT PROCEDURES'조항을 추가키로 함.

- 수정안 제 6항 서비스 교역 이사회의 검토대상과 관련 운수권등도 동 대상에 포함된다는데 대부분 의견을 같이하고, 그표현과 관련 EC 가 동항끝에 'WITH A VIEW TO CONSIDERING THE POSSIBLE APPLICATION OF MULTILATERAL UNDER STNADING IN THIS SECTOR'를 추가할 것을 제의하였음.

- 사무국 DRAFT 7항(정의)와 관련

0 EC 는 동항(A) 사무국 수정안에서 '...WITHRAWN FORM SERVICES' 란 표현이 삽입됨으로써 항공수선 유지서비스의 범위가 지나치게 제한적으로 되었다고 하고 이는 2항과 동시 검토가 필요하다고 하는 한편 LINE MAINTENANCE 와 관련 항공기 PAINTING등은 포함되어야 한다는 입장을 밝힘.

0 (D) 운수권의 정의와 관련 EC 는 동항 용어중 'PERSONS'는 'PASSENGERS' 로,'PROPERTY' 는 CARGO 로 수정하자고 하였음.

한편 현행 수정안상의 지정 항공사(AIR-LINES TOBE DESIGNATED) 란 표현을 수정하여 지정 항공사의수, 소유권 및 지배로 하자는 것에 대해서는 의견이 대립되었음.

2) 조세문제

- 사무국은 서비스협정상의 조세조치 예외에 대해 별첨 자료를 통하여 어떤 조세가 14조 적용대상이 될려면 제 17조 또는 제 2조 의무를 위반한 경우이어야 한다고하고, 대부분의 조세조치는 제 17조또는 제 2조에 합치되며 제 14조 대상은 별로없을 것임을 설명하고, 특히 내국민 대우 차별판단 요건의 하나인 LIKENESS 에 비추어 거주자인공급자와 비거주자인 공급자는 LIKENESS 가 없으므로 거주여부에 기초를 둔조세조치는 내국민대우 위반이 되지 않을 것이라고 하였음.

0 이에대해 일본은 사무국에 예시를 들어 보다 구체적으로 문서를 재작성하여

줄것을 요청하였고, EC 는 거주자 문제를 제 14조 논의대상에서 완전 배제하는 것은 곤란하다고 지적하였음.

- 조세문제에 대해서 미.EC 는 12.12(토)일자 자국안(기송부)의 입장을 견지하였으며 각국의 이견도 상존하여 논의가 진전되지 못하였음.

0 다만, 미국의 22조에 대한 수정안에 대해서는 일부 자구문제를 제외하고 별다른 반대가 없었음. 첨부: 1. 21조 협정문 수정안

2. 12.14 일자 항공부속서 및 뉴질랜드측 수정제안

3. 조세관세 관련 사무국측 설명문 각 1부

(GVW(F)-0758).끝

(대사 박수길-국장)

0771

주 제 네 바 대 표 부

번 호 : GVW(F) - 0758 년월일 : 21216 시간 : 1720

수 신 : 장 관 (통기, 경기원, 재무부, 교통부, 체신부)

발 신 : 주 제네바대사

제 목 : UR/GNS 비공식 협의(3)

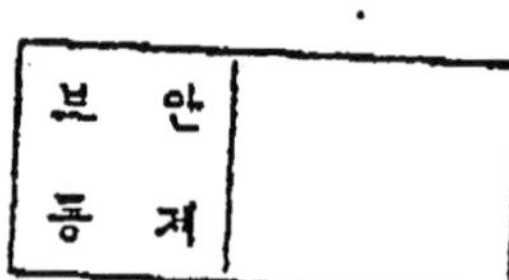
보 안	
통 제	

외신국	
통 제	

총 10 매(표지포함)

배부처	장관실	차관실	一차보	二차보	외정실	분석관	아주국	미주국	구주국	중아국	국기국	경제국	통상국	문협국	외연원	청와대	안기부	공보처	경기원	상공부	재무부	농수부	동자부	환경처	과기처	교통부	체신부
													O						/		/					/	/

758-10-1

0242

16/12/92 20:13 KOREA MISSION GENEVA → 736 7792 NO.640

DRAFT

14.12.92

Group of Negotiations on Services

ARTICLE XXI: MODIFICATION OF SCHEDULES

1. (a) A Member (hereafter in this Article referred to as the "modifying Member") may modify or withdraw any commitment in its Schedule, at any time after three years have elapsed from the date on which that commitment entered into force, in accordance with the provisions of this Article.

(b) A modifying Member shall notify its intent to modify or withdraw a commitment pursuant to this Article to the Council on Trade in Services no later than three months before the intended date of implementation of the modification or withdrawal.

2. (a) At the request of any Member whose benefits under this Agreement may be affected (hereafter "an affected Member") by a proposed modification or withdrawal notified under paragraph 1(b), the modifying Member shall enter into negotiations with a view to reaching agreement on any necessary compensatory adjustment. In such negotiations and agreement, the Members concerned shall endeavour to maintain a general level of mutually advantageous commitments not less favourable to trade than that provided for in schedules of specific commitments prior to such negotiations.

(b) Compensatory adjustments shall be made on a most-favoured-nation basis.

3. (a) If agreement is not reached between the modifying Member and any affected Member before the end of the period provided for negotiations, such affected Member may refer the matter to arbitration. Any affected Member that wishes to enforce a right

958-10-2

0243

20-ART2

that it may have to compensation must participate in the arbitration.

(b) If no affected Member has requested arbitration, the modifying Member shall be free to implement the proposed modification or withdrawal.

4. (a) The modifying Member may not modify or withdraw its commitment until it has made compensatory adjustments in conformity with the findings of the arbitration.

(b) If the modifying Member implements its proposed modification or withdrawal and does not comply with the findings of the arbitration, any affected Member that participated in the arbitration may modify or withdraw substantially equivalent benefits in conformity with those findings. Notwithstanding Article II, such a modification or withdrawal may be implemented solely with respect to the modifying party.

5. The Council on Trade in Services shall establish procedures for rectification or modification of schedules of commitments. Any Member which has modified or withdrawn scheduled commitments under this Article shall modify its schedule according to such procedures.

758-10-3

0244

20-ART2

Draft
14.12.92

ANNEX ON AIR TRANSPORT SERVICES[1]

1. This Annex applies to measures affecting trade in air transport services, whether scheduled or **non-scheduled**, and ancillary services.

2. The Agreement shall not apply to measures affecting:

(a) traffic rights, **however granted**; or

(b) **services directly related to the exercise of traffic rights,**

except as provided in paragraph 3 of this Annex.

3. The Agreement shall apply to measures affecting:

(a) aircraft repair and maintenance services;

(b) the selling **and** marketing of air transport services;

(c) computer reservation **system** (CRS) services.

4. Each Party shall ensure that access to and use of publicly available services offered within or from its territory is accorded to air services providers of other Parties on reasonable and non-discriminatory terms and

---

[1] Text in bold indicates changes from the draft contained in the Final Act.

0245

158-10-4

N-MISC5

16/12/92 20:14 KOREA MISSION GENEVA → 736 7792 NO.640 D04

conditions where commitments for such **publicly available services** have been made and unless otherwise specified in its schedule.*

5. **The dispute settlement procedures of the Agreement shall not apply to the rights and services described in paragraph 2.** The dispute settlement **procedures** of the Agreement may be invoked only where obligations or commitments have been assumed by the concerned Parties and where dispute settlement procedures in **bilateral and other multilateral regimes** have been exhausted.

6. **The Council for Trade in Services shall review periodically, or at least every five years, the operation of this Annex and air transport and ancillary services.**

7. Definitions:

(a) "aircraft repair and maintenance **services**" **mean** activities, **during which an aircraft is withdrawn from service,** required on a regular or *ad hoc* basis in order to guarantee the operational airworthiness of aircraft. **These activities do not include line maintenance.**

(b) **"selling and marketing of air transport services" mean** opportunities for the air carrier concerned to sell and market freely its air transport services including all aspects of marketing such as market research, advertising and distribution. **These activities do not include the pricing of air transport services nor the applicable conditions.**

---

*The content of this paragraph will depend on the outcome of the work relating to legal clarification of the definitions contained in Article XXXIV.

758-10-5 N-MISC5 0246

(c) "computer reservation system (CRS) services" mean services provided by computerized systems that contain information about air carriers' schedules, availability, fares and fare rules, through which reservations can be made or tickets may be issued.

(d) "traffic rights" mean the right for scheduled and non-scheduled carriers to operate and/or to carry persons, property and mail for remuneration or hire from, to, within, or over the territory of a Party, including points to be served, routes to be operated, types of traffic to be carried, capacity to be provided, tariffs to be charged and their conditions, and airlines to be designated.

958-10-6

N-MISC5 0247

Pour Mémoire

- It has been suggested that in drafting the Annex on Air Transport Services there was a common understanding among participants that nothing in the Agreement should undermine or diminish rights and obligations that exist through the network of aviation bilateral and multilateral agreements, including the Chicago Convention. In that regard, the following language has been proposed to be added to the end of paragraph 1:

"Commitments made or obligations assumed under this Annex shall not diminish parties' rights and obligations under pre-existing bilateral and multilateral regimes."

- Based on the understanding that the excepting of measures affecting traffic rights from the Agreement relates solely to the application of Article II on m.f.n. treatment, it has been proposed that the following language be inserted after "traffic rights," in paragraph 2(a):

"when granted in a manner not consistent with Article II.1 of the Agreement;"

- Matters relating to paragraph 4 have been the subject of inconclusive consultations.

- It has been suggested that the addition of "number, ownership and control of" before "airlines" in the sixth line of paragraph 7(d) could provide for greater clarity. Those not in favour of the addition have noted that ownership and control of flag airlines are not necessarily subsumed under the notion of "designation of airlines" and could, in the absence of any mention under paragraph 7(d), be subjected to the application of the Agreement.

758-10-7 N-MISC5 0248

16/12/92 20:15 KOREA MISSION GENEVA → 736 7792 NO.640

1

NZ

Below are suggested alternatives to language contained in the draft Annex on Air Transport Services dated 14.12.92. Changes are shown in bold typeface.

para. 2

(I)

2 **Save to the extent that a specific commitment has been inscribed in a Member's schedule** the Agreement...

or

2 bis

Notwithstanding paragraph 2 above nothing in this Annex shall prevent a Member from inscribing in its schedule a specific commitment on a measure affecting trade in air transport services within the meaning of this Annex.

para. 6.

(II)

6 ...ancilliary services. **A review shall include an**

958-10-8

0249

16/12/92 20:16 KOREA MISSION GENEVA → 736 7792 NO.640 D1

examination of whether the conditions which created the need for [this Annex] [paragraph 2 of this Annex] still prevail and consider possible multilateral undertakings on measures [affecting trade in air transport services within the meaning of this Annex] [falling within its scope].

2.

158-10-1

0250

16/12/92 20:16 KOREA MISSION GENEVA → 736 7792 NO.640

DRAFT

15.12.92

EXEMPTIONS FOR TAX MEASURES IN THE GATS

Tax measures affecting service suppliers require no justification under Article XIV (General Exceptions) unless they violate an obligation or commitment under the Agreement. The two relevant provisions in this respect are Article XVII (National Treatment) and Article II (M.f.n).

Under Article XVII, at least three conditions must be met before a tax (or any other) measure constitutes a violation of national treatment: the service suppliers must be "like"; the distinct treatment must be based on the national origin of the service or service supplier; and the treatment must be less favourable. To the extent that service suppliers in different jurisdictions are not "like", a tax measure based on residency would not violate national treatment. Further, distinctions without a link to national origin would not normally violate national treatment provisions, such as distinctions based on objective criteria like rates of taxation or level of distribution of profits. Finally, any formally different treatment accorded would have to result in conditions of competition less favourable. Measures designed to ensure the neutrality or integrity of the taxation system can be viewed as ensuring that service suppliers, in the structuring of their transactions, do not benefit from conditions of competition more favourable than others in similar circumstances. In Article II (M.f.n.) these considerations also apply: for a violation to occur, there must be likeness between service suppliers, a distinction based on national origin and conditions of competition less favourable.

In summary, it would appear that relatively few tax measures (affecting service suppliers) require justification under Article XIV (General Exceptions). Most tax measures providing distinct treatment to different categories of service supplier appear to deal with unlike service suppliers, be based on objective considerations, or not in fact accord less favourable conditions of competition.

158-10-10

0251

원 본

외 무 부

종 별 :

번 호 : GVW-2406 일 시 : 92 1218 2000

수 신 : 장관(수신처 참조)

발 신 : 주 제네바 대사

제 목 : UR/ 서비스 양자 협상(3)

수신처:통기,통이,경기원,재무부,법무부,농림수산부,상공부,문화부,건설부,교통부,체신부,보사부,과기처,공보처,환경처,항만청)

연: GVW-2388

12.16(수) 개최된 미국(금융이외) 및호주(금융이외), 스위스와의 표제 양자 협상내용을 하기 보고함.

1. 각국 공통 논의사항

- 미국 및 호주는 각각 자국의 수정 OFFER초안(미국: 3차 수정, 호주: 2차 수정)을 전달하고 동초안의 주요 내용을 설명함.

0 양국 공히 서비스 공급형태를 구분하여 작성하였으며, 포괄범위가 일부 확대됨.

- 아국은 최종 양허표 초안을 작성중에 있다고 밝히고 동 초안상의 주요 내용을설명하는 한편동 초안을 '93년 1월중 배포할 계획이나 최종배포 여부는 전체 협상의진전 상황에 달려있다고 함.

0 스위스 역시 수정 OFFER 작성 과정에 있으며, '93년 1월중 배포할 예정이라고함.

- 한편, 아국은 MFN 일탈과 관련 외국인 토지취득에 관한 상호주의 조치를 추가한 MFN 일탈신청 목록을 갓트 사무국에 제출할 계획이라고 밝혔는바, 미국은 동 일탈신청으로 인하여 아국 OFFER 상의 리스에 대한 COMMITMENT 까지도 철회된다면 심각한문제라고 강한 우려를 표명

- 기본 통신분야 시장접근 협상 참여 문제와관련 아국은 협상 방식 MFN 문제등을논의하는 절차적 토의에는 계속 참여하겠으며, 시장접근 협상에의 참여 여부도 동 분야의 기술발전, 소비자 수요등을 고려하여 아국입장을 재검토하고 있다고 밝혔는바,미국 및 호주는 제한적인 것이기는 하나 긍정적 진전이라고 환영함.

2. 국가별 논의 사항

통상국 법무부 보사부 문화부 체신부 경기원 재무부 농수부
상공부 건설부 노동부 과기처 해항청 환경처 공보처 통상국

PAGE 1 92.12.19 09:58 CJ

외신 1과 통제관

0252

가. 미국

1) 한.미 양자간 합의사항 이행의 서면 보장 문제

- 미국은 지난 10월 협의에 이어 새로운 포괄적협정이 과거의 양자간 합의를 OVERRIDE 하는것이 선례라고 하면서 '80년대 이후 한.미간 서비스분야 합의사항을 UR 결과 발효이후에도 계속 이행하겠다는 서면 보장을 해줄것을 강력히 요구하였는바

0 아국은 양허표라는 것은 최소한의 대우(최대한의 규제)를 약속하는 것이기 때문에 보다 나은 대우부여를 배제하지 않는다는 점, 손해 보험의 경우 한.미간 합의대로 양허할 경우 제 3국(일본)이 미국회사에 앞서 진입할 것이기 때문에 미국의 상업적 이익이 침해된다는 점, 다자간 협상에서 새로운 양자 협정을 체결할 경우 전체 UR팩키지에 대한 국내 동의를 얻기 어렵다는점등을 들어 이를 거부함.

- 이에 대해 미국은 다른 가능성(양자 채널에서의 해결등)을 찾아보겠다고 하였는바 아국은 양자채널을 통해 해결코자 한다면 UR/다자간 협상이 종료된 이후에 협의를 시작하여야 할 것이라고 지적함.

2) 회계 서비스

아국은 국내 회계법인과 국제회계법인과의 제휴, 국제적 상호의 병기 사용등 현재 허용되고있는 사항과 미국법인과 한국법인과의 실제제휴 현황등을 상세히 설명하였는바, 미국은 이에 대해 상당한 만족을 표시하였으며, 다만 동내용을 양허표에 어떻게 반영할 것인지 그방법에 관하여 상호 연기키로 함.

3) 법률 서비스

- 미국은 현재 법률 분야의 각국 OFFER 내용이 매우 부실한 상황이라고 전제하고다른 나라들의 OFFER 가 충분하지 못할 경우에는 동 분야에 MFN 일탈을 추가하겠다고하는 한편 UR 서비스협상에서 법률 서비스 개방을 더이상 요구하지않는다고 하여 그것이 미국의 관심이 철회되는것으로 오해되어서는 안되며, 오히려 동 문제를 양자차원에서 보다 강력히 촉구하겠다는 의도임을 강조함.

4) 보험

- 미국은 독립대리점업 허용, 외국보험사의 토지취득 허용범위 확대, 국내재보험사 우선 출재의무 폐지, 신상품에 대한 인가제도 개선등을 요구하였는바

- 아국은 독립대리점, 국내재보험사 우선 출재에대해서는 기존입장에 변화가 없음을 밝히고, 신상품에 대한 인가의 경우에는 신상품의 99퍼센트가 사전 허가없이 도입 되고 있음을 설명함.

0 외국 보험사의 토지취득 허용범위에 대해서는 내국민 대우(총 자산의 10 퍼센트 이내에서의 부동산 취득)가 이루어지고 있다는 점을 납득하였으나, 부동산 취득전일정기간 영업실적 요건(지사 7년, 합작투자 5년) 및 최소 자산보유조건 (지사 20억원, 자회사 200억원)에 대하여는 내국민 대우 위반이라는 문제가 지적됨.

나. 호주

- 호주는 호주 회계사의 자격인정, 법률분야 OFFER를 계속 요청하였으나 아국은수용불가 입장을밝힘.

다. 스위스

- 스위스는 금융분야와 관련 ECONOMIC NEEDS TEST에 대한 우려를 표명하였으며,유통분야의 경우일반 무역업과 무역 중개업이 제외된점과 ECONOMIC NEEDS TEST 에 대한 우려를 표명하였는바, 아국은 일반 무역과 무역 중개업은 아국에 특수한 업태이며 CPC 상의 일반적인 도매업에는 별다른 제한이 없으며, ECONOMIC NEEDSTEST 도 일반도매시장등 극히 한정된 사항에한하여 적용되고 있다고 설명하였음. 끝

(대사 박수길-국장)

0141

원 본

외 무 부

종 별 :

번 호 : GVW-2407 일 시 : 92 1218 2000

수 신 : 장관(수신처 참조)

발 신 : 주 제네바 대사

제 목 : UR/서비스 양자 협상(4)

수신처:(통기,경기원,재무부,법무부,농림수산부,상공부,문화부,건설부,교통부,체신부,보사부,과기처,공보처,환경처,항만청)

연: GVW-2406

12.17(목)-12.18(금)간 개최된 EC, 카나다,태국과의 표제 양자 협상 주요 내용 하기 보고함.

1. 각국 공통 사항

- EC 및 카나다는 각각 자국의 수정 OFFER 초안과 NATIONAL 스케쥴 초안의 주요내용을 설명하였는바, 양국 모두 서비스 공급 형태를 구분하여 작성하였으며, (EC 의경우 해외 소비와 국경간 공급구분이 어려웠음을 언급), 포괄범위가 일부 확대되었음을 설명하였음.

- 아국은 각국 수정 OFFER 에 대한 향후 COMMENT를 유보하고, 한국도 최종 양허표 초안을 작성중에 있다고 밝히고, 동 초안상의 주요내용을 설명하는 한편, 동 초안을 93년 1월중 배포할 계획이나 최종 배포여부는 전체 협상의 진전 상황에 달려 있다고 설명하였음.

2. 국가별 논의사항

가. EC (12월 17일 오전)

- EC 는 자국 수정 OFFER 설명과 관련 금융분야에서 금번 OFFER 작성시 폐지한 제한사항 목록을 아측에 전달하였으며, 아울러 96년까지 철폐 예정이던 부가가치 통신제한 사항을 GATS 발효와 동시에 철폐할 것임과 해운분야의 경우 최근 해운 비공식협의시 논의되고 있는 거의 모든 분야를 OFFER 하였으나 다만 미국을 고려, 조건부 OFFER 임을 명시하였음을 설명하였음.

- EC 는 한국에서의 외국인 부동산 취득과관련 건물과 토지를 분리하여 매매가

통상국		법무부	보사부	문화부	교통부	체신부	경기원	재무부
농수부	상공부	건설부	과기처	해항청	환경처	공보처		

PAGE 1 92.12.19 07:38 DW

외신 1과 통제관

0255

가능하다 하나 실제에 있어 분리매매되는 경우는 별로 없는 상황에서 토지 취득제한을한다는 것은 사실상 건물 취득 자체도 어렵게 하는 것이라고 지적하면서 한국정부가건물과 토지의 분리 매매 할성화방안을 모색해 볼 것을 제의하였음.

0 이에 대해 아측은 건물과 토지의 동시 매매는 민간 계약상의 문제로서 정부가분리 매매활성화를 요구하는 것은 곤란하다고 한바, EC측은 구체적 IDEA 를 제시할수는 없지만 한국정부가 추가 검토해 줄것을 재차 요청함.

- EC 는 특히 해운분야가 금융분야 다음으로 높은 관심 분야라고 하면서 한국의 OFFER 범위를 질의한바, 아측은 CARGO HANDLING SERVICES, CUSTOMS CLEARANCE SERVICES, CONTAINER STATION SERVICES 등은 OFFER 에서 제외될 것임을 설명하였음.

0 이에 대해 EC 는 많은 나라의 예에 따라 우리나라 OFFER 도 카알라일 PAPER 방식에 따른 양허가 필요하다고 하면서 주요국가의 해운분야에서의 자유화가 진전되어야만 미국도 해운MFN 원칙 일탈을 철회를 고려할 것이며, 그렇지않을 경우 해운 분야 자체가 서비스 협정에서 빠져버릴 위험이 있으므로 아측의 극히 신중한 검토(VERY CAREFUL CONSIDERATION)를 요청하였음.

나. 카나다(12월 17일 오후)

- 카나다는 기본 통신 개방관련 아측 입장을 질의하였던바, 아측은 현재 진행중인 기본통신 개방협상의 범위, MODALITY, 기간, MFN문제등 절차적 논의에는 계속 참여할 것이나, 기본통신 개방 협상 자체에 대한 참여여부는 검토중이며 이는 동 절차적논의결과에 영향을받을 것임을 설명하였음.

- 기본 통신 비공식 협의시의 카나다측 제안문서(기송부)와 관련하여 아측이

(1) 기본통신 개방 협상 참여 및 탈퇴에 대한 법적 기속력 여부

(2) MFN 원칙 유보등과 관련된 내용을 질의한바

0 카나다측은 자국문서상 개방 협상 참여 또는 협상 중간에서의 탈퇴에 대해 법적(LEGAL) 기속력이 있는 것은 아니며, 정치적(POLITICAL) 문제라고 설명하는 한편

0 협상 종료 시점까지의 동 협상기간중의 MFN일탈 중지, 협상력을 제고하기 위한조치나 MFN원칙에 불일치하는 조치의 STANDSTILL 을 의미한다고 하고, 다만 미국은동 협상기간중에도 자국 상호주의 조치에 따라 CASE BY CASE 로 인가여부를 결정하려는 입장으로 보인다고 지적하였음.

- 금융분야와 관련 카측은 3단계 BLUE PRINT상의 조치등 미래 시행예정 조치의 BINDING요구, 원화자금 조달과 관련된 사항(CD발행한도 추가 확대, CALL MARKET,

SWAP한도확대, 외은 지점 신탁업 허용등) 및 정책 대출 특히 중소기업 의무대출 비율 폐지 등을 요구하였는바, 기존 우리입장에 따라 설명하였음.

다. 태국(12월 18일 오전)

- 아측은 유통서비스를 OFFER 할 것을 요청한바, 태국은 이를 검토중이며, 아울러 태국 수정 OFFER는 93. 1월경 제출 예정이라고 하였음.

- 또한 아측은 모든 분야에 적용되는 49 퍼센트지분 제한의 폐지를 계속 요청하는 한편 49퍼센트이상의 외국인 투자가 허용되는 분야가 있는지 확인(해운분야등에 100 퍼센트 투자가 허용된다고함) 하고 그와 같은 경우 태국이 OFFER 에 49퍼센트 지분제한 조치를 유보하더라도 MFN원칙에 의하여 똑같은 혜택이 모든 회원국에 적용되어야 함을 지적하고 동 분야의COMMITMENT 수준 개선을 요청함.

3. 아울러 본부 훈령(WGV-1959) 에 따라 12월 17일별첨 아국 잠정 MFN 일탈 LIST를 GATT사무국에 제출하였으며, 금번 양허 협상기간중 배포된 각국의 수정 양허표들은 본부대표단 지참 귀국 예정임.

첨부: GATT 제출 아국 잠정 MFN 일탈 LIST1부

(GVW(F)-0765).끝

(대사 박수길-국장)

주제네바대표부

번 호 : GVW(F) - 765 년월일 : 21218 시간 : 1800

수 신 : 장 관 (통기, 경기원, 재무부, 법무부, 농림수산부, 상공부, 문화부, 건설부 교통부, 체신부, 보사부, 과기처, 공보처, 환경처, 항만청)

발 신 : 주 제네바대사

제 목 : UR/서비스 양자협상(4)

보 안	
통 제	

총 6 매(표지포함)

외신국	
통 제	

765-6-1

0258

PERMANENT MISSION OF THE REPUBLIC OF KOREA

GENEVA

14 December 1992

H.E. Mr. F. JARAMILLO
Chairman
Group of Negotiations on Services
General Agreement on Tariffs & Trade
Centre William Rappard
Rue de Lausanne, 154
1211 GENEVA 21

Dear Felipe,

Pursuant to the letter of 12 March, I enclose the list of measures for which the Republic of Korea seeks exemptions from the obligations of Article II.1 of the Final Draft Agreement on Trade in Services.

I would be grateful for the distribution of the attached to the negotiating parties who have made offers.

Sincerely yours,

Sam Hoon Kim

KIM, Sam Hoon
Ambassador
Deputy Permanent
Representative
to the GATT

165-6-2

0259

The Republic of Korea
MFN Exemptions Under GATS Article II.2 -
Revised Provisional List

1. While recognizing that the MFN principle is important for the GATS to be an effective agreement, the Republic of Korea has consistently maintained that the scope of MFN exemptions should be limited to the necessary minimum. The Republic of Korea is concerned about the current, excessive requests for MFN exemptions and reemphasizes its position that for the successful conclusion of the services negotiations, every participant should limit its exemptions to specific measures confined to specific areas.

2. Maintaining this basic position, the Republic of Korea submits the attached revised provisional list for MFN exemptions, which is in substitution of its initial list dated March 16, 1992, pursuant to Article 2 and its Annex under the GATS.

3. The Republic of Korea reserves its right to revise this list for MFN exemptions prior to the final outcome of the negotiations on the framework and initial commitments. In particular, the ROK reserves its right to revise this list in case a wide-ranging exemption in the financial services sector is sought. The ROK will also review MFN exemptions for horizontal bilateral agreements, such as visa agreements, according to the results of future negotiations on those agreements.

165-6-3

0260

I. Sector or Sub-sector: Maritime Transport Services

a. Description of the measures:

- Since the ROK-Japan Service Line is overcrowded, particularly by many small domestic businesses, the ROK strictly restricts new entrances to the route regardless of the nationality of the shipping firm.

b. Treatment inconsistent with Article II: 1 of the Agreement

- Operation of the ROK-Japan Service Line is permitted only to foreign firms which, for historical reasons, were licensed by the ROK government.

c. Intended duration of the exemption:

- Until January 1995.

d. Conditions which create the need for the exemption:

- This exemption is temporary, and the ROK will respect the MFN principle after the abolishment of this restriction in January 1995.

765-6-4

0261

II. Sector or Sub-sector: Computerized Reservation Services (CRS)

a. Description of the measures:

- Access to foreign CRS through the SITA network is restricted to a group of persons specified by the Minister of Communications, since such access is considered as third party use of international leased lines.

- The Minister of Communications permitted domestic travel agencies to use the SITA network for access to CRS designated by U.S. carriers.

b. Treatment inconsistent with Article II: 1 of the Agreement

- Domestic travel agencies are allowed to access SITA only when they access CRS designated by US carriers.

c. Intended duration of the exemption

- Indefinite

d. Conditions which create the need for the exemption:

- Access to foreign CRS through the SITA network could be limited or otherwise affected in relation to the negotiations on granting or receiving traffic rights.

0262

165-6-5

III. Sector or Sub-sector: Reciprocity measures on foreign acquisition of land in Korea

a. Description of the measures:

- Prohibitions or restrictions may be imposed on foreign nationals or juridical persons seeking to acquire or lease land in the ROK when Korean nationals or juridical persons are placed under similar prohibitions or restrictions in the country of the foreign nationals or juridical persons seeking to acquire or lease land in Korea (Article 2 of the Alien Land Law).

b. Treatment inconsistent with Article II: 1 of the Agreement

- Measures based on reciprocity

c. Intended duration of the exemption:

- Indefinite

d. Conditions which create the need for the exemption:

- To secure the right of Korean nationals and juridical persons to acquire land in a foreign country.

0263

이시

원 본

외 무 부

종 별 :

번 호 : GVW-2416 일 시 : 92 1221 1500

수 신 : 장 관(수신처 참조)

발 신 : 주 제네바대사

제 목 : UR/GNS 비공식 협의(6)

수신처 :통기, 경기원, 재무부, 법무부, 농수산부, 상공부, 문화부, 건설부, 교통부, 체신부, 보사부, 과기처, 공보처, 환경처, 항만청

연: GVW-2383

12.16(수)-12.18(금) 간에 표제관련 협의 주요내용하기 보고함.

1. 협의개요

- 12.16 및 17 양일간에 걸쳐 34조(정의), 기본통신, 항공부속서, 스케쥴링 및 협정문 밖의 조치관련 협의가 진행되었으나, 기존의 쟁점에 대한 자세한 논의는 행해지지 못하고 추가적 검토가 필요한 사항만을 적시하였음.

- 12.18.15:00 에 개최된 GNS 전체 비공식회의에서도 그간의 주요국간 서비스 비공식협의 결과를 의장이 보고하고 향후 협상일정은 TNC회의 결과에 따르기로 하였음.

2. 협의내용

가. 12.16-17일간의 비공식 협의

1) 34조

- 34조 관련 주요 쟁점은 대부분 정리되고 사무국안(12.3일자)중 (F)항 ORGIN OFSERVICE 및 이와 관련한 31조(협정혜택 부여 거부), (K)항영주권자의 국민 인정 문제등이 추가 논의가 필요한 사항으로 지적됨.

- 아울러 스웨덴은 (N), I) 항 법인 소유와 관련 3개국(예: 회원국, 비회원국, 회원국)이지분을 1/3식 공유하고 있는 경우 분쟁발생시 AFFECTED PARTY 등의 문제를다시 제기함.

2) 기본통신

- 연호 GVW-2360 대로 기본통신은 미국이 MFN문제와 관련 이들 협상의

통상국 법무부 보사부 문화부 교통부 체신부 경기원 재무부 농수산부
상공부 건설부 과기처 해항정 환경처 공보처

PAGE 1 92.12.22 07:54 WH

외신 1과 통제관

0264

수단으로삼지 않겠다는 입장을 서면으로 제출하고, 카나다는 기본통신 PROTOCOL을 제안하였으나, 자세히 논의되지는 못했음.

3) 항공부속서

- 12.14 자 항공부속서 수정안을 사무국이 그간의 논의 내용을 반영하여 수정 초안을 다시 작성, 배포한 바, 대부분의 기술적 쟁점은 정리되고 제4항 및 동항관련 제 2항(B)의 수정 문제가주된 쟁점으로 남아있음.

4) 협정문 밖의 조치

- 스웨덴은 GATS 협정문의 적용범위와 MFN 일탈 목록제출 여부와 관련 북구 인력공동시장 협정이 서비스 협정 대상인지 여부에 대해 법적 명료성 확보가 필요함을 강하게 주장한 바, 참가국간의 의견이 일부 상이하였으나 대체로 협정적용 밖이라는 의견이 지배적이었음.

- EC,오스트리아, 스위스등은 이외에도 투자보장협정, 사회보장협정, HEALTH CARE 등도 명료화 할필요가 있다고 한 바, 대부분의 국가들이 협정밖이라는데 의견을 같이 했으나, 다만 투자보장 협정에 대해서는 의문이 제기되었음.

- 사무국은 이러한 협정등이 이협정적용 대상인지여부는 상기 각 협정상의 구체적 조치 내용 및 유형등에 따라 판단해야 할것이며 단순히 협정명만으로 판단하기 곤란할 것이라고 언급한 바, 사무국이 동 문제에 대한 검토 의견을 작성, 추가 논의키로하였음.

5) 스케쥴링

- GVW-2338 관련 스케쥴링 논의사항을 반영하여 사무국이 별첨 수정 EXPLANATORYNOTE 를 제시한데 대해 별다른 이견이 제시되지는 않았으나, 국경간 공급, 해외소비MODE 에 있어서 외국서비스 공급자의 내국민 대우 문제 및 16조 제한사항이 MAXIMUM인지 MINIMUM 인지가 추가적으로 검토되어야 할것으로 지적되었음.

나. GNS 전체 비공식 회의(12.18)

- GNS 전체 비공식 회의시 상기 이슈들에 대한 의장 보고내용도 상기와 동일하였으며, 동 보고내용중 이들 이슈외의 사항들은 다음과 같음.

0 21조(양허표 수정) : TEXT 수정은 합의되었으며, 양허 수정절차와 관련해서는당분간 논의 유보 또는 계속 논의 여부에 대해서 추가 협의 필요

0 분쟁해결: DFA 상의 분쟁해결 절차와 GATS상의 절차간의 불일치 문제가 있는바 추후 논의예정

0 조세 : 추가 논의 필요

0 해운: 양허협상을 통한 분야별 자유화 문제

0 통신 부속서: 원가지향 가격 책적 관련 일부국의 문제 제기가 있음.

- GNS 의장은 상기 보고후 결론적으로 서비스 협상과제와 관련하여 항공부속서는주요국간의 BARGAINING 문제이며, 실질적 작업과제는 협정밖의 조치, 조세문제, 분쟁해결, 스케쥴링등이라고 언급하였음.

첨부: 1. 기본통신 미국측 LETTER 및 카나다 제안

2. 항공부속서 수정안(12.18 일장)

3. 12.18일자 스케쥴링 설명 NOTE수정안(12.28일자)

4. 조세문제에 대한 사무국 비공식 NOTE(12.18일자) 각 1부

(GVW(F)-0769).끝

(대사 박수길-국장)

UNITED STATES TRADE REPRESENTATIVE
1-3 AVENUE DE LA PAIX
1202 GENEVA, SWITZERLAND

December 16, 1992

Ambassador David Hawes, Co-Chairman
Group of Negotiations on Services
Permanent Mission of Australia to the GATT
Rue de Moillebeau 56
1209 Geneva

Dear Ambassador Hawes,

This letter responds to your suggestion that I provide in writing the ideas put forward in the group concerning the behavior of Parties during the proposed extended period of negotiations on basic telecommunications.

In the several meetings that have taken place among interested countries, it was generally agreed that some form of "Peace Clause" should be adopted for these extended negotiations, a clause which would be a political understanding similar to such a provision in the Punta del Este Declaration. Generally, countries have proposed that participants not take measures to improve their negotiating positions. In particular, reference has been made to measures that are not consistent with Article II. In addition, we propose that the legal obligation on MFN, as required in the Annex to Article II, be left open for all Parties until the conclusion of these extended negotiations.

I have pointed out on numerous occasions that the trade and economic value of an MFN commitment is of virtually no significance for a country who provides basic telecommunications services through a monopoly. Thus, it has no practical value during the time frame of the negotiations, except for those countries who allow competition. The United States, as a country which provides competition in basic telecommunications services on a comprehensive basis, has found it necessary on some occasions to administer its regulatory and trade statutes in a manner that is not consistent with MFN.

0267

161-32-2

As part of the maintenance of the status quo, it must be clearly understood that a Party's use of such measures is not viewed as an improvement in a Party's negotiating position. Such measures can serve as a necessary lever for a Party whose market is largely open to deal with those Parties whose markets are closed. In keeping with the general principle of standstill inherent in the peace clause, Parties should commit to resist only future legislation that would be inconsistent with MFN.

An additional issue concerns the question of bilateral agreements that may be entered into during the negotiations and their potential effects on the negotiating climate. Clearly, if Parties enter into contractually binding agreements that deal with the telecommunications relationship in a comprehensive manner, the basis for these negotiations will be undermined. At the same time, there must be no question over the right of parties to negotiate bilaterally on license applications and technical regulatory matters, including, for instance, the resolution of uniform settlement rates.

The United States has negotiated a series of arrangements, usually in the form of an exchange of letters, with some of its trading partners that deal with International Value-Added Network Services (IVANS). These arrangements, which in a few instances touch on some aspects of basic telecommunications services, are meant to provide greater clarity and transparency to the complicated web of regulations affecting telecommunications, and must not be viewed as undertakings that would improve the negotiating position of Parties.

Finally, there are numerous commercial arrangements that private providers of basic telecommunications services undertake with foreign PTTs. While it is clear that the GATS deals strictly with government-to-government measures, the Peace Clause should underscore this fact. It must be clearly understood among the parties that this extended negotiation is somehow used as an excuse for a government entity's refusal to reach an understanding with a private provider of basic telecommunications services.

I have previously stressed that the successful completion of these extended negotiations is the only possible basis on which basic telecommunications services can be provided on an MFN basis. If Parties insist that <u>all</u> types of measures must be administered on an MFN basis during the short duration of these negotiations, I fear that the GATS will have lost a major

0268

opportunity to liberalize this important sector according to its own rules. As countries begin to liberalize their telecommunications markets, they may find it more convenient to do so on a bilateral, non-MFN basis. At that point, the GATS will have lost its opportunity forever. It is for these reasons that I urge early agreement to a Protocol that would commence these negotiations at the earliest possible time.

Sincerely Yours,

Richard Self
US Negotiator for Services

0269

16/12/92
CANADA

D R A F T

Non-Paper

Protocol on Basic Telecommunications
(Part of the Final Act of the Uruguay Round)

Purpose — 1. Ministers, meeting on the occasion of the conclusion of the Uruguay Round, have decided to pursue trade liberalization negotiations on telecommunications transport networks and services (herein called "basic telecommunications").

NGBT — 2. A Negotiating Group on Basic Telecommunications (NGBT), responsible to the Services Council, is established to carry out the negotiations. It shall report from time to time to the Services Council on progress in implementing its mandate, and present a final report within the time frame set out in paragraph 4 below.

Members — 3. The negotiations in the NGBT shall be open to all Members of the Services Council. To date, the following Members have committed to take part in the negotiations: .....

Timing — 4. The NGBT shall hold its first negotiating session beginning no later than one month after this concluding ministerial conference of the Uruguay Round. It shall terminate its work and make its final report within [two/three] years.

Scope — 5. Without prejudice to their outcome, the negotiations shall be comprehensive in scope, with no telecommunications transport network or service excluded *a priori*.

Schedules — 6. Any commitments resulting from the negotiations, including the date of their entry into force, shall be inscribed in national schedules to the General Agreement on Trade in Services (GATS) and be subject to all the provisions of the GATS.

96P-32-5

0270

MFN

7. Unless an item covered by paragraph 5 above is already inscribed in a national schedule, Article II of the GATS and its Annex shall only enter into force for such commitments:

- on the date of entry into force of any commitments resulting from the NGBT negotiations;

or
{should the negotiations fail}

- on the date of the final report of the NGBT including the inscription of any MFN exemptions in the Article II Exemptions Annex.

Standstill

8. Commencing immediately and continuing until the formal completion of the work of the NGBT, it is understood that no Member would enter into any preferential agreements or arrangements regarding, or take other measures affecting, trade in basic telecommunications services (as defined in paragraph 5):

- inconsistently with Article II (paragraph 1) of the GATS;

- and which may improve its negotiating position.

Surveillance

9. The implementation of paragraph 8 above shall be subject to surveillance in the NGBT. Any participant may bring to the attention of the NGBT any actions or omissions it believes to be relevant to the fulfilment of this undertaking. Such notifications shall be addressed to the Secretariat.

0271

168-32-6

DRAFT
18.12.92

ANNEX ON AIR TRANSPORT SERVICES[1]

1. **This Annex applies to measures affecting trade in air transport services, whether scheduled or non-scheduled, and ancillary services. It is confirmed that any specific commitment made or obligation assumed under this Agreement shall not reduce or affect a Member's obligations under bilateral or multilateral agreements that are in effect at the entry into force of this Agreement.**

2. **The Agreement, including its dispute settlement procedures, shall not apply to measures affecting:**

(a) traffic rights, **however granted;** or

(b) services directly related to the exercise of traffic rights,*

except as provided in paragraph 3 of this Annex.

*.

3. The Agreement shall apply to measures affecting:

(a) aircraft repair and maintenance services;

(b) the selling **and** marketing of air transport services;

(c) computer reservation system (CRS) services.

---

[1]Text in bold indicates changes from the draft contained in the Final Act.

(*) Indicates that drafting proposals/amendments are under consideration.

0272

Q-MISC5

76P-32-1

4. Each Member shall ensure that access to and use of publicly available services offered within or from its territory is accorded to air services suppliers of other Members on reasonable and non-discriminatory terms and conditions where commitments for such publicly available services have been made and unless otherwise specified in its schedule.*

5. The dispute settlement procedures of the Agreement may be invoked only where obligations or commitments have been assumed by the concerned Members and where dispute settlement procedures in bilateral and other multilateral regimes* have been exhausted.

6. The Council for Trade in Services shall review periodically, or at least every five years, the operation of this Annex and air transport and ancillary services.*

7. Definitions:

(a) 'aircraft repair and maintenance services' mean such activities when undertaken on an aircraft while it is withdrawn from service and do not include so-called line maintenance.

(b) 'selling and marketing of air transport services' mean opportunities for the air carrier concerned to sell and market freely its air transport services including all aspects of marketing such as market research, advertising and distribution. These activities do not include the pricing of air transport services nor the applicable conditions.*

(c) 'computer reservation system (CRS) services' mean services provided by computerized systems that contain information about air carriers' schedules, availability, fares and fare rules, through which reservations can be made or tickets may be issued.

0273

Q-MISC5

16-32-8

(d) "traffic rights" mean the right for scheduled and non-scheduled carriers to operate and/or to carry passengers, cargo and mail for remuneration or hire from, to, within, or over the territory of a Member, including points to be served, routes to be operated, types of traffic to be carried, capacity to be provided, tariffs to be charged and their conditions, and * airlines to be designated.

Drafting proposals/amendments under consideration

Paragraph 2(b)

The following text has been proposed at the end of paragraph 2(b):

"except where a Member has made a specific commitment in its schedule".

Text to follow paragraph 2

"Notwithstanding paragraph 2 above, nothing in this Annex shall prevent a Member from inscribing in its schedule a specific commitment on a measure affecting trade in air transport services within the meaning of this Annex."

Paragraph 4

The retention of paragraph 4, identified in the Draft Final Act as subject to further consideration, has not been agreed among the delegations.

Paragraph 5

Replace "regimes" by "arrangements".

Q-MISC5 76P-32-P 0274

Paragraph 6

The following text has been proposed at the end of paragraph 6:

", with a view to considering the possible further application of multilateral understandings in this sector."

Paragraph 7(b)

It has been proposed that the last sentence in paragraph 7(b) be deleted.

Paragraph 7(d)

The following text has been proposed before the word "airlines" in paragraph 7(d):

"number, ownership and control of"

18.12.92

Informal Note by the Secretariat

The attachment contains a revised version of the Secretariat Note entitled "Scheduling of Initial Commitments in Trade in Services: Explanatory Note", dated 4 December 1992.

This note incorporates suggestions made during informal discussions among participants. Proposed changes are indicated in bold type. As discussions on matters relating to scheduling are continuing, particularly in the light of the negotiation of initial commitments, this note is subject to further revision.

0276

768-32-11

FF-INIT2

18.12.92

SCHEDULING OF INITIAL COMMITMENTS IN TRADE IN SERVICES:

EXPLANATORY NOTE[1]

Introduction

1. This informal note is intended to assist in the preparation of offers, requests and national schedules of initial commitments. Its objective is to explain, in a concise manner, how commitments should be set out in schedules in order to achieve precision and clarity. It is based on the view that some standardization of **the terms used in schedules** is necessary to ensure comparable and unambiguous commitments. The note cannot answer every question that might occur to persons responsible for scheduling commitments; it does attempt to answer those questions which are most likely to arise. The answers should not be considered as an authoritative legal interpretation of the GATS.

2. The GATS contains two sorts of provisions: general obligations which apply uniformly; and specific commitments, which are negotiated sectoral undertakings particular to each GATS signatory. Specific commitments, upon the conclusion of negotiations, are to be recorded in national schedules which will be attached to, and form an integral part of, the GATS. By virtue of Article XXVIII:1, every signatory must attach to the GATS its national schedule.

---

[1]This note is circulated by the Secretariat in response to requests by participants. It is a revised version of a draft entitled Scheduling of Commitments in Trade in Services: Explanatory Note 4 December 1992. **The changes indicated in bold are subject to further discussion and, as with previous versions, the whole text** is subject to further revision as thought necessary by participants. References to the General Agreement on Trade in Services (GATS) are based on the text contained in MTN.TNC/W/FA of 20 December 1991, as adjusted by the Legal Drafting Group and distributed as an Informal Note by the Secretariat (Review of Individual Texts in the Draft Final Act, No. 1161, 25 June 1992).

0277

1b P-32-12 FF-INIT2

This note addresses two main questions: what items should be entered on a schedule, and how should they be entered.

PART I

WHAT ITEMS SHOULD BE SCHEDULED?

3. A schedule contains the following main types of information: a clear description of the sector or sub-sector committed, limitations[2] to market access, limitations to national treatment, and additional commitments other than market access and national treatment. If a Member undertakes a commitment in a sector then it must indicate, for each mode of supply in that sector:

- what limitations, if any, it maintains on market access;
- what limitations, if any, it maintains on national treatment; and
- what further commitments, other than market access and national treatment, it may decide to undertake.

A. Limitations on Market Access (Article XVI)

4. A Member grants full market access in a given sector and mode of supply when it does not maintain in that sector or mode any of the types of measures listed in Article XVI. The measures listed comprise four types of quantitative restrictions (subparagraphs a-d), as well as limitations on

---

[2]The term "limitations" will be used throughout this note to refer to the "terms", "conditions", "limitations", and "qualifications" used in the GATS, in particular in Articles XVI and XVII.

0278

FF-INIT2

기 P-32-12

forms of legal entity (subparagraph e) and on foreign equity participation (subparagraph f). The list is exhaustive and includes measures which may also be discriminatory according to the national treatment standard (Article XVII). The quantitative restrictions can be expressed numerically, or through the criteria specified in sub-paragraphs (a) to (d). They do not relate to the quality of the service supplied, or to the ability of the supplier to supply the service (i.e. technical standards or qualification of the supplier).

Examples of limitations:

(a) Number of service suppliers:

- License for a new restaurant based on a needs test.
- Annually established quotas for foreign medical practitioners.
- Government or privately owned monopoly for labour exchange agency services.
- Nationality requirements for professional services.

(b) Total value of transactions/assets:

- Foreign bank subsidiaries limited to x percent of total domestic assets of all banks in country (making offer).

(c) Total number of service operations/quantity of service output:

- Restrictions on broadcasting time available for foreign films.

(d) Total number of natural persons:

- Foreign labour should not exceed x percent and wages xy percent of total.

(e) Restrictions/requirements on legal entity or joint venture:

0279

FF-INI

- Commercial presence excludes representative offices.
- Foreign financial institutions required to establish subsidiaries.
- In sector x, commercial presence must take the form of a partnership.

(f) Participation of foreign capital:

- Foreign equity ceiling of x percent for a particular form of commercial presence.

A Member which maintains a measure listed in Article XVI in a sector and mode of supply in which it is making a commitment has a choice: in the light of the results of negotiations it may either remove the measure, or it may record the measure on its schedule as a limitation to market access.

B. Limitations on National Treatment (Article XVII)

5. A Member grants full national treatment in a given sector and mode of supply when it accords in that sector and mode conditions of competition no less favourable to services or service suppliers of other Members than those accorded to its own like services and service suppliers. This requirement may result from treatment which is either formally identical or formally different; the standard thus covers both *de jure* and *de facto* discrimination. Unlike Article XVI, the national treatment commitment is not defined through an exhaustive listing of the types of measure which would constitute limitations.

Example: A measure which provides for domestic preference in the audiovisual sector is applied to frequency allocation for transmission within the national territory. (Such a measure discriminates explicitly on the basis of the origin of the service supplier and thus constitutes formal or *de jure* denial of national treatment).

0280

FF-INI

C. Additional Commitments (Article XVIII)

8. A Member may, in a given sector, make commitments other than market access and national treatment. Such commitments can include, but are not limited to, undertakings with respect to qualifications, technical standards, licensing procedures, and other domestic regulations referred to in Article VI, even though these measures may be consistent with full market access (Article XVI) and national treatment (Article XVII). Unlike market access and national treatment, additional commitments are expressed in the form of undertakings, not limitations.

D. Exceptions

9. All measures falling under Article XIV (General Exceptions) are excepted from all obligations and commitments under the Agreement, and therefore need not be scheduled. Clearly, such exceptions cannot be negotiated under Part III of the Agreement. Likewise, any prudential measure justifiable under paragraph 2:1 of the Annex on Financial services constitutes an exception to the Agreement and should not be scheduled. **Such exceptions apply only to the financial services listed in the Annex and not to other service sectors.** Measures falling under Article XII are also exceptions and should not be scheduled. Article XII provides for separate disciplines for such measures, including notification and consultation.

E. Specific Commitments and MFN Exemptions

10. A Member taking a national treatment or a market access commitment in a sector must accord the stated minimum standard of treatment specified in its schedule to all other Members. The m.f.n. obligation requires that the most favourable treatment actually accorded must also be accorded to all other Members. Where an m.f.n. exemption has been granted in a sector, a Member is free to deviate from its Article II obligations, but not from its

0282

76P-32-17

FF-INIT2

Example: A law requires that all accountants be graduates of local universities. Although the measure does not formally distinguish service suppliers on the basis of national origin, it de facto offers less favourable treatment to foreign service suppliers by modifying in an unfavourable way the conditions of competition in relation to the like service supplier of national origin.

Regarding the need to schedule residency requirements, it should be decided on a case-by-case basis which types of requirement (e.g. the need to live in the country as opposed to having a mailing address in the country) constitute a de facto national treatment restriction and therefore must be scheduled.

6. Article XVII applies to subsidy-type measures in the same way that it applies to all other measures. Article XV (Subsidies) merely obliges Members to "enter into negotiations with a view to developing the necessary multilateral disciplines" to counter the distortive effects caused by subsidies. Therefore, any subsidy which is a discriminatory measure within the meaning of Article XVII would have to be either scheduled as a limitation on national treatment or brought into conformity with that Article. Subsidy-type measures are also not excluded from the scope of Article II (M.f.n.). An exclusion of such measures would require a legal definition of subsidies which is currently not provided for under the GATS.

7. Measures may exist which are inconsistent with both Articles XVI and XVII. Article XX:2 stipulates that such measures shall be inscribed in the column relating to Article XVI on market access. Thus, while there may be no limitation entered in the national treatment column, there may exist a discriminatory measure inconsistent with national treatment inscribed in the market access column. However, in accordance with the footnote to Article XVI:2, any discriminatory measure can be challenged as a violation of Article XVII.

76P-32-16

Example: A law requires that all accountants be graduates of local universities. Although the measure does not formally distinguish service suppliers on the basis of national origin, it de facto offers less favourable treatment to foreign service suppliers by modifying in an unfavourable way the conditions of competition in relation to the like service supplier of national origin.

Regarding the need to schedule residency requirements, it should be decided on a case-by-case basis which types of requirement (e.g. the need to live in the country as opposed to having a mailing address in the country) constitute a de facto national treatment restriction and therefore must be scheduled.

6. Article XVII applies to subsidy-type measures in the same way that it applies to all other measures. Article XV (Subsidies) merely obliges Members to "enter into negotiations with a view to developing the necessary multilateral disciplines" to counter the distortive effects caused by subsidies. Therefore, any subsidy which is a discriminatory measure within the meaning of Article XVII would have to be either scheduled as a limitation on national treatment or brought into conformity with that Article. Subsidy-type measures are also not excluded from the scope of Article II (M.f.n.). An exclusion of such measures would require a legal definition of subsidies which is currently not provided for under the GATS.

7. Measures may exist which are inconsistent with both Articles XVI and XVII. Article XX:2 stipulates that such measures shall be inscribed in the column relating to Article XVI on market access. Thus, while there may be no limitation entered in the national treatment column, there may exist a discriminatory measure inconsistent with national treatment inscribed in the market access column. However, in accordance with the footnote to Article XVI:2, any discriminatory measure can be challenged as a violation of Article XVII.

0281

76P-32-16

FF-INIT2

C. Additional Commitments (Article XVIII)

8. A Member may, in a given sector, make commitments other than market access and national treatment. Such commitments can include, but are not limited to, undertakings with respect to qualifications, technical standards, licensing procedures, and other domestic regulations referred to in Article VI, even though these measures may be consistent with full market access (Article XVI) and national treatment (Article XVII). Unlike market access and national treatment, additional commitments are expressed in the form of undertakings, not limitations.

D. Exceptions

9. All measures falling under Article XIV (General Exceptions) are excepted from all obligations and commitments under the Agreement, and therefore need not be scheduled. Clearly, such exceptions cannot be negotiated under Part III of the Agreement. Likewise, any prudential measure justifiable under paragraph 2:1 of the Annex on Financial services constitutes an exception to the Agreement and should not be scheduled. **Such exceptions apply only to the financial services listed in the Annex and not to other service sectors.** Measures falling under Article XII are also exceptions and should not be scheduled. Article XII provides for separate disciplines for such measures, including notification and consultation.

E. Specific Commitments and MFN Exemptions

10. A Member taking a national treatment or a market access commitment in a sector must accord the stated minimum standard of treatment specified in its schedule to all other Members. The m.f.n. obligation requires that the most favourable treatment actually accorded must also be accorded to all other Members. Where an m.f.n. exemption has been granted in a sector, a Member is free to deviate from its Article II obligations, but not from its

0282

768-32-17

FF-INIT2

Article XVI and XVII commitments. Therefore, in such cases, a Member may accord treatment in that sector more favourable than the minimum standard to some Members, as long as all other Members receive at least that minimum standard of Article XVI or XVII appearing in its schedule. **In such cases, it is not possible for a Member to accord less favourable treatment to certain Members than that specified in its schedule, e.g. reciprocity cases.**

PART II

HOW SHOULD ITEMS BE SCHEDULED?

11. Schedules record, for each sector, the legally enforceable commitments of each Member. It is therefore vital that schedules be clear, precise and based on a common approach and terminology. This section describes how commitments should be entered in schedules.

The main elements are:

A. horizontal measures;
B. sector-specific measures;
C. sectoral classification;
D. modes of supply; and
E. use of common terms.

A. Scheduling of horizontal measures

12. A horizontal measure is a measure which affects trade in services in a number of service sectors. In order to avoid repetition, it is practicable to enter these measures in a separate section at the beginning of the schedule. The entry should describe the measure concisely, indicating the elements which make it inconsistent with Articles XVI or XVII. Some horizontal measures may be specific to only one mode of supply:

0283

76P-32-18

FF-INIT2

Example: Legislation may refer to foreign investment, formation of corporate structures or land acquisition regulations. Such measures affect above all commercial presence.

Example: Legislation may stipulate requirements regarding entry, temporary stay and work as well as define the scope of personnel movement covered by a particular offer. Such measures affect above all the presence of natural persons.

Other horizontal measures may affect more than one mode of supply:

Example: Legislation may provide for tax measures which are contrary to national treatment. Such measures would normally affect the supply of services in several modes.

B. Scheduling of sector-specific measures

13. A sector-specific measure is a measure which affects trade in services in a particular sector. Such a measure, if maintained and contrary to Articles XVI or XVII, must be entered as a limitation in the appropriate column (either market access or national treatment) for the relevant sector. The entry should describe the measure concisely, indicating the elements which make it inconsistent with Articles XVI or XVII.

14. Given the legal nature of a schedule, it should contain only descriptions of bound measures. Any additional information for clarification purposes should not be entered in the schedule. A reference to the legal basis of a scheduled measure (i.e. the relevant law or regulation) may be entered if thought necessary. In any event, such information will be subject to the obligations of Article III.

C. Sectoral Classification

0284

76 p - 32 - 1 p

FF-INIT2

15. **To the extent possible,** the classification of sectors and sub-sectors should be based on the secretariat's revised Services Sectoral Classification List.[3] Each sector contained in the secretariat list is identified by the corresponding Central Product Classification (CPC) number. Where it is necessary to refine further a sectoral classification, this **may** be done on the basis of the CPC. The most recent breakdown of the CPC, including explanatory notes for each sub-sector, is contained in the UN Provisional Central Product Classification.[4]

Example: A Member wishes to indicate an offer or commitment in the sub-sector of map-making services. In the secretariat list, this service would fall under the general heading "Other Business Services" under "Related scientific and technical consulting services" (see item 1.F.m). By consulting the CPC, map-making can be found under the corresponding CPC classification number 86754. In its offer/schedule, the Member would then enter the sub-sector under the "Other Business Services" section of its schedule as follows:

Map-making services (86754)

If a Member wishes to use its own sub-sectoral classification or definitions it should, **to the extent possible,** provide concordance with the CPC in the manner indicated in the above example.

---

[3] Document MTN.GNS/W/120, dated 10 July 1991.

[4] Statistical Papers Series M no. 77, Provisional Central Product Classification, Department of International Economic and Social Affairs, Statistical Office of the United Nations, New York, 1991.

0285

76p-32-20

FF-INIT2

D. Modes of supply

16. The four modes of supply listed in the schedules correspond to the scope of the GATS as set out in Article I:2. The modes are essentially defined on the basis of the origin of the service supplier and consumer, and the degree and type of territorial presence which they have at the moment the service is delivered. This classification is intended to correspond to the categories of regulatory measures which commonly affect trade in services. The modes of supply may be illustrated as follows:

MODES OF SUPPLY

Supplier Presence	Other Criteria	Mode
Service supplier not present within the territory of the Member	Service delivered within the territory of the Member, from the territory of another Member	CROSS-BORDER SUPPLY
	Service delivered outside the territory of the Member, in the territory of another Member, to a service consumer of the Member	CONSUMPTION ABROAD
Service supplier present within the territory of the Member	Service delivered within the territory of the Member, through the commercial presence of the supplier	COMMERCIAL PRESENCE
	Service delivered within the territory of the Member, with supplier present as a natural person	PRESENCE OF NATURAL PERSON

17. It is important to have a common interpretation of what each mode covers along the lines of what is suggested above. Further examples and explanations are given below.

0286

76 p-32-21

FF-INIT2

(a) Cross-border supply

18. The supply of a service through telecommunications, mail, and services embodied in goods (e.g. a computer diskette, or drawings) are all examples of cross-border supply, since the service supplier is not present within the territory of the Member where the service is delivered.

(b) Consumption abroad

19. This mode of supply is often referred to as "movement of the consumer". The essential feature of this mode is that the service is delivered outside the jurisdiction of the Member taking the measure. Often the actual movement of the consumer is necessary as in tourism services. However, activities such as ship repair abroad, where only the property of the consumer "moves", or is situated abroad, are also covered.

20. Whatever the mode of supply, obligations and commitments under the Agreement relate directly to the treatment of services and service suppliers. They only relate to service consumers insofar as services or service suppliers of other Members are affected.

21. The "service consumer of any other Member" mentioned in Article I:2(b) may be from any Member. In practice however, a Member may only be able effectively to impose restrictive measures affecting its own consumers, not those of other Members, on activities taking place outside its jurisdiction.

(c) Commercial Presence

22. This mode covers not only the presence of juridical persons in the strict legal sense, such as corporations, but also other legal entities such as partnerships, joint ventures, representative offices, and branches, which share some of the same characteristics (see Definitions: Article XXXIV).

0287

76P-32-22

FF-INIT2

(d) Presence of natural persons

23. This mode covers natural persons who are themselves service suppliers, as well as natural persons who are employees of service suppliers.

(e) Relationship between modes of supply

24. Where a service transaction requires in practical terms the use of more than one mode of supply, coverage of the transaction is only ensured when there are commitments in each relevant mode of supply.

Example: A Member has made a commitment in the cross-border supply of architectural services (e.g. by telecommunications or by mail). This commitment alone does not extend to the presence of natural persons (e.g. visits by architects). A separate commitment would have to be taken under "Presence of natural persons" to cover this case.

E. How should commitments be recorded?

25. Since the terms used in a Member's schedule create legally binding commitments, it is important that those expressing presence or absence of limitations to market access and national treatment be uniform and precise. Depending on the extent to which a Member has limited market access and national treatment, for each commitment four cases can be foreseen:

(a) Full commitment

26. In this case the Member does not seek in any way to limit market access or national treatment in a given sector and mode of supply through measures inconsistent with Article XVI and XVII. The Member in this situation should mark in the appropriate column: NONE. However, any relevant horizontal limitations will still apply.

0288

76p-32-27

FF-INIT2

The schedule should make clear in its horizontal section which measures constitute limitations on the various categories of natural persons which are covered e.g. "Unbound except for the entry and temporary stay of natural persons in the following categories ...".

(b) Commitment with limitations

27. Two main possibilities can be envisaged in this case. The first is the binding of an existing regulatory situation ("standstill"). The second is the binding of a more liberal situation where some, but not all, of the measures inconsistent with Articles XVI or XVII will be removed ("rollback"). Here, the Member must describe in the appropriate column the measures maintained which are inconsistent with Articles XVI or XVII. The entry should describe each measure concisely, indicating the elements which make it inconsistent with Articles XVI or XVII. It would not be sufficient to merely enter in a column words such as "bound", "freeze" or "standstill".

(c) No commitment

28. In this case, the Member remains free in a given sector and mode of supply to introduce or maintain measures inconsistent with market access or national treatment. In this situation, the Member must record in the appropriate column the word: UNBOUND. This case is only relevant where a commitment has been made in a sector with respect to at least one mode of supply. Where all modes of supply are "unbound", and no additional commitments have been undertaken in the sector, the sector should not appear on the schedule.

(d) No commitment technically feasible

29. In some situations, a particular mode of supply may not be technically feasible. An example might be the cross-border supply of hair-dressing services. In these cases the term UNBOUND* should be used. The asterisk should refer to a footnote which states "Unbound due to lack of

0289

160-32-28

FF-INIT2

technical feasibility". Where the mode of supply thought to be inapplicable is in fact applicable, or becomes so in the future, the entry means "unbound".

FF-INIT2

18.12.1992

Group of Negotiations on Services

TAXATION AND GATS

Informal Note by the Secretariat

1. During the course of the year, it was brought to the attention of the Secretariat that some technical matters concerning the manner in which taxation measures are dealt with in the draft General Agreement on Trade in Services (MTN.TNC/W/FA) may require some further clarification to achieve the drafting intention and ensure the certainty needed for the functioning of national tax systems. Articles XI, XIV and XXII have been mentioned specifically in this context. In this informal note by the Secretariat, some of these technical matters raised by participants are addressed, taking into account comments made in the process of informal consultations.

Article XIV

National Treatment

2. Taxation measures applied to preserve the integrity of the taxation system often do not violate the national treatment standard. If such measures are not in conformity with national treatment they may be maintained, however, in accordance with Article XIV, if -

(i) they meet the criteria of the chapeau to Article XIV that they "are not applied in a manner which would constitute a means of arbitrary or unjustifiable discrimination between countries when like conditions prevail, or a disguised restriction on trade in services";

76P-32-26

K-TX 0291

(ii) the difference of treatment is "aimed at ensuring the equitable or effective imposition or collection of taxes" (Article XIV:d);

(iii) the taxes are on "the income of service suppliers of other Members" (Article XIV:d); and

(iv) "under the Member's relevant tax measures, the service suppliers are not deemed to reside in the Member's territory" (Article XIV:d).

Comments:

3. In the light of comments by participants, it would appear that the following points are relevant in terms of the criteria:

- If a measure does not violate national treatment, no exception is needed and the criteria will not apply.

- The drafting intention in Article XIV(d) was to permit exceptions to national treatment only for those measures designed to preserve the integrity of the tax system, rather than for all measures which may violate national treatment.

- In this respect, is the criterion in (ii) above appropriate or necessary to meet the concerns relating to the preservation of the integrity of the tax system (i.e. in light of (a) the existence of the chapeau or (b) questions regarding the meaning of "equitable or effective")?

- The drafting intention in (iii) above was to capture "income taxes including capital gains taxes". (Should other taxes be included; taxes on capital, taxes on services?)

- Regarding the criterion in (iv), is it sufficient that the exemption only covers discrimination against non-residents or

/.

K-TX

0292

76f-32-27

are similar discriminatory measures also applied to residents on the basis of nationalities?

4. Tax measures not in conformity with national treatment, and which do not meet the criteria specified in Article XIV, may be maintained if they are listed in a member's schedule as a limitation or condition on national treatment.

Most-Favoured-Nation Treatment

5. Article XIV:e provides for an exception for measures inconsistent with Article II providing "that the difference in treatment is the result of an international agreement relating to the avoidance of double taxation". There are, however, other types of agreements that contain measures relating to double taxation of the kind contained in double taxation agreements. In order to provide for these, it has been suggested that it may be preferable to associate the requirement "relating to the avoidance of double taxation" to the measures covered by an agreement rather than to the type of agreement.

6. It has been suggested that tax measures related to the avoidance of double taxation that are contained in domestic legislation or based on the concept of reciprocity and not linked to international agreements should also be covered by the scope of Article XIV(e). This seems to be largely linked to transport services. In addition, it has been suggested that tax measures other than those relating to agreements on the avoidance of double taxation may be inconsistent with Article II also but applied to protect the integrity of the tax system. Tax havens have been cited as an example and discussed in this respect.

7. In the course of informal consultations held in June 1992, participants addressed the question of whether an exception from m.f.n. treatment for tax haven measures may be necessary.

K-TX

160-32-20

8. It was suggested that treatment based on objective criteria would not normally constitute a m.f.n. violation. Consequently, the scope of Article XIV may not need to be extended beyond the current Article XIV:e exception to Article II with respect to double taxation. An outline of the reasoning advanced in the consultations is attached.

Comments

- Is this attachment a reflection of the current thinking relating to tax havens?

- Are there measures other than tax havens that may be relevant in this respect?

9. Tax measures not in conformity with the m.f.n. obligation and which do not meet the criteria of Article XIV:e may be notified in accordance with the M.f.n. exemption procedures.

Article XI - Payments and Transfers

10. A clarification has been sought as to whether taxation measures, such as withholding taxes, could be considered "restrictions on international transfers and payments from current transactions" in terms of Article XI:1. Article XI:2 makes clear that it is not the intention of Article XI to prohibit measures considered permissible by the International Monetary Fund. Pursuant to request from participants, the Secretariat has consulted informally with representatives of the IMF on this matter. The IMF has provided the following explanation:

"For purposes of the Fund's jurisdiction, a withholding tax on the payment of income to non-residents is not an exchange restriction, unless the tax is only levied on the remittance abroad of the income. The remittance may take the form of a payment or transfer. In practice, therefore, a distinction must be made between (i) genuine

0294

K-TX

16P-32-2P

"income taxes", which are levied both on domestic and foreign payments or transfers, and (ii) "remittance taxes", which are only levied on foreign payments or transfers and constitute exchange restrictions."

Article XXIII:3 Consultation

11. The current provisions of Article XXII:3 would allow a Member to pursue tax matters under the GATS dispute settlement procedures after they have been pursued under the relevant tax treaty if a matter is covered by both agreements. It has been suggested that the intentions of Article XXII:3 could be clarified to ensure that tax matters falling under the non-discrimination provisions of a double taxation treaty in force should be exclusively addressed under the relevant procedures of that agreement, in order to avoid that the GATS become an "appeal board". Under this approach, it would, in all instances, be the non-discrimination provisions of the tax agreement that would prevail, thus recourse to the GATS provisions, for the parties to such an agreement would not be possible. In cases where the parties concerned disagree on the appropriate forum, it would nevertheless be possible to request a GATS determination as to whether a particular tax measure is covered by the exemption or is subject to the GATS.

0295

K-TX

16P-32-30

ATTACHMENT

The question addressed in this attachment is whether Article XIV should include exception to Article II for measures designed to counter practices used by firms where funds are diverted out of a particular tax jurisdiction to avoid or reduce taxes paid.[1]

A number of reasons have been cited as to why such measures may not be inconsistent with m.f.n. obligations:

- the aim of the measure is not discrimination per se, but rather to address deliberate tax avoidance;
- the criteria used in applying such measures are not based on nationality, but on "neutral" objective tests for determining whether the parent company's main purpose was to avoid taxes; and
- the maintenance of a list either of "qualifying" or "excluded" countries with respect to the measure would not, in itself, be inconsistent with m.f.n. treatment, if the list simply reflected the application of non-discriminatory criteria.

It was also noted in consultations that if the measure itself is consistent with m.f.n. obligations, any discrimination that might be necessary for enforcement of the measure could be justified under the exception of paragraph (c) of Article XIV.

---

[1]In applying measures to counter such practices, tax experts have indicated that the tax authority concerned typically applies a set of objective criteria to determine whether avoidance was the main purpose for a parent firm's relationship with a particular subsidiary.

0296

K-TX

76P-32-31

Approaching the issue from another perspective, it was unclear that m.f.n. treatment, or discrimination among foreign suppliers, would be relevant, since the country taking these measures was applying them to resident parent firms (whether or not foreign-owned or controlled).

Regarding the possible indirect affects of such measures, it is relevant that under the Agreement, the subsidiary company concerned may qualify as a service supplier "of another Member" and thus be entitled to m.f.n. treatment. In this respect, the following considerations were relevant:

- Since the measure would usually apply only if the subsidiary was not found to be engaged in commercial activities, it is unclear how such a company could qualify as a "service supplier";

- Since the measure would apply only if the subsidiary was under the overall control of the parent company, under certain circumstances the subsidiary could also be deemed to be a service supplier of the country applying the measure and, as such, m.f.n. treatment would not be relevant; and,

- As cited above, the measure is not applied to the parent firm on the basis of nationality of a subsidiary, but as a result of applying neutral criteria to determine whether tax avoidance was the main purpose (i.e. if a parent company can prove that it does not use its subsidiary for the purpose of tax avoidance, the measures will not be applied, even if the subsidiary benefits from low tax rates or special tax incentives offered in the country where it is doing business).

0297

K-TX

7ᄉP-32-32

정 리 보 존 문 서 목 록					
기록물종류	일반공문서철	등록번호	2020030078	등록일자	2020-03-10
분류번호	764.51	국가코드		보존기간	영구
명 칭	UR(우루과이라운드) / 서비스 분야 양허협상, 1992. 전6권				
생 산 과	통상기구과	생산년도	1992~1992	담당그룹	
권 차 명	V.6 양허협상 대책회의				
내용목차					

0001

경　제　기　획　원

우 427-760 / 경기도 과천시 중앙동1 정부제2청사 / 전화 503-9149 / 전송 503-9141

문서번호 통조삼 10502-10

시행일자 1992. 1. 14.

(경유)

수신 수신처참조

참조

선결			지시		
접수	일자 시간	92. 1. 15	결재·공람		
	번호	1661			
처리과					
담당자					

제목 UR/서비스 양허협상을 위한 관계부처 회의개최

1. 그동안의 양자협의결과를 바탕으로 1월 27일주에 미국등 주요국들과 본격적인 UR/서비스 양허협상을 진행할 예정입니다.

2. 이에 따라 상대국의 주요관심사항(별첨1 양자협의 회의록 참조)에 대한 협상대책을 마련하기 위한 관계부처회의를 별첨2와 같이 개최하니 분야별 협상대책자료를 지참하고 반드시 참석해 주기 바랍니다.

첨부 : 1. UR/서비스 양자협의 회의록 1부.
　　　2. '92년 1월 UR/서비스 양허협상 추진대책 1부. 끝.

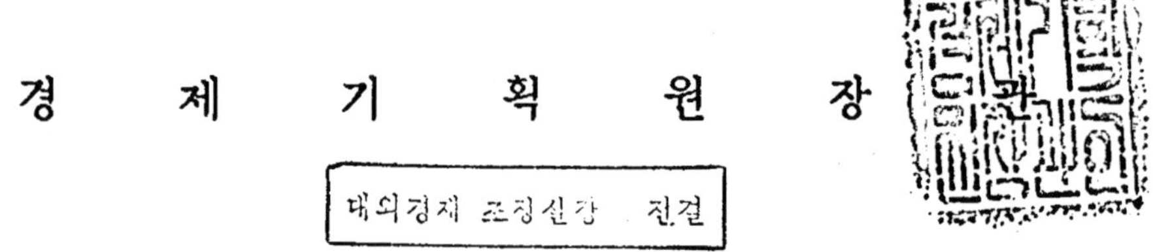

경　제　기　획　원　장

대외경제 조정실장 전결

수신처 : 외무부장관, 내무부장관, 재무부장관, 법무부장관, 교육부장관, 문화부장관, 농림수산부장관, 상공부장관, 보건사회부장관, 건설부장관, 교통부장관, 노동부장관, 동자부장관, 체신부장관, 체육청소년부장관, 과학기술처장관, 환경처장관, 공보처장관, 경찰청장, 특허청장, 해운항만청장, 대외경제정책연구원장, 한국개발연구원장

0002

'92年 1月 UR/서비스 讓許協商 推進對策

Ⅰ. 讓許協商槪要

가. 全般的인 動向

- 전반적인 UR협상 추진일정상 서비스 讓許協商(Negotiation)은 1月末~3月末까지 두세차례의 讓許協商을 하여 마무리 지을 계획

  o 현재 우리에게 公式으로 Request를 제시한 국가는 美國, EC, 日本, 캐나다, 濠洲, 스위스, 스웨덴, 핀랜드, 노르웨이, 印度등 10개국이며 우리도 노르웨이, 印度를 제외한 8개국에 대하여 Request를 제출

  o 同 Request를 바탕으로 이중 美國, 캐나다와는 2회, EC, 濠洲, 스위스, 스웨덴, 핀랜드와는 각각 1회씩 兩者協議(Consultation)를 진행

- 美國등 主要協商國은 서비스 일반협정 제정을 위한 協商이 일단락 지워짐에 따라 각국 서비스시장의 개방확대를 위한 讓許協商을 본격적으로 진행시키겠다는 계획

  o 이제까지의 協議(Consultation)와는 달리 이번부터는 協商(Negotiation)으로 성격 규정

  o 1回 協商期間도 2週씩으로 연장할 전망

0003

나. 協商對象國家

- 우리에게 Request한 10개 국가가 모두 要請할 것으로 전망

- 한편 우리가 추가로 Request할 예정으로 있는 인도네시아, 印度, 泰國등 3개국가와도 협상할 가능성 존재

다. 協商對象分野

- 金融과 通信을 포함한 全分野

- 一部分野協議를 별도로 진행할 지 여부는 불분명

라. 協商日程

- 1월 27일 週間으로 추진중

  o 美國이 1월 20일을 제시하였으나 현재 1월 27일주로 연기 요청중

마. 場所

- 대부분 GATT內 會議室에서 진행

바. 議題

- Request를 바탕으로 各國 서비스시장 개방에 대한 구체적인 협상

- 특히 지금까지의 兩者協議에서 구체적으로 부각된 主要關心事項을 중심으로 논의할 가능성이 큼.

0004

Ⅱ. 推進對策

1. 協商代表團의 構成

가. 出張期間 : 1.26~2.2(잠정)

나. 代表團構成

- 首席代表 : 經濟企劃院 第2協力官
- 代　　表 : 主要關係部處의 擔當課長
- 諮 問 官 : KIEP, KDI의 專門家

2. 협상대책마련을 위한 關係部處 實務級會議 開催

- 場　　所 : 經濟企劃院 第2協力官室(과천청사 3동 225호)
- 參席範圍 : 經濟企劃院 第2協力官(會議主宰)
  關係部處의 擔當課長
  KIEP 박태호, 성극제, 김태준 研究委員
  KDI 김지홍 研究委員
- 持參資料

① 相對國의 主要關心事項에 대한 協商對策

② 우리의 Request에 대한 具體的인 說明資料 및 要求論理

0005

- 各部處別 會議日程 및 對象業種

日　　時	對象部處	對　象　業　種
1.16(木)		
10:00~12:00	法 務 部	法務서비스
14:00~16:00	交 通 部	貨物運送周旋서비스, 會議用役
16:00~17:00	遞 信 部	通信
1.17(金)		
10:00~11:00	動資部, 環境處	地質, 環境關聯서비스
11:00~12:00	科 技 處	엔지니어링, R&D
14:00~16:00	保 社 部	病院管理
1.20(月)		
14:00~15:00	財 務 部	會計, 稅務서비스
15:00~17:00	財 務 部	銀行, 保險, 證券

3. UR對策 實務委員會 開催

- 日時 및 場所(暫定) : 1.22(水) 14:00~17:00,
  經濟企劃院 小會議室

- 參席範圍 : 經濟企劃院 對外經濟調整室長(會議主宰)
  〃 第2協力官
  各部處 擔當局長

- 議題 : 상기 實務級 會議結果를 토대로 이번 讓許協商에 대한 政府次元의 協商對策 確定(具體事項 추후통보)

0006

외무 4 (3)

UR對策 實務委員會 資料

관리번호	92-87

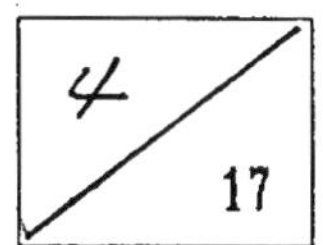

UR/서비스協商 關聯對策

1992. 1. 23

經 濟 企 劃 院
對外經濟調整室

0007

目　　次

0008

Ⅰ. 讓許協商對策(案)

1. 協商日程

- 전반적인 UR협상 일정상 3월말까지의 서비스 讓許協商日程은 다음과 같이 결정됨.
  - o 제1차 讓許協商 : 1.20～1.31
    - * 2.10까지 修正 Offer 제출
  - o 제2차 讓許協商 : 2.17～2.28
  - o 제3차 讓許協商 : 3. 9～3.20(商品分野와 서비스분야 協商結果 綜合評價)
    - * 3.9까지 讓許協商結果를 반영한 National Schedule 제출
  - o 3. 31 : 서비스協定에 부속될 최종 National Schedule 제출

- 제1차 讓許協商期間中 현재(1.21)까지 우리와의 협상이 확정된 국가는 EC, 스웨덴, 핀랜드, 美國, 뉴질랜드, 濠洲등 6개국임.

日 時	對象國家	分 野
1.28(火)		
09:00	E C	金融 및 通信分野를 포함한 전분야
15:00	스웨덴	〃
1.29(水)		
09:00	핀랜드	〃
14:00	美 國	通信分野 포함, 金融分野 포함여부는 未定
1.30(木)		
16:00	뉴질랜드	金融 및 通信分野를 포함한 전분야
1.31(金)		
15:00	濠 洲	金融分野포함 통신분야 제외

- 우리에게 Request를 한 餘他國家들도 兩者協商을 요청할 가능성
  - o 日本, 카나다, 스위스, 노르웨이, 印度등

2. 基本對應方向

- 앞으로 있게될 3차례의 讓許協商過程을 고려하여 우리의 최종 입장을 정립하되 이를 업종별로 상황변화에 따라 伸縮性있게 대처

① 基本的으로 Initial Offer 수준에서 대응

o 分野別로 상대방의 요구가 불명확한 사항에 대해서는 상대측의 요구를 보다 正確하게 파악

② '90.11월이후 개방화가 이루어진 通信, 流通, 金融, 運送, 觀光分野등은 기본적으로 MFN原則이 적용될 것임과 同 追加自由化 內容을 향후 수정 Offer에 반영할 것임을 언급

③ 그간 1~4회의 兩者協議를 통하여 제기된 각국의 關心事項중 다수국가가 공동으로 요구하거나 요구강도가 높고 우리측의 대응논리가 취약한 사항에 대하여는 國內的 影響을 최소화하는 수준에서의 自由化計劃을 마련하여 대응

o 旣 開放되었으나 우리의 讓許表에 기재하지 않고 있는 業種으로 추가포함이 가능한 분야

· 의료시설관리, 산업폐기물 처리, 자연과학 연구용역 등

o 資格關聯規制 內容變更이 가능한 분야 : 법무, 회계, 엔지니어링등

- 상기 협상과정에서 우리의 協商力 強化를 위하여 주요국에 대한 Request List 제출

- 상대측의 요구수준이 낮거나 단순한 確認要請事項에 대해서는 관련되는 자료 및 정보를 성의있게 제공하는 선에서 대응

3. 分野別 對策

(1) 法務서비스

- 要求事項(美國, EC, 濠洲, 스웨덴, 핀랜드)
  - o 外國法 및 國際法 자문허용
  - o 國內法 諮問會社 설립허용
    - · Partnership 認定
    - · 한국인 변호사 고용가능

- 對策
  - o 1차적으로 現 司法制度의 유지를 위하여 讓許不可하다는 기존입장을 견지하고
  - o 최종적으로는 外國人에 대하여 내국인과 동일한 조건으로 辯護士 資格取得을 허용하는 수준(國籍要件 廢止)으로 대응
    - · 이경우 외국인이 資格取得時 업무영역 및 영업형태에 있어 내국인과 동등한 대우를 한다는 약속은 불가피

(계속 追加的인 開放要求가 있을 경우)

- o 양국의 當事者團體인 대한변호사협회와 상대국변호사 협회의 협의를 통한 意見交換을 선행시키고 그 결과를 참고로 兩國政府가 다시 협의토록 하자는 方式을 제시

(2) 公認會計서비스

- 要求事項(美國, EC, 카나다, 濠洲, 스웨덴, 핀랜드)
  - o 略式試險을 거쳐 자격인정된 外國 CPA의 業務領域制限 폐지
  - o 正式試險을 거친 외국인 CPA의 營業形態制限(고용된 경우만 가능)을 폐지
  - o 會計法人設立을 위한 외국인투자 또는 外國 CPA와의 Partnership의 인정

0011

- 對策

  - o 略式試驗을 거치는 資格認定事項은 Offer에서 제외
  - o 정식으로 국내 CPA시험에 합격한 外國人에 대하여는 업무영역 및 영업형태상 內國人과 동등한 대우(法務서비스와 同一)
  - o 國內 CPA취득자가 아닌 者의 國內 商業的駐在는 불인정

(3) 엔지니어링

- 要求事項(美國, EC, 카나다, 日本, 濠洲, 스웨덴, 핀랜드)
  - o 外國用役發注承認制 및 主契約者 制度 폐지
  - o 登錄制 폐지
    - · 일정수의 기술사 확보의무등 現 登錄要件의 폐지 요구
- 對策
  - o 현재 개정추진중인 技術用役育成法의 改正(案)을 중심으로 讓許計劃表 수정
    - · 現 外國用役發注 承認制, 主契約者制度 및 登錄制度를 申告制로 전환

(4) R&D

- 要求事項(카나다)
  - o R&D業種의 추가자유화
- 對策
  - o R&D의 주종을 이루고 있는 自然科學硏究開發業 部門에 대하여 제한없음을 Offer
    - · 현재 外國人投資 자유화업종

0012

(5) 地質關聯서비스

- 要求事項(카나다)

  o 地質關聯서비스의 자유화

- 對策

  o 同 部門에 아무런 제한없음을 Offer
    · 현재 外國人投資 자유화업종

(6) 環境關聯서비스

- 要求事項(카나다)

  o 산업폐기물 처리업의 개방

- 對策

  o 산업폐기물 처리업(수집 · 운반, 중간처리, 최종매립) 및 폐수수탁처리업을 修正 Offer에 포함

  o 허가요건을 갖추었을 경우 外國人의 進出이 가능하나 허가과정에서 처리업자수 및 영업구역등에 대해 제한이 가능함을 명기

(7) 醫療施設管理서비스

자본투자없는 관리.

- 要求事項(美國)

  o 醫療施設管理서비스의 개방

- 對策

  o 현행법규상 同 分野에 외국인 진출을 제한하는 규정은 없으므로 修正 Offer에 포함(제한없음)

0013

(8) 通信

- 要求事項(美國, EC, 카나다, 濠洲, 스웨덴, 핀랜드)
  - o 外資制限 撤廢時期('94.1) 단축
  - o 기업내 통신의 개방범위 확대

- 對策

※ 기본적으로 韓·美 通信協商과 같은 입장으로 대응

(i) 外資制限 撤廢時期는 기존입장 견지

- o 현재도 50%까지 外國人의 參與가 허용되어 있어 부분적 참여가능
- o 韓國의 통신관련 Offer List에는 패킷교환서비스등 데이타 단순전송서비스까지 포함되어 있기 때문에 他國에 비해 開放範圍가 상대적으로 광범위
- o 최근에야 國內通信業界에도 VAN사업에 대한 경쟁이 도입되어 있기 때문에 대외개방에는 '94.1까지 준비 기간이 필요

(ii) 기업내 통신의 開放範圍擴大에 대해서는 韓·美通商會談(1.22~24)의 결과에 따라 同一立場으로 대처

(9) 貨物運送周旋서비스 NVOCC.

- 要求事項(EC, 카나다, 스웨덴)
  - o 貨物運送周旋業에 대한 구체적 개방일정 제시

- 對策
  - o 海上貨物運送周旋業에 대하여 현행 Offer에서는 外國人 投資持分을 50%미만으로 제한하고 있으나['96.1부터는 외자지분제한을 폐지하는 것으로 修正 Offer에 기재] 로 confirm.

0014

(10) 人力移動

- 要求事項

  o 人力移動의 범위확정(美國, EC, 카나다, 스위스)

  o 單獨代表者(sole representative)의 포함요구(EC)

- 對策

  o 修正 Offer의 전문에 商業的駐在에 필수적인 상급관리자, 임원, 전문가의 이동이 허용된다는 事項을 포함

  o 또한 국내에 商業的駐在가 없더라도 서비스판매를 위한 협상을 하거나 계약을 체결하기 위한 일정한 기업의 대표자는 國境間移動을 허용

0015

Ⅱ 修正 Offer List 提出對策

1. 提出經緯

- '91년 12월말 현재 總43個國家가 Offer List 제출

  o OECD국가들 뿐만 아니라 南美國家, 아세안, 印度, 이집트, 中國등 開途國들도 Offer를 제출

- 그런데 이들 各國은 Offer List 作成에 대한 통일된 기준 없이 다양한 형태로 작성

  o 이에 따라 '91년중 讓許表 作成方法에 대한 기술적인 논의를 계속하여 '91년 12월 讓許表 作成方法에 대한 대체적인 합의형성

    < 새로운 讓許表 作成方式의 주요내용 >

    ① 市場接近을 제한하는 量的인 제한조치(예 : 수급사정을 고려한 면허 및 인가제도, 독점, 자산규모 및 영업 총액에 대한 제한조치등)는 讓許表에 기재하지 않으면 없는 것으로 간주

    ② 內國人과 차별적인 제한조치는 讓許表에 기재하지 않으면 없는 것으로 간주

    ③ 서비스의 質을 유지하기 위한 단순한 면허 · 인가 · 등록제도 및 同要件등 무차별적인 · 질적인 규제는 기재할 필요없음.

- 이러한 새로운 讓許表 作成方式에 따라 美國, EC, 스위스, 濠洲가 수정 Offer List를 각국에 배포했으며 日本, 캐나다 등 주요협상국들도 조만간 GATT에 제출예정

0016

2. 修正 Offer의 槪要

① 構造

- 수정 Offer는 개괄적인 설명과 공통적인 규제사항이 포함되어 있는 前文(headnote)과 分野別 自由化約束으로 구성
- 共通的인 規制事項에는 모든 업종에 공통적으로 적용되는 외국인투자, 외환관리, 부동산취득, 인력이동에 대한 사항을 包括的으로 기재

② 分野別 自由化約束

- 業種羅列順序는 GATT사무국 분류표(MTN · GNS/W/120)에 가능한 일치시킴.
- 업종의 명칭 및 포괄범위는 가급적 GATT事務局 分類表에 일치시키되 國內標準産業分類 및 國內規制制度와 일치하지 않는 경우 후자에 따름.
- 記載方法은 새로운 讓許表 作成方式에 따라 기재
  - o 특히 各部處가 면허, 인가, 등록제도등을 수급여건 및 國內産業保護를 위해 재량적으로 운영하는 경우, 또한 시장질서유지등을 위하여 영업총액, 자산규모등에 대한 量的인 제한을 하는 경우는 반드시 讓許表에 해당사실을 기재
- 自由化水準
  - o 기본적으로는 '90년 11월 initial offer에 명시된 自由化水準을 견지하되 추가적으로 다음사항을 포함.
    - ① '90년 11월이후 추가 자유화한 사항 : 영화, 광고, 통신, 유통, 금융, 운송, 관광분야등
    - ② 兩者協議過程에서 상대국이 지속적인 관심을 보인 사항중 추가 Offer가 가능한 事項(關係部處間 實務協議에서 조정) : 법무, 보건시설관리, 산업폐기물 R&D, 환경 및 지질관련서비스등

③ Initial Offer와 修正 Offer의 形式面에서의 差異

	Initial Offer	修正 Offer
① 人力移動	- 追加檢討事項으로 유보	- 서비스공급에 必須的인 上級管理者, 任員, 專門家, 서비스販賣者는 양허
② 業種羅列 順序	- 英文表記(A,B,C)順序 및 主務部處別로 나열	- GATT 事務局 分類表 순서에 따름.
③ 市場接近 및 內國民 優待 制限措置	- 無差別的 · 質的規制 措置(면허, 등록제도 자체) 일부포함.	- 無差別的 · 質的規制 措置는 삭제 - 量的인 制限措置(독점 등) 포함.
④ 包括業種	- 시청각, 事業, 통신, 건설, 유통, 금융, 관광등 8개분야	- 법무, 의료시설관리, 산업폐기물처리, R&D, 지질관련서비스등을 추가하고 旣 包含分野도 세분
⑤ 凍結時点	- '90년 11월	- '91년 12월

3. 修正 Offer 提出을 위한 作業計劃

- 2月 1日까지 : 별첨 "修正 Offer(案)"에 대한 각부처의 수정, 추가의견 수렴

- 2月初旬 : 對外協力委員會등을 통한 修正 Offer 확정 및 GATT 제출(GATT 提出時限 2월 10일)

6-1

회의 참석 결과 보고

1. 회 의 명 : UR 대책 서비스 분야 실무소위원회

2. 개최일시 및 장소 : 92.2.12(수) 15:00-17:30, 경기원 회의실

3. 회의 참석

   o 경제기획원 대조실 제2협력관 (회의 주재)

   o 외무부, 내무부, 재무부, 법무부등 UR/서비스 협상 관련 18개부처 실무 담당과장 (외무부 : 통상기구과 조현 서기관 참석)

   o KIEP, KDI 연구관

4. 회의 결과

   o 아국의 UR/서비스 협상 수정 양허표(안) 확정

   - 91.1.9 갓트에 제출한 최초의 양허 계획표(Initial offer list)를 기초로 재작성

   - 최초 양허 계획표상의 8개분야 42개에서 15개를 추가 양허하고 업종을 세분화하여 11개분야 57개로 등재

     ※ 기본적으로 최초 양허계획표에 양허한 수준을 갓트사무국 서비스 분류표에 따라 재작성한 것으로서 91년도중 양자간 양허 협상 결과에 따라 일부 부담이 적은 업종을 추가한 것과 90.11월 이후 추가 자유화 사항을 반영한것 이외에는 최초 양허계획표와 큰 차이가 없음.

   o 수정 양허표 제출 계획 확정

   - 2.13(목) 수정 양허계획표의 최종 정리
   - 2.14(금) 대외협력위원회 서면 결의 및 국내언론 발표
   - 2.15(토) 주 제네바 대사에 수정 양허표를 갓트에 제출토록 지시
   - 2.17(월) 수정 양허표 갓트 제출. 끝.

안 고 재	통상기구과	92 년 2월 13일	담 당	과 장	심의관	국 장	차관보	차 관	장 관
			조현	(서명)	(서명)	(서명)			

0019

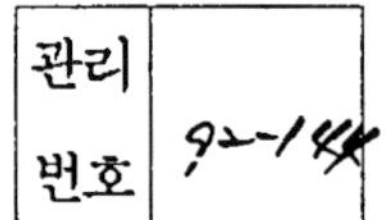
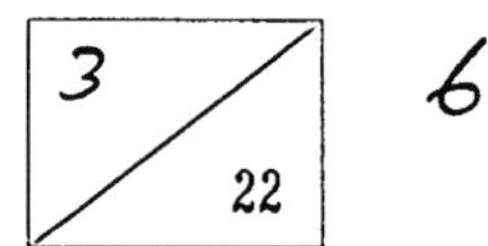

경 제 기 획 원

우 427-760 / 경기도 과천시 중앙동1 정부제2청사 / 전화 503-9149 / 전송 503-9141

문서번호 통조삼 10502-14	선결			지시	
시행일자 1992. 2. 13	접수	일자 시간	:	결재·공람	
(경유)		번호			
수신 수신처참조		처리과			
참조		담당자			

제목 제14차 대외협력위원회 개최(서면결의)

1. 대외협력위원회 규정(대통령령 제12535호)에 의거 UR대책 서비스 실무소위원회(2.12)에서 관계부처간 실무협의를 거친「한국의 수정양허계획표 제출대책 및 한국의 수정양허계획표(국·영문)」안을 제14차 대외협력위원회에서 서면 의결코자 합니다.

2. 동 안건을 검토하시고 반드시 위원(장관, 청장)의 서명을 받아 그 결의내용을 2월 14일까지 당원에 통보하여 주시기 바랍니다.

첨부 : 1. 서면의결서 1부.
2. 한국의 수정양허계획표 제출대책 및 한국의 수정양허계획표(국·영문) 1부.

끝.

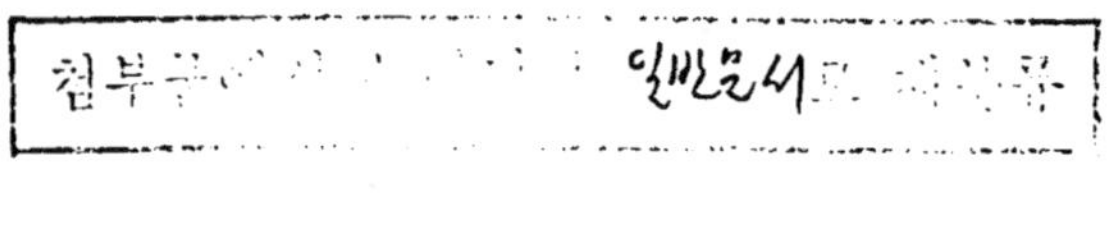

경 제 기 획 원 장

수신처 : (대외협력위원회 위원)
국가안전기획부장, 외무부장관, 재무부장관, 농림수산부장관, 상공부장관, 동력자원부장관, 건설부장관, 보건사회부장관, 노동부장관, 교통부장관, 체신부장관, 과학기술처장관, 환경처장관, 대통령비서실장(경제수석비서관, 외교안보수석비서관), 국무총리 행정조정실장
(특별위원)
내무부장관, 법무부장관, 문화부장관, 공보처장관, 항만청장

0020

관리 번호	

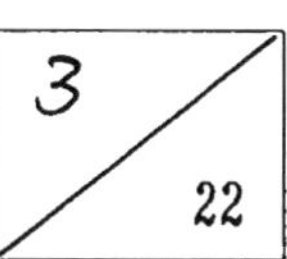

UR/서비스協商關聯

韓國의 修正讓許計劃表 提出對策

1992. 2. 13

對外協力委員會

0021

目　　次

0022

Ⅰ. 修正讓許計劃表 提出經緯 및 向後協商日程

- UR/서비스 협상과 관련하여 우리정부는 1991.1.9 對外協力委員會의 議決을 거쳐 최초의 讓許計劃表(Initial Offer List)를 GATT에 제출

- 그간 UR협상의 진전에 따라 1991.12.20 全體協商議題에 대한 最終協定文案(Draft Final Act)이 제출되었으며 서비스분야 일반협정초안도 거의 합의된 상태로 제시

  o 서비스 讓許表 作成方式에 대한 합의형성

  o 향후협상일정

    · '92.1~3월중 2~3차에 걸친 國家別 讓許協商 진행
    · '92.2.10까지 각국의 修正讓許計劃表 제출
      (현재 美國, EC, 日本, 濠洲, 뉴질랜드등 제출)
    · '92.3.9까지 讓許協商結果를 반영한 양허표 및 MFN 逸脫事項(3.6) 제출
    · '92.3.31까지 서비스 一般協定에 포함될 國家別 最終讓許計劃表 확정

- 政府는 그동안 關係部處 實務協議를 거쳐 새로운 讓許計劃表 作成方式과 그간의 國家別 兩者協議(1~4회) 및 讓許協商(1.28~1.30, 美國, EC등 7개국)結果를 반영한 修正讓許計劃表案을 마련

- 同 讓許修正計劃表를 대외협력위원회의 의결을 거쳐 第2次 讓許協商이 진행되는 2월중순까지 GATT에 제출

0023

Ⅱ. 讓許計劃表 主要修正內容

1. 修正讓許計劃表上 등재업종의 調整

가. 業種分類의 變更

- 우리의 1次 讓許計劃表는 8개분야 43개 細部業種을 등재
- 修正讓許計劃表 業種分類는 GATT사무국 서비스 분류표에 따라 11개분야중 8개 분야(教育서비스, 保健社會서비스, 文化娛樂서비스 제외)를 등재하고 韓國標準産業分類 및 國內法規에 의거 55개(12개 증가) 세부업종을 등재

< 業種分類 比較 >

最初의 讓許計劃表		修正 讓許計劃表	
分　　野	細部業種	分　　野	細部業種
1. 視聽覺서비스	2	1. 事業서비스	20(10)
2. 事業서비스	10	2. 커뮤니케이션	5 (-)
		가. 通信	3 (-)
		나. 視聽覺서비스	2 (-)
3. 通信	3	3. 建設	2(-1)
4. 建設	3	4. 流通	2 (-)
5. 流通	2	5. 環境關聯서비스	2 (2)
6. 金融	7	6. 金融	9 (2)
7. 運送	12	7. 觀光	3(-1)
8. 觀光	4	8. 運送	12 (1)

*(　　)내는 業種의 細分化 및 追加讓許에 따른 증가업종수

0024

나. 讓許業種數 增加內容

① 業種의 細分化에 따른 業種數增加

- 엔지니어링서비스 → 엔지니어링서비스, 종합엔지니어링 서비스
- 컴퓨터관련서비스 → 컴퓨터설비자문업, 소프트웨어시행 서비스, DP서비스, DB서비스
- 銀行 → 預金 및 관련업무, 貸出 및 관련업무, 外換업무
- 여행알선서비스 → 여행알선서비스, 통역안내서비스

② 各國의 讓許協商結果에 따른 業種追加

- 이미 外國人投資가 자유화된 업종으로서 협상과정에서 상대국의 요구가 비교적 강하고 讓許하여도 우리로서는 부담이 적은 것으로 검토된 업종을 추가
  - o 도시계획 및 조경설계서비스, 自然科學 R&D서비스, 시장조사및 여론조사, 지질조사 및 탐사서비스, 속기사, 특정폐기물 처리, 폐수수탁 처리 (11개)

③ 最初 讓許計劃表('90.11월기준) 작성이후의 追加自由化 事項 반영

- 廣告(외자지분 제한폐지), 通信(국제서비스 허용), 流通(매장면적 및 점포수 확대), 陸運分野(개방시기 단축)의 자유화수준 반영
- 鐵道小運送業은 업종추가 — 1개

④ 除外業種 : 外國人專用 觀光紀念品 販賣業

0025

2. 讓許表 作成方式의 變更에 따른 修正

- UR/서비스 일반협정초안에서 제시된 讓許表 作成方式에 따라 前文 및 分野別 記載事項을 수정

< 讓許表 前文 >

o 최초의 양허표에서는 商業的駐在(외국인투자 및 외국환 관리법상의 공통제한사항), 토지취득및 이용, 外換管理에 대하여 共通制限事項을 명기

o 修正讓許表에서는 기본적으로 외국인투자, 토지취득 및 이용에 대하여는 國內制度를 보다 명료하게 기재하고 外換管理에 관한 실질적인 제한사항은 各 業種別로 記載

o 人力移動에 있어서는 상업적주재에 따른 必須人力의 범위를 정의하고 同 人力의 일시적 입국을 양허

< 分野別 自由化約束 關聯事項 >

o 최초의 양허표에서는 國境間 供給, 海外消費, 商業的駐在 등 3가지 서비스 거래형태에 대한 규제사항을 기재하였으나 修正讓許表에서는 去來形態에 대한 구분없이 각종 규제사항만을 기재

o 최초의 양허표에서는 일부 登錄·許可要件을 기재하였으나 修正讓許表에서는 시장접근에 따른 수량제한등 制限措置(일반협정 16조관련)와 內國民待遇上의 차별 사항(17조관련)만을 기재하고 內·外國人이 동등하게 적용되는 등록요건등은 不記載(필요시 주석으로 명기)

o 최초의 양허표에서는 現存規制水準 讓許를 Standstill로 표기하였으나 修正讓許計劃表에서는 규제내용을 구체적으로 기재하여 양허

0026

Ⅲ. 向後 讓許協商 關聯對策

1. 讓許協商對策

가. 主要國의 開放要請(Request)에 대한 對應

- 현재 우리에게 서비스시장 개방을 요청하고 있는 나라는 美國, EC, 日本, 濠洲, 뉴질랜드, 카나다, 스위스, 스웨덴, 노르웨이, 핀랜드, 印度, 폴란드등 모두 12개국이며, 이번 修正讓許計劃表에서는 이들 국가의 요청사항중 일부만 반영

< 主要國의 開放要求事項 >

	開 放 要 求 業 種	備　考
美國	회계, 광고, 시청각, 보건시설관리, 통신, 엔지니어링, 건설, 프랜차이징, 보험, 법무, 소매업, 관광	엔지니어링 반영
EC	법무, 회계, 세무, 컴퓨터관련서비스, 광고, 통신, 건설, 유통, 금융, 호텔, 관광, 해운, 항공, 육운, 금융, 사업서비스(종합엔지니어링, 도시계획, R&D, 광업관련서비스, 속기서비스, 패션디자인, 시장조사 및 여론조사, 환경관련서비스)	事業서비스, 環境關聯서비스 반영
日本	사업서비스(장비임대, 전문직서비스, 엔지니어링), 시청각, 금융, 해운	-
캐나다	금융, 보험, 통신, 해운, 항공, 관광, 건설, 컴퓨터 및 소프트웨어 서비스, 사업서비스, R&D, 시장조사 및 여론조사, 광업관련서비스, 지질관련서비스, 환경관련서비스, 화물주선서비스	事業서비스, 環境關聯서비스 반영
濠洲	회계, 광고, 항공, 건설, 엔지니어링, 금융, 법무, 해운, 통신	-
스위스	유통, 금융	-
北歐(스웨덴, 노르웨이, 핀랜드)	통신, 건설, 유통, 금융, 해운, 육운, 법무, 회계, 설계, 엔지니어링, 광고, 컨설팅, 관광, 환경, 컴퓨터관련서비스	-
뉴질랜드	농업(축산)관련서비스, 교육서비스등	-

0027

- 앞으로 讓許協商에서 각국이 공식적으로 개방을 요청한 사항에 대해서는 보다 강도높은 압력 예상

o 1차적으로 현재의 修正讓許計劃表上에 제시된 수준을 가지고 讓許協商에 대응

o 각국이 계속 追加的인 自由化約束을 요구할 경우에는 다음 代案을 가지고 신축성있게 대응

① 法務서비스(外國法에 대한 法律諮問 허용)

· 변호사 자격요건중 國籍要件을 폐지한 수준에서 양허표에 등재용의 표명(방침 기확정)

② 醫療施設管理서비스

· 의료시설의 소유권과는 별개 용역업으로서의 開放 檢討意思 표명(방침 기확정)

③ 公認會計서비스(상호사용 및 업무제휴등)

· 國內規制制度의 본질을 침해하지 않는 범위내에서 수용여부 검토

④ 현재 국내제도상 자유화된 업종중 讓許表에 등재되지 않고 있는 업종

· 同 業種에 대해서는 이미 개방키로 결정한 사항으로서 일부국가에는 이미 약속된 상황이므로 開放 計劃을 철회할 의사가 없는 한 등재 불가피

· 同 業種에 대한 개방요구에 대해서는 個別法 및 外換管理上의 規制등을 검토한 후 신축성있게 대응

⑤ 기타 새로운 要求事項은 별도검토

o 金融서비스에 있어서는 美國, EC등 선진국들의 MFN原則 適用 제한움직임을 정확히 파악하여 대응

나. 우리가 開放要請한 事項에 대한 對策

- 그동안 우리나라는 美國, EC, 日本등 15개국에 대하여 금융, 유통, 통신, 건설등 업종에서 상대국의 서비스市場 開放을 요청

  ㅇ 美國등은 유통등 일부분야에서 追加讓許

- 우리가 중점적으로 개방을 요청한 나라들은 대부분 先進國으로서 우리와의 개방격차가 큰 실정이기 때문에 동등한 협상력을 발휘하는데는 한계가 있으나 우리의 입장을 방어하는 차원에서 開放要請事項을 계속 주장

< 우리의 開放要請事項 >

主 要 國	開 放 要 請 事 項	備 考
美國	통신, 건설, 유통, 은행, 보험, 육운, 창고, 관광, 엔지니어링	流通반영
EC	통신, 건설, 유통, 은행, 보험, 육운, 관광	-
日本	통신, 건설, 유통, 은행, 육운, 관광	-
캐나다	통신, 은행, 유통	-
濠洲	통신, 은행, 유통	-
스위스	통신, 은행, 증권	-
스웨덴, 핀랜드 노르웨이,뉴질랜드, 홍콩, 멕시코	통신	-
인도네시아	엔지니어링, 통신, 유통	-
泰國	엔지니어링, 유통	-
中國	영화 및 비디오, 보험, 통신, 건설	-

0029

2. 最惠國待遇(MFN) 逸脫對策

- 그간 最惠國待遇原則은 다자간 서비스협상의 기본원칙으로써 반드시 준수되어야 함을 강조

  o 이에 따라 우리는 最惠國待遇 逸脫要請은 가급적 최소한에 그치겠다는 입장표명

- 금년 1월 들어 美國, EC, 日本등 상당수의 국가들이 MFN 逸脫意思를 표명하고 있기 때문에 우리도 이에 伸縮性있게 대응필요

- 2월중 讓許協商 過程에서 우리의 MFN 일탈사항을 조건부로 제시함으로써 우리의 協商力 強化(공식제출시한 : 3.6)

  ① 콤퓨터 豫約서비스(CRS)

    o 韓·美 航空協定('91.6)에 따라 美國에 개방키로 한 SITA를 통한 CRS공급('92.4) 서비스는 美國을 제외한 여타국에 대하여 개방을 유보

    o 상기 MFN 逸脫內容은 UR/서비스협상에서 각국의 CRS 개방에 대한 開放約束程度에 따라 변경 가능

  ② 海運

    o 定期外航貨物船의 국적선 우선이용제도에 대한 適用免除 對象國은 우리나라와 해운협정을 맺고 있는 美國, 獨逸, 덴마크, 싱가폴, 台灣, 파키스탄, 노르웨이, 말레이지아, 나이지리아에 한정(海運産業育成法에 근거)

    o 1995.1월부터 同 制度 폐지가능

3. 協商關聯 國內對策의 차질없는 推進

- 우리의 修正讓許計劃表는 대부분 현재 개방된 업종 및 자유화수준을 반영하고 있으나 일부 분야에서 開放日程計劃 및 國內規制의 緩和를 양허하고 있기 때문에 이를 차질없이 추진해 나가는 것이 필요

① 開放日程 提示業種

o 建築設計 : 한국건축사와 공동계약 허용('96.1)

o 附加通信 : 외국인 지분제한 폐지('94.1)

o 一般建設 : 외국인 지분제한 폐지('94.1) 및 지사설치 허용('96.1)

o 專門建設 : 외국인 지분제한 폐지('94.1) 및 지사설치 허용('96.1)

o 海　　運 : 정기선 화물국적선 이용제도 폐지('95.1)

o 航　　空 : 항공기 수선 및 항공서비스 판매 합작투자 허용('97.1)
컴퓨터예약업 외국인 지분제한 폐지('94.1)

o 貨物트럭킹 및 鐵道小運送 : 연차적으로 영업지역 확대 ('97.1부터 전국 허용)

② 技術用役育成法의 改正

o 外國用役發注承認制의 신고제전환 및 주계약자제도의 폐지

o 登錄制를 申告制로 전환

0031

UR/서비스협상 관련 양자협의 대책

30

I. 상대국의 요청사항

1. 미 국

- UR 서비스협상을 촉진하기 위하여 미국은 Initial Offer를 제출한 9개국과 양자협의 제의
  - o 북구와 카나다는 Gulf전쟁으로 연기한 상태이며 호주, 뉴질랜드 등은 요청에 응할 예정임.

    【호주(1.28), 이국(1.29), 뉴질랜드(1.30)등과 양자협의 예정】
  - o 일본은 Framework와 분야별 부속서에 대한 협상이 선행되어야 한다는 점을 들어 미국요구에 답변을 미루고 있음.

- 참 석 자
  - o USTR의 N.Adams외 7명(USTR2, 상공부 3, 체신부 1, 노동부 1)

  * 동신분야는 한·미 쌍무간 동신우선협상대상국(PFC)지정과 관련 동신 협상도 병행

- 주요협의 요청사항
  - o 미국의 관심분야에 대한 시장접근 및 내국민대우 요구
    - · 회계, 광고, 시청각서비스, 건축설계, 건설, 엔지니어링, 법무서비스, 통신, 관광, 보험, 은행, 증권 및 기타금융서비스, 컴퓨터서비스, 컨설팅, 리스, 프랜차이징

0032

o '90. 6 미국이 아측에 요구한 사항

· 회계법인에 대한 시장접근, 보험중개업에 대한 시장접근, T·V광고 등에 대한 시장접근, 동신시스템 컨설턴트에 대한 자격요건등

o 동신분야에 대한 포괄적인 사항

o 금융분야에 대한 요구사항

· 금융서비스의 광범위한 개방약속과 동등한 경쟁기회(ECO) 보장 요구

· 금융분야의 Initial Offer는 최소한 현존 자유화수준(standstill) 이 되어야 함.

2. E C

- 복수국가간의 비공식협의를 요청

o 일 시 : 1.30일경(잠정)

o 장 소 : 스위스 제네바

o 참석범위 : Offer List를 제출한 10개국가 및 기타 관심국가

o 의 제 : 각국의 Offer List에 대한 설명(Clarification)및 서비스 협정 Framework에 대한 협의로 대부분의 국가가 이와같은 비공식 협의에 지지

0033

Ⅱ. 아국의 대응방안

1. 기본방향

- 아국의 주요교역 상대국인 미국과 EC 양자의 요청사항을 적절히 충족시키는 선에서 양자협의 및 협상에 대응
  - o 일단 미국과 EC의 요청에 따라 협상에 참가

- Initial Offer List이외에 추가적인 개방약속하는 문제에 대해서는 소극적으로 대응
  - o 금번협의는 각국의 Initial Offer에 대한 설명 및 기본입장을 제시하는 것에 한하며,
  - o 아직까지 Framework와 분야별부속서 제정작업이 완료되지 않은 상태이며, EC 등 조건부로 Offer List를 제출한 국가 및 Offer List 미제출국가들과도 협상진행상 전체적인 균형유지가 필요

- 특히 금융분야는 FPT등 양자협의를 통하여 주요쟁점에 대해서는 충분히 이해가 된 상태이므로 Offer List에 대한 설명 및 금융부속서에 대한 아국입장을 설명토록 함.

2. 협상팀 구성

- 미국의 협상팀 규모와 비슷하게 아측의 본부대표단은 10여명으로 구성하되 수석대표는 경제기획원 제2협력관이 담당하고 각분야별로 협상책임자가 참석
  - o 당부는 국제금융과(금융서비스) 증권업무과(회계서비스) 사무관이 참석토록 함.

0034

3. 협상대책자료 준비

- 금융분야 Initial Offer에 대한 자료
  - o 금융주석서에 대한 기본입장 및 우리의 금융제도에 대한 설명

- 미국의 Request List에 대한 아국입장 및 미국의 Offer List에 대한 질문사항 준비

가. 보험서비스 : 보험중개업(Broker system)개방

- 현황
  - o 보험중개업은 아직까지 국내에서도 시행되고 있지 않는 제도로서
  - o 다만 외국으로부터의 Broker제도 개방압력에 능동적으로 대처하기 위해 '88.12 외국보험중개회사등에 대한 대리점 허가기준을 제정하여, 현재 국내에서 시행되고 있는 전속대리점의 형태에 한해 외국사의 국내진출근거를 마련하였음.
  - o 동 규정에 의해 '90.12 Johnson & Higgins 중개사의 전속대리점 본인가를 해주었음.

- 검토의견
  - o 현재 우리 보험시장은 상품이 다양치 못하고 대부분 협정요율이기 때문에 보험Broker 제도도입이 불필요하며,
  - o 국내 보험 모집질서가 미처 확립되지 않은 현 단계에서는 이를 성급히 도입할 경우 향후 소비자보호에 큰 문제점에 야기될 수 있음.
  - o 따라서 동제도가 시행되기 위해서는 다양한 보험상품과 범위요율체계 및 건전한 보험모집 질서가 확립되어 소비자들로부터 이제도에 대한 자발적 수요가 충분히 형성되어야 할 것임.

0035

나. 회계서비스 : 회계법인 설립 및 업무범위 제한

- 현 황

o 외국인 국내공인회계사 시험응시에 아무런 제한이 없으며, 합격한 경우 업무범위에도 제한이 없음.

o 단 한국의 회계사자격을 인정하는 국가에서 자격을 취득한 외국 공인회계사는 국내상법·세법등 일부과목에 대한 시험을 거쳐 국내영업인가를 받을 수 있으며, 이러한 경우 업무범위는 본국기업이 50%이상 출자한 합작기업이나 본국기업이 이해관계를 가진 기업체에 대한 회계감사업무 수행가능

· 현재까지 13명의 외국인 국내공인회계사 자격을 취득

o 외국인의 회계법인 설립 또는 투자는 허용되지 않고 있음.

· 다만 외국회계법인은 국내회계법인과 업무제휴를 통하여 자국회계사를 국내회계법인에 파견하여 업무를 수행하고 있음. (Technical Adviser로서 국내영업인가를 받지않고 있음)

- 검토의견

o 외국공인회계사로서 국내영업인가를 받은 경우의 업무범위 제한

· 당분간 국내공인회계사의 경쟁력 제고등 수용태세 정비를 위하여 일정기간 경과후 업무제한 철폐가 가능하며,

o 외국인의 회계법인 설립 및 투자허용

· 국내회계법인의 수용태세 정비를 위하여 일정기간 경과후 단계적으로 허용할 예정이며, 회계법인은 공인회계사로 구성되는 인적단체이므로 회계사 자격을 갖고 있는 자에 한함.

0036

경 제 기 획 원

우 427-760 / 경기도 과천시 중앙동1 정부제2청사 / 전화 503-9149 / 전송 503-9141

문서번호 통조삼 10502-60
시행일자 1992. 4. 1
(경유)
수신 수신처참조
참조

선결			지시		
접수	일자 시간	92. 4. 2	결재·공람		
	번호	11086		국장	
처리과				심의관	
담당자				과장	

제목 UR/서비스 양허협상 대책회의 개최

그간 3차에 걸친 양허협상결과 주요쟁점으로 부각된 사항들을 논의하기 위하여 UR/서비스 양허협상관련 대책회의를 다음과 같이 개최하니 각 회의의제에 대하여 책임있는 결정을 할 수 있는 각부처의 담당과장이 별첨 회의결정 필요사항에 대한 입장을 정립하여 참석해 주기 바랍니다.

- 다 음 -

- 일 시 : '92. 4.7(화), 15:00~18:00
- 장 소 : 경제기획원 대회의실(과천청사 1동 727호)
- 참석범위 : 경제기획원 제2협력관(회의주재)
  외 무 부 통상기구과장
  재 무 부 국제금융과장
  법 무 부 국제법무담당검사, 출입국기획과장
  문 화 부 영화진흥과장
  상 공 부 유통산업과장
  건 설 부 해외협력과장
  교 통 부 국제협력과장
  노 동 부 인력수급과장
  체 신 부 통신협력과장
  과 기 처 기술협력2과장
  항 만 청 진흥과장
  KIEP 성극제 선임연구위원
  KDI 김지홍 연구위원

0037

우 427-760 / 경기도 과천시 중앙동1 정부제2청사 / 전화 503-9149 / 전송 503-9141

첨부 : 서비스협상대책관련 주요결정 필요사항 1부. 끝.

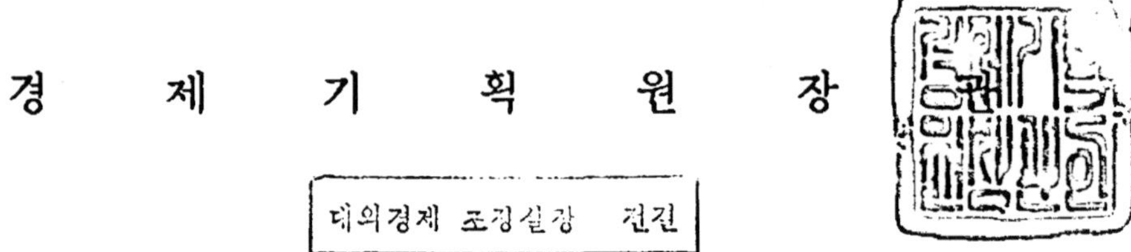

경 제 기 획 원 장

대외경제 조정실장 전결

수신처 : 외무부장관, 재무부장관, 법무부장관, 문화부장관, 상공부장관, 건설부장관, 교통부장관, 노동부장관, 체신부장관, 과학기술처장관, 해운항만청장, 대외경제정책연구원장, 한국개발연구원장

0038

< 別添 > 서비스協商對策關聯 主要決定 必要事項

課 題	主要決定 必要事項	主管部處
1. 人力移動	① 서비스販賣者(Service Seller) 및 單獨代表者(Sole Representative)의 정의확정 및 양허여부 * Service Seller는 양허하기로 기 결정하였으나 同 人力에 대한 定義가 명료하지 못하여 修正 Offer에는 일단 제외한 상황 ② 專門家(Specialist)의 범위에 資格所持者 포함여부 ③ 人力移動의 制限事由로 "Labor management disputes"를 제시한 근거마련	勞動部
2. MFN逸脫	① 韓・日間 시청각서비스교류 제한사항 - 韓・日間 文化交流에 대한 기본 입장 정립 - MFN逸脫 根據對象 : 영화 및 비디오 수입, 각종공연, 영화제작・배급업 등 * 同 事項의 MFN일탈문제는 매우 광범위하기 때문에 韓・日間 文化交流次元에서 장기적인 정책방향을 바탕으로 검토되어야 하며, 특정 국가에 대한 특혜배제라는 점에서 國際的非難을 고려한 신중한 접근이 필요	文化部

0039

課　題	主要決定 必要事項	主管部處
	② 韓·日航路에 있어서의 제한사항 - 우리가 이미 제출한 Waiver의 MFN逸脫事項과 연결시켜 韓·日 航路의 制限事項 추가 MFN일탈여부 검토	海運港灣廳
	③ 貿易業에 대한 MFN 適用排除問題	商工部
	※ 상기 ①~③은 현재 추진중인 韓·日 貿易逆調改善問題와 관련하여 검토 필요	
	④ 金融分野	財務部
3. 通信	① 基本通信分野 미국의 Request에 대한 각 항목별 우리의 입장을 명확히 정리	遞信部
	② 基本通信分野의 다자화협상 참여여부 - 美國이 동건관련 多者化協商을 요구한 12개국의 국가별 입장파악·정리 - 協商參與與否에 대한 입장 및 동 입장에 대한 설명논리 정립	
4. 航空	① 航空附屬書에 대한 세부항목별 우리의 입장정립	交通部

0040

課　題	主要決定 必要事項	主管部處
5. 海運	① GATT事務局이 제시한 海運附屬書案 및 EC, 北歐國家등이 제시한 입장에 대한 항목별 우리의 대응입장 정립 ② 海運補助서비스 각 업종별 다자화시한 등 우리의 입장정립 - 遞信部, 鐵道廳등 관계부처의 입장 종합	海運港灣廳
6. 會計	① 國際提携(affiliation) 許容要求에 대한 우리의 입장정립	財務部
7. 法務	① 國際提携(affiliation) 許容要求에 대한 우리의 입장정립	法務部
8. 保險	① 無配當 保險商品 認可指針과 관련 허용범위확대 및 예정이율 인하요구에 대한 우리입장의 정립	財務部
9. 建設	① 都給限度額制度 廢止要求에 대한 우리입장의 정립 ② 3년마다의 新規免許 發給制度, 免許更新制度에 대한 우리의 입장정립 ③ 外國建設技術者의 資格認定基準에 대한 우리의 입장정립	建設部

0041

課　題	主要決定 必要事項	主管部處
※ 其他	① 相對國의 要求事項 및 우리의 요구 사항에 대한 지금까지의 협상결과 종합정리 ② 修正讓許表 記載業種의 포괄범위 명료화	各部處

0042

경 제 기 획 원

우 427-760 / 경기도 과천시 중앙동1 정부제2청사 / 전화 503-9149 / 전송 503-9141

문서번호 통조삼 10502-70
시행일자 1992. 4. 6
(경유)
수신 수신처참조
참조

선결			지시		
접수	일자 시간	92 . 4 . 7	결재·공람		
	번호	11785			
처리과					
담당자		(서명)			

제목 UR/서비스 양허협상 대책회의 개최일시 변경통보

1. 통조삼 10502-67('92.4.1) 관련입니다.

2. 각부처의 보다 면밀한 검토를 바탕으로 각 쟁점사항에 대한 우리의 입장을 최종적으로 결정하는 회의가 될 수 있도록 UR/서비스 양허협상 대책회의를 '92.4.14(화), 15:00로 변경, 개최코자 하니 철저히 준비해 주시기 바랍니다.(개최일시 변경이외의 여타사항은 종전과 동일)

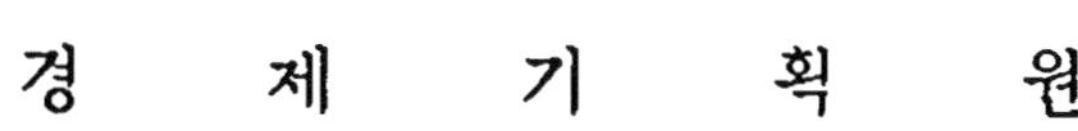

제 2협력관 전결

수신처 : 외무부장관, 재무부장관, 법무부장관, 문화부장관, 상공부장관, 건설부장관, 교통부장관, 노동부장관, 체신부장관, 과학기술처장관, 해운항만청장, 대외경제정책연구원장, 한국개발연구원장

0043

最近에 提示된 UR서비스協商 關聯資料

- Request

  - o 캐나다의 追加 Request
  - o 스리랑카의 Request
  - o 아이슬란드의 Request
  - o 中國의 Request
  - o 스위스의 追加 Request
  - o 오스트리아의 Request

- 修正 Offer

  - o 美國의 金融分野에 대한 修正 Offer

- MFN逸脫 List

  - o 21개국의 List
  - o 中國의 List
  - o 베닌의 List

0044

91무
20-1

UR對策 서비스
實務小委員會 資料

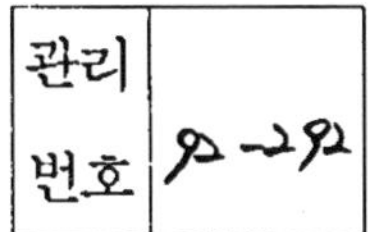
관리 번호 92-292

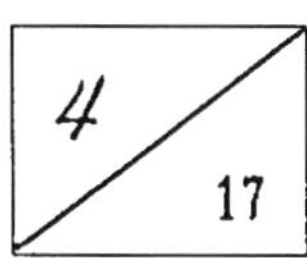
4 / 17

最近 UR/서비스協商의 進展狀況과 對應方向

1992.6.30에 예고문에 의거 일반문서로 재분류됨

'92. 4. 14

經 濟 企 劃 院
對外經濟調整室

0045

目　　次

0046

I. 協商進行狀況

- 서비스 一般協定(GATS)의 制定作業은 '91년 12월 20일 UR 最終協定文案(MTN.TNC/W/FA)이 제출된 이후 기술적 논의에 국한하여 非公式的 協議가 계속 진행되고 있는 상태

  o 항공부속서 내용중 空港設備利用權保障(제4항)의 해석에 대한 문제와 海運附屬書의 追加制定與否를 둘러싼 非公式的 協議
  o 協定文 제34조(定義)에 대한 비공식협의
  o 양허표작성을 위한 共通基準制定을 위한 논의
  o 법제화그룹에서 共同紛爭解決節次등 타분야와 관련되는 사항의 기술적 논의등

- 서비스 國家別 讓許協商은 그간 3차에 걸쳐 진행되었으며 ~~주요협상참가국들은~~ 협상종결을 위해서 수차례의 追加協商이 ~~필요하다는 인식~~

  o '92년 4월 13일 현재 Offer를 제시한 국가는 47개국(修正 Offer 제출국 24개국)으로 主要國은 수정 Offer를 모두 제출하고 開發途上國의 Offer제출을 기다리고 있는 상태

- MFN逸脫 對象目錄은 '92년 4월 13일 현재 32개국이 제출하였으나 일탈목록이 지나치게 광범위하고 공통규율이 없는 상태로서 앞으로 MFN逸脫事項의 정리가 서비스협상 진전의 주요 변수로 대두

  o 특히 美國이 기본통신, 해운, 항공, 금융분야등 주요한 분야를 망라한 MFN 逸脫事項을 제출

Ⅱ. 우리의 對應現況

- 서비스 一般協定 및 同 附屬書에 대한 현단계에서의 협의는 제네바 대표부를 중심으로 對應하고 있는 상황

- 수정 Offer List를 새로운 讓許表 作成方式에 따라 작성하여 지난 2월 17일 GATT에 제출
  - o 協商對象國의 Request가 있었던 업종중 일부 自由化業種을 Offer에 추가 반영

- MFN 逸脫事項은 해운 Waiver제도, 항공 CRS등 2개분야를 대상으로 作成하여 3월 12일 GATT에 제출

- 讓許協商에는 정부대표단을 구성하여 3차례 참여
  - o 第1次(1.28~31) : 미국, EC, 일본, 호주, 뉴질랜드, 스웨덴, 핀란드등 7개국
  - o 第2次(2.24~28) : 미국, EC, 일본, 카나다, 호주, 뉴질랜드, 스위스, 스웨덴, 핀란드, 노르웨이, 태국등 11개국
  - o 第3次(3.19~20) : 미국, EC, 일본, 중국등 4개국

- 양허협상에서는 修正讓許計劃表의 범위내에서 대응하였으며 추가적인 자유화 약속요구에 대하여는 현재 수준이상의 양허가 곤란함을 구체적으로 설명하는 線에서 대응
  - o 또한 우리의 相對國에 대한 要求 및 確認事項도 계속 제기

0048

Ⅲ. 向後展望 및 對應方案

1. 協商展望

- 앞으로의 讓許協商日程은 아직 확정되지 않았으나 전체 UR협상과 연계되어 결정될 것으로 전망
  - ㅇ 4월 22일 美·EC 頂上會談이 UR협상 조기타결여부의 분기점이 될 것으로 예상
- 따라서 同 頂上會談을 전후하여 개최될 것으로 관측되는 TNC 會議에서 T1, T2, T3등의 協商日程이 제시될 것으로 보이며 T2(서비스 양허협상)은 빠르면 4월 27일 주간부터 再開될 가능성도 있음.

2. 向後 協商對應方案

가. 共通課題에 대한 대책

① 人力移動(노동부 안건검토)

- 서비스販賣者(Service Seller) 및 單獨代表者(Sole Representative)의 정의확정 및 양허여부
- 專門家(Specialist)의 범위에 資格所持者 포함여부
- 人力移動의 制限事由로 "Labor management disputes"를 제시한 근거마련

② 우리 讓許計劃表上의 業種包括範圍 확정(별첨자료 참조)

- 우리 讓許計劃表 業種範圍와 CPC 包括範圍 비교검토
- 우리가 Offer한 업종의 包括範圍를 명료화할 필요성이 있는 분야(즉 CPC 包括範圍와 다른분야)에 대하여 주석을 작성 제출(4.22)

③ 우리의 Request에 대한 相對國의 答辯內容 종합정리(별첨자료 참조)

- 所管事項에 대하여 經濟企劃院에서 작성한 내용을 修正·補完하여 제출(4.22)

나. 分野別課題에 대한 對策

- 다음사항에 대하여 각부처가 마련한 자료를 기초로 經濟企劃院과 關係部處가 協商對策을 합의 · 확정하도록 함.

  o 필요한 경우 별도의 關係部處會議를 개최

課　題	主要決定 必要事項	主管部處
1. MFN逸脫	- 韓 · 日間 시청각서비스교류 제한사항 - 韓 · 日航路에 있어서의 제한사항 - 貿易業에 대한 MFN 適用排除問題	文化部 港灣廳 商工部
2. 通信	- 基本通信分野 미국의 Request에 대한 각 항목별 우리의 입장을 명확히 정리 - 基本通信分野의 다자화협상 참여여부	遞信部
3. 航空	- 航空附屬書에 대한 세부항목별 우리의 입장정립	交通部
4. 海運	- GATT事務局이 제시한 海運附屬書案 및 EC, 北歐國家등이 제시한 입장에 대한 항목별 우리의 대응입장 정립 - 海運補助서비스 각 업종별 다자화시한 등 우리의 입장정립	海運港灣廳
5. 會計	- 國際提携(affiliation) 許容要求에 대한 우리의 입장정립	財務部
6. 法務	- 國際提携(affiliation) 許容要求에 대한 우리의 입장정립	法務部

0050

課 題	主要決定 必要事項	主管部處
7. 保險	- 無配當 保險商品 認可指針과 관련 허용범위확대 및 예정이율 인하요구에 대한 우리입장의 정립	財務部
8. 建設	- 都給限度額制度 廢止要求에 대한 우리입장의 정립 - 3년마다의 新規免許 發給制度, 免許更新制度에 대한 우리의 입장정립 - 外國建設技術者의 資格認定基準에 대한 우리의 입장정립	建設部
9. 外國人 投 資	- 外國人投資 改正作業을 우리의 수정 Offer 및 최종 자유화약속에 어느 범위까지 反映시키는가에 대한 검토	財務部

0051

21

경 제 기 획 원

우 427-760 / 경기도 과천시 중앙동1 정부제2청사 / 전화 503-9149 / 전송 503-9141

문서번호 통조삼 10502-96
시행일자 1992. 4. 16
(경유)
수신 수신처참조
참조

선결			지시		
접	일자 시간	92. 4. 16	결		
수	번호	13138	재 ·		
처리과			공		
담당자			람		

제목 UR/대책 서비스실무소위원회 결과통보

'92년 4월 14일 개최된 표제회의결과를 통보하니 각부처는 소관업종의 포괄범위에 대한 주석, 우리 Request에 대한 상대국의 대응결과, 최근의 추가 Request에 대한 대응방안을 4.22(수)까지 기일 엄수하여 경제기획원에 제출하는등 UR서비스 양허협상 대책추진에 만전을 기해 주시기 바랍니다.

첨부 : UR대책 서비스 실무소위원회 결과 1부. 끝.

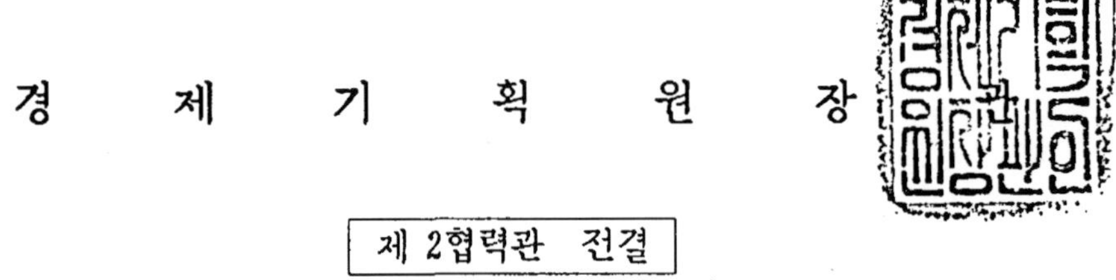

경 제 기 획 원 장

제 2협력관 전결

수신처 : 외무부장관, 재무부장관, 법무부장관, 문화부장관, 상공부장관, 건설부장관, 교통부장관, 노동부장관, 체신부장관, 과학기술처장관, 해운항만청장, 대외경제정책연구원장, 한국개발연구원장

0052

UR對策 서비스實務小委員會 結果

Ⅰ. 會議概要

- 日時 및 場所 : '92. 4.14(火), 15:00~18:00,
  經濟企劃院 大會議室

- 參席者 : 경제기획원 제2협력관(회의주재), 통상조정3과장, 외무부, 재무부, 법무부, 상공부, 문화부, 교통부, 노동부, 체신부, 해운항만청 담당과장, KIEP 성극제 연구위원, KDI 김지홍 연구위원등

- 議 題 : UR서비스 讓許協商對策

Ⅱ. 會議結果

1. 人力移動

① 서비스販賣者(Service seller)는 기본적으로 勞動部가 마련한 案을 중심으로 최종적인 양허표 제출시 Offer토록 함.

- 다만 구체적인 表現文句는 經濟企劃院, 法務部, 勞動部가 협의하여 결정하고 각부처에 추후통보

- 財務部 및 文化部는 소관분야에 대하여 현재의 방침대로 서비스판매자를 Offer하기 어려울 경우 이에 대한 대안을 마련하여 經濟企劃院, 法務部, 勞動部등 관계부처와 협의

0053

② 專門家의 Offer 關聯事項

- 공인된 資格所持者는 각국마다 資格認定制度가 상이하므로 이를 일률적으로 전문가로 인정할 수 없으므로 일단 현재의 Offer수준 유지

- 노동부가 專門家의 判斷基準과 관련하여 고도의 지식 보유조건과 해당기업에 대한 獨占的인 知識保有條件이 동시 충족되야 하는 조건인지 여부문제, 국내인력으로 대체가 불가능한 인력이라는 개념의 추가문제에 대하여 별도 검토하여 關係部處會議에서 정부입장을 결정

- 노동부는 分野別 專門家의 範圍를 설정하기 위한 구체적 작업계획을 수립·추진

③ 單獨代表者(Sole representative)는 출입국관리법에 해당되는 규정이 없고 EC외에 대부분의 國家가 Offer하지 않은 상태이므로 우리도 Offer하지 않도록 함.

④ 우리가 수정 Offer에 포함시킨 勞使關係와 관련한 인력이동에 대한 約束不適用 條項은 현행대로 유지토록 함.

2. Offer한 業種의 包括範圍 明瞭化作業

- 각부처가 Offer한 업종중 CPC분류와 包括範圍가 같지 않을 경우 註釋書(國·英文)를 회의자료에 포함된 양식에 따라 작성하여 4.22(수)까지 經濟企劃院에 제출토록 함.

3. 우리 Request에 대한 相對國 對應綜合整理 작업

- 우리가 Request한 사항에 대한 相對國의 對應結果를 회의자료를 바탕으로 수정·보완하고, 필요시 추가적인 Request를 발굴하여 4.22(수)까지 經濟企劃院에 제출토록 함.

0054

4. 追加 Request에 대한 對應

- 各部處는 최근에 캐나다(추가), 스위스(추가), 아이슬란드, 오스트리아, 폴란드, 中國, 스리랑카가 제시한 Request사항 중 소관분야에 대한 對應方案을 작성하여 4.22일(수)까지 經濟企劃院에 제출토록 함.

5. 分野別課題에 대한 對應

- 다음사항에 대해서는 會議結果를 토대로 向後協商에 대응토록 함.

① 한·일항로에 있어서의 制限事項은 추가 MFN 일탈목록의 제출계기가 마련되면 MFN逸脫을 신청

o 다만 지난번에 제출한 海運協定締結國에 대한 웨이버 면제제도의 MFN일탈신청사항과 대체토록 할 것인지는 추후 關係部處間 協議를 통해 결정

② 貿易業은 MFN일탈을 신청하지 않음.

- 시청각서비스, 통신, 항공, 해운, 회계, 법무, 보험, 건설, 외국인투자등 其他分野에 대해서는 각 과제별로 소관부처에서 이번 會議結果를 반영 추가적인 검토후 關係部處會議를 통하여 最終方針을 결정토록 함.

0055

경 제 기 획 원

우 427-760 / 경기도 과천시 중앙동1 정부제2청사 / 전화 503-9149 / 전송 503-9141

문서번호 통조삼 10502-99
시행일자 1992. 6. 12
(경유)
수신 수신처참조
참조

선결			지시	대리 참석	
접수	일자 시간	92. 6. 15	결재·공람		
	번호	21465		국장	
처리과				심의관	
담당자		이시형		과장	

제목 UR/서비스 실무소위원회 개최통보

1. 통조삼 10502-76('92.4.16) 관련입니다.

2. UR/서비스 제4차 양허협상이 6월 22일 주간에 개최될 예정으로 있어 이와 관련 대책회의를 다음과 같이 개최하니 참석하여 주시기 바랍니다.

- 다 음 -

가. 일 시 : '92. 6.18(목), 15:00

나. 장 소 : 경제기획원 대회의실(과천청사 1동 727호)

다. 참석범위 : 경제기획원 제2협력관(회의주재)
외 무 부 통상기구과장
재 무 부 국제금융과장
법 무 부 국제법무담당검사, 출입국 기획과장
문 화 부 저작권과장
상 공 부 국제협력과장
건 설 부 해외협력과장
교 통 부 국제협력과장
노 동 부 인력수급과장
체 신 부 통신협력과장
과학기술처 기술협력과장
환 경 처 정책조정과장
해운항만청 진흥과장
K D I 김지홍 연구위원
KIEP 성극제 〃 "끝"

경 제 기 획 원 장

대외경제조정실장 전결

수신처 : 외무부장관, 재무부장관, 법무부장관, 문화부장관, 상공부장관, 건설부장관, 교통부장관, 노동부장관, 체신부장관, 과학기술처장관, 환경처장관, 해운항만청장, 한국개발연구원장, 대외경제정책연구원장 0056

修正讓許表의 業種包括範圍 檢討

1. 註釋이 不必要한 業種

- 讓許業種 55개중 CPC 5單位와 業種名 및 包括範圍가 대체로 일치하거나 업종의 정의가 명확하여 주석이 필요없는 業種은 14개(3의 ×표)
  - o CRS는 GATT分類(MTN, GNS/W/120)나 CPC에 없지만 業種의 定義가 명확하여 주석이 불필요

2. 註釋이 必要한 業種

- CPC 5單位와 업종명이나 포괄범위가 상이하여 註釋이 필요한 業種(3의 ○표)은 41개이나 이중에는 讓許表의 業種名을 GATT분류나 CPC와 일치시키면 註釋이 불필요한 업종(3의 △)도 포함

< 修正讓許表와 CPC 比較 >

	대체로 一致	相 異
① 事業서비스	8	12
② 커뮤니케이션서비스	-	5
③ 建設서비스	-	2
④ 流通서비스	-	2
⑤ 環境關聯서비스	-	2
⑥ 金融서비스	-	9
⑦ 觀光서비스	2	1
⑧ 運送서비스	4	8
計	14	41

3. 業種包括範圍

修正讓許表의 業種	包　括　範　圍	備考
1. 事業서비스		
A. 專門職業서비스		
(1) 公認會計	0 CPC 862	△
(2) 稅務	0 CPC 863	△
(3) 建築設計	0 CPC 8671	×
(4) 엔지니어링	0 CPC 8672 + CPC 86754	○
(5) 綜合엔지니어링	0 CPC 8673	×
(6) 都市計劃 및 조경설계	0 CPC 8674	×
B. 컴퓨터 및 關聯 서비스		
(7) 컴퓨터設備 諮問業	0 CPC 841	×
(8) 소프트웨어施行	0 CPC 842	×
(9) DP	0 CPC 843	×
(10) DB	0 CPC 844	×
C. 硏究開發서비스		
(11) 自然科學部門 R&D	0 CPC 851	△
D. 賃貸서비스		
(12) 船舶貸與	0 CPC 83103	△
E. 其他事業서비스		
(13) 廣告	0 CPC 8711	△
(14) 市場調査 및 輿論調査	0 CPC 864	×

修正讓許表의 業種	包 括 範 圍	備考
(15) 經營컨설팅	0 CPC 86501, 86502, 86503, 86504, 86505, 86509	○
(16) 事業管理	0 CPC 86601	△
(17) 地質調査 및 探査	0 CPC 86751, 86752, 86753	○
(18) 國際會議用役	0 CPC 87909중 國際會議의 計劃, 準備, 進行등에 필요한 업무를 行事主管者로부터 위탁받아 代行하는 사업	○
(19) 번역	0 CPC 87905중 번역	○
(20) 速記士	0 CPC 87909중 速記士	○
2. 커뮤니케이션서비스		
A. 通信		
(21) 온라인 情報檢索 및 온라인 資料處理	0 CPC 75232	○
(22) 附加通信	0 CPC 75232	○
(23) 데이타單純傳送	0 CPC 75231	○
B. 視聽覺서비스		
(24) 映畵 및 비디오 製作·配給	0 CPC 96112, 96113	△
(25) 音盤製作·配給	0 音盤 및 테이프製作·販賣業 · GATT分類의 Sound Recording에 해당	△

修正讓許表의 業種	包 括 範 圍	備考
3. 建設		
(26) 一般建設(토목, 건축, 토건)	0 CPC 511, 512, 5131중 鋪裝工事業을 제외한 것, 5132, 5133, 5136중 發電設備工事業을 제외한 것, 5137, 5139	○
(27) 專門建設(특수, 전문, 전기, 전기통신, 소방시설)	0 CPC 5131중 鋪裝工事業, 5134, 5135, 5136중 發電設備工事業, 514, 515, 516, 517	○
4. 流通		
(28) 都賣		
< 除外業種 >		
0 穀物都賣業	0 CPC 62211	△
0 고기都賣業	0 CPC 62223	△
0 果實 및 채소都賣業	0 CPC 62221	×
0 原乳都賣業	0 CPC 62222중 原乳都賣業	○
0 알콜성飮料都賣業	0 CPC 62226중 알콜성 飮料都賣業	○
0 홍삼都賣業	0 CPC 62229중 홍삼都賣業	○
0 肥料都賣業	0 CPC 62276중 肥料都賣業	○
0 농약都賣業	0 CPC 62276중 농약都賣業	○
0 書籍 및 新聞都賣業	0 CPC 62262중 書籍 및 其他 印刷物都賣業	○

修正讓許表의 業種	包 括 範 圍	備考
0 連鎖化事業	0 백화점, 수퍼마켓, 편의점, 전문점 등과 같은 特定形態의 同一業種을 통일적 방법으로 운영하기 위하여 이를 經營者와 정형적인 체인계약을 체결하여, 그 運營에 필요한 각종 상품 및 용품을 자기 계정에 의하여 구입하여 繼續的, 總括的으로 공급하는 産業活動	○
0 一般貿易業	0 자기계정으로 구입한 專門 또는 綜合商品의 대외거래(수출 또는 수입)만을 전업으로 하는 事業體의 産業活動으로 다음과 같이 나누어 짐. ① 綜合貿易業 : 각종 상품을 綜合的으로 輸·出入하는 산업활동 ② 農畜産物, 飮食料品 및 담배 貿易業 ③ 家庭用品 貿易業 ④ 産業用 中間財 및 再生材料 貿易業 ⑤ 産業用 機械裝備 및 關聯用品 貿易業 ⑥ 달리 分類되지 않은 貿易業	○
0 貿易仲介業	0 CPC 621중 國境間 仲介業	○
0 農水畜産物(가축, 동물,화훼류포함) 도매시장	0 양곡류·청과류·화훼류·鳥獸肉類·어류·貝介類·해조류 및 林産物등을 도매 거래하게 하기 위하여 都市地域에 개설하는 市場	○

修正讓許表의 業種	包 括 範 圍	備考
<經濟的 必要性 檢討> 0 市場, 大型店, 都賣센타	0 市場 : 一定區域안의 건물 또는 지하도에 설치된 多數의 店鋪施設에서 都·小賣業者 및 이를 지원하는 용역업자가 계속적으로 商品을 賣買하거나 用役을 提供하는 營業場 0 大型店 : 都·小賣業이 이루어지는 하나의 점포로서 일정규모이상의 營業店 * 大型店의 基準 ① 賣場面積 : 1,000㎡이상 ② 運營基準 : 賣場面積中 상품의 판매에 직접 제공되는 營業場의 면적의 100% 直營 0 都賣센타 : 一定區域안의 건물에서 都賣業者가 근대적인 시설과 운영 체제를 갖추고 商品을 都賣하거나 用役을 提供하는 營業場 * 都賣센타의 基準 ① 賣場面積 : 3,000㎡이상 ② 運營基準 : · 賃借建物의 경우에는 10% 이상 直營 · 總商品賣出額의 100% 도매	○

修正讓許表의 業種	包 括 範 圍	備考
0 中古自動車賣買業	0 CPC 61111중 中古自動車 都賣業	○
0 가스都賣業	0 CPC 62271중 기체연료 및 關聯製品 都賣業	○
(29) 小賣		
< 除外業種 >		
0 담배小賣業	0 CPC 63108	×
0 골동품 및 예술품 小賣業	0 CPC 63299중 골동품 및 예술품 小賣業	○
0 醫藥品 小賣業	0 CPC 63211	△
0 化粧品 小賣業	0 CPC 63212	△
0 書籍小賣業	0 CPC 63253중 書籍(중고서적 포함) 및 其他印刷物 小賣業	○
0 穀物小賣業	0 CPC 63109중 穀物小賣業 0 CPC 63295중 飼料小賣業	○
0 고기小賣業	0 CPC 63103	△
0 原乳小賣業	0 CPC 63102중 原乳小賣業	○
0 家畜 및 動物 小賣業	0 CPC 63295중 家畜 및 動物小賣業	○
0 채소小賣業	0 CPC 63101	×
0 果實小賣業		×
0 달리 分類되지 않은 飲食料品 및 담배小賣業	0 CPC 63102, 63105, 63106, 63107, 63109	○
0 煉炭小賣業	0 CPC 63297	△
0 石油小賣業		△
0 가스小賣業		△

修正讓許表의 業種	包 括 範 圍	備考
0 注油所運營業 0 가스充電業	0 CPC 61300	△ △
<經濟的 必要性 檢討>		
0 市場, 大型店, 大規模 小賣店	0 市 場 : 都賣參照 0 大型店 : 都賣參照 0 大規模 小賣店 : 一定區域안의 건물에서 小賣業者가 근대적인 시설과 運營體制를 갖추고 直營 또는 賃貸의 형태로 商品을 小賣하거나 用役을 提供하는 營業場 * 大規模 小賣店의 種類 및 基準 ① 百貨店 · 各種 商品을 부문별로 구성하여 最終消費者로 하여금 일괄 구매할 수 있도록 直營爲主의 형태로 운영하는 大規模 店鋪 · 賣場面積 : 3,000㎡이상 · 運營體系 : 賣場面積의 50%이상 直營 ② 쇼핑센타 · 百貨店·수퍼마켓등 핵점포가 있고 각종 전문점과 레저시설·공공시설등 便益施設을 갖추고 통일적으로 管理·運營되는 직영 또는 임대형태의 소매업 집단	○

修正讓許表의 業種	包 括 範 圍	備考
	· 賣場面積 : 3,000㎡이상 · 運營體系 : 賃借建物의 경우는 賣場面積의 30%이상 직영	
0 中古自動車賣買業	0 CPC 61112중 中古自動車 小賣業	○
5. 環境關聯서비스		
(30) 特定廢棄物 收集處理	0 CPC 9402중 産業廢棄物을 수집, 운반 또는 처리하는 業 * 産業廢棄物의 種類 : 廢棄物管理法 제2조	○
(31) 폐수수탁처리	0 CPC 9401중 廢水處理施設을 갖추고 수탁한 산업체의 폐수를 再生·利用 외의 方法으로 처리하는 業	○
6. 金融		
< 銀行業 >		
(32) 預金 및 關聯業務	0 CPC 81115, 0 CPC 81116 중 預金의 수입, 유가증권 또는 기타 채무증서의 발행에 의하여 一般으로부터 債務를 負擔하는 업무	○
(33) 貸出 및 關聯業務	0 CPC 81131, 0 CPC 81132 중 자금대출, 어음할인 등 일반에게 이자수취를 목적으로 資金을 融資하는 業務	○
(34) 外換業務	0 CPC 81333중 外換의 賣買, 발행, 추심, 송금업무	○

修正讓許表의 業種	包　括　範　圍	備考
(35) 銀行附隨業務		○
0 商業어음賣出	0 CPC 81339중 商業어음 賣出業務	
0 貿易어음賣出	0 CPC 81339중 貿易어음 賣出業務	
0 相互賦金	0 CPC 81132중 相互賦金業務	
0 支給保證	0 CPC 8113중 支給保證業務	
(36) 信託業	0 CPC 81192, 0 CPC 81193 중 委託者가 수탁자에게 財産權을 위임하여 수탁자를 위하여 管理 處分하게 하는 업무	○
< 證券業 >		
(37) 證券業		○
0 自己賣買	0 CPC 81321중 自己賣買 業務	
0 委託賣買	0 CPC 81321중 委託賣買 業務	
0 引受業務	0 CPC 8132중 引受業務	
< 保險業 >		
(38) 원보험		○
0 生命保險	0 CPC 8121	
0 損害保險	0 CPC 8129중 재보험 및 재재보험업을 제외한 것	
(39) 재보험및 재재보험	0 CPC 81299중 재보험 및 재재보험업	○
(40) 보험계리업,	0 CPC 81404	○
손해사정업	0 CPC 81403중 손해사정업	

0066

修正讓許表의 業種	包 括 範 圍	備考
7. 觀光		
(41) 호텔(관광, 가족, 한국전통)	0 CPC 6411	△
(42) 旅行斡旋	0 CPC 7471	×
(43) 通譯案內	0 CPC 7472	×
8. 運送		
(44) 外航旅客運送	0 CPC 7211	×
(45) 外航貨物運送	0 CPC 7212	×
(46) 船舶維持 및 修繕	0 CPC 8868중 海上旅客 運送事業·海上貨物運送事業·船舶貸與業을 영위하는 자로부터 선박관리, 선원관리 및 해상보험등의 업무를 수탁하여 代行하는 事業	○
(47) 航空機修繕및 維持	0 CPC 8868중 航空機修繕 및 維持 서비스로서, 공항 또는 비행장의 계류장에서 航空機에 대한 비행전 점검등을 하는 사업	○
(48) 컴퓨터豫約	0 航空機 運航計劃, 가용좌석, 요금 및 항로에 관한 자료를 가지고 있는 컴퓨터 시스템을 통해 情報를 提供하는 業	×
(49) 航空서비스販賣	0 CPC 748의 일부 + 여객운송대리 ·航空運送總代理店業 : 航空運送事業者를 위하여 유상으로 항공기에 의한 여객 또는 화물의 國際運送契約締結을 대리(여권 또는 사증을 받는 절차의 대행제외)하는 사업	○

修正讓許表의 業種	包　括　範　圍	備考
	·航空貨物運送代理店業 : 航空運送事業者 또는 航空運送總代理店業者를 위하여 유상으로 항공기에 의한 화물의 運送契約 締結을 대리하는 사업	
(50) 貨物트럭킹	0 CPC 71233중 一定事業區域안에서 화물자동차를 이용하여 貨物을 運送하는 事業	○
(51) 鐵道小運送業	0 CPC 748중 鐵道에 의한 貨物運送代理業(철도를 이용하여 화물을 운송하고자 하는 자는 철도소운송업체에게 委託·運送하여야 함)	○
(52) 倉庫	0 CPC 742	×
(53) 海運代理店	0 CPC 748중 海上旅客運送事業 또는 海上貨物運送事業을 영위하는 자를 위하여 통상 그 事業에 속하는 去來代理를 하는 事業	○
(54) 海上貨物運送周旋	0 CPC 748중 자기의 명의로 선박에 의한 貨物의 운송을 周旋하는 事業	○
(55) 海運仲介業	0 CPC 748중 海上貨物 運送仲介, 또는 선박의 대여, 용대선, 매매를 仲介하는 事業	○

0068

UR 實務小委
會議資料

第4次 UR/서비스 讓許協商對策

1991. 6

經濟企劃院

0069

I. 讓許協商 經緯 및 日程

- 서비스 國家別 讓許協商은 그간 3차에 걸쳐 진행되었으며 협상종결을 위해서 앞으로도 수차례의 追加協商이 있을 전망
  - o '92.5.13 서비스 20개국 非公式協議에서 일부국에서 6月 讓許協商이 불필요하다는 유보의견이 있었으나 海運, 基本通信, 金融등의 주요난제외에 여러 技術的課題가 남아 있으므로 협상의 지속적 추진이 필요하다는 인식에 따라 협상을 속개키로 결정

- 금번 협상은 마지막 라운드가 아니므로 實質的 讓許交換이 곤란할 것이나 기술적 명료화 작업보다는 한단계 높은 Request와 Offer의 격차를 줄이기 위한 作業으로 성격규정 (카알라일 事務次長)
  - o 各國이 금번 협상에 임하는 수준은 일본외에는 대체적으로 小規模 代表團을 파견할 것으로 예상

- 우리나라의 금번 第4次 讓許協商對象 豫想國은 10개국임.

< 國家別 協商日程 및 各國의 參席水準 >

일자	시간	국가	참석수준
- 6. 23(火)	09:00	美 國	協商代表 및 金融專門家등 3~4명
	15:00	카나다	〃 및 金融, 通信, 運送, 人力移動 專門家
- 6. 24(水)	09:30	E C	未定
	15:00	濠 洲	서비스協商代表 2명
	17:00	뉴질랜드	〃 1명
- 6. 25(木)	09:30	노르웨이	本部代表 참석예정이나 代表團規模는 未定
	11:00	스웨덴	〃
	15:00	日 本	서비스協商代表 및 各 分野別 專門家등 완전한 협상팀
- 6. 26(金)	09:00	핀란드	未定
	11:00	스위스	〃

Ⅱ. 금번 讓許協商 對應基本方向

- 금번 讓許協商이 마지막 협상이 아니고, 또 UR全體協商의 進行速度가 늦어지고 있어 금번 협상에서 각국간에 實質的인 讓許交換 및 主要爭點에서의 의견접근은 곤란할 것으로 예상됨.

- 따라서 이번 讓許協商에는 다음의 基本立場으로 대응

  o 韓國政府는 그동안 서비스협상에 적극적으로 참여하여 왔으며 同 協商의 조속한 타결을 위하여 최선의 協調와 努力을 다할 것임을 강조

  o 業種別 讓許範圍에 있어서는 기본적으로 2.17 제출한 修正讓許計劃表의 範圍內에서, 쟁점별로는 기존의 입장을 견지하는 선에서 대응하고 MFN逸脫問題, 通信등 협상주요 쟁점에 대한 各國의 動向把握에 주력

  o 다만, 그간 各國이 우리에게 계속적으로 양허하기를 요구해 온 분야로서 最終讓許表 提出時 추가양허가 가능한 人力移動등 몇몇분야는 오늘 회의를 거쳐 肯定的으로 檢討하고 있음을 시사

- 또한 代表團規模는 대부분의 나라가 비교적 小規模 代表團을 파견할 예정이므로 우리도 협상총괄팀 중심의 대표단을 파견

Ⅲ. 主要爭點別 讓許協商 對應方向

主 要 爭 點	關聯國家	對 應 方 向
1. 人力移動分野 (서비스판매자 양허여부)	美, EC, 카나다, 오스트리아등	- 4.14 UR實務委에서 결정한 바와 같이 서비스 판매자는 最終讓許表 提出時 양허할 것이라는 입장을 표명 ※문화부 이의제기. 0 다만 금융부문의 서비스 販賣者 讓許適用 問題는 각국의 금융부문에의 양허내용 확인등 追加檢討結果에 따를 것임을 시사 * 기타 單獨代表者, 專門家範圍등 관련쟁점은 旣存立場 견지
2. MFN逸脫問題	모든 讓許協商 國家	- 금번 협상에 임하여서는 MFN逸脫 最小化라는 우리 基本立場에 변함없음을 표명하되, 다만 各國의 申請動向, 逸脫基準定立, 國內的 要求등을 감안 몇몇 분야에서 MFN逸脫與否를 구체적으로 검토중임을 언급하고 각국의 動向把握에 주력 * MFN逸脫 追加申請 관련해서는 현재 視聽覺分野, 韓·日航路, 貿易業, 外國人 土地取得上의 相互主義등을 공식 신청하고 금융분야에 대하여도 防禦的 MFN逸脫意思表明與否에 대한 검토가 진행중이나 政府方針은 이번 양허협상후 판단, 결정할 예정

0072

主 要 爭 點	關聯國家	對 應 方 向
3. 通信	美國, 스웨덴, 카나다등	- 美國의 기본장거리 통신시장개방 多者間 協商 要求에 대한 대응 0 현재의 제안 내용대로는 協商參與不可라는 기존입장을 견지 0 각 항목별 參與不可立場을 다시 설명 0 다만, MFN일탈 불가, 쌍무협상배제등 협상 참여의 前提條件에 대한 美側反應 타진 - 同 多者間 協商關聯 Sweden 제안에 대한 대응 0 同 案이 교착상태에 빠진 基本通信關聯 協商 打開를 위해 각국 입장을 비교적 균형되게 반영했다는 점에서 검토의 대상이 될 수 있을 것이라는 肯定的 意思表明
4. 金融	美, 카나다, EC 등	- 金融分野의 경우 기존의 입장을 견지하고 현행 우리 offer水準 및 현재 진행중인 blueprint 作業計劃을 자세히 설명
5. 會計 및 法務 서비스의 affiliation허용	美國	- 會計서비스 affiliation과 관련해서는 0 광범위하고 불명확한 int'l affiliation 개념의 受容이 곤란하다는 旣存立場 견지 0 投資를 통한 financial link 형태를 제외한 國際商號의 連繫使用등 affiliation의 주요 요소들은 실제 다 허용되고 있는데 이를 公式 讓許하라는 미측의 의도를 정확하게 파악 * 商業的駐在의 한 형태로서의 affiliation 개념 認定問題 검토중 - affiliation槪念의 법률서비스에의 적용에 대해서는 反對立場 견지

主 要 爭 點	關聯國家	對 應 方 向
6. 會議錄 作成問題	美國	- 먼저 美側提議에 대한 각국의 반응 타진한 후 0 會議錄(Record of Discussion)은 일반적으로 法的拘束力이 없는 형식이라는 점을 확인하고 또 기록된 사항에 대한 flexibility가 있어야 함을 강조하고 그런 점을 會議錄 head에 명기하는 條件으로 수용 0 法的拘束力이 있는 회의록에 대해서는 반대
7. 서비스業 外國人 土地取得 許容 問題	EC	- 外國人 不動産 取得制限은 한국의 특수한 역사적 경험에서 배태된 外國人 土地所有自體에 대한 일반국민의 거부감이라는 정서적 요인으로 인해 外國人 土地所有를 전면 허용시 정치적 문제화될 소지가 있어 당분간 현재의 제도유지는 불가피함을 설명 0 다만 앞으로 外國人 不動産取得 許容範圍를 점차 확대할 것임을 표명하고 현재 금융·호텔외에 추가로 R&D센타, 航空機·自動車 性能檢査등 제조업과 관련된 첨단서비스업 및 보험업에 대한 土地取得許容도 현재 검토중임을 설명
8. 海運·航空등		- 航空附屬書·海運關聯 EC의 Model 스케쥴 제안 등에 대해서는 交通部 및 海運港灣廳과 별도 협의하여 입장정립후 대응
9. 建設	日本	- 日本이 제기할 경우 旣存立場水準에서 대응
10. 其他		- 旣存立場 견지

경 제 기 획 원

우 427-760 / 경기도 과천시 중앙동1 정부제2청사 / 전화 503-9149 / 전송 503-9141

문서번호 통조삼 10502-118
시행일자 1992. 9. 17
(경유)
수신 수신처참조
참조

선결			지시		
접수	일자 시간	:	결재·공람		
	번호			국장	
처리과				심의관	
담당자				과장	

제목 호주와의 UR/서비스협상 관련 협의참석요청

호주측으로부터 UR/서비스협상과 관련한 문제에 대해 협의요청(주요관심사항은 서비스일반, 금융, 통신등이며 공식적협상은 아님)이 있어 다음과 같이 호주측과 비공식 협의를 가지고자 하니 귀부의 과장급 담당자가 참석하도록 조치하여 주시기 바랍니다.

- 다 음 -

가. 일 시 : '92. 9.23(수), 14:30~16:30

나. 장 소 : 경제기획원 소회의실(과천청사 1동 722호)

다. 참석범위 : 경제기획원 제2협력관(회의주재)
외 무 부 통상기구과장
재 무 부 국제금융과장
체 신 부 통신협력과장

첨부 : 호주측 대표단 및 주요 예상발언요지 1부. 끝.

경 제 기 획 원 장

제2협력관 전결

수신처 : 외무부장관, 재무부장관, 체신부장관

0075

RECEIVED FROM 5039141 1992.09.17 11:02 P. 1

UR/서비스 濠洲代表團 訪問關聯

1. 訪問日時 및 代表團構成

- 訪問日時 : '92. 9.23, 14:30
- 代 表 團 : Donald Kenyon(對外貿易部 Principal Adviser)외 數名

2. 訪問背景

- 濠洲代表團은 서비스협상문제등을 논의하기 위해 아시아 각국을 순방중임.
- 이번 訪問의 目的은 UR/서비스협상에 대한 논의외에 UR타결 지연시 양국간의 서비스部門 協力可能性을 타진하고자 하는 것임.

3. 主要 豫想發言要旨

- UR 協商全般 및 서비스協商 展望에 대한 양국의 의견교환 (미국의 신속처리권한 시한내 UR妥結可能性에 대한 濠洲의 평가 포함)
- 兩國의 offer에 대한 部門別 論議 및 美國의 MFN逸脫에 대한 대응방안 모색
- UR타결지연시 서비스부문에서의 兩國間 協議(bilateral work program)를 지속해 나갈 수 있는지 여부에 대한 논의
  - o 역내의 서비스交易을 촉진시키기 위해 양국이 협력할 수 있는 부문을 모색

0076

원 본

외 무 부

종 별 :

번 호 : AUW-0788 일 시 : 92 0918 1030

수 신 : 장관(통일,아동,사본:상공부)

발 신 : 주호주대사

제 목 : 호주 통상조사단 방한

1. 외무무역부 다자통상국 CON KENYON (PRINCIPAL ADVISOR, MULTI LATERAL TRADE DIV)을 단장으로 한 주재국 통상조사단이 9.22-24 방한 예정임.

2. 동 조사단은 방한중 9.23 오후 아측과 우루과이 라운드의 진전사항 검토와 특히 서비스 분야에 있어서 호주의 대 아국 진출 확대 가능성등을 타진 예정이라하며,동 방한 일정은 주한 호주대사관에서 주선중임.끝.

(대사 이창범-국장)

통상국 2차보 아주국 상공부

PAGE 1 92.09.18 21:02 CR

외신 1과 통제관

0077

지 급

경 제 기 획 원

우 427-760 / 경기도 과천시 중앙동1 정부제2청사 / 전화 503-9149 / 전송 503-9141

문서번호 통조삼 10502-121
시행일자 1992. 10. 2
(경유)
수신 수신처참조
참조

선결			지시		
접수	일자 시간	92.10.5 :	결재·공람	국장	[서명]
	번호	34903		심의관	[서명]
처리과					
담당자					

제목 UR/서비스 실무소위원회 개최통보

1. 통조삼 10502-109('92.7.16) 관련입니다.

2. UR/서비스 제5차 양허협상이 10월 12일 주간에 개최될 예정으로 있어 이와 관련 대책회의를 다음과 같이 개최하고자 하니 참석하여 주시기 바라며 별첨 회의자료에 대해서도 사전에 검토하여 주시기 바랍니다.

- 다 음 -

가. 일 시 : '92. 10.7, 10:00

나. 장 소 : 경제기획원 대회의실(과천청사 1동 727호)

다. 참석범위 : 경제기획원 제2협력관(회의주재)
외 무 부 통상기구과장
내 무 부 지적과장
재 무 부 국제금융과장
법 무 부 출입국 기획과장
농림수산부 국제협력과장
문 화 부 저작권과장
상 공 부 국제협력과장
건 설 부 해외협력과장
교 통 부 국제협력과장
노 동 부 인력수급과장
체 신 부 통신협력과장
과학기술처 기술협력과장
환 경 처 정책조정과장

0078

우 427-760 / 경기도 과천시 중앙동1 정부제2청사 / 전화 503-9149 / 전송 503-9141

해운항만청 진흥과장
KIEP 성극제 연구위원
한양대학교 김지홍 교수

첨부 : UR/서비스 제5차 양허협상대책 1부. 끝.

경 제 기 획 원 장

대외경제조정실장 전결

수신처 : 외무부장관, 내무부장관, 재무부장관, 법무부장관, 농림수산부장관, 문화부장관, 상공부장관, 건설부장관, 교통부장관, 노동부장관, 체신부장관, 과학기술처장관, 환경처장관, 해운항만청장, 대외경제정책연구원장, 한양대학교 총장

0079

외 무 부

110-760 서울 종로구 세종로 77번지 / (02)720-2188 / (02)720-2686 (FAX)

문서번호 통기 20644-

시행일자 1992.10. 5.( )

수신 통상1과장, 통상2과장

참조

취급		통 상 기 구 과 장
보존		
국 장		
심의관		
과 장	전 결	
기안	안 명 수	협조

제목 UR 서비스 협상

1. 10.12 주간에 개최될 예정인 UR/서비스 제5차 양허협상에 대비하여 UR 서비스 실무 소위원회가 10.7(수) 10:00 경제기획원에서 개최될 예정입니다.

2. 경제기획원이 동 UR 서비스 실무 소위원회 개최에 대비하여 작성한 대책 자료를 별첨 송부하니 귀업무에 참고하시기 바라며, ~~검토~~의견이 있는 경우 당과로 ~~송부하여~~ 통보하여 주시기 바랍니다.

첨부 : 제5차 UR/서비스 양허협상 대책자료. 끝.

통 상 기 구 과 장

0080

경 제 기 획 원

우 427-760 / 경기도 과천시 중앙동1 정부제2청사 / 전화 503-9149 / 전송 503-9141

문서번호 통조삼 10502-123
시행일자 1992. 10. 7
(경유)
수신 수신처참조
참조 통상기구과장

선결			지시	
접수	일자 시간	:	결재·공람		
	번호				
처리과					
담당자		안명기			

제목 UR/서비스 실무소위원회 개최일시 및 장소변경 통보

1. 통조삼 10502-121('92.10.2) 관련입니다.

2. 당초 10.7, 10:00 당원 대회의실에서 개최할 예정이었던 UR/서비스 실무소위원회를 당원 사정으로 다음과 같이 변경하여 개최하니 착오없으시기 바랍니다.

- 다 음 -

가. 일 시 : '92. 10,7, 15:00

나. 장 소 : 경제기획원 소회의실(과천청사 1동 721호)

경 제 기 획 원 장

수신처 : 외무부장관, 내무부장관, 재무부장관, 법무부장관, 농림수산부장관, 문화부장관, 상공부장관, 건설부장관, 교통부장관, 노동부장관, 체신부장관, 과학기술처장관, 환경처장관, 해운항만청장, 대외경제정책연구원장, 한양대학교 총장

0081

UR 實務小委
會議資料

第5次 UR/서비스 讓許協商對策

1992. 10

經 濟 企 劃 院
對外經濟調整室

0082

目　　次

0083

Ⅰ. 서비스協商의 全般的 進行狀況

- 서비스 一般協定(GATS)의 制定作業은 '91.12.20 최종협정문안(Dunkel초안)이 제시된 이후 기술적 논의에 국한하여 非公式協議가 계속 진행되고 있는 상태

  o 協定文 第34條(定義)의 구체화에 관한 논의, 분쟁해결절차등에 관한 기술적논의등

  o 우리는 제네바代表部를 중심으로 대응(현 단계까지의 作業內容은 관계부처에 旣 配付)

- 서비스 國家別 讓許協商은 그간 4차에 걸쳐 진행되었으며 주요협상참가국들은 협상타결을 위해서는 아직 수차례의 追加協商이 필요하다고 인식

  o '92.8말 현재 51개국이 自國의 讓許計劃表(offer list)를 제출했으며, 우리는 '92.2 修正讓許計劃表를 제출

  o 우리는 각국과의 양허협상에서 修正讓許表의 範圍內에서 대응해 왔고 추가적인 자유화 약속요구에 대하여는 현재 수준이상의 양허가 곤란함을 구체적으로 설명하는 선에서 대응해 왔으며 또한 우리의 相對國에 대한 要求 및 確認事項도 계속 제기

- MFN逸脫對象目錄은 '92.8말 현재 38개국이 제출하였으나 일탈목록이 지나치게 광범위한 관계로 앞으로 MFN逸脫問題가 서비스協商進展의 主要變數로 대두

  o 특히 美國이 기본통신, 해운, 항공, 금융분야등 주요한 분야를 망라하여 MFN逸脫事項을 제출

  o 우리는 海運 Waiver制度, 航空 CRS등 2개분야를 제출한 바 있으며 그동안 追加, 補完與否를 검토

Ⅱ. 이번 讓許協商經緯 및 對應의 基本方向

- 이번 讓許協商은 7.24(木) 카알라일 GATT 사무차장 주재로 개최된 35개국 非公式協議에서 결정된 것이며 10.5부터 2週間 兩者協商을 진행

  o 우리나라는 10.12부터 1週間 참여하여 8개국(美國, 日本, EC, 카나다, 핀랜드, 스웨덴, 뉴질랜드, 中國)과 협상예정

- 이번 讓許協商의 性格은 UR전체협상의 실질적인 진전여부에 영향을 받을 것으로 추정

  o 主要協商參加國들은 양허수준이 미흡한 국가의 추가적인 양보를 계속 要求, 協商하는 기회로 활용코자 할 것으로 예상

  o 그러나 전체적인 협상분위기의 전환이 없는 한 이번 讓許協商에서도 각국간의 실질적 양허교환 및 주요쟁점에서의 큰 의견접근은 어려울 것으로 豫想

- 이러한 상황인식하에서 이번 讓許協商에는 다음의 기본입장으로 대응

  ① 韓國政府는 그동안 서비스협상에 적극 참여하여 왔으며 동 협상의 조속한 타결을 위하여 最善의 協調와 努力을 다할 것임을 강조

  ② 讓許範圍는 기본적으로 수정양허계획표의 범위내에서, 쟁점별로는 기존의 입장을 견지하는 線에서 대응하되 그간 추가적인 검토가 완료되었거나 自由化方針을 마련한 인력이동, 해운등 몇몇분야는 最終讓許表 提出時 追加 讓許가 가능할 것임을 표명

  ③ MFN逸脫問題, 基本通信등 주요쟁점에 대한 각국의 입장과 全般的 動向을 면밀하게 파악

0085

Ⅲ. 主要爭點別 讓許協商 對應方向

1. 人力移動分野

가. 서비스 세일즈人力 讓許與否(美, EC, 카나다등)

< 經緯 >

- 4.14 UR/實務委에서 양허원칙이 결정되었으나 讓許部門에 대해서는 財務部가 금융부문제외를 명시해야 한다는 입장 제시

  o 美, EC, 카나다등은 金融分野讓許를 않고 있으며

  o 金融分野의 경우 계약체결만으로도 금융서비스 제공이 현실적으로 가능하므로 양허할 경우 金融分野가 추가적으로 개방될 우려

< 對應方向 >

- 그동안의 檢討結果

  o 주요국이 모두 실질적으로 金融部門도 포함하여 讓許(日本, EC는 양허를 명시, 美國은 cover note에 모든 분야적용을 명시)하고 있음을 확인.

  o 서비스 세일즈인력의 개념자체가 販賣協商, 契約締結만 할 수 있고 서비스를 직접 공급하는 효과를 가지는 행위를 할 수 없다는 것이므로 계약체결만으로 金融서비스의 제공이 이루어지는 행위는 당연히 同 人力의 범주에서 제외

- 따라서 최종양허표 제출시 금융부문을 포함한 모든분야에서 讓許(參考2. 人力移動部門 讓許計劃案)

나. 商業的駐在 設立目的의 代表人力 讓許與否(EC)

< 經緯 >

- 우리는 同 代表人力이 ① 出入國 管理法에 해당되는 규정이 없고 ② EC외에 美, 日, 카등 주요국이 offer 하지 않은 상태이므로 양허하지 않겠다는 立場으로 대응

< 對應方向 >

- 出入國管理法上 사업상의 입국자에 대해 短期綜合비자 (90日)가 발급되고 있어 사실상 상업적주재의 설립을 목적으로 하는 서비스 供給企業의 上級管理者 또는 重役이 입국하는데 아무런 제한을 가하지 않고 있고

- 商業的駐在를 인정하면서 이를 위한 人力의 事前的移動을 보장하지 않는다는 논리가 설득력이 없으며

- 同 代表人力의 範圍가 기업의 上級管理者級에 한정되어 서비스 세일즈인력보다 좁은 점을 감안할 때 서비스 세일즈인력을 양허하면서 代表人力을 양허하지 않는 것은 양허의 균형이 맞지 않고

- 또한 人力移動에 있어 제일 보수적인 EC가 offer했으며 美國, 日本, 캐나다등도 추가적으로 양허할 것임을 명백히 하고 있음.(4차 협상시 확인)

- 따라서 同 代表人力에 대하여도 최종양허표 제출시 追加 讓許. 단, 이번 협상에서는 同 人力範圍의 讓許與否에 대하여 肯定的인 檢討를 하고 있음만 示唆

2. MFN逸脫問題

< 經緯 >

- 우리는 航空 CRS, 海運分野의 waiver制度에 대한 MFN일탈을 공식 신청('92.3.12)

0087

- 韓·日間 視聽覺 및 韓·日航路등에 대한 MFN일탈 필요성 제기

  ㅇ 日本의 同 分野에 대한 지대한 관심 표시

〈 對應方向 〉

- 그동안 檢討結果를 토대로 이번 양허협상기간중 MFN逸脫 申請 變更內容을 설명하고 公式的으로 GATT에 제출 추진

- MFN逸脫 最小化라는 우리 기본입장에 변함이 없음을 표명하되 각국의 신청동향, 신청필요성등을 감안, 2~3개 분야에서 追加與否를 檢討中임을 언급(參考1. MFN逸脫追加申請案)

  ① Covernote

    ㅇ 最小化, 特定措置限定 基本立場 명시

    ㅇ 金融分野에 광범한 MFN일탈이 있을 경우 이에 대응할 수 있다는 權利留保立場 명시

  ② 視聽覺分野

    ㅇ 韓·日文化交流에 관한 정책변경이 당분간 없을 것이므로 역사적·문화적이유를 들어 日本과의 視聽覺 交流에 대한 MFN逸脫을 申請(문화부의견 수용)

  ③ 韓·日航路

    ㅇ 기존의 海運 waiver制度에 대한 逸脫申請을 철회하고 韓·日航路에 대해 MFN逸脫을 신청(항만청의견 수용)

  ④ 外國人 土地取得上 相互主義

    ㅇ 현행 외국인토지법상 상호주의에 의해 外國人의 土地取得을 制限할 수 있도록 규정되어 있어 이에 대해 MFN일탈을 신청(내무부의견 수용)

    ※ 對日貿易業 差別分野는 MFN일탈을 하지 않고 日本과의 雙務協議를 통해 해결(상공부 의견)

3. 通信分野

< 經緯 >

- 美國의 基本通信開放을 위한 다자간 협상요구('91.12.18) 에 대해 우리는 EC, 日本등과 함께 협상참여 곤란입장 표시

  o 美國은 主要協商國(12개국)들이 미국이 제시한 요구사항을 충족하는 경우에만 MFN逸脫을 撤回할 것임을 제안

- 스웨덴이 교착상태에 있는 通信讓許協商에 대해 중재안을 제시('92.5.8)함에 따라 우리立場 再定立 필요

  o 스웨덴은 UR終了前(협상시한 미정) GATS체제하에서 기본 通信分野 多者間協商을 추진하되 協商範圍에 제한을 두지 말고 開放程度는 국가별사정에 따라 균형있게 개방할 것을 제안('92.6.25 修正提案에서는 협상진행중 MFN逸脫不可文句를 삭제)

  o 美, 日, 카, 濠洲, 뉴질랜드, 핀랜드는 찬성, EC, 오스트리아, 스위스는 반대, 우리는 立場表明을 유보

< 對應方向 >

- EC의 입장변화없이는 協商開始가 사실상 불가능한 상황임을 감안 당분간 EC반응을 주시하면서 基本通信 市場開放을 전제로 한 多者間協商에는 참여할 수 없다는 기존입장 견지

- EC의 참여가 명백해 질 경우에는 다음 전제하에 스웨덴提案 基本通信 多者間協商에 참여의사가 있음을 표명

  o 多者間協商의 진행과 동시에 별도의 雙務協商이 요구되는 일이 없을 것

  o 協商이 개방을 전제로 해서는 안되며 開放程度는 국가별로 차등이 인정될 것

  o 협상기간중 MFN逸脫不可 그리고 협상의 결과 개방된 서비스에 대해서도 MFN原則을 적용할 것

0089

4. 會計서비스 affiliation 許容問題(美, EC)

< 經緯 >

- Affiliation 許容要求에 대해 우리는 재정적제휴를 포함한 광범위하고 불명확한 affiliation概念의 受容이 어렵다는 입장을 견지

- 4차협상시 美, EC는 direct investment link를 원하는 것이 아니고 worldwide조직에 membership가입과 共通經費分擔이 가능한 지 여부등을 문의

< 對應方向 >

- 韓國의 회계서비스는 외국회계법인이 한국회계법인에 출자하여 持分을 獲得(partnership)하는 것을 제외하고는 업무제휴를 포함한 모든 분야에서 개방되어 있다는 점을 언급

  o 國內會計法人이 국제조직에 加入(member firm) 또는 出資(partnership)하는 것이 가능하며 共通經費(membership fee)支給도 가능

  o 기타 감사자문 및 회원연수를 위한 인력교류, 정보교환, 상호고객알선, 국제상호 연계사용등이 가능

- Affiliation의 Commitment를 요구할 경우 最終讓許表에 footnote형태로 기재할 지 여부를 검토하겠다고 표명

※ Affiliation概念의 법률서비스에의 적용에 대해서는 反對立場 견지

5. 金融(美, 카나다, EC등)

- Blueprint등 金融開放計劃의 offer 반영요구

  o Blueprint 1, 2단계 조치와 保險市場開放案中 최종 양허표 제출시점까지의 自由化內容을 反映할 용의가 있으나

  o 이는 協商參加國들의 MFN일탈이 최소화되고 우리의 상대국에 대한 金融障壁 緩和要求를 상대국이 수용 한다는 전제가 있어야 가능함을 표명

- Standstill 要求

  o 그동안 우리는 修正 offer가 offer작성시점인 '91年末 현재를 기준으로 작성되어 사실상 standstill 約束이 반영된 것으로 설명

  o 그러나 어느 시점에서 standstill하는 것인지 구체적으로 명기되어 있지 않고 讓許表上의 市場接近 및 內國民待遇 制限들도 포괄적 규제가 있다는 식(例: restrictions, regulations등으로만 표시)으로 적시되어 있어 현존 규제수준보다 후퇴된 규제가 가능하다는 오해소지가 있는점 등을 감안할 때 standstill立場을 양허표상에 명백히 나타나도록 하는 것이 필요한 상황

  o 따라서 이번 협상에서는 美側의 standstill 要求立場을 다시한번 정확하게 타진한 후 우리의 standstill의도를 보다 명백하게 表現할 용의가 있음을 표명

- 金融 offer中 "Certain"과 같은 불명확한 부분의 구체적 기재요구등에 대해서는 最終讓許表에서 모든나라가 유사한 표현을 사용하지 않는다는 합의가 선행되어야 함을 언급

6. 海運分野(EC, 日, 카나다등)

- 海上貨物運送周旋業, 海運代理店, 海運仲介業의 지분제한 철폐요구

  o 美國에 約束한 內容('93.6말까지 持分制限撤廢)에 대해 MFN일탈의사가 없으며 具體的인 內容은 최종양허표 제출시 반영할 계획임을 언급

- 陸上트럭킹 區域擴大問題

  o 美國에 약속한 내용('94.3말까지 全國擴大實施)에 대해 MFN일탈의사가 없으며 具體的인 內容은 최종양허표에 반영할 계획임을 언급

- 指定貨物制度 撤廢要求등에 대해서는 기존입장견지

- EC모델 스케쥴에 대해서는 아직 각국간에 用語에 대한 개념조차 정립되지 않은 상태이므로 動向把握에 주력

7. 農林業分野(濠洲, 뉴질랜드)

- 식품, 고기가공등과 관련한 Consulting, Engineering

  o 우리 offer의 Engineering Services 및 Management Consulting Services부문에 포함되어 있으며 제한없이 許容可能함을 언급

- 畜産 및 獸醫師서비스

  o 畜産서비스는 구체적 요구내용을 확인한 후 필요하다고 판단될 경우 畜産法에서 허용하는 범위내에서 讓許與否를 검토해 보겠다고 언급(동 업종은 外國人投資 自由化業種임)

  o 獸醫師서비스는 外國人投資 制限業種으로서 양허가 곤란하다고 대응

- 林業서비스, 農業用 機械裝備 서비스業 및 作物生産關聯 서비스業에 대해 양허를 요구해 올 경우 最終讓許表에서 추가 반영할 것임을 언급(뒤의 2개업종은 外國人投資 自由化業種임)

8. 建設(日本)

- 新規免許 發給制限問題

  o 新規免許 發給制限은 최종양허표 제출시 시장접근사항으로 기재하되 免許發給週期 短縮을 檢討中임을 언급

  o 아울러 현재 우리 양허표상의 市場接近 約束事項은 지킬 것임을 표명

- 都給限度制 撤廢問題

  o 民間部門에 대한 도급한도제는 制度改善을 檢討中임을 언급

9. 環境(카나다)

- 環境分野全般에 걸쳐 광범위한 Commitment 요구

  o 현 단계에서 우리가 offer한 분야이외에 대해서는 追加讓許가 어려운 점을 설명

10. 外國人 土地取得(美國, 日本)

- 土地取得에 있어 내외국인간의 차별적 요소들을 漸次的으로 解消해 나갈 계획임을 설명

  o '92년말까지는 土地取得 許容範圍를 부분적으로 확대하고 同 基準을 명료하게 공개

  o '93년중에는 外國人 土地取得 關聯制度全般에 대한 改善作業을 추진

11. 外國人投資(濠洲)

- 外國人投資 追加自由化를 발표('92.5.1)한 서비스업종을 binding하는 문제

  o 금년말 關聯規程 改正作業이 완료된 후에야 양허여부에 대한 검토가 가능함과 外國人投資 自由化內容과 양허 내용이 반드시 일치할 수는 없음을 설명

12. 流通, 廣告등(美, 日, EC등)

- 旣存立場을 견지하는 線에서 대응

13. 其他事項

- 우리 修正讓許表上의 業種包括範圍를 확정, 배포할 예정임. (參考3. UR/서비스 修正讓許表上의 業種包括範圍)

0094

< 參考1 >

The Republic of Korea

MFN Exemptions Under GATS Article Ⅱ.2 - Revised Provisonal List

1. 大韓民國은 GATS가 제대로 기능을 발휘하기 위해서는 MFN원칙이 유지되어야 한다는 인식하에 그동안 MFN일탈이 최소한으로 제한되어야 한다는 입장을 견지해 왔음.

이러한 점에서 현재 각국의 과도한 MFN일탈시도는 우려할 만한 사항이라고 생각하며 따라서 協商의 成功을 위해서 MFN일탈은 일탈범위가 구체적으로 한정되는 특정조치에 한하여야 한다는 점을 再強調 함.

2. 이러한 기본입장을 견지하면서 大韓民國은 GATS 제2조와 그 부속서에 의거, 1992년 3월 16일에 기 제출하였던 MFN일탈 신청목록을 대체하는 다음의 修正 MFN逸脫 申請目錄을 제출함.

3. 대한민국은 협정문 및 국별양허협상이 끝나기 전까지 이 修正 目錄을 수정할 권리를 유보함. 특히 金融分野에 있어 향후 각국이 광범한 MFN일탈을 할 경우 大韓民國도 이에 대응할 수

있는 권리를 유보하며, 또한 비자협정등 일부 수평적 양자 협정이 GATS 適用對象인지 여부에 대한 협상결과에 따라 이들에 대한 MFN逸脫與否를 결정할 것임.

1. Sector or Sub-sector : Audio-Visual Services

a. Description of the measures :

- 역사적배경 및 문화적영향을 고려하여 일본에 대해 다음의 視聽覺서비스 供給에 대한 시장접근을 제한함.
(영화법, 음반 및 비디오에 관한 법률, 공연법 및 동법들의 관련규정)

  o 映畵 및 비디오제작업(합작제작 포함), 수입·배급업 및 상영업

  o 韓國 映畵에의 일본배우 출연

  o 일본 대중가요음반 수입 및 배급업

  o 가수의 일본 대중가요 공연 및 특정국 언어 가창

  o 韓國語로 공연하는 일본극단의 번역극 및 전통극을 제외한 연극공연

  o 희극공연 및 기타 연예물

b. Treatment inconsistent with Article Ⅱ : 1 of the Agreement

- 外國人에 대하여 상기 서비스 제공활동이 일반적으로 허용되나 日本에 대하여는 制限을 가하고 있음.

c. Intended duration of the exemption :

- 無期限

d. Conditions which create the need for the exemption :

- 大韓民國은 日本과의 특수한 역사적 경험을 고려하여 동 특정국가로 부터의 文化的影響에 대한 국내정치적 수용이 가능할 때까지 同 特定國家와의 文化交流를' 허용하기 곤란함.

0096

2. Sector or Sub-sector : Maritime Transport Services

a. Description of the measures :

- 韓·日航路는 한국에 근접되어 있는등의 특수성으로 인하여 국내 영세업체들이 과다하게 참여하고 있어 旣存 參與業體를 제외하고는 國·內外 船社를 막론하고 신규참입을 엄격하게 제한하고 있음.

b. Treatment inconsistent with Article Ⅱ : 1 of the Agreement

- 역사적이유에 의해 허가된 外國의 기존 참여업체 이외에는 新規參與를 制限하고 있음.

c. Intended duration of the exemption :

- 1995年 1月까지

d. Conditions which create the need for the exemption :

- 한시적 MFN일탈이며 1995.1월까지는 동 제한을 철폐하여 MFN원칙을 적용할 것임.

3. Sector or Sub-sector : CRS

a. Description of the measures :

- SITA 네트워크를 통한 外國 CRS接近은 국제 leased lines 의 제3자 사용으로 취급되므로 遞信部長官에 의해 지정된 자들에 한정됨.

- 遞信部長官은 구체적으로 美 航空社만을 특정하여 허용하고 있음.

b. Treatment inconsistent with Article Ⅱ : 1 of the Agreement

- 國際旅行社들은 미국 항공사가 지정하는 CRS를 사용할 때만 SITA 이용이 허용됨.

c. Intended duration of the exemption :

- 無期限

d. Conditions which create the need for the exemption :

- SITA 네트워크를 통한 外國 CRS接近은 運輸權 讓許協商과 관련하여 제한되거나 영향받을 수 있기 때문임.

0098

4. Sector or Sub-sector : 外國人 土地取得의 相互主義

a. Description of the measures :

- 大韓民國 國民 또는 大韓民國法人에 대하여 토지에 관한 권리의 향유를 금지하거나 조건 또는 제한을 가하는 국가에 속하는 外國人 또는 外國法人에 대하여 大韓民國에 있어서의 토지에 관한 권리의 향유에 관하여 동일 또는 유사한 금지를 하거나 조건 또는 제한을 가할 수 있음 (外國人 土地法 제2조)

  o 단, 현재 土地取得이 허용되고 있는 부문은 觀光業(호텔), 銀行業(은행지점)의 2개부문에 한정

b. Treatment inconsistent with Article Ⅱ : 1 of the Agreement

- 현재로서는 없음.

c. Intended duration of the exemption :

- 無期限

d. Conditions which create the need for the exemption :

- 韓國國民 또는 法人이 외국영토내에서 사업을 영위함에 있어서 土地關聯 權利取得에 있어 불리한 대우를 받지 않도록 하기 위함임.

The Republic of Korea

MFN Exemptions Under GATS Article Ⅱ.2 - Revised Provisional List

1. While recognizing that the MFN principle is important for the GATS to be an effective agreement, the Republic of Korea has consistently maintained that the scope of MFN exemption which each negotiating partner may seek should be limited to the necessary minimum. The Republic of Korea is concerned about the current, excessive requests for MFN exemption and reemphasizes its position that for the successful conclusion of the services negotiations, every participant should limit its exemptions to specific measures whose scopes are confined to specific areas.

2. Maintaining this basic position, the Republic of Korea submits the attached revised provisional list for MFN exemption, which substitutes its initial list dated March 16, 1992, pursuant to Article 2 and its Annex under the GATS.

3. The Republic of Korea reserves its right to revise this list for MFN exemption prior to the final outcome of the negotiations on the framework and initial commitments. In particular, the ROK reserves its right to revise this list in case a wide-ranging exemption in the financial services sector is sought. The ROK will also review MFN exemptions for horizontal bilateral agreements, such as visa agreements, according to the results of future negotiations on those agreements.

0100

1. Sector or Sub-sector : Audio-Visual Services

a. Description of the measures :

- In light of political sentiments based on its historical and cultural background, the Republic of Korea prohibits the market access of service suppliers of Japan in the following audio-visual sectors :

  o Motion picture and video tape production (including joint-production), import, distribution and performance;

  o Performance by a Japanese actor in a Korean movie;

  o Import and distribution of sound recordings of the specified country's pop songs;

  o Public performance of the specified country's pop songs by any singer, and the singing of any song in the specified country's language (except in the case of singing in an international ceremony);

  o Drama, except in the cases of traditional drama or drama not originating from Japan, both of which must be performed in Korean.

  o Comedy and other forms of entertainment (business or performance), excluding magic shows, circuses and dance performances.

b. Treatment inconsistent with Article II : 1 of the Agreement

- In general, the ROK permits the supply of services in the audio-visual sector by foreign parties, except in the case of Japan.

c. Intended duration of the exemption ;

- Indefinite

d. Conditions which create the need for the exemption :

- Until the political preparations to receive cultural exchange are set up, the Republic of Korea has, and will have, difficulties in allowing such exchange with the specified country, with which Korea has had a peculiar historical background.

0102

2. Sector or Sub-sector : Maritime Transport Services

a. Description of the measures :

- Since the ROK-Japan Service Line is overcrowded, especially by the many small domestic businesses, the ROK strictly restricts new entrance to the route regardless of the nationality of the shipping firm.

b. Treatment inconsistent with Article Ⅱ : 1 of the Agreement

- Operation of the ROK-Japan Service Line is permitted only to foreign firms which, for historical reasons, were licensed by the ROK government.

c. Intended duration of the exemption :

- Until January 1995.

d. Conditions which create the need for the exemption :

- This exemption is temporary, and the ROK will respect the MFN principle after the abolishment of this restriction on January 1995.

3. Sector or Sub-sector : Computerized Reservation Services

a. Description of the measures :

- Access to foreign CRS through SITA networks are restricted to a specified group of persons by the Minister of Communications since such access is considered as third party use of international leased lines.

- The Minister of Communications specifically permits U.S. carriers to use the SITA network for access to CRS.

b. Treatment inconsistent with Article Ⅱ : 1 of the Agreement

- International travel agencies are allowed to access SITA only when they access CRS designated by US carriers.

c. Intended duration of the exemption :

- Undecided

d. Conditions which create the need for the exemption :

- Access to foreign CRS through the SITA network could be limited or affected otherwise in relation to the negotiations on granting or receiving traffic rights.

0104

4. Sector or Sub-sector : Reciprocity measures on alien acquisition of land in Korea

a. Description of the measures :

- Prohibitions or restrictions may be imposed on foreign nationals or juridical persons to acquire or lease land in the ROK when Korean nationals or juridical persons are placed under similar prohibitions or restrictions in the country of the said foreign nationals (Article 2 of the Alien Land Law).

- However, the acquisition of land is currently limited to two sectors: hotels and banking

b. Treatment inconsistent with Article Ⅱ : 1 of the Agreement

- None, at present.

c. Intended duration of the exemption :

- Indefinite

d. Conditions which create the need for the exemption :

- To secure the right of Korean nationals and juridical persons to land in doing business in the territory of a foreign country.

< 參考2 > 人力移動部門 讓許計劃(案)

- 商業的駐在에 대하여 자유화약속을 한 분야에 있어서 다음범주의 기업내 필수인력은 一時的 移動이 허용됨.

  o 滯留期間은 최초 2년까지 허용되며 필요한 경우 연장 가능하나 최장 4年을 초과할 수 없음.

  < 企業內 必須人力의 定義 >

  o 韓國內에 설립된 支社, 子會社에 근무하면서 체재기간중 다음과 같은 직무에 계속 종사하고자 하는 자로서 該當 서비스 供給企業에 1년이상 고용된 者

    a) 上級管理者(Senior Manager) : 企業 또는 部署單位組織의 목표와 정책의 수립 및 시행에 책임을 지고 계획·지휘·감독에 관한 권한과 직원에 대한 雇傭 및 解雇權 또는 이에 관한 推薦權을 가지며, 다른 감독직·전문직·

       관리직 종사자의 업무를 결정·감독·통제하거나 일상 업무에 裁量權을 행사하는 者. 피감독자가 전문서비스 공급자가 아닌 한 일선감독자를 포함하지 않으며 직접적으로 서비스 供給行爲에 종사하는 者도 포함하지 않음.

    b) 任員(Executive) : 組織內에서 조직관리를 제1차적으로 지휘하며, 의사결정에 광범위한 권한을 행사하고 그 기업의 最高位 任員, 理事會, 株主로부터 일반적인 지휘감독만을 받는 자. 임원은 서비스의 실질적인 공급 또는 조직의 서비스에 관련된 業務는 직접 수행할 수 없음.

    c) 專門家(Specialist) : 當該企業 서비스의 연구·설계·기술·관리등에 필수적인 고도의 전문적이고 독점적인 경험과 지식을 가진 者

-1-

0106

- 商業的駐在에 대하여 자유화약속을 한 분야에 있어서 上級 管理者 및 重役의 범주에 속하는 者(기업내 필수인력의 정의중 a), b)항)로서 한국내에서의 서비스제공을 위한 商業的駐在 設置의 책임을 맡은 者에 대해서는 90일이내의 일시적이동이 허용됨.

  o 단, 이 자는 一般大衆에게 직접서비스를 제공하는 업무에 종사하거나 직접서비스를 제공해서는 안되며 韓國內에 서비스공급자의 事務所, 支店, 子會社등이 없어야 함.

- 다른 분야에 달리 규정된 바가 없다면 다음 범주의 인력에 대해서는 90일이내의 一時的 移動이 허용됨.

  o 각 개별 sector별로 양허된 범위내에서 韓國領土內에 소재하지 않는 특정한 서비스供給者를 代表하며 同 서비스공급자로부터 韓國領土내에서 보수를 지급받지 않는 사람으로서 同 서비스 공급자의 서비스를 판매하기 위한 협상을 목적으로 또는 서비스 販賣契約을 체결할 목적으로 일시적으로 입국하고자 하는 사람. 단, 이 자는 공중에게 직접서비스를 제공하거나 同 서비스를 販賣하는 業務에 관여할 수 없음.

- 서비스提供을 위하여 일시적 입국이 허용된 자는 出入國管理法, 勞動關係法등을 준수해야 하며, 인력이동에 관한 약속은 勞使關係에는 적용되지 아니함.

0107

Temporary Movement of Natural Persons

(1) Unbound except for the temporary movement of natural persons as defined below for those sub-sectors in which commitments on commercial presence are made:

Natural persons who are employees of firms that provide services through branches or subsidiaries established in Korea and who have been in the prior employ of their firms for a period of not less than one year immediately preceding the date of their application for admission and who are one of the following:

(a) Senior Managers - persons within an organization who primarily direct the organization or a department of the organization; supervise and control the work of other supervisory, professional or managerial employees; have the authority to hire and fire or recommend hiring, firing or other personnel actions; and exercise discretionary authority over day-to-day operations. Senior managers do not include first-line supervisors, unless the employees supervised are professionals, nor do they include employees who primarily perform tasks necessary for the provision of the service.

(b) Executives - persons within the organization who primarily direct the management of the organization, exercise wide latitude in decision-making, and receive only general supervision of direction from higher-level executives, the board of directors, or shareholders of the business. Executives would not directly perform tasks related to the provision of the service or services of the organization.

(c) Specialists - persons within an organization who possess knowledge at an advanced level of expertise and who possess proprietary knowledge of the organization's service, research equipment, techniques or management.

Temporary entry of natural persons as defined above is limited to a two-year period that may be extended for a term not to exceed four years.

(2) For those sub-sectors in which commitments on commercial presence are made, temporary movement for not more than 90 days of the following category of natural persons is permitted in Korea.

(a) Natural persons meeting the criteria of category (1)(a) or (1)(b) and who are responsible for the setting up, in Korea, of a commercial presence of a service provider of a Party when:

- o the persons are not engaged in making direct sales or supplying services and
- o the service provider has no representative, branch or subsidiary in Korea.

(3) For those sub-sectors in which commitments are made, unless otherwise specified in individual sectors/subsectors, temporary movement for not more than 90 days of the following category of natural persons is permitted in Korea:

(a) Natural persons not based in the territory of Korea and receiving no remuneration from a source located within Korea, who are engaged in activities related to representing a services provider for the purpose of negotiating for the sale of the services of that provider where: a) such sales are not directly made to the general public and b) the persons are not engaged in supplying the service.

(4) Natural persons whose temporary entries are permitted shall observe the Immigration Control Law and the labor laws of Korea. It should be also noted that Korea's commitments regarding temporary movement of natural persons do not apply in cases of labor-management disputes.

0109

< 參考3 >

THE SECTORAL COVERAGE OF REVISED CONDITIONAL OFFER

1992. 10

THE REPUBLIC OF KOREA

0110

TABLE OF CONTENTS

0111

1. BUSINESS SERVICES

A. Professional Services

Sub - sector	Coverage
Certified Public Accountant (CPA) services	CPC 862
Certified Tax Accountant(CTA) services	CPC 863
Architectural services	CPC 8671
Engineering services	CPC 8672
Integrated engineering services	CPC 8673
Urban planning and landscape architectural services	CPC 8674

B. Computer and Related Services

Sub - sector	Coverage
Consultancy services related to the installation of computer hardware	CPC 841

Sub - sector	Coverage
Software implementation services	CPC 842
Data processing services	CPC 843
Data base services	CPC 844

C. Research and Development Services

Sub - sector	Coverage
Research and Development services on natural science	CPC 851

D. Rental/Leasing Services without Operators

Sub - sector	Coverage
Rental services relating to ships without operators	CPC 83103

E. Other Business Services

Sub - sector	Coverage
Advertising services	CPC 8711
Market research and public opinion polling services	CPC 864

0113

Sub - sector	Coverage
Management consulting services	CPC 865(excluding 86506)
Project management services	CPC 86601
Geological and prospecting services	CPC 8675
Convention agency services, excluding demonstration and exhibition services	Planning, preparation and related services regarding international meetings and events for convention organizer under CPC 87909
Translation services	Translation services under CPC 87905
Stenography services	Stenography services under CPC 87909

2. COMMUNICATION SERVICES

A. Telecommunication Services

Sub - sector	Coverage
On-line database and remote computing services	CPC 75232
Computer communication services	
Data transmission services	CPC 75231

B. Audiovisual Services

Sub - sector	Coverage
Motion picture and video tape production and distribution services	CPC 96112, 96113
Record production and distribution services	2.D.e(sound recording) in MTN. GNS/W/120

3. CONSTRUCTION SERVICES

Sub - sector	Coverage
General construction work	CPC 511, 512, 5131(excluding pavement works), 5132, 5133, 5136(excluding power plants works), 5137, 5139
Special construction(specialist, specialized, electrical, telecommunication and fire-fighting facility work)	Pavement works under CPC 5131, 5134, 5135, power plants works under CPC 5136, 514, 515, 516, 517

4. DISTRIBUTION SERVICES

A. Wholesale Trade Services

Sub - sector	Coverage
Wholesale trade services(excluding wholesale of grain, meats, fruits and vegetables,	CPC 61111, 6113(excluding retail sales of parts and accessories of motor vehicles),

0115

Sub - sector	Coverage
raw milk, alcoholic beverages, red ginseng, fertilizers, pesticides, books and news-papers, and brokers-chain market services, general foreign trade services and foreign trade broker services)	6121(excluding retail sales of motorcycles and snowmobiles and related parts and accessories), 621(excluding foreign trade brokers services) and 622(ex-cluding CPC 62211, 62221, wholesale trade services of raw milk under CPC 62222, 62223, wholesale trade services of aloholic beverages under CPC 62226, wholesale trade services of red ginseng under CPC 62229, wholesale trade services of books and other printed matter under CPC 62262, wholesale trade services of fertilizers under CPC 62276 and wholesale trade services of agricultural medicines under CPC 62276) "Brokers-chain market services" (not listed in CPC and MTN. GNS/W/120) refers to a business which makes a chain contract with retail shops such as department stores,supermarkets, convenience stores, specialty stores systematically and which

Sub - sector	Coverage
	buys and supplies various goods necessary to manage those shops on its own account continuously. "General foreign trade services" (not listed in CPC and MTN.GNS/W/120) refers to a business which wholly engages in foreign trade of goods on its own account. * "Wholesale trade services of used cars" in the M.A column refers to CPC 61111 * "Wholesale trade services of natural gas" in the M.A column means wholesale trade services of gaseous fuels and related products under CPC 62271

B. Retailing Services

Sub - sector	Coverage
Retailing services (excluding retailing of tobacco; antiques and works of art; grain; meats; vegetables; fruits; raw milk; livestock and animals; food, beverages and tobacco n.e.c.; pharmaceuticals; cosmetics; books; coal bri-quettes; fuel oil; bottled gas; service stations for gasoline; gas recharging)	CPC 61112, 6113(excluding wholesale trade services of parts and accessories of motor vehicles), 6121(excluding wholesale trade services of motorcycles and snowmobiles and related parts and accessories), 63104 and 632(excluding CPC 63211, 63212, retail sale of books and other printed matter under CPC 63253, retail sale of animal fodder under CPC 63295, retail sale of livestock and animals under CPC 63295, CPC 63297 and retail sale of works of art and antiques under CPC 63299) * "Retail sale of used cars" in the M.A column refers to CPC 61112.

5. ENVIRONMENTAL SERVICES

A. Sewage Services

Sub - sector	Coverage
Refuse water disposal services	Collection and treatment services of industrial waste water under CPC 94010

B. Refuse Disposal Services

Sub - sector	Coverage
Industrial refuse disposal services (collection and transportation, intermediate processing and final processing)	Collection, transportation and disposal services of industrial waste under CPC 94020

6. FINANCIAL SERVICES

A. Banking

Sub - sector	Coverage
Deposit and related business	Deposit and related business under CPC 81115 and 81116
Loans and related business	Loans and related business under CPC 81131 and 81132
Foreign exchange business	Foreign exchange business under CPC 81333

0119

Sub - sector	Coverage
Services auxiliary to banking (sales of commercial bills, sales of trade bills, mutual installment deposits and payment guarantees)	Sales of commercial and trade bills under CPC 81339 and mutual installment deposits and payment guarantees under CPC 8113
Trust business	Trust business under CPC 81192 and 81193

B. Securities business

Sub - sector	Coverage
Dealing, broking and under-writing	Dealing, broking and under-writing under CPC 8132

C. Insurance

Sub - sector	Coverage
a. Direct insurance	
i) Life insurance	CPC 8121
ii) Non-life insurance	CPC 8129 (excluding reinsurance and retrocession)
b. Reinsurance and Retroces-sion	Reinsurance and retrocession under CPC 81299
c. Actuarial services and claim settlement services	CPC 81404 and claim settlement services under CPC 81403

7. TOURISM AND TRAVEL RELATED SERVICES

A. Hotels and Restaurants

Sub - sector	Coverage
Tourist hotels, family hotels and traditional Korean hotels	CPC 6411

B. Travel Agencies and Tour Operator Services

Sub - sector	Coverage
Travel agencies	CPC 7471

C. Tourist Guide Services

Sub - sector	Coverage
Tourist guide services	CPC 7472(excluding own-account tourist guide services)

8. TRANSPORT SERVICES

A. Maritime Transport Services

Sub - sector	Coverage
International passenger transportation services	CPC 7211
International freight transportation services	CPC 7212

0121

Sub - sector	Coverage
Maintenance and repair of vessels	Services such as repair and management of vessels, management of crew, marine insurance, etc., on behalf of a person (including foreigners) who operates maritime passenger transportation business, maritime cargo transportation business and vessel leasing business under CPC 7459 and 8868

B. Air Transport Services

Sub - sector	Coverage
Aircraft repair and maintenance services	Aircraft repair and maintenance services performed at the apron of the airport or airfield prior to its flight under CPC 7469 and 8868
Computer reservation services	Reservation and ticket issuing services through computerized systems that contain information about air carriers schedules, seat availability, fares and far rules.

Sub - sector	Coverage
Selling and marketing of air transport services	Services defined in provisions 24 (general air transporation agent services) and 25 (air cargo transportation agent services) of Article 2 of the Korea Aviation Act. "General air transportation agent services" refers to an enterprise which undertakes to make contracts of international transportation of passengers or cargo by aircraft (excluding the service of acting for other persons in the application procedure for visa or passport) on behalf of air transportation service firms for compensation. "Air cargo transportation agent services" refers to an enterprise which undertakes to make contracts of cargo transportation by aircraft on behalf of air transportation services firms or general air transportation agent services firms for compensation.

0123

C. Road Transport Services

Sub - sector	Coverage
Domestic general local freight trucking services	Freight transport services by truck within the designated business activities regions under CPC 71233

D. Services Auxiliary to All Modes of Transport

Sub - sector	Coverage
Railway freight forwarding services	Freight transport agency services by railway under CPC 748 (Arrangements regarding the shipping of freight by rail must be made through a railway freight forwarder.)
Storage and warehouse services (excluding services for agricultural, fishery and livestock products)	CPC 742(excluding services for agricultural, fishery and livestock products)
Shipping agency	Agency services which carry out transactions on behalf of maritime passenger transportation business or maritime cargo transportation business(including foreign transportation businesses) under CPC 748

Sub - sector	Coverage
Maritime freight forwarding services	Cargo forwarding services by vessels in the name of the forwarder (including any foreign forwarders under contract) under CPC 748
Ship brokering services	Brokering services of maritime cargo transportation or of chartering, leasing, purchasing and selling of vessels under CPC 748

0125

UR/서비스 실무 소위원회

1. 제5차 UR/서비스 양자 협상(10.12-16, 제네바)과 관련, 대책 실무회의가 10.7. 경기원 제2협력관 주재로 개최(외무부, 내무부, 재무부, 문화부 등 관계부처 실무자 참석)

2. 회의 내용

가. 양자협의 대책

- o 92.2. 제출한 아국의 수정 양허 계획표 상의 기존입장 견지
- o 그동안 추가 검토가 완료되었거나 자유화 방침을 마련한 인력이동, 해운분야 등 몇몇 분야에서는 최종 양허표 제출시 추가양허 가능 표명
- o MFN 일탈 신청과 관련 변경사항 GATT에 제출
  - 시청각 서비스분야와 관련, 문화부 의견 추가 반영
- o UR/서비스 수정 양허표상 업종포괄 범위를 협상대상국에게 제시
  - 금융 서비스분야와 관련, 재무부 의견 추가 반영

나. 대표단 구성

경기원을 중심으로 소규모 대표단 파견. 끝.

공람	통상기구과	92년 10월 7일	담 당	과 장	심의관	국 장	차관보	차 관	장 관
			[signature]	[signature]	[signature]	[signature]			

0126

경 제 기 획 원

우 427-760 / 경기도 과천시 중앙동1 정부제2청사 / 전화 503-9149 / 전송 503-9141

문서번호 통조삼 10502- 125
시행일자 1992. 10. 9
(경유)
수신 수신처참조
참조 통상기구 과장

선결			지시		
접	일자 시간	92. 10. 12 :			
수	번호	35788	결재·공람		
처리과					
담당자					

제목 UR대책 서비스 실무소위원회 결과통보

지난 10월 7일 개최된 제5차 UR/서비스 양허협상 대책회의결과를 별첨과 같이 통보하니 업무에 참고하기 바랍니다.

첨부 : UR대책 실무소위원회 회의결과 1부. "끝"

경 제 기 획 원 장

제 2협력관 전결

수신처 : 외무부장관, 내무부장관, 재무부장관, 법무부장관, 농림수산부장관, 문화부장관, 상공부장관, 건설부장관, 교통부장관, 노동부장관, 체신부장관, 과학기술처장관, 환경처장관, 해운항만청장, 대외경제정책연구원장

0127

UR對策 實務小委員會 會議結果

Ⅰ. 會議概要

- 日時 및 場所 : '92.10.7(水), 15:00~16:00
  經濟企劃院 小會議室

- 參席者 : 經濟企劃院 第2協力官(會議主宰), 通商調整3課長
  外務部, 內務部, 財務部, 法務部, 農林水産部,
  文化部, 商工部, 建設部, 交通部, 勞動部, 遞信部,
  科學技術處, 環境處, 海運港灣廳 擔當官,
  KIEP 諮問官

Ⅱ. 會議結果

- 이번 協商('92.10.12~16)에는 既 配付한 「第5次 UR/서비스 讓許協商對策」에 의거 대응하되 회의시 논의가 있었던 몇가지 쟁점은 다음과 같이 대응

  o MFN逸脫問題는 그동안 검토결과를 토대로 이번 양허협상 기간중 MFN逸脫申請 變更內容을 설명하고 공식적으로 GATT에 제출을 추진

    · 협상대책자료중 「MFN逸脫最小化 ..... 檢討中임을 言及」이라는 문장은 삭제

    · MFN일탈 추가대상업종중 視聽覺部門은 文化部와 協議를 거쳐 문안 확정

  o 회계서비스중 國內會計法人이 國際組織에 出資(partner-ship)하는 것도 허용하려고 하였으나 追加檢討가 필요하다는 의견이 있어 이번 협상에서는 허용하지 않는다는 입장으로 대응

0128

o 금융분야중 Blueprint등 金融開放計劃의 offer 반영요구
에 대해서는

· 主要協商參加國들이 MFN 부적용을 최소화하고 우리의
金融障壁 緩和要求를 상대국이 수용할 수 있는 경우

· Blueprint 1, 2단계 조치와 보험시장 개방계획중
旣 自由化된 내용의 양허여부를 검토할 용의가 있다는
입장으로 대응

o UR/서비스 修正讓許表上의 업종포괄범위중 金融部門은
別添資料로 대체

0129

6. FINANCIAL SERVICES

A. Banking

Sub - sector	Coverage
Deposit and related business	Acceptance of deposits and other repayable funds from the public under CPC 81115 and 81116
Loans and related business	Lending of all types under CPC 81131 and 81132
Foreign exchange business	Purchase, sale, issuance, remittance, and collection of foreign exchange under CPC 81333
Services auxiliary to banking (sales of commercial bills, sales of trade bills, mutual installment deposits and payment guarantees)	Sales of commercial and trade bills under CPC 81339 and mutual installment deposits and payment guarantees under CPC 8113
Trust business	Activities where the trustee manages assets of the truster, having been delegated the authority under CPC 81192 and 81193

0130

B. Securities business

Sub - sector	Coverage
Dealing, broking and under-writing	Dealing, broking and under-writing under CPC 8132

C. Insurance

Sub - sector	Coverage
a. Direct insurance	
i) Life insurance	CPC 81211
ii) Non-life insurance	CPC 8129 (excluding reinsurance and retrocession)
b. Reinsurance and Retroces-sion	Reinsurance and retrocession under CPC 8129
c. Actuarial services and claim settlement services	CPC 81404 and claim settlement services under CPC 81403

0131

관리번호	92-710

원본

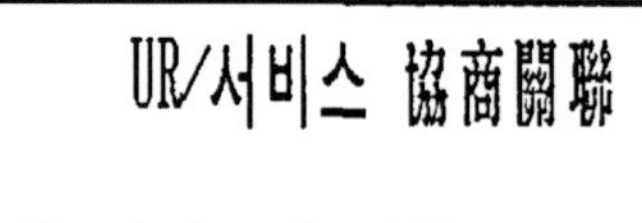

UR/서비스 協商關聯

視聽覺 서비스에 대한 對日 差別問題

(회의 자료)

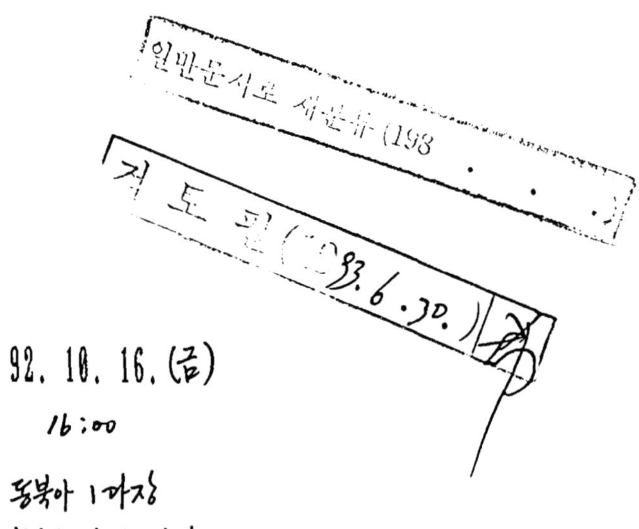

92. 10. 16.(금)

16:00

동북아 1과장

문화협력1과장

통상1과장

通 商 局

0132

- 목 차 -

0133

1. UR/서비스 협상 개요

o 91.12.20. 던켈 갓트 사무총장이 UR 협상 협정초안(Draft Final Act)을 제시한 이래, 서비스 협상 그룹은 현재까지 5차례에 걸쳐 양자협상 개최

- 각국은 관심분야의 서비스 시장개방을 상대국에 요청하고, 당사국은 개방 계획을 제시하고 관심국간 양자협상을 하는 형식

- 우리나라는 5차례(92.1,2,3,6,10월에 각 1회)에 걸쳐, 미, 일, EC, 호주, 뉴질랜드, 스위스, 스웨덴, 핀랜드, 중국 등 주요 서비스 교역국과 양허협상 진행

o 우리나라는 91.1월 최초의 양허계획을 제출하였으며, 92.2. 수정안을 제출하였음.

- 최초 양허계획서는 금융, 통신, 운송, 유통, 건설, 관광, 사업서비스(전문직 서비스, 컴퓨터 및 관련 서비스 등), 시청각 서비스 포함. 교육, 보건서비스, 유통서비스중 무역업, 사업서비스중 법무서비스는 제외

- 수정 양허계획은 분류표 변경에 따른 것으로 내용은 최초 양허계획과 동일

2. UR/서비스 협상과 MFN 일탈 문제

가. 관련 규정

o UR 서비스 일반협정(GATS) 초안은 서비스 교역의 특수성을 감안, MFN 원칙 적용을 배제할 수 있는 경우를 인정, 각국이 사전 신청토록 규정 (제2조 2항)

- 협정 발효후에 MFN 일탈을 희망하는 경우에는 Waiver를 받아야 함. (24조)

나. MFN 일탈신청 기준

o 현재 UR 서비스 협상 차원에서 MFN 일탈 신청과 관련, Modality 나 대상에 대한 합의가 없음.
  - 각국 사정에 따라 임의대로 제출
  - 관계국간의 양자협상 과정에서 협의, MFN 일탈 내용을 확정한다는 것이 참가국의 양해사항

다. 각국의 MFN 일탈 신청 현황과 유형

o 현재 38개국이 광범위한 MFN 일탈 신청, 서비스 협상의 주요변수로 대두
  - 미국은 기본통신, 해운, 항공, 금융 등 주요분야를 망라하여 상호주의를 적용키로 하고 MFN 일탈을 신청, 각국의 반발 초래

o 각국의 MFN 일탈 신청 유형
  - 특정국과의 양자협상 내용의 제3국 부적용
  - 국제협정 미가입국에 대한 부적용
  - 상호주의에 의한 시장접근 인정
  - 특정 외국회사에만 시장접근 허용 등

라. 우리의 MFN 일탈 신청

o 기본적으로는 서비스 분야에서도 MFN 원칙이 지켜져야 하며, 따라서 MFN 일탈은 최소화 하여야 한다는 기본입장

o 92.3.12. 1차로 MFN 일탈 신청

  - <u>콤퓨터 예약서비스(CRS)</u> : 한.미 항공협정(91.6)에 따라 미국에 개방키로 한 CRS 공급서비스는 미국을 제외한 여타국에 대해 개방 유보

- 해운 Waiver제도 : 해운산업 육성법에 의거, 정기 외항 화물선의 국적선 우선 이용제도에 대한 웨이버 신청의무 면제 대상국은 우리나라와 해운협정을 맺고 있는 국가(9개국)에 한정. (단, 95.1월부터 동 제도 폐지)

o 92.10.13-16간 개최되는 양허협상 기간중 수정된 MFN 일탈 신청

- 한.일간 시청각 분야 : 한.일간 문화교류에 관한 정책 변경이 당분간 없을 것이므로, 역사적.문화적 이유를 들어 일본의 아래 우리나라 시청각 서비스 시장접근을 불허
  . 영화업(제작업, 수입, 배급업)에 대한 일본의 투자
  . 일본영화(video 포함), 대중가요의 제작, 수입 및 배급
  . 일본 드라마, 대중가요 및 기타 오락물의 공연

- 한.일 항로 : 한.일 항로에 대한 과다 취항에 따라 국적선 및 외국선사에 대해 공히 신규 참여 제한 (95.1월 폐지)

- 외국인의 토지 취득 : 외국인 토지법상 상호주의에 의해 외국인 토지 취득을 제한할 수 있게 규정

- CRS : 1차 신청과 동일

3. 한.일간 시청각 서비스관련 MFN 일탈 문제

가. 경 위

o 문화부의 요청으로 한.일 시청각 서비스에 대한 MFN 일탈 문제를 국내적으로 계속 검토
  - 92.4. UR 서비스 대책회의에서는 일본과의 관계 등을 고려, 일탈 신청을 일단 보류하고 계속 검토키로 함.

o 92.1-6월간 4차례의 한.일간 UR 서비스 양자협상시 일측은 우리의 시청각 서비스 분야 MFN 일탈 여부에 관심을 표명하고, 우리측이 일탈 신청을 자제하고 있음을 환영한다는 반응을 보임. (아측은 논평 유보)

o 92.7. 일 외무성 문화교류부장 방한시, 우리 문화협력국장과 면담에서 일측은 일본영화의 한국내 상업적 상영제한을 재검토해 줄 것을 요청

o 92.10.7. UR 서비스 대책회의(경기원 주관)에서 문화부의 요청으로 금번 양자협상 개최에 동 MFN 일탈을 신청하고 일측에도 설명키로 결정

나. 일측의 이의 제기 및 대응

o 10.14. 양자협상시 우리측의 상기 시청각 분야 MFN 일탈 신청 설명에 대해 일측은 강한 반대의사를 표시하고, 협상 계속을 위해서는 우선 동 일탈 신청 철회를 요청

- 일측은 일본만을 대상으로 하는 MFN 일탈 신청이 공식 제출되는 경우 의회의 반발등 국내적으로 문제가 되므로 양국간 협의를 통해 조용히 해결할 것을 희망

- 일측은 동 일탈신청 철회 조건으로, 필요하다면 현행 대일 시청각 분야 차별 조치에 대한 갓트차원의 challenge 의사 없음을 UR/서비스 협상 수석대표가 구두 보장하겠다고 제의

o 경기원, 문화부와 협의, 10.15. 주 제네바 대표부에 대해 일단 MFN 일탈 신청을 보류하고 대표단 귀국후 우리입장을 재검토하여 최종 입장을 결정키로 하였음을 훈령

4. 대 책

가. 고려사항

o UR 조기타결 전망이 불투명한 현시점에서 UR에서의 대일 협력관계 전반에 손상을 줄지도 모를 사안을 무리하게 추진할 필요는 없을 것으로 판단

o 본건은 일반적인 MFN 일탈과 달리 특정국가 만을 명시, MFN 대상에서 제외하는 점에서 일본측이 끝까지 문제시 하는 경우 관철 전망 불투명

나. 대 책

o 상기 감안, 일측이 아래 대안중 하나를 수락할 경우, 동 MFN 일탈 신청을 철회

① 우리가 현행 시청각 서비스 분야의 대일 차별 정책을 계속 유지 하는데 대하여 일본은 GATT 차원에서 challenge 하지 않는다는 내용의 구두약속을 일본측이 제공할 것.

② 상기 약속을 Record of Discussion 등 형식의 문서로 할 것.

o 일본 시청각 서비스 진출의 국내적 민감성을 고려할때 상기 대안 ②가 바람직. 끝.

예고	발행처 : 93.12.31. 까지
	접수처 : 93. 6.30. 파기

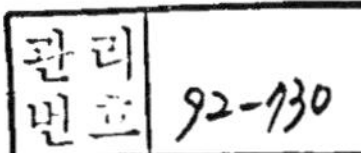

대일 시청각 서비스 제한 관련 UR/서비스 협상 대책 회의 결과

1. 일 시 : 92. 10. 16.(금) 16:00-17:00

2. 참 석 : 통상국장 (주재), 동북아 1과장 , 문화협력 1과장, 통상 1과장 (대리), 동상기구과장.

3. 안 건 : 별첨 회의 자료 참조

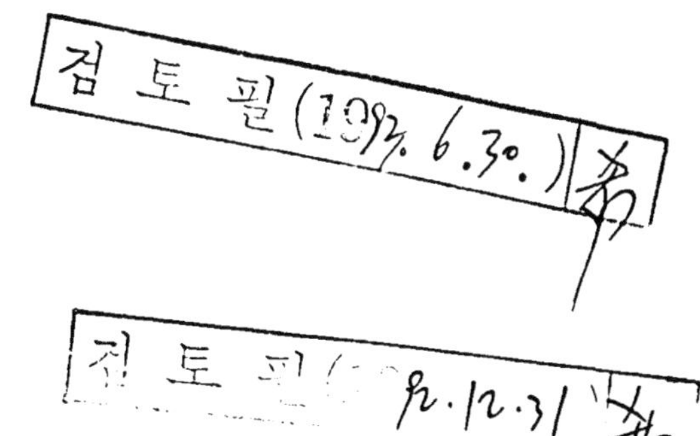

4. 토의 내용

o 동북아 1과장

- 일본이 평소 모든 약속을 문서로 받으려 하는 관행을 감안, 반드시 문서로 assurance 를 받을 필요가 있음.

- 문서화 하는경우, 일본측이 우리측의 MFN 일탈 희망범위를 그대로 수용 하기는 어려울 것이므로 포괄적 표현 사용 필요.

- CIS 지원국 회의차 장관님 방일 기회에 한.일 외무장관회의 (10.30)가 예정되어 있어, 동 기회에 일측이 이 문제를 제기할 경우에 대비, 아측입장 마련 요망.

o 문화협력 1과장

- 92.7월, 일 외무성 문화교류부장 방한시 우리 문화협력국장과 면담, 일본 영화의 상업적 상영 금지 재고를 요청한데 대해 우리측이 전향적 검토 시사.

0139

- 문화부 입장은 비교적 강경 (별첨 문화부 입장)

- 93년 1-2월경 한.일간 회담이 예정되어 있어 그동안 공청회등 국내 의견 수렴 예정.

o 통상기구과장

- 일본으로서는 일본이 특정되어 MFN 에서 배제되는 내용의 공식문서가 회람되는 것을 막는것이 급선무 이므로 서면 보장을 수락할 가능성도 있음.

- 우리로서는 종래의 정책을 유지코자 새로운 UR 체제 출범시 그 근거를 마련하려는 것으로 일측의 보장을 요구하는 것이 무리는 아님.

o 통상국장

- 협상 대표단이 귀국하는 대로 국내 조정업무를 담당하는 경제기획원 주재로 관계부처 회의를 개최, 아측입장을 조속히 확정 (ROD 형식의 보장을 받고, MFN 일탈 신청을 철회) 하되,

- 서면보장 내용등에 관한 구체적 대일 교섭은 UR협상 진전 상황을 보아 추진 ~~도 가급적 조속 종결~~. 끝.

공람	통상기구과	93년 10월 17일	담당	과장	심의관	국장	차관보	차관	장관
			이 손	(서명)					

0140

管理番號	92-848

경 제 기 획 원

우 427-760 / 경기도 과천시 중앙동1 정부제2청사 / 전화 503-9149 / 전송 503-9141

문서번호 통조삼 10502-124
시행일자 1992. 11. 19
(경유)
수신 외무부장관, 문화부장관
참조

선결			지시	
접수	일자 시간	92.11.19	결재·공람	
	번호	41848		
처리과				
담당자				

제목 UR/서비스협상 대일 시청각서비스관련 회의소집

1. 통조삼 10502-117(10.28) 관련입니다.

2. 대일 시청각서비스 문제와 관련하여 다음과 같이 관계부처 국장급회의를 소집하니 참석하기 바랍니다.

- 다 음 -

가. 회의일시 : '92.11.20(금), 14:30~

나. 회의장소 : 경제기획원 대외경제조정실장실(제2청사 1동 726호)

다. 참석범위 : 경제기획원 대외경제조정실장(회의주재)
경제기획원 제2협력관
외 무 부 통상국장
문 화 부 예술진흥국장 "끝"

경 제 기 획 원 장

대외경제조정실장 전결

0141

이시

對日 視聽覺서비스 關聯

1. 交涉經過

- 10.15 : MFN逸脫申請 保留, 日側 書面保障 約束(제네바)
- 10.23 : 日側, non-paper 傳達方案提示
- 10.29 : 우리側, ROD(兩國 首席代表署名)方式 수정제안
- 11. 4 : 日本側, ROD는 수용하기 어렵다는 立場表明(ROD는 法的意味의 文書이므로 양측이 서로 양보할 수 없는 부분을 포함시키고자 할 것이므로 文書作成이 현실적으로 매우 어려움 강조)
- 11. 6 : 日側, 既存提議(non-paper방식)을 반복하면서 修正代案으로 ① 日側이 작성한 ROD方式(일측주장내용만 반영)으로 하되, 이를 우리측이 수정할 경우 받아들이기 어렵다는 입장 ② 日側 首席代表가 우리측 수석대표에게 書翰을 보내는 方案을 제시
- 11.17 : 우리側, 日側이 제시한 書翰內容(별첨)中 3항의 삭제를 요구
- 11.19 : 日側, 同 3項의 削除要求를 수용하되, 3項의 內容을 口頭傳達하겠다고 제시

2. 검토의견

- 日側이 그간 제시한 non-paper方式, ROD方式, 書翰方式은 공히 동문제가 政治·社會的으로 민감하기 때문에 日本側은 이를 多者間 방식으로 다루기를 원치 않는다는 내용을 포함하고 있으며 ROD에는 이에 2가지 사항(GATT上 權利·義務 留保, 兩國間 視聽覺問題 協議)을 추가하여 제시

0142

- 上記 3가지 方案을 檢討할 때

  o Non-paper方式 : 확실한 保障方式이 되지 못함.

  o ROD方式 : 日側 主張內容만 반영한 것으로서 수용곤란 (우리가 修正할 경우 수용하기 어렵다는 입장)

  o 書翰方式 : 위 2가지 方式을 배제할 경우 수용을 검토할 수 있는 유일한 方案

- 따라서 그간 협의된 대로 日側 首席代表 書翰을 받고 현재 GATT에 보류되어 있는 MFN逸脫申請書를 철회하는 것으로 同 問題를 종결짓는 것이 바람직하다고 판단됨.

  o 우리가 현존 對日 視聽覺措置를 당분간 유지하더라도 日本이 多者次元에서 문제제기를 하지 않도록 하려는 목적은 어떤 형식으로든 日本의 書面保障이 있는 한 達成되는 것으로 보아야 할 것임.

  o 同件과 관련한 兩國間의 그동안의 協議過程에서 일단 日本이 우리가 MFN逸脫申請을 하지 못하게 한 후 이를 악용하여 GATT次元에서 동건 MFN 違背問題를 제기코자 하는 의도는 없다는 點을 확인할 수 있었다고 봄.

  o 한편 현 시점에서 MFN逸脫申請을 다시 추진할 경우에 이의 貫徹可能性이 불투명하고 이에 따른 파장에 대한 충분한 고려가 있어야 할 것임.

3. 檢討事項

① 書翰方式 受容與否

② 書翰受容경우, 書翰傳達方式

- 日本側 首席代表가 駐日韓國大使館을 통해서 우리 首席代表에게 전달
- 〃 우리 首席代表에게 직접 전달

③ MFN逸脫申請 撤回時期 其他

0143

Draft

November , 1992

Dear Mr. Lee,

On behalf of the Japanese delegation to the initial commitment negotiations under the draft General Agreement on Trade in Services of the Uruguay Round (GATS), I wish to inform you of the following in view of the practical solution of the issue, on the basis of the understanding shared by the Japanese and Korean sides in the course of their consultations:

1. It is the view of the Japanese side that under the current circumstances the issue of the existing Korean measures on Japanese audio-visual services in the Republic of Korea is a sensitive socio-political issue. In light of the sensitivity of this issue, the Japanese side considers it inappropriate to address the issue further in the multilateral context of the Uruguay Round.

2. In view of the above, the Japanese side has no intention of taking advantage of the lack of derogation by the Republic of Korea from the most favoured nation treatment obligation under Article II of the GATS with respect to the existing Korean measures on Japanese audio-visual services in the Republic of Korea.

3. It is confirmed that this letter does not affect the legal rights and obligations of the Japanese side under the GATS.

Sincerely yours,

Koji Tsuruoka
Head of Japanese delegation
to the initial commitment
negotiations under the GATS

0144

管理番號	92-936

경 제 기 획 원

우 427-760 / 경기도 과천시 중앙동1 정부제2청사 / 전화 503-9149 / 전송 503-9141

문서번호 통조삼 10502-140
시행일자 1992. 12. 4
(경유)
수신 수신처 참조
참조 통상기구과장

선결			지시		
접수	일자 시간	:	결재·공람		
	번호	4188			
처리과					
담당자		이시형			

제목 대일 시청각서비스 관련 회의결과 통보

1. 통조삼 10502-124('92.11.19), 영진 35175-91('92.11.24)등의 관련입니다.

2. 대일 시청각서비스와 관련하여 관계부처 장관회의를 개최한 바 그 결과를 다음과 같이 통보합니다.

- 다 음 -

가. 회의실시 및 장소 : '92.12.3, 10:10~10:20
정부종합청사 부총리집무실

나. 참 석 자 : 부총리, 문화부장관, 외무부차관

다. 회의결과

- UR/서비스협상에서의 대일 시청각서비스 MFN일탈신청문제와 관련하여 그간 한·일 양측이 최종 절충한 서면보장방식대로 우리측이 UR/서비스협상 일측 수석대표의 서한을 접수하고 현재 GATT사무국에 보류되어 있는 동건 MFN일탈신청을 철회하기로 함. "끝"

경 제 기 획 원 장 관

대외경제조정실장 전결

수신처 : 외무부장관, 문화부장관

0145

경 제 기 획 원

우 427-760 / 경기도 과천시 중앙동1 정부제2청사 / 전화 503-9149 / 전송 503-9141

문서번호 통조삼 10502-139
시행일자 1992. 12. 5
(경유)
수신 수신처 참조
참조

선결			지시	
접수	일자 시간	92 . 12. 8 :	결재·공람	
	번호	42107		
처리과				
담당자		이시형		

제목 UR/서비스 실무소위원회 개최통보

1. 통조삼 10502-132(11.3) 관련입니다.

2. UR/서비스 제6차 양허협상이 12월 14일 주간에 개최될 예정으로 있어 이와 관련 대책회의를 다음과 같이 개최하고자 하니 참석하기 바랍니다.

- 다 음 -

가. 일 시 : '92.12.8(화), 14:00
나. 장 소 : 경제기획원 대회의실(과천청사 1동 727호)
다. 참석범위 : 경제기획원 제2협력관(회의주재)
외 무 부 통상기구과장
내 무 부 지적과장
재 무 부 국제금융과장
법 무 부 출입국기획과장
농림수산부 국제협력과장
문 화 부 저작권과장
상 공 부 국제협력과장
건 설 부 해외협력과장
교 통 부 국제협력과장
노 동 부 인력수급과장
체 신 부 통신협력과장
과학기술처 기술협력과장
환 경 처 정책조정과장
산 림 청 임정과장
공업진흥청 검사행정과장

0146

우 427-760 / 경기도 과천시 중앙동1 정부제2청사 / 전화 503-9149 / 전송 503-9141

해운항만청 진흥과장
철 도 청 국제협력담당관
KIEP 성극제 연구위원

"끝"

경 제 기 획 원 장

대외경제조정실장 전결

수신처 : 외무부장관, 내무부장관, 재무부장관, 법무부장관, 농림수산부장관,
문화부장관, 상공부장관, 건설부장관, 교통부장관, 노동부장관,
체신부장관, 과기처장관, 환경처장관, 산림청장, 공업진흥청장,
해운항만청장, 철도청장, 대외경제정책연구원장

0147

UR 實務小委
會議資料

UR/서비스 第6次 讓許協商對策

1992. 12

12/8

經 濟 企 劃 院
對外經濟調整室

0148

目　　次

0149

Ⅰ. 最近 協商動向과 展望

- 서비스 一般協定(GATS) 制定作業은 '91.12.20 제시된 최종 협정문안에 대해 技術的事項에 국한하여 협의가 진행되고 있으며 현재의 협정문안에 대한 큰 수정없이 마무리될 전망

- 서비스 讓許協商은 '93.2말까지 2~3차례 마무리협상이 있을 것으로 예상되는 바, 앞으로 진행될 협상에서 金融, 基本通信, 海運分野가 주요관건이 될 것으로 보이며, 美·EC등은 이들 분야에 대한 Common Approach를 모색

  o 金融 : 11.20 美·EC間 농산물분야 타결시 共同步調宣言 (日本, 韓國 및 ASEAN등에 대하여 높은 수준의 自由化約束 요구예상)

  o 基本通信 : UR종료후에도 基本通信分野 開放을 위한 협상을 계속, 동 결과에 따라 MFN문제 결정 (미국, 북구주도, 한국포함 12개국에 참여 요청)

  o 海運 : 共通讓許表에 따라 주요 해운국가들이 자유화약속을 함으로써 美國의 參與를 유도(EC주도, 한국포함 13개국 참여중)

- 海運 및 基本通信은 주로 미·EC간 대립되어 온 분야로서 양국간 農産物分野 合意를 바탕으로 하여 타결전망이 가능하며, 금융분야는 先·開途國間 對決構圖로서 美·EC의 공동노력에 의한 압력가중 예상

  o 海運은 미국의 MFN일탈 완전철회(또는 일탈범위 축소), 基本通信은 EC의 시장개방협상 참여동의, 美國의 MFN 일탈 철회하는 식으로 타결될 가능성

  o 先進國들은 금융분야에 가시적인 성과가 없을 경우 전체 UR/서비스협상을 無意味한 것으로 해석

0150

Ⅱ. 금번 讓許協商對應의 基本方向

- 이번 양허협상은 美·EC間의 農産物分野 協商妥結을 계기로 소집된 11.26의 TNC회의에서 Track별로 협상의 재개를 추진키로 합의함에 따라 12.7부터 2주간 개최

  o 우리나라는 12.14(月)부터 1주간 참여하여 美國, 日本, EC, 캐나다, 濠洲등과 협상 예정

- 이번 讓許協商의 性格은 UR 전체협상의 마무리라는 측면에서 그동안 제기된 主要爭點에 대한 타결노력이 본격화될 것으로 보이며 各國間에 讓許水準을 둘러싼 보다 활발한 협상전개 예상

- 우리는 그동안의 協商結果를 토대로 다음과 같은 方向으로 대응

  ① 韓國政府는 그동안 同 協商의 成功的妥結을 위해 노력해 온 바와 같이 협상의 완결시까지 최선의 協助와 努力을 계속해 나갈 것임을 강조

  ② 讓許範圍는 수정양허표 제출이후 추가자유화가 이루어졌거나 향후의 자유화계획이 마련된 분야를 대상으로 그동안의 양허협상을 통해 추가양허가 가능한 부분을 밝힌 상태이므로 이번 協商에서는 이러한 기본입장을 견지하되 지난번 양허협상이후 추가로 검토된 통신, 환경등 분야에서는 동 검토내용을 표명

  ③ 아울러 우리의 最終讓許表 草案을 다음 양허협상시 제시하겠다는 의사를 밝히고 金融, 基本通信, 海運, MFN逸脫問題등 주요쟁점에 대한 각국의 입장과 최종양허표 제출 동향등 全般的 動向을 면밀하게 파악

0151

Ⅲ. 部門別 讓許協商 對應方向

1. 人力移動部門

- 人力移動部門 讓許計劃에 서비스 세일즈인력, 상업적주재의 설치를 위한 代表人力을 포함시킨다는 방침을 協商相對國에 通報

- 美國, 日本등이 요구한 전문직업인의 일시적이동과 중국의 契約條件附(contractual basis) 入國者에 대한 인력이동 요구에 대해서는 국내노동시장 수급여건상 追加讓許가 어렵다는 입장을 표명(美國, 日本, 中國)

2. 外國人 投資企業의 土地取得

- 자유화된 서비스업종에 대한 外國人 投資企業의 토지취득 허용요구에 대해서는 현시점에서 추가 양허하기는 어려우나 外國人 投資企業의 土地取得을 확대 허용하기 위한 制度改善 計劃이 있음을 표명(美國, 日本)

  o 아울러 12.1부터 시행된 保險業 및 尖端서비스業種에 대한 外國人 土地取得 內容을 설명

- 外國人이 토지와 별개로 건물만 취득 가능한지 여부에 대해서는 제도적으로는 建物取得이 가능함을 표명(EC)

3. 外國人投資

- 外國人 投資持分 制限이 없어지면 신고대상 자유화업종으로 되는지 여부에 대해서는 신고만으로 사업영위가 가능하나 개별법상의 登錄要件, 免許要件은 충족해야 함을 설명(美國, 日本)

0152

4. 金融分野

- Blueprint등 金融開放計劃의 offer 반영요구에 대해서는 blueprint 내용과 保險市場開放計劃中 최종양허표 제출 시점까지의 자유화내용을 양허표에 반영할 용의가 있음을 표명

- Standstill 요구에 대해서는 우리 양허표가 사실상 standstill을 전제로 하고 있음을 설명하고 최종양허표에 우리의 standstill의도를 보다 명백하게 표현할 용의가 있음을 표명

5. 事業서비스

- 法務서비스는 양허가 곤란하다는 기존입장 견지(美國, 핀랜드)

- 會計서비스와 관련 외국 C.P.A가 한국내에 있는 自國會社의 支社, 子會社등에 대해 회계서비스를 제공하는 것이 가능한지 여부에 대해서는 단독으로 會計서비스를 제공하는 것은 不可하다는 입장을 표명(濠洲)

  o 다만, 外國會計法人과 國內會計法人과의 업무제휴를 통해 외국회계법인 소속 C.P.A가 국내회계법인에 일정계약 기간동안 근무하면서 自國會社의 支社, 子會社등에 대해 회계제도에 관한 자문, 회계감사자문, 감사기술을 전수하는 것 등은 가능

- 敎育서비스와 관련 事務所(representative office)의 설치가 가능한 지 여부에 대해서는 國內事務所 設置가 가능하나 국내에서의 활동은 弘報活動, 資料蒐集등에 제한됨을 설명(뉴질랜드)

사무기기 및 장비 수리유지.

- 컴퓨터관련서비스중 CPC 845 양허요구에 대해서는 最終讓許表에 추가로 등재할 계획임을 표명(中國)

- 試險檢査서비스(CPC 8676)의 양허요구에 대해서는 CPC 86761중 測定代行業(대기, 수질, 소음, 진동)과 檢査代行業(대기, 소음, 진동) 및 CPC 86764(技術檢査서비스)를 추가로 양허할 계획임을 표명(캐나다)

6. 通信

- 基本通信 多者間協商 參與要求에 대해서는 다음과 같은 전제하에 협상에 참여할 의사가 있다는 우리측 基本立場을 표명(美國, 캐나다, 스웨덴)
  - o 多者間協商이 진행되는 동안 雙務協商을 요구하지 않을 것
  - o 多者間協商이 반드시 참여국의 基本通信 市場開放을 의미해서는 안되며 시장개방의 정도는 各國의 通信産業 發展程度를 고려해야 할 것임.
  - o MFN原則은 협상기간중 그리고 협상이 끝난 후에도 적용될 것

7. 海運

- 貨物留保制度 對象品目의 축소요구에 대해서는 향후 점진적으로 대상품목을 축소해 나갈 방침이나 具體的內容을 양허표에 反映할 단계는 아님을 설명(日本, 濠洲)

- 合作海運船社 設立에 대한 제한사항 완화요구 및 해운보조서비스 추가양허요구에 대해서는 追加讓許가 곤란함을 설명(中國, 스웨덴)

8. 航空

- 航空 CRS MFN逸脫 撤回要求에 대해서는 철회곤란 입장 견지(EC)

9. 流通

- 流通業 ENT, 賣場面積 및 賣場數 制限 撤廢要求에 대해서는 기존입장 고수(美國, 中國)

- 종합무역상사의 輸入業 許容要求에 대해서는 곤란함을 표명(日本)

10. 環境關聯서비스

- 환경서비스중 CPC 9403, 9404, 9405, 9406, 9409에 대한 양허요구에 대해서는
  - o CPC 9406중 環境影響評價代行業 및 CPC 9409중 環境影響評價代行業을 추가로 양허할 계획임을 표명(캐나다, 핀랜드)
  - o CPC 9404중 大氣汚染 防止施設業 및 CPC 9405중 騷音振動 防止施設業은 건설 및 엔지니어링분야에 旣反映되어 있음을 설명

11. MFN逸脫問題

- 이번 양허협상기간중 航空 CRS, 韓·日航路, 外國人 土地取得 및 리스關聯 相互主義 등 세 분야에 대한 MFN 일탈 신청서를 GATT에 공식제출('92. 3.12. 제출하였던 逸脫申請書와 대체)
  - o 對日 視聽覺 서비스分野는 제외
- 단, 外國人 土地取得 및 리스關聯 相互主義에 대한 MFN일탈 신청은 ① 현재까지 한번도 적용된 사례가 없었고 ② 사실상 대부분의 나라가 양허표에서 토지취득·리스와 관련하여 아무런 제한사항을 기재하지 않고 있는 상황에서 經濟的 實益이 크지 않고 ③ 동종의 MFN逸脫申請을 했던 일본이 이를 철회하기로 했고 ④ 土地取得許容도 되지 않는 상황에서 리스의 경우까지 제한가능성을 유지하는데 따라 우리 양허의 全般的인 質이 저하된다는 미국등의 강력한 불만표명이 있는 등 문제가 있으므로 이번 讓許協商의 結果를 본 후 그 유지여부를 다시 검토

12. 其他

- 韓·美 兩者間에 논의된 사항을 서신교환등의 형태로 추가 약속하는 문제에 대해서는 기존 韓·美間 合意가 UR협정에 의해 무효화되지 않는다는 것이 우리 法律專門家들의 견해이며 우리정부는 기존의 韓·美間 合意를 충실히 이행할 의지가 확고하나 새로운 문서화는 곤란함을 표명(美國)

The Republic of Korea

MFN Exemptions Under GATS Article Ⅱ.2 - Revised Provisional List

1. While recognizing that the MFN principle is important for the GATS to be an effective agreement, the Republic of Korea has consistently maintained that the scope of MFN exemptions should be limited to the necessary minimum. The Republic of Korea is concerned about the current, excessive requests for MFN exemptions and reemphasizes its position that for the successful conclusion of the services negotiations, every participant should limit its exemptions to specific measures confined to specific areas.

2. Maintaining this basic position, the Republic of Korea submits the attached revised provisional list for MFN exemptions, which is in substitution of its initial list dated March 16, 1992, pursuant to Article 2 and its Annex under the GATS.

3. The Republic of Korea reserves its right to revise this list for MFN exemption prior to the final outcome of the negotiations on the framework and initial commitments. In particular, the ROK reserves its right to revise this list in case a wide-ranging exemption in the financial services sector is sought. The ROK will also review MFN exemptions for horizontal bilateral agreements, such as visa agreements, according to the results of future negotiations on those agreements.

0156

1. Sector or Sub-sector : Maritime Transport Services

a. Description of the measures :

- Since the ROK-Japan Service Line is overcrowded, particularly by many small domestic businesses, the ROK strictly restricts new entrances to the route regardless of the nationality of the shipping firm.

b. Treatment inconsistent with Article Ⅱ : 1 of the Agreement

- Operation of the ROK-Japan Service Line is permitted only to foreign firms which, for historical reasons, were licensed by the ROK government.

c. Intended duration of the exemption :

- Until January 1995.

d. Conditions which create the need for the exemption :

- This exemption is temporary, and the ROK will respect the MFN principle after the abolishment of this restriction in January 1995.

0157

2. Sector or Sub-sector : Computerized Reservation Services

a. Description of the measures :

- Access to foreign CRS through SITA networks is restricted to a group of persons specified by the Minister of Communications since such access is considered as third party use of internationally leased lines.

- The Minister of Communications specifically permits U.S. carriers to use the SITA network for access to CRS.

b. Treatment inconsistent with Article Ⅱ : 1 of the Agreement

- International travel agencies are allowed to access SITA only when they access CRS designated by US carriers.

c. Intended duration of the exemption :

- Indefinite

d. Conditions which create the need for the exemption :

- Access to foreign CRS through the SITA network could be limited or otherwise affected in relation to the negotiations on granting or receiving traffic rights.

0158

3. Sector or Sub-sector : Reciprocity Measures on Foreign Acquisition of land in Korea

a. Description of the measures :

- Prohibitions or restrictions may be imposed on foreign nationals or juridical persons seeking to acquire or lease land in the ROK when Korean nationals or juridical persons are placed under similar prohibitions or restrictions in the country of the foreign nationals or juridical persons seeking to acquire or lease land in Korea(Article 2 of the Alien Land Law).

b. Treatment inconsistent with Article Ⅱ : 1 of the Agreement

- Measures based on reciprocity

c. Intended duration of the exemption :

- Indefinite

d. Conditions which create the need for the exemption :

- To secure the right of Korean nationals and juridical persons to acquire land in foreign country.

0159

MFN 일탈 신청내역(92.12)

1. 해운 servise

- ROK - Japan Liner
- 1995.1까지

2. 컴퓨터 예약 Servise

- SITA를 통한 해외 CRS 접근은 체신부장관이 지정한 그룹에 국한
- 무기한

3. 외국인 토지취득

- 상호주의에 의거 외국 국적인 혹은 외국법인이 토지취득 혹은 임차시 제한
- 무기한. 끝.

0160

경 제 기 획 원

우 427-760 / 경기도 과천시 중앙동1 정부제2청사 / 전화 503-9149 / 전송 503-9141

문서번호 통조삼 10502-142
시행일자 1992. 12. 10
(경유)
수신 수신처 참조
참조 통상기구과장

선결			지시		
접수	일자 시간	92. 12. 11 :	결재·공람		
	번호	42496			
처리과					
담당자		이시형			

제목 UR대책 서비스 실무소위원회 결과통보

지난 12월 8일 개최된 UR/서비스 제6차 양허협상 대책회의 결과를 별첨과 같이 통보하니 업무에 참고하기 바랍니다.

별첨 : UR대책 실무소위원회 회의결과 1부. "끝"

경 제 기 획 원 장

제 2협력관 전결

수신처 : 외무부장관, 내무부장관, 재무부장관, 법무부장관, 농림수산부장관, 문화부장관, 상공부장관, 건설부장관, 교통부장관, 노동부장관, 체신부장관, 과기처장관, 환경처장관, 산림청장, 공업진흥청장, 해운항만청장, 철도청장, 대외경제정책연구원장

0161

< 別添 >

UR/對策 實務小委員會 會議結果

1. 會議槪要

- 日時 및 場所 : '92. 12.8(火), 15:00~16:00
  經濟企劃院 大會議室

- 參席者 : 經濟企劃院 第2協力官(會議主宰), 通商調整3課長,
  外務部, 內務部, 財務部, 法務部, 農林水産部,
  文化部, 商工部, 建設部, 交通部, 勞動部, 遞信部,
  科學技術處, 環境處, 山林廳, 海運港灣廳,
  工業振興廳, 鐵道廳 擔當官, KIEP 諮問官

2. 會議結果

- 이번 讓許協商('92.12.14~18)에는 經濟企劃院에서 준비하여 회의안건으로 상정·배포한「UR/서비스 第6次 讓許協商對策」에 의거 대응키로 합의

- 회의시 각부처에 배포한「Draft Schedule of Specific Commitments of the Republic of Korea Under the General Agreement on Trade in Services」은 이번 양허협상이후 최종마무리 작업이 가능하도록 각 부처에서 所管分野에 대하여 철저히 검토하여 그 의견을 조속히 經濟企劃院에 送付

0162

외교문서 비밀해제: 우루과이라운드2 24
우루과이라운드 서비스 분야 양허 협상 3

초판인쇄 2024년 03월 15일
초판발행 2024년 03월 15일

지은이 한국학술정보(주)
펴낸이 채종준
펴낸곳 한국학술정보(주)
주 소 경기도 파주시 회동길 230(문발동)
전 화 031-908-3181(대표)
팩 스 031-908-3189
홈페이지 http://ebook.kstudy.com
E-mail 출판사업부 publish@kstudy.com
등 록 제일산-115호(2000. 6. 19)

ISBN 979-11-7217-126-1 94340
979-11-7217-102-5 94340 (set)